PRAISE FOR

BORDER WARS

"Essential reading for those searching for the 'beating heart' of the Trump administration. . . . Davis and Shear are scrupulously fair reporters. . . . [They] are right: Immigration demagogy is at the 'heart' of the Trump show—and the Trump show is at the heart of our tragic decline as a civil and humane society."

—Joe Klein, *The New York Times*

"A stark account of the Trump administration's ongoing attempts to disembowel the nation's immigration policy. . . . Davis and Shear had only to state the facts and allow readers to draw their own conclusions. Trump had already taken care of impaling himself."

—Oscar Cásares, *The Washington Post*

"The book reveals much about how Trump thinks, why he instinctively 'grasped for the solution that looked toughest,' and, in hair-raising insider detail, how he governs from day to day. If journalism is the first draft of history, this volume is a solid second draft."

—Jessica T. Mathews, *Foreign Affairs*

"An excellent way to understand recent U.S. immigration policy. While the book's revelations about Donald Trump advocating for alligator-filled moats have received the most attention, there is much more to learn about immigration from Davis, Shear and their well-researched book."

—Stuart Anderson, Forbes.com

"A vivid, revelatory account of President Trump's attempts to overhaul the U.S. immigration system. . . . Davis and Shear's fast-paced, richly detailed narrative underscores the chaos surrounding the White House without minimizing the fact that it's now 'more dangerous and costly to be undocumented' in America than it has been in decades."

—*Publishers Weekly*

BORDER WARS

Inside Trump's Assault on Immigration

JULIE HIRSCHFELD DAVIS

AND

MICHAEL D. SHEAR

SIMON & SCHUSTER PAPERBACKS

New York   London   Toronto   Sydney   New Delhi

Simon & Schuster Paperbacks
An Imprint of Simon & Schuster, Inc.
1230 Avenue of the Americas
New York, NY 10020

First Simon & Schuster paperback edition November 2020

SIMON & SCHUSTER PAPERBACKS and colophon are registered trademarks of Simon & Schuster, Inc.

For information about special discounts for bulk purchases, please contact Simon & Schuster Special Sales at 1-866-506-1949 or business@simonandschuster.com

The Simon & Schuster Speakers Bureau can bring authors to your live event. For more information, or to book an event, contact the Simon & Schuster Speakers Bureau at 1-866-248-3049 or visit our website at www.simonspeakers.com.

Interior design by Joy O'Meara

Manufactured in the United States of America

10 9 8 7 6 5 4 3 2 1

Library of Congress Control Number: 2019946685

ISBN 978-1-9821-1739-9
ISBN 978-1-9821-1740-5 (pbk)
ISBN 978-1-9821-1741-2 (ebook)

For our families:
Jonathan, Claire, Harry, and Rose
Caitlin, Sam, and Sophie

CONTENTS

The question is about your legacy. Will you be remembered
as Donald Trump, the xenophobic president?

"I hope not. Because I'm not that way. I hope
not—I think you're right—I think the perception
might be more that way than the other. I hope not.
I would like to have a great immigration policy, I'd
like it to be fair. I do not want criminals coming
into our country. I don't think you do either."

Donald J. Trump
The Oval Office
June 25, 2019

BORDER WARS

PROLOGUE

PRESIDENT TRUMP WAS OBSESSING AGAIN.

It was the afternoon of December 4, 2018, just two days after his return to Washington, D.C., from a quick, three-day trip to Buenos Aires. The world was mourning the death of George H. W. Bush over the weekend, and the screens of the many televisions Trump had installed in the White House were filled with glowing tributes to the ninety-four-year-old icon. Trump was in the Oval Office, where he had just finished signing a bill to fund the Coast Guard. But as his guests were ushered out, Trump asked Kirstjen Nielsen, his secretary of homeland security, to stay behind. He wanted to talk about the wall.

That was no surprise to Nielsen. In almost every conversation she had with the president, no matter the topic, Trump eventually found his way to the wall. He raised it in the middle of meetings that had nothing to do with immigration or border security. He buttonholed her at social occasions, like after a movie screening in the White House family theater, to ask, "Kirstjen, what about the wall?" He called her at home, usually before 7 a.m., to complain or muse about it, often flinging f-bombs about how ugly the existing wall looked and demanding that she do something about it. Sometimes, his outburst was prompted by a fleeting image of a section of the wall during a segment on Fox News or a snarky tweet from a critic about his demands for a barrier on the southern border. Other times, it seemed to come out of nowhere. But in Trump's mind, those close to him could see, the building of the wall and its physical appearance were directly correlated to his own success as president—they were an extension of himself. And if there was one thing Trump loved to talk about, it was himself.

"It's got to be steel bollards," Trump told Nielsen that afternoon, describing his vision for what seemed like the millionth time. This was his latest infatuation. During his campaign, Trump had said he wanted a wall built of precast cement slabs, and as president he had proudly posed for the cameras in front of massive, concrete prototypes that towered over him. But he had since shifted his focus. Border officials didn't like concrete walls because they made it impossible to know who or what was on the other side. Besides, his homeland security advisers had explained to him, concrete was exceedingly easy to break apart. All you had to do was drill a small hole and inject expanding grout—available cheap from any Home Depot—and within twenty-four hours, the cement would begin to collapse. After many months of painstaking conversations, Trump had been convinced that heavy-duty steel posts were the way to go instead, and that was what his Department of Homeland Security had signed contracts to have built.

"Love that design. Gotta be steel bollards," Trump told Nielsen. "But it's got to be the bollards right next to each other. Just the bollards." He showed with his hands what he meant—kind of like toothpicks standing straight up, right next to each other.

That might work, Nielsen said, as she explained, once again, that such a design would require some kind of stabilizing bar at the top. Otherwise, the engineers said it would be too easy for someone to pull down individual poles or spread them apart and slip through the barrier into the United States.

No. No. No, Trump said. If you have a bar at the top, people can throw a rope over it and climb over the fence. Plus, it's ugly. This has to be beautiful. Think of it like flagpoles, he told Nielsen, using his hands again to demonstrate a series of lines placed close together. A flagpole next to a flagpole next to another flagpole. "I have the best flagpole guy in the country," Trump assured her. "I'll put you in touch with him." And also, he continued, the tops of the poles have to be sharp and pointy, so that no one will dare try to climb over it. And the pointy parts should be painted black, so that they get hot in the bright sun. That will help to deter anyone trying to climb up.

By now, everyone around Trump had become accustomed to the president's extraordinarily detailed lectures about the wall. He saw it as the embodiment of his presidency, a hulking physical reflection of his giant political brand, and he was obsessed with every aspect of it, down to the kind of black paint that should be used. "Flat black!" he would insist, both because it would draw in the most heat and make the structure too hot to touch, and because it would be "beautiful," he said. He was reluctant to let go of the idea even after Nielsen informed him that his preferred matte black paint would cost an additional $1 million per mile of wall. Nor was Trump discouraged by the practical challenges associated with building the structure, which involved a painstaking, often impossible process of poring over property records—some so outdated they were still on microfiche—to identify who owned the land where it would be erected. Just take the land and let them sue us, Trump would say. In one meeting with a group of Republican senators at the White House, Trump had veered off topic and offered another reason the border wall had to be sharp and hot on top. It was so that birds would be less likely to land on it and take a shit, sullying his beautiful edifice.

But the president's overarching goal was to make the experience of crossing the border into the United States as terrifying and perilous as possible. At one point, Trump became enamored of the idea of digging a trench along the border, so much so that Nielsen asked the Army Corps of Engineers to calculate the cost. (Twice to three times as expensive, they reported back.) Discussions with his advisers ensued about what would be inside the ditch: Water? Alligators? Snakes? Some of the president's proposals were so outlandish that aides could not even tell whether he was serious. Trump was crystal clear on one point, though: the wall should be dangerous enough to dissuade immigrants from even attempting to scale it. More than once, he had instructed officials at the Department of Homeland Security to look into whether the wall could be electrified so that anyone touching it would receive a shock. He wanted the spikes on top to be sharp enough to pierce human flesh in an instant. He wanted concertina wire everywhere. Trump had vivid descriptions of what he wanted immigrants to experience if they tried to scale the wall: They would be burned, maimed, cut to pieces by the wire. I want these people to be in horrible shape if they climb up, the president would say.

It was stunning. The president was openly advocating for illegal border crossers to be maimed and burned at the border, the kind of treatment usually associated with brutal dictators or military strongmen. In fact, Trump was envious of Kim Jong-un, the ruthless leader of North Korea, for the security of his border, fortified with land mines and policed by armed guards who shot to kill. "When you talk about a wall, when you talk about a border," he said in 2019 before a visit to the Demilitarized Zone, "that's what they call a border. Nobody goes through that border." Trump expressed no sympathy for people clamoring to enter the United States. To the president, they were all criminals, the kinds of dangerous people he so frequently warned about during his rallies. He was determined to keep them out, and his aides were alarmed at what he was willing to do to get his way.

On that particular day in early December, Nielsen left the meeting with yet another detailed presidential vision for his wall. This time, though, she had an idea. She would take Trump's musings and make them into something tangible that she could use to mollify him the next time he spun into one of his regular rages about immigration. When she got back to DHS headquarters, Nielsen gave the staff at Customs and Border Protection the specs and asked them to develop a mock-up of what the president had described. She didn't mention that it was Trump who had dictated the requirements to her in meticulous detail in the Oval Office. She had no intention of actually instructing her department to scrap its plans and build what Trump had described instead, nor was she planning to present the design to the president proactively. But Nielsen figured that having a printout of the president's dream vision for the wall might be useful the next time Trump got angry at her for failing to be tough enough at the border and she needed a way to calm him down. A diversion of sorts. Just as Trump had used it on the campaign trail.

Donald John Trump never meant for a giant wall across the entire southwestern border to be the totem of his presidential campaign or the icon of his presidency. And he certainly never thought it would be the omnipresent reminder of his biggest frustrations in the White House. But it became all of those things, and the story of how it did is the story of Trump's assault on immigration.

Conceived of almost by accident, out of political expediency and sheer marketing power, the wall perfectly captured the us-versus-them spirit that animated Trump's candidacy, becoming a symbol of the same working-class disaffection and sense of alienation that he had first tapped into by questioning Barack Obama's birthplace. For a politically inexperienced president who was untethered from any particular ideology, the wall was a centering force, an organizing principle for his promises. He would fix what was broken in the country, and what better symbol of America's problems than a deeply dysfunctional immigration system that had become a third rail of politics, too charged for either party to touch? Trump vowed to cut through all of that—a Manhattan developer who would take a figurative hammer and nails to the task. In doing so, he would gleefully raise a middle finger to "political correctness" and to a Republican establishment that was looking for ways to appeal to Hispanic voters. And while he was at it, Trump would fan the flames of fear and insecurity by promising to wall off the United States from the threats he imagined were just across the threshold, the "them" who looked and sounded different than "us."

Was it racism? Nativism? Xenophobia? Trump and those who knew him best swore that it was not. But Trump's instincts clearly tended toward bigotry—the belief that foreigners were a threat, and that native-born Americans were inherently more deserving. And his agenda held deep appeal to white supremacists and others who had felt shut out of politics in America for years, chastised for their views and obsessed with an agenda of racial purity. The appeal for Trump was much simpler and more basic.

He was a marketing genius, a branding maven. And fear of the other, he discovered at his campaign rallies, sells like gangbusters. It worked as well on audiences in places like Michigan, Ohio, and Pennsylvania whose once thriving industrial manufacturing workers felt displaced and distraught as it did in states on the border with Mexico that had been profoundly changed by immigration and immigrants.

But as potent a campaign message as the wall became for Trump, and as strong as its gravitational pull grew after he took office, it also stood as a symbol of everything that plagued his immigration policy. It reflected Trump's fixation with ideas that had political power but were often impossible to implement. His ever-changing dictates about its dimensions and materials were the most concrete examples of the whims of a fickle and deeply insecure president who always grasped for the solution that looked toughest. He pursued the wall over the objections of the career public servants who always knew that a wall was not the solution, just as he would disregard their advice and legal counsel on so many other immigration matters. It was a one-dimensional approach to a complex problem, in large part based on his own ignorance. His determination to build the wall over the objections of Congress reflected his cavalier approach to the law, which invited court challenges at almost every turn. The years-long war he waged over the wall revealed the bundle of contradictions that was Trump himself: a resident of one of the most diverse cities on the planet who married two immigrants, but was hostile to outsiders; a businessman enamored of cheap and readily available labor who pressed for cuts to legal immigration; a self-styled master negotiator who could not cut a deal with Congress on immigration to save his life.

"Build that wall!" was the incessant soundtrack of Trump's frenzied campaign rallies, but once in office he discovered that doing so was an operational, legislative, and legal quagmire that would swallow up his political capital and leave him deeply frustrated. It was a pattern that played out on every level of Trump's immigration agenda. His Muslim ban was an early indication of how the rush to fulfill his campaign promises could sow chaos and spark court challenges. Plotted in secret because Trump's advisers were certain "deep state" bureaucrats would kill it in the cradle, the travel order embodied the president's approach: Propose something outrageous, divisive, and potentially illegal. Watch your political opponents lose their minds criticizing it. Ask questions and provide policy rationales later. Trump's decision to end protections for Dreamers—the undocumented young immigrants who had been brought into the United States as children—set the stage for months of fighting with Congress and revealed his conflicting instincts: a desire to be seen as compassionate even as he disparaged "shithole countries" in Africa and unleashed bare-knuckled tactics on immigrants. His decision to separate migrant children—some just a few months old—from their parents at the border pointed up profound conflicts inside his administration. Some had warned of the dire consequences of a plainly cruel tactic while others argued that it was the only effective way to deter a horde of migrants from rushing the border. It was one of the only times that Trump retreated under pressure, unwilling to endure a backlash that included members of his own family.

And a curious thing—perhaps predictable, in retrospect—happened as Trump's immigration crackdown unfolded throughout the country: an actual crisis, different but no less urgent than the one he was constantly warning Americans about, began to develop and worsen at the border. Desperate groups of migrants, fleeing for their lives and looking for better opportunities from Central America, surged across the border, pleading for asylum and further clogging a system that was already under intense strain. Trump's harsh rhetoric fueled a sense of urgency for these migrants, many of whom hastened their journey north because they believed the new American president was about to seal off the border. His deterrence tactics acted as a perverse incentive; as the administration clamped down at legal ports of entry, migrants went around them, crossing illegally. They formed caravans that were a constant irritant for Trump, a living, breathing personification of his inability to get control of the border. It was a vicious cycle perpetrated by the sitting president of the United States: Clamp down on the flow of migrants being processed at the border, prompting them to look for other ways to get across. Watch as border apprehension numbers rise. Become enraged at the uptick. Crack down still harder. Rinse and repeat.

Through it all, Trump chafed under the strictures of the law and the institutions of government itself, raging profanely about the lawmakers who rejected his demands, the judges who blocked his directives, and the bureaucrats who were unable or unwilling to execute on his wishes. Refusing to be constrained by any of them, he tried to make immigration policy on his own, through declarations on Twitter or out-of-the-blue utterances shouted over the sound of helicopter rotors on his way to Marine One. Trump grasped for ever-more extreme ways to get his hands around the border crisis, ordering the National Guard, and then the active-duty military, to the border over the wishes of his defense secretary. He defied a recalcitrant Congress and declared a national emergency to fund his border wall, drawing a legal challenge that could take years to resolve. He overruled his own homeland security secretary when she refused to turn away migrants at the border and instructed the top Border Patrol official to do just that, promising a presidential pardon if there were consequences. None of it worked. The big, beautiful wall does not exist, and at this writing in the summer of 2019, as Trump looks toward his reelection, border crossings are at their highest levels since he took office, outpacing what they were under Obama.

But for all its frustrations and failures, Trump's attempt to upend the nation's immigration system has had its share of successes, with vast impact on the nation. Through little-noticed rules and regulations, his administration made it more dangerous and costly to be undocumented in the United States. They targeted undocumented immigrants who had lived in the United States for decades, tagging them for immediate removal. It now takes much longer to get a visa to come to America, and the wait to become a naturalized citizen has doubled. The number of refugees admitted to the United States has plummeted to its lowest level in more than three decades.

Through demagoguery and sheer force of messaging, Trump has upended many decades of bipartisan consensus in favor of immigrants and immigration, swinging the pendulum on an issue that is fundamental to America's vision of itself. Since the country's founding, immigration has been at the heart of the American ideals of freedom and democracy, diversity and inclusion, opportunity and upward mobility. But it has also been at the core of the nation's struggles with its own identity, at times yielding darker moments in which leaders have turned inward in hopes of preserving a bygone era.

Trump is one of them.

In the end, Trump always came back to the "big, beautiful wall." His obsession with building it infuriated world leaders and eroded alliances, egged him on to force a damaging government shutdown, frustrated his attempts to cut deals with Democrats, and tortured his own immigration officials every day.

No one was more tortured than Nielsen. But on December 21, just four days before Christmas in 2018, she got her chance to use the mockup of the wall that Trump had described in such detail several weeks earlier. Trump was fuming about the government shutdown that was looming and Nielsen needed a way to distract him. "Sorry to interrupt," she said, pulling out a copy of the artist rendering. Instantly, his mood brightened. This was exactly what he wanted! "That is beautiful," he exclaimed as he yelled out for Dan Scavino, his social media guru and the keeper of the Trump Twitter feed. "I gotta tweet this out!" Nielsen had a moment of heartburn. This wasn't a serious design. Her department wasn't really examining how, or if, it could be built. There might be environmental concerns or operational restrictions. And if the president of the United States tweeted new specs, it could affect the contracts that were already in the works for rebuilding parts of the aging fences along the border. They could probably alter the existing contracts, but the change orders to do so could be costly. It's not really ready to be tweeted, she protested. But Scavino wasn't about to tell Trump no, and it wouldn't have mattered anyway. This was a president who did what he wanted.

At 5:14 that evening, Trump posted the sketch that Nielsen had handed him on Twitter. "A design of our Steel Slat Barrier which is totally effective while at the same time beautiful!" The picture showed what looked like tall, black flagpoles with pointy tops, one after another, towering over a Customs and Border Protection Jeep. It quickly became an internet meme, Trump's proudest achievement instantly transformed into the object of relentless ridicule. The president's tweet drew thousands of replies, including some that showed dogs, cats, and even people squeezing through the flagpole-like slats and into the interior of the United States.

Trump's moment of triumph that day in the Oval Office would be just that: a moment. It quickly gave way to frustration with his inability to get funding for the wall and the broader predicament of a border crisis that seemed impossible to solve. His wall—like his immigration agenda itself—remains a work in progress, as divisive as it is ambitious, as politically powerful as it is practically limited, as much a private disappointment as it is a public source of pride. Trump's assault on immigration became the beating heart of his administration, reflecting deep truths about the most unconventional of presidents, about whom he trusts and how he governs, and about the ways in which he has impacted the country he leads.

This is how it happened.

— 1 —

THE VESSEL

SOARING HIGH ABOVE IOWA in his private jet, Donald J. Trump permitted himself to imagine a successful campaign for the White House.

The year was 2013, and Trump had just finished a short trip to Ames, where he had spoken to the Family Leadership Summit, a gathering of evangelical Christian conservatives that had become a mandatory Midwest stop for aspiring presidential candidates. During his speech, Trump lamented the decline of the country, which he said was on the brink of collapse. He mercilessly ridiculed Mitt Romney's losing presidential campaign and what he said was the failed strategy of Republican operatives like Karl Rove. He warned that Hillary Clinton would be tough to beat in 2016 and cautioned Republicans against cutting any immigration deal that would allow undocumented immigrants to gain citizenship. That would be "a death wish" for the party, he said, given that all 11 million illegal immigrants would certainly vote for Democrats. He threw in some signature Trumpian flourishes, too, drawing chuckles from the audience when he said he'd much rather talk about himself than Romney. "It's very hard for me to build up somebody else," he told the crowd of devout, churchgoing Christians. "But what the hell."

In fact, Trump was preoccupied with building himself up on that trip.

He was already sixty-seven years old and thinking about seizing what his advisers were telling him would be his final chance at mounting a winning presidential campaign. As a Manhattan real estate magnate and political neophyte, he had donated to liberal Democrats but done little more than flirt on the fringes of Republican politics. He had no obvious policy platform on which to run and no core set of beliefs with which the public identified him. He was known for his boastful air as a businessman, his glitzy buildings and golden hair, his brash "You're fired!" television persona— and not much else. But Trump had a gut feeling that he could build a movement that would capture the imagination of a group of disaffected Americans who disdained conventional politics and felt that they were being talked down to by politically correct elites. He imagined harnessing their anger and sense of exclusion to create a powerful groundswell. Trump knew they existed, and he knew how to speak to them because he had been cultivating them for years. These were the same people who had bought into a pet cause that had recently gained purchase as he traveled around the country: Trump's quest to prove that Barack Obama was an African born in Kenya, making him an illegitimate—indeed an illegal—president.

Trump had been stoking the birther lie for two years, bringing it up in television interviews, embracing fringe conspiracy theorists who offered detailed purported evidence, and tweeting false claims about Obama's birth certificate. Trump repeatedly taunted the sitting president to prove that he belonged in the Oval Office. Sam Nunberg, the foul-mouthed political operative from New York City who worked for Trump, had seen the result: Trump's popularity among hard-core Republican primary voters had skyrocketed. Nunberg thought that people who believed in the birther conspiracy could represent at least 5 to 7 percent of Trump's base if he ran for president. But running openly as a birther was a nonstarter. The trick, Nunberg told Trump that summer, was to weave the birther theme into a legitimate campaign platform, without losing those voters.

"It's going to be immigration," Nunberg told Trump that day as they flew back from Iowa to New York on his private 757, emblazoned with "TRUMP" in giant white letters. Birtherism was an attempt to stoke fear about installing in the Oval Office a dark-skinned foreigner whose loyalties and patriotism were in question. The voters who appreciated the theory were also moved by Trump's blunt talk about the evils of immigration, and they harbored deep anxiety about people who looked and sounded different from themselves. "It's interconnected," Nunberg said later. "We would be able to keep those people."

Trump was captivated throughout the flight, peppering Nunberg with questions. A communications operative who relished the same kind of in-your-face politics that animated Trump, Nunberg first drew attention for his fierce opposition to construction of a mosque two blocks from Ground Zero in New York. He was a volunteer for Mitt Romney's first presidential campaign in 2007 and signed on with Trump in 2011, long before the real estate mogul was taken seriously as a potential candidate. That day on the plane, they discussed the Republican Party's "autopsy," in which the party leaders had called for renewed outreach to Hispanics after Romney's loss in 2012. In a campaign, Trump would take the opposite approach, seizing on the threats posed by immigrants as a way of doubling down on the fears of American citizens who were struggling economically. Immigration dovetailed perfectly with Trump's protectionist impulses and his long-standing antipathy for multilateral trade agreements, which riled up voters who felt exploited by globalization. And it had the advantage of setting Trump apart from some of the Republican Party's leading lights, like Jeb Bush, the former governor of Florida, and Marco Rubio, the Florida senator—two possible rivals whose positions on immigration were squishy at best. Nunberg ranted during the flight about John McCain, the Arizona senator who had tried, and failed, to pass a liberal immigration compromise with Democrats. "Nobody kissed the Spanish people's asses more than Juan McCain, okay?" Nunberg told Trump. "And he got less votes from the Spanish than even Mitt Romney did in 2012," Nunberg told him (though the opposite was true). "This shit is not how you get their votes." Immigration was an issue Trump could take on without any real financial risk to his business, Nunberg promised. "I don't think those people are getting married at Trump Tower or Mar-a-Lago," Nunberg said with a laugh. "It's not going to cost you business."

If there was any doubt in Nunberg's mind that immigration would be

Trump's issue, the flight dispelled it. It was, he said later, like pushing on an open door.

Trump did not know it at the time, but seven months earlier, three men had gathered in Washington, D.C., and sketched out what would become the contours of Trump's immigration-centered campaign. They met in the shabbily chic, ornate dining room of a townhouse on Capitol Hill known as the Breitbart Embassy, which served both as Steve Bannon's home and the headquarters of Breitbart News, the right-wing media empire he oversaw. Bannon had invited Jeff Sessions, the Republican senator from Alabama, and Stephen Miller, one of the senator's top aides, for a dinner that would last for five hours and serve as the spark for a political alliance that would change history.

A onetime Navy officer and Goldman Sachs investment banker, Bannon in 2013 looked like neither, with his unkempt, ragged mane of salt-and-pepper hair, chinos and multiple layers of shirts, open at the collar and usually stacked under a khaki barn jacket. He was not yet a universally recognizable figure on the national stage, assailed by the left as an anti-Semite or lampooned by *Saturday Night Live* as a Grim Reaper–like figure behind a childlike president. But as the chairman of Breitbart, the hard-right internet outlet backed by the conservative Mercer family, he was well known in media circles and within the Republican Party as a political anarchist. Bannon had spent $1 million of his own money making *The Undefeated*, a hagiographic documentary about Sarah Palin, McCain's ill-fated 2008 Republican vice presidential nominee, which had been panned by critics. Bannon used his clout at Breitbart and the megaphone of a satellite radio show popular with the far-right conservatives and white supremacists who make up the alt-right to torment establishment Republicans. He prodded the party toward a darker view of American society and culture—one in which whites felt threatened by immigrants, radically left-leaning Democrats, and, most importantly, by mainstream Republicans who he argued had forsaken the people who sent them to Washington. There was, Bannon argued, a "collective unconsciousness" among working-class voters, who believed that immigrants were to blame for the social and economic problems they were suffering. But politicians had to find a way to tap into those concerns, and he needed to find the perfect vessel to carry the message. Bannon railed against elites even as he eagerly rubbed shoulders with Washington reporters while pitching them on the dangers of a corrupt ruling class. A fan of apocalyptic imagery and the 1973 French novel *The Camp of the Saints*, in which mass migration to the West from the Third World leads to the destruction of Western civilization, Bannon argued that the "Judeo-Christian West" was engaged in a war against Islamic fascism.

Jefferson Beauregard Sessions III had strong views on immigration shaped by his experience as a young politician in rural Alabama. He had watched as an influx of immigrants had moved into his state's white working-class communities, taking the grueling, low-wage jobs in poultry plants that had once been the exclusive domain of poor, unskilled Americans. During more than a decade as a federal prosecutor and state attorney general, and twenty years in the Senate, Sessions came to believe that legal and illegal immigrants posed a direct threat to the country by depressing wages, committing crimes, and competing for welfare benefits. At sixty-six years old, he was deeply influenced by the work of George Borjas, a Harvard economist who has said that immigrants have an adverse impact on the economy. An apple-cheeked, almost elfin white-haired man with a glint in his eye, Sessions was as courtly as his deep southern accent suggested. He was no fire-breather, and he did not set out to become the leading anti-immigrant voice in the United States Senate. He had never worked much on the issue before 2006, when George W. Bush had set out to forge a bipartisan comprehensive immigration reform bill that would give the undocumented immigrants living in the United States—then estimated at around 12 million—a pathway to citizenship. But during a meeting in his Senate office that year with Roy Beck, the executive director of NumbersUSA, a group that pressed for less immigration, it dawned on Sessions that he might be the only person willing to take up the cause and try to block Bush's "amnesty." Sessions turned to look out his window, clasping his hands behind his back as he pondered a future as the leading anti-immigration voice in Congress. "I guess if I don't do it," Sessions finally said, "nobody's going to do it."

Miller, then in his mid-twenties, had found a home on Capitol Hill as a spokesman and strategist for Sessions. By day, he drafted the senator's strongly worded speeches lamenting how Congress was too complacent in the face of Obama's overly permissive immigration policies. By night, he would pelt journalists with barrages of emails arguing that immigrants were taking advantage of native-born Americans, depressing wages, living off welfare, and posing threats to their communities. He forged an informal alliance with Breitbart, pumping out a steady stream of tips and critiques that the news site would dutifully publish, making life exceedingly uncomfortable and politically dangerous for those seeking a consensus for a comprehensive immigration overhaul.

Together, the trio couldn't have been further out on the fringes of the Republican Party establishment in 2013. But they were convinced that their views represented those of the majority of voters. And they were determined not to give up on their vision of a very different future for America, one where secure borders meant that immigrants were no longer threats to the economic and physical safety of the native-born.

The dinner unfolded at Bannon's home at a dark time for Republicans. Obama's reelection victory over Romney two months earlier had sent dejected party leaders searching for answers for how they could have suffered defeat in two consecutive presidential elections. Some argued that Romney's harsh approach on immigration—he had proposed making life so untenable for undocumented immigrants that they would "self-deport"—had cost Republicans the election, driving away Hispanic voters who helped Obama win key states like Colorado, Nevada, and Virginia. Miller thought that analysis was disastrously stupid. What was needed, the trio agreed, was not a more inclusive party but a raw, populist appeal to the grievances and concerns of white working-class voters. Those men and women felt betrayed by liberal politicians like Obama, who constantly cried foul about "inequality" but did nothing to confront the trade agreements and immigration policies that created job loss, low wages, and disappearing economic opportunity. Over steak and fish from

Dean & DeLuca, the three men discussed an article entitled "The Case of the Missing White Voters" by Sean Trende, a right-wing writer. More than six and a half million white voters did not show up in 2012, Trende wrote, because they could not stomach Romney, who had allowed himself to be caricatured as a wealthy elitist and failed to articulate an agenda that spoke to their fears and insecurities.

As the clock ticked close to midnight, talk shifted to 2016, and Bannon turned to Sessions with an out-of-the-blue idea: "We have to run you for president." Bannon told Sessions the same thing that he had told both Sarah Palin and Lou Dobbs, the Fox anchor, during similar conversations years before. He wouldn't win the presidency. But a Sessions campaign could catapult trade and immigration to the top of the Republican agenda and reshape the party in the process. The argument was simple. Mass illegal immigration was just a scam perpetrated by the Chamber of Commerce and corporate-backed Republicans to suppress wages for unskilled black and Hispanic workers, Bannon said, and legal immigration was doing the same to skilled workers. Trade agreements were nothing more than a permission slip for unfair foreign competition, hurting working people while fattening the wallets of the elites who ran the companies that benefited. It was the same set of arguments Sessions had been making in the Senate for many years, Bannon argued. If he took it national in a presidential campaign, the populist right could seize control of the Republican machinery in Washington.

The Alabama senator demurred. I'm not the guy, he said. Even if he thought the strategy could elevate the issues that he had been toiling quietly for years to highlight, a presidential campaign would dredge up the nasty accusations of racism that his enemies raised during his failed bid to be a federal judge in 1986. In his Senate confirmation hearings that year, an African American prosecutor testified that Sessions had called him "boy." Sessions had always denied the story, but if he ran for president, that would all come up again, he told Bannon and Miller. Still, the three men were captivated by the idea of finding a candidate who could seize on the deep resentments of white, working-class Americans toward the large influx of immigrants entering the country.

Sessions believed there was a cleavage between where the American people were and where the political establishment was. Bannon saw it, Stephen Miller saw it, and Sessions saw it, along with a few others. Why not give the American people what they want? What's wrong with a lawful system of immigration that serves the national interest? The energy generated from the clash between elites and everybody else was what generates populism, Sessions liked to say. And if a politician was serving the people, instead of the elites, there was nothing wrong with honest populism.

Even if they didn't know it that night in early 2013, the three men were setting in motion an absurdly unrealistic takeover of the Republican Party and an improbable presidency, which would usher in an equally audacious effort to upend decades of law and policy that had opened the United States to generations of immigrants. By the time their project had come to fruition, they would erode a public consensus in favor of immigration that was more fragile than most in Washington had thought it to be.

The notion of finding a candidate who could catapult those ideas to the forefront of the Republican Party was still on Bannon's mind two months after their dinner when he heard Trump speak at the Conservative Political Action Conference, CPAC, in Washington. Trump was not a candidate for anything at the time. But his speech touched on all of the themes that Bannon, Sessions, and Miller had talked about at dinner: China's rise, the danger of 11 million "illegals" gaining the right to vote, the decline of the manufacturing sector in the United States. "You're on a suicide mission," Trump told Republicans. "Our country is a total mess—a total and complete mess, and what we need is leadership." Bannon's ears perked up. Suddenly, the conversation that had started two months earlier was no longer in the realm of the hypothetical. Trump was the living, breathing embodiment of what Bannon, Sessions, and Miller had agreed was needed to bring their party back from the dead. Miller was impressed, too. Within months, Miller would tell friends that he hoped that Trump would run for president.

Raised in Queens and a longtime resident of Manhattan, Trump spent most of his life in places defined by diversity, where differences of language and national origin are a reality and multiculturalism is a fact of life. But even in his childhood, Mr. Trump and his family sought the homogeneity afforded by wealth and privilege that set him apart. Jamaica Estates, the neighborhood where he grew up, was a cloistered and mostly white enclave in a sea of more pluralistic communities, where he attended a private school before being sent to a military academy. As an adult, Trump was equally removed from the clash of cultures on the streets of New York City, overlooking them from the windows of his glitzy triplex apartment in Trump Tower. He once observed that from the top floor of his building "we looked down on the sidewalk and there were thousands and thousands of people, they looked like ants, little people going all over—boom boom boom—so little, because when you're sixty-eight floors, they look really small, but there were a lot of them."

The president himself is a grandson of immigrants, as Michael D'Antonio notes in the biography of Trump that he wrote a year before the 2016 election. Friedrich Drumpf, Trump's grandfather, immigrated in the 1890s from Bremen, a German city on the banks of the Weser River in the northwest part of the country. He arrived in New York at Castle Garden, an entry point at the southern tip of Manhattan, where immigration officers conducted many inspections before stamping their approval, and the name Trumpf, on his papers. A barber in Germany, Friedrich Trumpf followed the mining boom of that decade to the Pacific Northwest, and later renounced his allegiance to his home country and became an American citizen. He eventually returned to New York like many immigrants, wealthier and more prosperous than he was when he arrived. After traveling back to Germany to marry, D'Antonio writes, Friedrich Trump (by then he had dropped the "f") returned to New York with a pregnant wife.

If Trump took anything profound from his grandfather's experience as an immigrant to America, there is little evidence of it. Despite having been the subject of attention and scrutiny for much of his adult life,

Trump rarely built his grandfather's immigrant story into the narrative of his own life. (In fact, one of Trump's most curious fabrications involves claiming that his father, not his grandfather, had been born and raised in Germany, a false assertion that he has repeated at least three times as president.) His early upbringing was not without exposure to some other kinds of people; his family occasionally vacationed at the Concord in the Catskills, where they "ate dinner together at tables piled with platters of kosher food," writes Gwenda Blair in her book *The Trumps: Three Generations of Builders and a President.* But there are few stories about Trump's exposure to people from other cultures during his time at the New York Military Academy, where he attended high school, and later at Fordham University and the Wharton School of Business. Those early years offered few clues to explain his later embrace of xenophobia and anti-immigrant sentiment as a path to political power.

In the early 1970s, the Justice Department sued Trump and his father, alleging that the pair refused to rent apartments to African Americans, a charge that Trump vigorously denied. As Blair observed, the future president learned a lesson from the episode about surviving accusations about racism: "He had also seen that being charged with discrimination did not seem to deter anyone in the public or private realm from doing business with him," she wrote. "Indeed, practically speaking, the entire matter appeared to add up to little more than 'a spit in the ocean.'"

In the 1980s and 1990s, Trump's instincts about race and immigration became public fodder when he called for the death penalty in the case of the Central Park Five, four African Americans and a Hispanic man who were convicted of brutally beating and raping Trisha Meili, a white woman who was out for a nighttime jog in Central Park. In full-page ads that he took out in the city's four major newspapers, Trump assailed what he called "roving bands of wild criminals," and later, in an interview with Larry King, he said that, "maybe hate is what we need if we're gonna get something done." Twelve years later, the convictions of the five men were thrown out after a serial rapist linked by DNA confessed to the crimes, but Trump never apologized. Then in 2011, Trump revived the birther conspiracy about Obama, instinctively tapping into a fear of "the other" that he felt strongly himself.

Bannon had no elegant theory about where Trump's views on immigration came from. "We needed a vessel" for the anti-immigration presidential campaign, Bannon would say later, and this guy was it; it was as simple as that. He saw Trump as a modern-day Archie Bunker the "lovable bigot," as the television producer Norman Lear once called his fictional character, sitting in his armchair ranting about the threat to the common folk. Trump, who lived in a gilded tower bearing his name in the heart of Manhattan, was about as far as he could be from the blue-collar Archie in his working-class home in Queens, but when he opened his mouth, it was sometimes hard to tell the difference. Some who knew Trump said the prejudice ran deep and had been building for years. "He's always been fearful where other cultures are concerned and always had anxiety about food and safety when he travels outside the United States," said D'Antonio, who spent hours talking with Trump before he became president. "His objectification and demonization of people who are different has festered for decades, and he has sought out the safety of the same." Over time, those views hardened and became part of a more insidious story Trump told himself about people from outside the United States.

By the time he entered politics, Trump had grown to see immigration as a zero-sum issue: what is good for immigrants is bad for America. But even as Trump embraced those hard-line views, he remained conflicted, often describing himself to friends as benevolent and wanting to be liked by the many immigrants he employed. As a budding politician, he harbored ambitions of appealing to Hispanic voters who he believed would share his anger at illegal immigrants because they were competing unfairly for jobs. Two weeks after returning from Iowa with Nunberg in 2013, Trump met with Antonio Tijerino, the president of the Hispanic Heritage Foundation, to discuss whether the group might honor him at their annual gala. Tijerino arrived at Trump Tower with three guests, young undocumented immigrants. Sitting in Trump's office, they shared their stories one by one, describing how they had been brought to the United

States as children and raised as Americans, but each lacked the legal status to attend college, serve in the military, or work.

"I came to this country when I was five and a half years old," José Machado told Trump. Machado had awoken one morning years earlier at the age of fifteen to find his mother had vanished—deported, he later learned, back to Nicaragua. Trump was shocked. "Honestly, he had no idea," Machado would say later.

Trump was preoccupied with the politics of the Hispanic community. He quizzed his young guests about what they thought of the potential Republican presidential candidates—Marco Rubio, Jeb Bush, Rick Perry, Chris Christie—and asked who they thought would win their community's support in the next election. He mused about his own personal experiences with immigrants, at one point saying that some of the employees keeping the lawns beautiful and green at his hotel and golf properties were probably "illegals." But the future president displayed no understanding of how the immigration system worked. "Well, why don't you just hire an attorney and get legal?" Trump asked them, appearing perplexed when they insisted that it was not that simple. "What do you mean that's not possible, to just pay someone to make sure you can stay?"

Trump was friendly and charming, and seemed touched by the Dreamers' personal stories. But he also displayed flashes of what would later become his America First philosophy, at one point asking the young immigrants "so who deserves to go to college? A young man who's in a wheelchair, or one of you?" The question hung in the air awkwardly. As the meeting wound down, Trump insisted that his guests accompany him downstairs to his gift shop for souvenirs for them and their families. In the elevator on the way to the lobby, Trump became quiet, looking at his visitors and seemed to come to a conclusion in his own head. He nodded slightly and said quietly, "You convinced me."

Before the group could react, Trump was showing them around the gift shop, choosing watches, books, and neckties for them to take home. As soon as they left Trump Tower, the activists—stunned to have apparently won his support—rushed to draft a press release memorializing his stance. "Perhaps the most poignant part of the meeting was when Donald

Trump told José, Diego and Gaby 'You've convinced me,' " the release said. Trump was irate that his words had been made public. Days later, Estuardo Rodriguez Jr., a lobbyist who had attended the meeting and drafted the statement, received a call from Trump's assistant, Rhona Graff, who said that Trump wished the group had not issued a press release without clearing it with him first.

"We never heard from him again," Rodriguez said.

By 2014, Nunberg and his political mentor, Roger Stone, were the two primary consultants urging Trump to run for president. Stone was a legend in Manhattan, a Republican political assassin and former aide to Richard Nixon who made money in the 1980s and 1990s by parlaying his connections into a Washington lobbying firm. Nunberg and Stone shared a palpable disdain for the establishment, an appreciation of the outrageous, a tendency to be profane, and an on-again-off-again friendship with Trump. Nunberg would frequently be fired by the mercurial Trump (in 2014 for arranging an article that turned out to be unflattering) only to be rehired again, and then fired once more (in August of 2015, for racist Facebook posts). Stone would eventually get caught up in the Russia election meddling probe after bragging during the campaign that he had connections with Julian Assange and knew what WikiLeaks planned to release before Election Day.

In April of 2014, the pair arranged for Trump to attend the New Hampshire Freedom Summit at the Executive Court Banquet Facility in Manchester. Organized by Americans for Prosperity and Citizens United, the event gave Trump a chance to mock Jeb Bush, who had just claimed that people who enter the United States illegally do so out of "love." Trump was merciless in his skewering of Bush and the audience loved it. "That's one I never heard of before. I've heard money. I've heard this. I've heard sex. I've heard everything. But one thing I've never heard of is love." A few months later, Trump attended a fundraiser in Iowa for Steve King, the virulently anti-immigrant congressman, and called for a ban on travel from parts of Africa hit by an Ebola outbreak. "He said, why the fuck is it our problem that these idiots went to Africa?" Nunberg recalled.

But getting Trump to remember to talk about immigration was tricky. He rarely stuck to a script on anything. Nunberg and Stone knew they needed a gimmick to make sure that their candidate would never forget his anti-immigration screed. One day that summer, Nunberg called up Stone with what he thought would be the perfect mnemonic. Trump loves two things: boasting about himself and talking about building things. Let's have him promise to build a wall on the southwestern border with Mexico. And tell him to say he'll cut foreign aid to Mexico to pay for the construction. Trump fancied himself above all else a master of the construction trade. He wouldn't be able to resist talking about building a giant edifice as only he could, and from there it would be easy. He would promise to crack down on illegal immigration, lament the problems at the border, and warn of the threat of violence and disease from migrants swarming into the United States.

In January of 2015, Trump tried out a version of the idea during a return visit to Iowa for the Freedom Summit. "We have to build a fence—and it's got to be a beauty," Trump said. "Who can build better than Trump? I build. It's what I do. I build. I build nice fences. But I build great buildings. Fences are easy—believe me." Trump then went on to deliver the rest of his immigration attack, saying that the political responses to the border had been "incompetent" and asserting that he had seen video of immigrants crossing the border illegally and walking right past armed members of the military. The crowd loved it.

Trump loved their reaction even more.

The "build-a-wall" message was cemented four months later, when Trump gleefully delivered it during a little noticed visit to the Texas Patriots, an ultraconservative political group with roots in the antigovernment Tea Party movement. Sitting on a stage in a big leather-backed chair in a large auditorium, Trump laid it on thick: Mexicans were pouring "illegals" and cheap cars across the border with the United States like so much "vomit." He let out a sound effect to mimic throwing up for emphasis, drawing laughs from his audience. "These are people—and some are very fine, I'm sure—but they're sending their killers, their rapists, their murderers, their drug lords. This is what we're getting," he told the audience. "One thing I can tell you—I'm a great builder. I would build the greatest wall that anybody's ever seen. Believe me." There was enthusiastic hooting and a sustained round of applause.

Trump was hooked. The wall would become a permanent part of his campaign machinery and a potent symbol for everything that he stood for, taking on totemic significance and shaping his presidency. It would ultimately prompt a government shutdown as Trump battled with Democrats over border security, and the declaration of a national emergency of dubious constitutionality. The populist, anti-immigrant appeal that Bannon, Miller, and Sessions had envisioned at their dinner years earlier was a perfect fit for Trump as he prepared to hijack a Republican establishment that he viewed as soft on crime, weak on the border, and gripped by political correctness.

That was the plan as Trump prepared to officially announce his bid for the presidency on June 16, 2015.

In the few minutes before Trump walked out to start the show, Nunberg had just one final opportunity to offer some advice. (First, though, Trump kicked him out of the holding room so he could make a last-minute switch from a black suit to a navy blue one.) Remember, Nunberg said when Trump let him back in, you have to get in as much about immigration as you can. He pleaded with Trump not to forget, as the developer-turned-celebrity prepared to face the cameras. The speech that Nunberg had helped write included a critical section about Mexico beating the United States on trade. It repeated Trump's call for a "massive wall to secure our southern border," along with a Trumpian boast that "nobody can build a bigger and better wall than Donald Trump." But this was Trump. He was infamous for paying little attention to prepared remarks. And so on that day in June, Nunberg was nervous about what he might—or might not—say.

Moments later, Trump emerged with his wife, Melania, at the top of an escalator in the grand, marble-and-brass-adorned lobby of Trump Tower, his fortress in midtown Manhattan. With Neil Young's "Rockin' in the Free World" blaring, Trump made his way down the escalator and onto a flag-lined stage, where his daughter Ivanka gave him a peck on the cheek. Nunberg didn't need to hold his breath for long. After a few introductory remarks to the packed room, Trump delivered only six words from the written speech—"Our country is in serious trouble"—before veering off script. Within forty-six seconds, Trump was talking about Mexico beating the United States at the border. And fifty seconds after that, he delivered a rant about immigration and the line that would forever define his campaign and his presidency.

"The U.S. has become a dumping ground for everybody else's problems. It's true. And these aren't the best and the finest. When Mexico sends its people, they are not sending their best. They are not sending you. They are not sending you. They are sending people that have lots of problems, and they are bringing those problems with us. They are bringing drugs; they are bringing crime. They're rapists. And some, I assume, are good people."

Bannon, listening to Trump wandering off script, was thrilled. Turning to Alex Marlow, Breitbart's editor in chief, he said, "That's the sound bite! Get it pulled." Bannon was gleefully anticipating the outrage that was to come. "They're going to go full meltdown," he said. "Nobody's ever talked like this. People don't talk like this—you can't! This is the way you cut through the vernacular."

His prediction did not play out immediately. Initial reports about Trump's announcement focused on his bombastic promise to make America great again, and hardly mentioned his comments about Mexico. But after a twenty-one-year-old white supremacist killed nine African Americans at a church in South Carolina the next day, Hillary Clinton suggested that Trump's comments about immigrants could "trigger people who are less than stable" to commit such acts, and she condemned Trump for saying "some very inflammatory things about Mexicans." Trump offered a video retort on Instagram, calling it "pretty pathetic" that Clinton had blamed him. But when the fierce backlash to Trump's comments finally came over the course of the next week, it proved financially costly for Trump. NBC and Univision dumped Trump's Miss USA and Miss Universe programs. Macy's canceled its line of Trump-branded menswear. Mattress-maker Serta said it would stop selling the Trump Home collection of bedding. José Andrés, the famed Spanish-born chef, backed out of a restaurant deal for Trump's new hotel in Washington. NASCAR decided not to hold its annual banquet at the Trump National Doral resort in Miami. "Why did you have to say they're rapists, Donald?" Don Lemon, the CNN anchor, asked during a telephone interview with Trump. Trump was defiant and fired back. "Well, somebody's doing the raping, Don."

On July 8, three weeks after Trump's announcement, Reince Priebus, the chairman of the Republican National Committee, called to beg Trump to tone down the immigration rhetoric. Donors and activists were worried that Trump's attacks on Mexicans were going to stain them all, Priebus warned. We are working really hard at the RNC to build Hispanic and black coalitions, and we can't do it if these are the words that you are using. It would cost the party crucial votes among people of color, and hand the White House to Democrats. When the call from Priebus leaked to the press, Trump lied about it in a tweet, calling the story "totally false reporting" and saying that Priebus had merely told him his speech had "hit a nerve." Trump refused to back down and later told NBC News that he had "nothing to apologize for." He filed a lawsuit against Univision. And on Fox News, he doubled down, saying that "some of the people coming here are very violent people—not all."

But Nunberg was ecstatic about the Priebus flap. The Republican establishment, the left-wing liberals, and the familiar cast of immigration-reform characters were all whining that Trump's over-the-top rhetoric about the Mexicans should disqualify him as a candidate. In three short weeks, Trump had drawn a line in the sand, setting himself apart from his rivals, especially Jeb Bush and Marco Rubio. For every Republican voter who was frustrated about immigrants, there was now a clear choice between Trump and the rest of the political world. "It was a tremendous advantage for us," Nunberg said. The seeds of Trump's embrace of immigration as a political weapon had been planted years earlier, by Nunberg and others. It had taken a while. But in the days after Trump's announcement at Trump Tower, they finally bore fruit.

"They thought they were going to knock us out for that," Nunberg recalled with a sneer. Trump had been at number eight in some polls when he was at the top of the escalator before his announcement. Within weeks, he had shot up to the top of the Republican pack. "It helped us. It didn't help business-wise; he lost millions of dollars. But it helped us politically."

— 2 —

BREAKING THE APOLOGY-RETREAT CYCLE

JEFF SESSIONS WAS IN his car heading to a Republican event in Mobile, Alabama, when he heard the news on the radio: Donald Trump was in town.

It was a Friday in August of 2015, about two months after the launch of Trump's campaign, and no one had given Alabama's junior senator a heads-up that the candidate was planning a visit to his hometown. But Sessions had been watching Trump's campaign with growing interest. The immigration rhetoric was spot-on, he thought. Over the previous decade, Sessions had waged his lonely battles in the Senate to stop a bipartisan effort to grant amnesty to nearly 11 million illegal immigrants, a move that he believed would further devastate middle America. In floor speeches, Sessions had derided colleagues from both parties as self-anointed "masters of the universe" who wanted to do more for immigrants than for the struggling workers in the United States. Surveys showed that most Americans wanted the border secured for good before any action was taken to legalize millions of people who had entered the country illegally. Congress needed to listen to that sentiment. Sessions was also skeptical of free trade agreements, which he viewed as a giveaway to foreign countries and detrimental to workers in the United States. As far as Sessions was concerned, Trump was the only candidate who was addressing the issues that he and Miller and Bannon had talked about during their dinner years earlier—speaking boldly, and with clarity, about both trade and immigration.

If Trump was appearing in his backyard, Sessions was going to make sure he was onstage with him. He turned his car around and headed back toward home, dialing George Gigicos, Trump's advance man and an Alabama native, as he drove. Come to the airport, Gigicos told him. Once there, Trump invited Sessions onto the plane for a pre-rally chat. A few hours later, Sessions was in the audience at the Ladd-Peebles Stadium, home to the University of South Alabama Jaguars, along with at least 20,000 people, nearly half of the stadium's capacity. The senator could not believe that in a matter of days Trump's staff had managed to schedule a rally of this size; it dawned on Sessions that this candidate was like no other he had ever seen. After entering the arena to "Sweet Home Alabama" and raucous applause from the crowd, Trump singled out Sessions.

"We have a great politician here. We have a man here. He's been so spot-on. He's so highly respected. Has anybody ever heard of Senator Jeff Sessions?" At Trump's urging, Sessions clambered up onto the stage. "Look at him, he's like twenty years old. Unbelievable guy," Trump bellowed as Sessions briefly donned a white baseball cap with the words Make America Great Again. While not endorsing Trump's nascent presidential bid, Sessions made it clear to the audience that he appreciated Trump's rhetoric. "The American people, these people, want somebody in the presidency who stands up for them, defends their interests and the laws and traditions of this country," Sessions said at the microphone. "We welcome you here, thank you for the work you put into the immigration issue. I'm really impressed with your plan. I know it will make a difference. And this crowd shows that a lot of people agree with that."

There were real numbers behind Sessions's gut feeling, he would soon learn. In the fall of 2015, Kellyanne Conway, a Republican pollster, was working for Senator Ted Cruz of Texas and publicly criticizing Trump as offensive and extreme. But she confided in Sessions that she had studied the polling data on immigration, and Trump's message was resonating strongly. It was remarkable, she told Sessions. By the following July, Conway was working for Trump's campaign.

For Sessions, Trump had seized on a cause that was both politically powerful and desperately needed. During the next several months, the senator from Alabama would offer informal counsel and advice to Trump. Then, at a February 2016 rally in Madison, Alabama, just outside Huntsville, Sessions delivered the formal endorsement that had been long in coming, declaring that Trump was leading a movement, not a campaign. His enthusiastic public backing of Trump was a *Good Housekeeping* seal of approval for many hard-line activists and voters who had yet to be convinced that Trump could succeed in taking their anti-immigration agenda all the way to the White House. But even more important was something less visible that Sessions helped to deliver to Trump in the days after his endorsement: Stephen Miller.

In Miller, Sessions had found a kindred spirit who channeled his restrictionist thinking into speeches, press releases, and a seemingly endless stream of indignant emails to reporters. The Trump campaign was also a natural fit for Miller, who began informally advising the candidate on immigration issues while still working for Sessions. Steve Bannon, who built a symbiotic relationship with Miller on Capitol Hill as the young aide fed Breitbart a steady stream of anti-immigration story lines, was relentless in urging the campaign to hire Miller full-time. Once they did, Miller became Trump's primary speechwriter and sharpened the campaign's immigration agenda. Before long, Miller became a mini-celebrity of sorts on the Trump campaign circuit, a fixture as an opening act at the candidate's arena rallies. Sporting sideburns and skinny ties, Miller specialized at whipping supporters into a frenzy by reciting a litany of broken promises he said had been made to them for decades on trade, jobs, and border security and exhorting them to think about all the ways in which they had been betrayed by the political establishment. He spoke in grandiose, nationalistic terms and hyperbole. Trump's crowds lapped it up.

At an event in Johnstown, Pennsylvania, about two weeks before Election Day, Miller told a hall full of working-class voters that the steel mills had closed and their jobs and opportunities been shipped overseas not because of globalization and a modernizing economy, but "because some politician in Washington, D.C., got a little bit of graft"—he rubbed his fingers together for effect—"and decided to look the other way when they started dumping the products into your community." That event was personal for Miller and offered a hint of the history that shaped his political ideology. His mother, Miriam Glosser, grew up in Johnstown, where Miller told the audience his "immigrant ancestors" opened a chain of grocery stores. "It broke my heart to see what happened to Johnstown when the steel mill shut down and the jobs left and the industry died and they went to foreign countries," Miller told the crowd. Now, he said, they only had "one chance" that would "never come again" to vote for Trump and to "show the whole, entire world that Donald J. Trump is going to save this country!" Miller concluded his diatribe as he often did, by flashing a "V" for victory sign and introducing the candidate, leaving the crowd seething with excitement and rage.

For Miller, the Trump campaign was a revelation. For years, he had felt a sense of deep disappointment with Republican politicians, who in his view repeatedly betrayed their voters, especially when it came to immigration. Republican candidates would latch on to a get-tough-on-immigrants message to win an election, often airing intense television ads in the final days of the campaign. But once in office, the tough talk would evaporate, replaced by compromise with Democrats or a desire to move on to other issues. Miller called it the "apology-retreat cycle," and it happened again and again.

"There's a profound disenfranchisement, which also speaks to the emotional power of the issue. In many GOP primary voters—and I relate intensely with this emotion, right?—there's a feeling of powerlessness," Miller said during a lunch interview in the White House Mess, the basement cafeteria, near the end of Trump's first year in office. "And so you keep feeling like you're winning at the ballot box and then you're losing at the policy."

Miller recalled knowing instantly that Trump was different. The fact that Trump said what he did at his announcement speech—calling some Mexicans "rapists," and then refusing, amid weeks of criticism, to apologize for it—sent an unmistakable message to voters, Miller believed. It was a simple way of describing Trump's worldview, which Miller said is rooted in a belief that it is the responsibility of leaders to provide advantages to those who reside in their countries, not to those who live elsewhere. By not using the carefully poll-tested language of other politicians, Republicans and Democrats alike, to introduce himself to voters, Trump made it clear that voters who felt disenfranchised by other politicians could trust him not to waver on his anti-immigrant agenda if he made it to the White House. "The fact that he, as I say, doubled down, breaking that apology-retreat cycle, gave enormous confidence to a lot of people," Miller recalled.

And yet Trump's willingness to dehumanize immigrants, his obsession with building a border wall, and his lack of understanding of policy specifics alarmed some immigration hard-liners, leaving them worried that he would be an unreliable and imperfect ally for the restrictive policies they had long championed. When it came time for NumbersUSA, the organization that advocates for less immigration, to grade Trump on his immigration agenda the month after he declared his candidacy, he initially earned a C, in part because of comments Trump made suggesting he wanted more legal immigration and might be open to legal status for some undocumented immigrants—not the "bad ones," Trump said. Shortly after releasing the mediocre grade, NumbersUSA Chief Roy Beck got a call from Sam Clovis, who had signed on as Trump's national campaign chairman. During a meeting with Beck in the glassed-in conference room of the NumbersUSA office suite in Crystal City, Virginia, Clovis pleaded for a better rating for Trump. I'm with you guys entirely, Clovis told Beck. I want to represent you to Mr. Trump, and help educate him, and help get him around to your point of view. Bottom line, Clovis asked: "What do we need to do to get the grade up?"

Beck was frank about what he saw as Trump's shortcomings. "Well, there's ten categories here," he told Clovis, gesturing toward a sheet of paper that listed his group's criteria for evaluating presidential candidates.

"And calling Mexicans rapists *actually isn't on here*. You get no points for that." If Trump wanted the group's support, Beck said, he would have to endorse major policy changes, things like ending chain migration, a loaded term for what immigrant rights advocates call family-based immigration, the long-standing policy of allowing immigrants to sponsor members of their extended families for citizenship in the United States. To get a better grade, Trump would have to call for eliminating the diversity visa lottery that gave away visas to tens of thousands of immigrants around the world, and for requiring every employer in the country to clear potential employees through E-Verify, the federal electronic system that checked their immigration status to make sure they were legal to work in the United States. A wall wasn't mentioned. It wasn't even on Beck's list of priorities.

At the same time, establishment Republicans fretted privately that Trump's over-the-top immigration rhetoric was damaging the party. In early December of 2015, Representative Michael McCaul, the Republican chairman of the House Homeland Security Committee, watched with horror as Trump called for a "total and complete shutdown of Muslims entering the United States" in the wake of terror attacks by Muslim perpetrators in Paris and San Bernardino, California. That idea of a ban on Muslims was antithetical to everything the party and the country stood for, McCaul told colleagues. This had to stop. The next day, McCaul reached out to Rudy Giuliani, a Trump confidant who had been mayor of New York City during the September 11, 2001, terrorist attacks. Together with Michael Mukasey, a former Republican attorney general under George W. Bush, and Andrew C. McCarthy, a former federal prosecutor who worked at *National Review*, McCaul drafted a two-page memo for Trump. In it, they argued that the idea of a Muslim ban was borderline unconstitutional and would not help Trump win the White House. You don't really want a Muslim ban, they wrote. They urged him to focus on policies that would aggressively weed out known and suspected terrorists while facilitating lawful entry. They suggested that Trump use the phrase "extreme vetting" as a way of signaling how tough he would be in protecting the country. It seemed to work. In the weeks that followed, Trump dropped calls for a complete ban on Muslims. "We dodged a bullet," McCaul said privately.

But Miller had other ideas. He couldn't care less what establishment Republicans thought was best for the party. Miller believed that Trump's views on immigration and the incendiary ways in which he expressed himself on the issue were an asset, not a liability. They created the kind of stark contrast with his rivals that voters craved when they were trying to make a decision about whom to support. "The most popular message to say is that you want to grow the economy," Miller explained. "Everybody agrees with that. Well how are you going to distinguish yourself on that? How are you going to build a coalition? How are you going to mobilize a movement? How are you going to inspire people to wait in line for ten hours? To go in the cold, the sleet, the snow, the rain?" For Miller, the obvious answer was: you can't provide that kind of motivation with a feel-good message that all politicians deliver. There was a reason, Miller thought, that Republicans had lost the previous two presidential campaigns, and were likely to do so again. Only issues where there is absolute clarity are powerful enough to win, he said. And voters needed to know that even if he took criticism for it—*especially* if he did—Trump would not back down, he'd dig in further. Immigration was the perfect battleground on which to prove that.

"This issue's potency, because it affects every other issue—health care, education, tax base, economic conditions, social conditions—has the power in ways that the GOP establishment never understood to move elections," Miller said.

Even as Muslim activists condemned Trump for his Islamophobic statements, Trump doubled down yet again. In Cedar Falls, Iowa, he seized on the lyrics of a 1968 Motown song to drive home his fearful message about the hidden dangers of refugees. To the delight of about 1,300 Republican caucus voters, Trump read from "The Snake," made famous by Al Wilson, in which a woman takes in an injured snake and nurses him back to health, only to have the reptile kill her with a venomous bite. In Trump's view, vulnerable-seeming refugees might seem sympathetic and in need of help, but what if they were in fact conniving, vicious snakes, preying on the benevolence of unsuspecting Americans, only to turn on their benefactors at the first opportunity? And in case there was any doubt, Trump made it clear. "I read it and I just thought it put it together," he said. "We have no idea what we are doing. We have no idea who we are taking in, and we'd better be careful."

On August 13, 2016, three weeks after Trump triumphantly claimed the Republican nomination in Cleveland, Bannon sat down with him. Things were in a dark place, amid news reports that the campaign was foundering and off message. Trump was down 16 points to Hillary Clinton in internal polling, and it was getting worse. You have to simplify your agenda, Bannon counseled: bring back jobs, get out of foreign wars, and cut legal and illegal immigration to get our sovereignty back. Trump had gotten wildly off track, with unfathomable plans on education, women's empowerment, and entrepreneurship. Bannon told Trump that the only way to salvage his shot at the presidency was by returning to the themes that helped win him the nomination. Four days later, Trump named him the chief executive of the campaign.

But Trump continued to struggle. While he loved to talk tough at rallies, Trump was by nature a pleaser; he hated face-to-face confrontations and often told people what they wanted to hear, saying whatever would get him through the next five to ten minutes. During a private meeting with Hispanic evangelical leaders at Trump Tower on a Saturday afternoon, Trump said he was open to granting legal status to undocumented immigrants who had not committed crimes beyond their immigration offenses. The statement was at odds with his promise one year before to employ a large "deportation force" to quickly remove undocumented people. The following day, Kellyanne Conway went on CNN's *State of the Union* and was pressed about the inconsistency. Was Trump going to stand up a deportation force or not? It was, Conway said, "to be determined." Trump's base was up in arms. "Are you flip-flopping?" Trump was asked on Fox News the following morning. "No, I'm not flip-flopping," he insisted. "We want to come up with a really fair, but firm answer. It has to be very firm. But we want to come up with something fair."

Behind the scenes, Trump's team knew he had created a big problem for himself. The candidate was scheduled to give a major immigration speech in Colorado that Thursday, and Miller had been toiling away on it for weeks. Now Trump was facing new questions about what his policy actually was, and he was casting about for a way to back off of the idea of mass deportations without alienating his core supporters. With forty-eight hours' notice, his staff summoned three prominent immigration hard-liners—NumbersUSA's Roy Beck, Steven Camarota of the Center for Immigration Studies, and George Borjas, the Harvard labor economist—to an emergency meeting at Trump Tower in Manhattan to strategize with the candidate on how to get him out of the box in which he had put himself.

They gathered on a Monday morning on the fifteenth floor, with Trump at the head of the table along with Beck, Camarota, Borjas, and his campaign brain trust: Bannon, Conway, Miller, and Sessions. For an hour, Trump aggressively quizzed the immigration hawks about what he could say in his speech that wouldn't look like he had abandoned the grass roots. What would the troops be willing to tolerate? he asked. How could he square this circle? Borjas spoke first, giving a lengthy and dry, academic answer that seemed to bore Trump. "No," the candidate said, with an emphatic shake of his head. Camarota was next. "That's not it," Trump responded, his frustration mounting. Then it was Beck's turn. Trump was still not satisfied, and he was starting to act angry, snapping at his guests. He seemed to want them to say it was okay not to insist on a deportation force. Sessions intervened, imploring Trump to tone it down. "Donald, you dug this hole," Sessions said to him, pointing out that none of them had pushed for mass deportations. "These people didn't make you do it." All the while, Trump barked orders at Miller, who was typing away furiously on a laptop as he made late revisions to the speech. "Stephen, you gotta write that!" Trump kept saying. But it soon became clear that the candidate was nowhere near ready to deliver the speech. We're going to have to postpone this, Conway said, as heads nodded around the table. You can stop working on that one, Trump told Miller, gesturing at his computer. He would have to write an entirely new speech.

Sessions and Miller got to work rewriting the speech, adding specific proposals drawn from the hard-core agenda that they had pursued for years, packaged in a ten-point plan. They included Trump's wall, but they went further. Trump would call for an end to "catch and release" policies at the border, an embrace of "zero tolerance" when it came to prosecuting illegal border crossers, the elimination of funding for so-called "sanctuary cities"—those that limited their cooperation with federal immigration authorities—and an overhaul of legal immigration that would prioritize the admission of people with certain skills rather than those whose family members were already living legally in the United States. Trump insisted on calling for an end to Obama's "illegal executive amnesties," now targeting the Dreamers he had met with at Trump Tower years earlier. He would keep the idea of a deportation force, but it would be a team of agents within existing immigration enforcement agencies that would focus on the most violent criminals. And Trump would reassure his base there would be "no amnesty" for undocumented immigrants.

The speech was rescheduled for the following week in Phoenix, immediately after Trump was to return from a trip to Mexico City where he would meet with Mexican president Enrique Peña Nieto. On Trump's jet on the way back, Sessions made the case that he should seize the opportunity to make it clear that he would prioritize the deportation of criminals, not the removal of undocumented immigrants who had lived in the United States for years or decades without incident. What he needed to emphasize, Sessions told Trump, was that the fate of those people would only be addressed once his restrictive and punitive policies—the rest of the ten-point plan—were in place. The conversation turned into an argument. It was too complicated, Trump complained, and it would sound like a retreat. Other politicians are for amnesty, and I'm against it, Trump told Sessions. He said he didn't want to muddle his message. But Sessions persisted, and in the end, they reached a compromise of sorts. Trump would use his signature tough rhetoric, but he would also say that his first order of business would be to kick out criminals and secure the border against future illegal immigration, stopping short of saying he would immediately deport other undocumented immigrants. "Then and only then will we be in a position to consider the appropriate disposition of those individuals who remain," Trump said toward the end of the speech, speaking to 7,500 people at the Phoenix Convention Center.

Some news accounts described Trump's speech that day as a characteristic doubling down by Trump on his hard-core anti-immigration rhetoric, but others had precisely the take that he had told Sessions he feared. *The Washington Post* noted that Trump never clarified whether he meant to forcibly remove the nation's 11 million undocumented immigrants, and *The New York Times* even used the word Trump had on the plane ride to Phoenix, saying that the candidate had "muddled" his message. Still, for Miller and Sessions, it was a triumph. They had finally gotten Trump to lay out a point-by-point plan for what he would do on immigration if he was elected. It was the roadmap they needed.

Just hours after CNN declared Trump the winner at 2:47 a.m., on November 9, 2016, Mario Diaz-Balart was on American Airlines flight 1533 for the short trip back to Washington from Miami.

A Cuban American whose aunt had been Fidel Castro's first wife, the Republican congressman from Miami had spent more than a decade in the House working to forge consensus on immigration issues and watching two presidents fail miserably to solve the problem. George W. Bush had made a run at a deal with Ted Kennedy, the Senate's liberal icon, that would have given millions of illegal immigrants a path to citizenship, but ran into a buzz saw of opposition from conservative talk radio hosts and hard-liners like Sessions. When Congress blocked Barack Obama's efforts at a similar deal, he gave up on legislation and tried to use the power of his office to protect millions of immigrants from deportation, only to be stopped by the courts. Now, the nation had elected as its president a man who won the office by trashing immigrants. In their early-2013 post-election autopsy, Republican leaders had concluded the party needed to repair its image with Hispanic voters if they had any hope of winning back the presidency. Trump had not just rejected that approach; he had obliterated it.

But Diaz-Balart was an optimist by nature. As he waited at Washington's airport to be picked up after the flight, he ran into Doug Rivlin, a top aide to one of his Democratic colleagues. Rivlin, the communications director for Luis Gutiérrez of Chicago, was also rushing back to Washington after staying up all night watching Hillary Clinton lose to Trump. He was tired and despondent, and Diaz-Balart could see it all over his face.

"No, no, no. This could work out. He's a dealmaker," Diaz-Balart told Rivlin. Overhauling the nation's outdated, broken immigration system had always failed in large part because conservatives demanded harsh measures to secure the border in exchange for anything that might look like amnesty for the illegal immigrants already living here. Trump wouldn't need to bend over backward to prove he's tough. He comes into office with the credibility among immigration hard-liners that Bush and Obama never had, but also with the hubris of a billionaire-celebrity-mogul-turned-politician who is certain he can succeed where his predecessors had failed.

"Think Nixon going to China," Diaz-Balart told Rivlin. "He wants to make deals that no one else can make."

— 3 —

THE HAMILTON GROUP

THE EMAILS STARTED ARRIVING the morning after the election.

Across Washington, a small cadre of congressional staffers received invitations from Gene Hamilton, a thirty-three-year-old lawyer from Georgia who was a top legal adviser to Sessions. The unimaginable had actually happened; Trump had won the presidential election, in no small measure on the power of his promises of cracking down on immigration, building a border wall, and banning Muslims and other refugees from the United States. But Trump had been too superstitious to plan for his own transition to the White House. And he was too toxic as a candidate to have attracted the usual throng of young, eager policy experts angling for plum posts in his nascent administration. Now the president-elect needed people who could help draft an aggressive new set of immigration measures to match his tough campaign rhetoric. And it needed to happen fast. It fell to Hamilton to quickly assemble a team.

Their assignment would be shrouded in secrecy; unlike government workers, the members of Hamilton's group could not speak about their work to anyone and would have to sign nondisclosure agreements of the kind usually used to guard corporate secrets. They weren't even supposed to alert Republican Party leaders on Capitol Hill. But the pitch was attractive: they would be part of a small but influential team charged with restoring the rule of law and reversing decades of liberal mismanagement of the nation's immigration system. No longer would they be relegated to the sidelines, grousing about the perverse incentives and dysfunctional practices that had long governed the way the country treated immigrants and immigration. They would have a free hand to rewrite the rule book. Trump had promised as a candidate that were he to win the presidency, he would waste no time in beginning to deport undocumented immigrants who had committed crimes—"My first hour in office, those people are gone," he had vowed. He wanted to strip the legal protections Obama had provided to the Dreamers, those who had been brought to the United States as children, and block immigrants from what he called "terror-prone" countries.

Bannon and Miller knew that time was of the essence. They were convinced that Trump's refusal to back down from his divisive rhetoric and extreme policy proposals on immigration during the campaign had won him the presidential race, earning him the undying affection of white working-class voters who were sick of seeing both political parties mince words and shrink from harsh measures when it came to immigrants. The pearl-clutching outrage of liberal Democrats and even mainstream Republicans was of no concern to them or to Trump; they courted and invited it. So Trump's first order of business was to do what he said he would on immigration, the more shocking the better. Speed, Miller believed, would be critical if Trump was to maintain the credibility on immigration that he had built up during the campaign. It was also vital because of what Miller and Bannon considered the liberal leanings of the "deep state," career officials who had served for years and had no loyalty to the elected president. If they were given the chance, they would use all the bureaucratic tools at their disposal to stall and obstruct and thwart Trump's plans. Better to go fast—use a "shock and awe" approach—so there wouldn't be time for them to resist.

Much of official Washington would try to stop them, they knew. For more than fifty years, both political parties in the United States had largely embraced the idea of opening the country's borders to immigrants from all over the world. Democrats pushed to expand refugee and asylum programs as part of their bid to treat immigration as a new civil rights cause. Republicans wanted new ways to recruit workers from overseas for high-tech companies and vast agribusinesses.

Now that Trump had been elected, his inner circle knew they were pushing against a bipartisan consensus in favor of immigration that would be difficult to counter. In Trump-world, the level of suspicion toward the government bureaucrats who handled immigration issues bordered on paranoia, and informed Hamilton's planning from the start. Trump and his advisers believed that the people running the country had betrayed working-class Americans with liberal trade and immigration policies that had cost them their jobs, their wages, and their dignity, bringing foreigners from faraway places who spoke different languages into their communities. As they began to put together their team, Hamilton and the others closest to Trump felt they could not trust any of the experts on immigration policy: the diplomats, lawyers, analysts, or migration specialists who worked at the Department of Justice, the Department of Homeland Security, or the National Security Council. They would be cut out of the process altogether. What he would need instead, Hamilton decided, was a group of loyal immigration experts who thought like Trump.

Andrea Loving received one of Hamilton's invitations. She was the whip-smart general counsel at the House Judiciary Committee and a top immigration adviser to Bob Goodlatte, the committee's hard-line Republican chairman from Virginia. George Fishman, a veteran immigration lawyer for Goodlatte, got an email from Hamilton, as did Dimple Shah, a first-generation American who speaks Hindi and handled immigration issues for the committee. Art Arthur, a former immigration judge who had worked for Goodlatte, was on the list. Hamilton invited Kathy Nuebel Kovarik, a top aide to Republican senator Chuck Grassley, who chaired the Senate Judiciary Committee, and Lee Francis Cissna, the son of a Peruvian immigrant and career civil servant who had worked at the State Department and the Department of Homeland Security, then alongside

Hamilton and Miller after having been assigned to work on Grassley's staff. And Hamilton requested help from Tracy Short, who had worked with him years earlier as a lawyer in the Atlanta office of Immigration and Customs Enforcement, ICE.

About fifteen people in all, they took leaves from their jobs after receiving clearance from congressional ethics offices to work for the transition. What they shared, in addition to Trump's restrictionist views about immigration, was status in Washington as political and policy outcasts. For more than a decade, they had labored mostly on the fringes of the immigration debate, shunned not only by Democrats on Capitol Hill, but also by mainstream Republicans in their own party, who saw them as too strident, too unwilling to compromise, too aligned with the agenda of racist hate groups that opposed immigration at all costs. When Republicans from moderate districts wanted to compromise with Democrats on immigration, these staffers gave no quarter, putting principle over politics and earning scorn from their party leaders as they quietly blew up deal after potential deal. But over the years, their success had been almost entirely defensive, a matter of killing immigration measures they viewed as too soft by tapping into the party's nativist base and whipping "no" votes. They had rarely been in the position to go on offense, scoring legislative victories of their own.

Over the years, the members of the group had pushed unsuccessfully for passage of bills that would deny benefits to undocumented immigrants, eliminate family-based immigration rules, drastically slash the number of visas for legal immigrants, end birthright citizenship for babies born in the United States, require a biometric system to allow companies to screen for illegal immigrants, and deport millions of immigrants. It didn't seem to matter whether a Republican or a Democrat occupied the White House; no president supported an agenda designed to protect the country against what Miller, Hamilton, and their colleagues saw as the ravages of immigration. It was clear that they were doomed to remain on the fringe until someone came along who would embrace their restrictionist ideology and enable their agenda. And now someone had.

Even as Hamilton began assembling his team, Dan Stein faced reporters at the National Press Building blocks away from the White House to unveil the latest immigration wish list compiled by his group, the Federation for American Immigration Reform. For years, Stein and FAIR had been part of a network of restrictionist activists who tried, largely without success, to prod lawmakers and presidents toward their anti-immigration views and funneled their work to hard-right publications like Breitbart News and conservative television and radio hosts like Mark Levin and Sean Hannity.

A graduate of Indiana University and the law school at Catholic University, Stein was a disciple of John Tanton, a retired Michigan ophthalmologist and white nationalist who had founded FAIR in 1979 and begun a crusade against immigrants, warning about what he called a coming "Latin onslaught." By the time Trump arrived on the political scene, Stein was in charge at the group, having spent two decades arguing for the kinds of restrictions that the new president embraced. "Immigrants don't come all church-loving, freedom-loving, God-fearing," Stein said in 1997. "Many of them hate America; hate everything that the United States stands for." Until Trump's arrival, Stein and his counterparts at other groups that advocated for much lower rates of immigration—people like Roy Beck at NumbersUSA and Mark Krikorian at the Center for Immigration Studies—were shunned as extremists by the Republican establishment, the business community, religious groups, and others. The Southern Poverty Law Center, an organization that tracks and monitors hate groups, condemned their work and listed some of them as hate groups, on par with neo-Nazis and the Ku Klux Klan.

Trump's victory held out the promise of a president who would finally advance their agenda. But in the days after the election, Stein, Beck, and Krikorian felt uneasy. It was true that as a candidate, Trump had done what none of their groups had been able to achieve in more than two decades of trying: he had turned immigration politics in America on its head. By calling public attention to the dangers and downside of immigration, Trump had mobilized millions of blue-collar voters, beating back the Washington coalition of liberal activists and big-business donors who had long pushed for higher and higher levels of immigration. And as he prepared to take office, there was no doubt that with him in the Oval Office—particularly with Sessions and Miller at his side—the anti-immigration groups would be welcomed into the fold of legitimacy and influence.

But it was hardly certain that Trump would be a reliable advocate for their primary goal: substantially reducing legal immigration into the United States. The numbers were clear, they believed. Over the next four decades, they argued, 75 million immigrants would flood into the country, crowding out wealth and opportunity for native-born citizens and radically changing the very definition of what it means to be an American. They were inherently suspicious of Trump, who after all was a businessman whose financial interests depended on the ready availability of cheap labor. And during the campaign, Trump had repeatedly waffled on whether he would try to cut legal immigration. In a Republican debate in October of 2015, Trump had heartily endorsed the desire of tech executives like Mark Zuckerberg, the founder of Facebook, to bring in workers from all over the world. "As far as Mark is concerned, as far as the visas are concerned, if we need people, it's fine. They have to come into this country legally," Trump said. Illegal—bad; legal—good. It was exactly the kind of pro-business formulation that NumbersUSA and the Center for Immigration Studies had been battling for years.

Trump's racist rhetoric was not exactly helpful, either. Over the years, Beck and the others had learned to steer clear of divisive comments and refrain from attacking immigrants themselves, even if their policy goals were indisputably intended to keep them out of the United States. They had had some success; Krikorian and Beck were frequently quoted in news articles written by mainstream publications during debates over immigration legislation. Trump's attacks on Mexicans as rapists and murderers were aimed at demonizing illegal immigrants who in the president-elect's view were pouring across the southern border unimpeded. And the wall was a potent symbol for Trump's anti-immigrant policies. But restrictionists knew it would do virtually nothing to stop the millions of immigrants who arrive in the United States legally, most of them on planes that would soar over Trump's wall no matter how high he made it. To people like Krikorian, who frequently warned of the dangers of too much legal immigration, the wall was little more than a meaningless gimmick.

And yet, Trump's move into the White House meant that the doors of the agencies that make immigration policy in the United States would for the first time be open to them and their allies. The groups were asked to send the names and résumés of potential appointees for the Trump administration, some of whom would go on to take plum posts in the nascent government. Jon Feere, one of Krikorian's legal policy analysts at CIS, who had taken a leave of absence to join Trump's campaign, was installed as a senior adviser at Immigration and Customs Enforcement. In early 2017, Julie Kirchner, who for eight years was Stein's top staffer at FAIR, left the group to work in the Trump administration, first at Customs and Border Protection and later as the ombudsman for U.S. Citizenship and Immigration Services, USCIS, the agency that processes immigration and citizenship applications and is a key part of immigration policymaking within the Department of Homeland Security.

At the press building event during the transition, Stein handed out copies of a report titled "Immigration Priorities for the 2017 Presidential Transition." The document was a blueprint of sorts, laying out a series of hard-line policy changes to seal the American border and remove illegal immigrants from the United States. And while the group remained suspect in the eyes of many mainstream Republicans, this time it had a direct line to the next president and his aides. "The right to come to this country is not a civil right; it is something given by the American people," Stein said that day. "The right to live in this country can be given but it can never be taken—but for too long there have been organizations and individuals in this country who believe that the right to live in this country can and should be taken. This has to end."

For seventy-two days after Trump won, however, it would still be Barack Obama's government. The outgoing president, who had been impressed by the professionalism of George W. Bush's transition, had ordered a similarly smooth handover of power—no matter who won.

Susan Rice, the soon-to-be-former national security adviser, was determined to make that happen. On the day after the election, Rice consoled staffers during an all-hands meeting in the first-floor auditorium of the Eisenhower Executive Office Building, the majestic warren of offices next to the White House. "It feels like it's the end of the world," one staffer recalled she told them. "It's not." And she repeated Obama's promise of a seamless transition. Her staff had spent months assembling binders full of detailed reports on national security issues that they all assumed would be handed over to Hillary Clinton's team. Instead, they would be briefing Trump's people. And they owed them the best effort, regardless of what they thought of the new president's politics. Weeks later, though, Rice's staff was still waiting. At the NSC Office of Multilateral Affairs and Human Rights, which coordinates policy on refugees and migrants, Rice had directed staff to tweak their transition memos for the incoming administration. "Then, nothing," said one senior NSC official. The silence went on for weeks, followed by a single, hour-long meeting with a few officials from the Trump transition. "Clearly, the people hadn't opened the memos we wrote."

One group of officials was not sitting idle: regulatory lawyers in the general counsel's office at the Department of Homeland Security. Five years earlier, the Obama administration had ended the use of a registry for tracking noncitizens visiting the United States. Created after the 9/11 attacks, the program, known as the National Security Entry-Exit Registration System, or NSEERS, had a checkered history; tens of thousands of visitors, many of them Muslims, had been entered into the system, but no terror cases ever produced convictions. The ACLU had called it ineffective. Others said it was nothing more than religious and ethnic profiling. But when officials ended use of the program in 2011, they didn't actually remove it from the books. In November of 2016, it was still there, waiting to be turned back on if the next president wanted to. (On Sunday, November 20, Kris Kobach, the Kansas secretary of state and immigration hard-liner, was photographed visiting Trump at the president-elect's

Bedminster estate carrying a partially visible document titled "Kobach Strategic Plan for First 365 Days." The first item on the list was: "Update and reintroduce the NSEERS screening and tracking system" and noted that with NSEERS, "all aliens from high-risk areas are tracked.") Fearing that Trump might do exactly that, the DHS lawyers raced to make sure it couldn't happen. Normally, it would take months to unwind the regulatory structure for a program like that. But the lawyers found exceptions in the law that allowed them to formally end NSEERS without lengthy public hearings. On December 23, just weeks before Trump's inauguration, they succeeded in pulling the plug.

Others were worried, too. Members of the U.S. Digital Service, a technology strike force drawn from the ranks of Google, Facebook, and other Silicon Valley firms, had spent months inside DHS building efficient computer systems to identify the Dreamers so the Obama administration could provide them protection from deportation under a program known as Deferred Action for Childhood Arrivals. Now, with Trump about to take office, the technology whizzes were distraught. The systems they built could be used by the new Trump administration for just the opposite—to find the undocumented immigrants and deport them. One member of the Digital Service darkly joked to friends that they should sabotage the computer system. Instead, many of them just quit.

Still, across most of the government, officials who dealt with immigration issues had little to do. Despite Trump's pledge to ramp up vetting of immigrants to counter terror threats, Obama officials waited throughout November and December for someone to seek their counsel. "We had a team and we were expecting them to tell us, okay we have heard from the Trump transition team and here's what's going to happen," one senior security official said. "For days and days and stretched into weeks, we just heard nothing from them. We did all this work. We've got the books and binders and everything. The most prevalent rationale was that the Trump campaign just had not prepared for this. They had not prepared for the possibility of winning the election." At the National Counterterrorism Center, which oversees the kind of threat assessments that might have informed Trump's "extreme vetting," top personnel didn't meet with the new president's team until early December, and then only for a perfunctory, two-hour session that one participant described as "NCTC 101," not a substantive policy discussion.

One Homeland Security official said it seemed like the new Trump administration wasn't interested in anything they had to say. He put it bluntly: "We were twiddling our thumbs."

There was so little contact between the Obama officials and their Trump administration successors that some people in senior positions had no idea whether they would still have jobs after the inauguration. Tom Bossert, the new president's homeland security adviser, had hinted early on that he wanted Nick Rasmussen, the barrel-chested head of the Counterterrorism Center, to stay on. But then Rasmussen heard nothing for weeks. On January 19, the day before Trump was to be sworn in, Rasmussen returned to his office from one final meeting to find a voicemail from his wife and a pink sticky-note from his assistant stuck to his desk chair. While he was in the meeting, Sean Spicer, the soon-to-be White House press secretary, had read from a list that he said contained fifty names of Obama officials Trump wanted to stay on. The message from Rasmussen's wife said she had heard Spicer read his name on NPR.

On Friday, January 13, just seven days before the inauguration, forty-one of the most senior Obama administration officials, including most of the cabinet, gathered in room 350 of the Eisenhower Executive Office Building, across from the West Wing, for a transition disaster exercise that was required by law. Sitting next to most of the Obama officials at the large, square table were their counterparts in the incoming administration. Jeh Johnson, Obama's secretary of homeland security, was there, sitting next to John Kelly, the former Marine general Trump had selected to replace him. Sally Yates, the deputy attorney general, was seated next to Jeff Sessions. Ash Carter, the secretary of defense, and his soon-to-be-successor, General James Mattis, were seated together. And Cecilia Muñoz, who ran Obama's Domestic Policy Council and oversaw immigration issues for the president, sat down next to Stephen Miller.

Muñoz and Miller didn't speak to each other before the exercise started, and they sat silently as Lisa Monaco, Obama's homeland security and counterterrorism adviser, laid out the challenges of responding to three possible disasters, all of which could involve mass casualties or other disastrous consequences: a devastating cyberattack, a pandemic, and a major hurricane. Miller paid little attention, pecking away at his phone and rarely looking up. Muñoz recalled thinking he would have to soon shake the habit of texting during such meetings, since anything he sent as a government official would be considered a presidential record that would need to be preserved.

About halfway through the presentation, Monaco took a break and Muñoz turned to Miller to introduce herself. A lifelong immigrant advocate and activist who was the daughter of Bolivian immigrants, Muñoz was Miller's polar opposite. She had spent two decades at the National Council of La Raza, a Hispanic advocacy group, and in Obama's White House had helped to develop the executive order that sought to shield millions of young illegal immigrants from deportation—the order that Miller repeatedly called an unconstitutional abuse of presidential power. Miller's intended assault on the immigration system offended her. Still, with just a week left in a West Wing office that Miller would soon take over as his own, Muñoz was under orders to be gracious. "Is there anything I can do to be of help?" she asked. His response caught her off guard.

"You run immigration. How do you maneuver so that you're making the decisions and not the NSC?" she recalled him asking, referring to the National Security Council. "How do you elbow them out of the way so that you are controlling the decision making?"

Muñoz was perplexed. Having the NSC and officials from across the government involved in policy discussions was a vital part of the process. "You won't make good decisions if you're elbowing people out of the room," she explained, getting ready to launch into an elaborate discourse on how to run an effective policy process from the White House. But Miller wasn't interested; he quickly returned to his phone and the conversation came to a halt. Muñoz was struck by the exchange—the only one that would take place between the two of them before she left the White

House and Miller moved in. "The impression I was left with was, 'Oh, you Obama people. Aren't you cute with your collaboration?'"

Collaboration with the rest of the government was the last thing on Gene Hamilton's mind as his group raced to finish a series of executive orders that Trump could sign as soon as he took office. On most days, the group gathered together for sixteen-hour marathon sessions at the campaign's transition offices at 1717 Pennsylvania Avenue, a block away from the White House. Often, Kris Kobach would join by teleconference from his office in Topeka to offer support and to urge them to move quickly once Trump assumed the presidency. The team had virtually no contact with the official DHS transition group, which was in charge of the more mundane duties of helping the new government assume operational control of the day-to-day functions of the bureaucracy. Their charge was to make sure the president could begin executing his immigration promises the minute he took office.

Hamilton had long taken a hard-line approach to immigration, first in the general counsel's office at DHS, then as a top lawyer in the Atlanta ICE office, where immigration judges denied more asylum claims than almost any other ICE facility in the nation, and later on Capitol Hill, where he became a key legal adviser for Sessions. Married with young children, Hamilton was an eminently likable man—even his political adversaries would routinely marvel out loud about how gosh-darn nice he was—and he had personal connections to immigrants. His best friend from the high school he attended in Georgia had been born in Central America. And his brother's wife was going through the excruciatingly long process of trying to immigrate legally to the United States. But like Bannon, Miller, and Sessions, Hamilton was frustrated by what he viewed as a terrifying erosion of enforcement and a deliberate refusal to stop illegal immigration, especially during the Obama years. It wasn't fair to those trying to come in legally, he thought, and it was dangerous. In Trump, Hamilton saw possibilities. If you could look past the undisciplined rantings about immigrants and the insensitive comments, Trump seemed like he could be the president to restore the rule of law in America's immigration system. Hamilton was the honey to Miller's vinegar, the soft-spoken Boy Scout to Miller's loudmouthed enfant terrible. But the two shared hard-edged goals on immigration and a passionate belief that what was needed to achieve them was someone who could get beyond the usual platitudes offered by traditional politicians.

Like the others in his group, Hamilton had largely failed to see his immigration vision become reality. Now, he and his ad hoc team of im-migration specialists had a tantalizing assignment from the White House–in–waiting: come up with all of the immigration ideas that you never got the chance to put into practice. It was an almost round-the-clock effort. On the days when Hamilton stayed at the office past the 11:30 p.m. clos-ing time for Washington's Metro, he would call an Uber to take him back to his house in Fairfax for four hours of sleep before returning the next morning.

But as hard as the group was working, it was not up to them to de-cide what the president would do first or when he would do it. Hamilton thought of himself as the head of a strategic planning team, not unlike a group of advisers that might be sent over by a major management consult-ing firm or lawyers performing legal work. (Almost all of his team mem-bers were attorneys.) They would look at the problem and deliver a menu of potential solutions to their client, in this case the president, and he would be the one to decide which course to take. But his group had a clear path to follow: the ten-point plan that Hamilton had helped to author, and Trump had delivered, for the speech in Phoenix during the campaign. Unlike so much else that Trump said—most of which was undisciplined and unfocused—that speech contained policy promises that were specific and actionable. As president, Trump could turn them into promises kept. But it would be up to Hamilton to work out the steps that would get him there.

They churned out draft after draft of executive orders, including one aimed at removing the shackles that Obama had placed on immigration enforcement agents in the country. Another would end the Obama execu-tive order protecting the Dreamers, many of whom were poised to enroll in college or join the military. A third would temporarily ban travel into the United States from countries—predominantly Muslim ones—that they viewed as posing grave threats to the country's security. Still others were designed to vastly reduce legal immigration, begin construction of Trump's border wall, and allow immigrants to be barred from permanent legal status or even deported if they became overly reliant upon public benefits like food stamps or the Children's Health Insurance Program, CHIP. In the past, when they had proposed such ideas on Capitol Hill, they would inevitably run into staunch opposition from Democrats and the more moderate members of their own party. But there was no one pushing back now. Through Hamilton, they sent their drafts to the White House, uncertain of what might happen next.

Officially, Hamilton's group reported to the senior transition officials, including Andrew Bremberg and Rick Dearborn. But Hamilton was in constant touch with Miller, who spent most of his time at Trump Tower in New York, close to the president-elect. Through Hamilton, Miller kept on top of the group's work, checking in by phone multiple times each day. But despite their frequent contact, Hamilton had almost no knowledge of what the president thought of his team's work, which executive orders he intended to sign, and how quickly that might happen. Once the orders were drafted and sent into the chaotic vortex of the soon-to-be-administration, Hamilton largely lost control over them.

As inauguration day approached, there was little doubt in Trump's mind where to start. His promise to block foreign terrorists from infiltrating the United States—initially pitched as a Muslim ban, but modified in the face of public backlash to be described as "extreme vetting" to protect the nation—was the clearest distillation of his get-tough approach. Hamilton's group had discovered a law enacted under President Obama in 2015 that cited security concerns with seven predominantly Muslim countries—Iran, Iraq, Libya, Somalia, Sudan, Syria, and Yemen—as grounds for barring dual nationals from using the visa waiver program, a special status that allows foreigners to enter the United States without express permission. There was no time to do a worldwide review of foreigners entering the United States, so they would adopt Obama's criteria as their own. A ninety-day ban on travelers from those countries seemed straightforward, the group agreed. They included a 120-day halt to refugee admissions and a complete ban on Syrian refugees, following through on the president's campaign-trail promise to block anyone from the civil-war-torn nation from taking refuge in the United States "until we can figure out what the hell is going on."

In his inaugural address on January 20, the president vowed to "protect our borders from the ravages of other countries" and promised to "unite the civilized world against radical Islamic terrorism." To the Hamilton group, it was inspiring, a sea change from Barack Obama's address four years earlier, which did not even include the words "terror," "border," or "Islam." To others, Trump's message was a foreshadowing of a darker time.

Luis Gutiérrez, the fiery Democratic lawmaker from Illinois, had made a public show of his decision to skip the inauguration to protest Trump's election. (The video of his floor speech announcing his decision was viewed more than seven million times on Facebook.) Instead, he would join his wife, Soraida, at the women's march on the National Mall the next day. When they arrived at the airport outside Washington the night of the inauguration Gutiérrez saw crowds of women wearing pink knit hats with little cat ears. They had caught on as a popular form of wearable protest among Trump-haters after he boasted in leaked audio from outtakes of an appearance on *Access Hollywood* that women would allow him to "grab 'em by the pussy" because he was a celebrity. But Gutiérrez had no idea what they were. Soraida urged him to go over and politely inquire. "Oh, these are pussy hats," one of the women responded, leaving the congressman stunned. "Fuuuuck," Gutiérrez thought to himself, turning to his wife to relay the news. "Tomorrow's going to be really interesting."

— 4 —

FORTY-THREE MINUTES

ON SATURDAY, JANUARY 21, as more than a half a million people gathered a few blocks away for the women's march to protest Trump's inauguration, Jason Galui, an Army lieutenant colonel who had served as the deputy executive secretary in Obama's National Security Council and was in the same position for Trump, received a call from his counterpart at the Pentagon. We've heard about a bunch of national-security-related executive orders, including a travel ban and a cyber-security directive, but our lawyers haven't seen them. Have you? Galui, whose job largely involved managing the flow of national security information in the White House, had not. At just after 9:30 a.m., he walked over to see Rob Porter, Trump's staff secretary, who had been on the job for about twenty-one hours. The orders were real, Porter confirmed, and they were among scores of executive directives that Trump wanted to sign as soon as possible. Galui was alarmed. As far as he knew, no one in the NSC, at the Defense Department, or anywhere else for that matter had seen the documents. You have to slow this down, give us time to review them, he said. Porter, a former senior Senate aide with undergraduate and law degrees from Harvard, was defensive. He had been working nonstop on vetting the orders, as had lawyers who worked on the transition and in the White House counsel's office. Attorneys in the Justice

Department's Office of Legal Counsel were reviewing them to make sure they met the basic "form and legality" standard for presidential actions. When Galui suggested that career national security officials should sign off on the documents before the president signed them, Porter pushed back. It wasn't clear who they could trust at the NSC, and Mike Flynn, Trump's new national security adviser, has already approved this, Porter said. It's handled.

What Galui didn't yet understand was how profoundly things had changed overnight. Under Obama, NSC's executive secretary cleared every national security policy decision, running it through layers of review by career officials in a carefully managed process. But Trump's team didn't trust anyone inside the bureaucracy, and that was especially true at the NSC, which was filled with Obama administration holdovers like Galui and aides on loan to the NSC from the State Department and other agencies whose loyalties were unknown. Reince Priebus, who was now Trump's chief of staff, and Flynn had decided that, at least for now, they were going to bypass the traditional NSC clearance process, which would have involved showing the draft executive orders to scores of officials who they believed might leak them or seek to sabotage them. At the same time, Porter, whose position gave him responsibility for vetting every piece of paper that came across the president's desk, was under immense pressure from Bannon and Miller to produce a barrage of signature-ready executive orders by yesterday. "We've gotta flood the zone!" Bannon would say, demanding that Porter pick up the pace so the president could sign five executive orders a day. Priebus was agitating as well, terrified of incurring Trump's wrath if they didn't deliver. The problem was, many of the dozens of draft executive orders that had been produced by the transition teams were in a shambles, presenting a host of legal and policy problems. The travel ban was one of them. Porter saw it as extraordinarily aggressive, potentially at odds with the president's policy goals, and fraught with constitutional issues as well as potential operational problems. The Office of Legal Counsel didn't like it either; attorneys there strenuously objected that it needed further review.

The president did not announce the orders on Saturday, but the clock was clearly ticking. On Monday, Josh Black's smartphone buzzed at around 7 p.m. The acting senior director for the NSC Bureau of Multilateral Affairs and Human Rights, he looked down to see an email from Galui with an attachment: the draft of the travel ban. "WTF?" Black emailed a colleague. They were flabbergasted. By Tuesday morning, Black and several members of his team were huddled over a printout of the draft in their third-floor offices of the Eisenhower Executive Office Building. Multilateral Affairs didn't have any Trump appointees yet, so the career staffers considered it a "safe space" to openly discuss their concerns. On that day, the conversation was simple: What to do? Did the new White House really want their input? Could they share the document with others? It wasn't clear, but inside the NSC, the emails started flying.

At 10:37 that morning, Sarah Cross, the director for human rights and refugee protection in the bureau, dashed off an email to her NSC counterparts, urging a government-wide legal review of the order. "Given the significant implications for the work of relevant departments and agencies (State, DHS, DOD, ODNI, and FBI), it is also our recommendation that, prior to issuance, they have an opportunity to provide input." Two minutes before noon, Joshua Harris weighed in. The director of Iraq for the NSC, Harris was worried. The executive order as written could affect international cooperation in the fight against the Islamic State terror group, and might even undermine efforts to protect U.S. forces in the Middle East, he wrote. He proposed that the NSC's Middle East bureau could lead an interagency review aimed at making sure that the president's executive order would have "no adverse implications on the counter-ISIL campaign and other U.S. priorities in the Middle East, including the safety and security of U.S. personnel." Five minutes later, Andrew Fausett, the deputy legal adviser for the NSC, responded. "NSC-LEGAL strongly concurs with the recommendation for an interagency lawyers' group to review the draft executive order in expedited fashion."

By Wednesday morning, the plaintive calls from inside the NSC for a review grew even more urgent. At 10:47 a.m., Yael Lempert, the senior director for the Levant, Israel, and Egypt at the NSC, wrote in an email that State Department officials have been "calling to express concerns" and to request time for an interagency policy review. Lempert laid out three immediate steps for the NSC: an "expedited interagency legal review"; an "expedited interagency policy review"; and an "interagency-coordinated diplomatic and public rollout plan" that would include guidance to all American embassies, complete with "talking points for use with our partners, and White House–approved press guidance."

The emails were ignored. In desperation, aides who handled the Middle East and North Africa and defense issues convinced David Cattler, the just-named deputy assistant to the president for regional affairs, to send an urgent memo to Flynn. The memo contained all the same warnings: the likelihood of "broad political fallout," the possibility of calls for boycotts of American goods, "significant political problems" for American allies, "public outcry" among travelers from affected countries, and increased "risks undermining U.S. foreign policy interests in Africa." The mention of safe zones in Syria was also a huge problem, they warned. Cattler's memo listed the number of countries with refugees already in the pipeline to be resettled in the United States. Among them: 72,000 from Iraq, 26,615 from Kenya, 25,000 from Jordan, and 15,000 from Turkey. In short, Cattler wrote, the executive order "could have broad and far reaching implications for U.S. foreign policy, security, and economic interests across several regions."

Flynn never responded.

By Wednesday, the travel ban and five other executive orders had leaked to the press, prompting a hunt for whoever was responsible. Miller and Porter were convinced the leak had come from one of the Obama holdovers working at the NSC. As word trickled out about what was to be included in the order, even some members of Hamilton's team were taken aback. They had presented the incoming president with a wide-ranging menu of the toughest possible actions he could take on immigration; instead of picking and choosing, he had opted to order the all-you-can-eat buffet.

Across town, the leaked copy of the travel ban found its way to the offices of the Refugee Affairs Division at U.S. Citizenship and Immigration Services. Refugee Affairs was the opposite of ICE, the better-known agency that was filled with gung ho, law-and-order types eager to crack down on illegal aliens. The civil servants who worked in Refugee Affairs had spent years finding ways to welcome desperate refugees, helping them to escape persecution and torture by resettling them in the United States. In addition to offices in Washington, D.C., and almost two dozen other countries, Refugee Affairs hired hundreds of "circuit riders" each year to travel around the world conducting interviews with displaced people to see whether they qualified for refugee status. In the days after Trump's inauguration, dozens of circuit riders, in Washington for training, were scheduled to leave for several months on the road conducting interviews in refugee camps all over the world.

Suddenly, that made no sense. At Refugee Affairs headquarters, officials were stunned by what they read in the draft travel ban. In addition to banning entry of people from seven mostly Muslim nations, the document called for a worldwide suspension of all refugees entering the United States for 120 days. It would reduce by more than half the total number of refugees that could be admitted in 2017, and permanently block Syrian refugees. If the president actually signed this, top officials knew, the circuit riders would have nothing to do for the foreseeable future. That afternoon, Barbara Strack, the chief of the Refugee Affairs Division, fired off an email to every employee in the agency. It was carefully worded to sound as neutral as possible, but it was also candid. We don't know what's coming, she wrote. But in light of what might happen, she was ordering a pause of all circuit rider teams that were scheduled to deploy overseas until at least mid-February.

For the moment, the Refugee Affairs office was grounded.

On Twitter the next morning, the president lashed out at Enrique Peña Nieto, his Mexican counterpart, for refusing to accept that his country would finance Trump's border wall. It was an early beginning to the fraught and erratic relationship with Mexico that would only get worse over the next two years. By the end of the day, the social media temper tantrum would lead Peña Nieto to abruptly cancel a face-to-face White House meeting set for the following week. Perhaps fittingly given its intended audience of one, the Mexican president announced the cancellation on Twitter after posting a video that could not have been clearer: "Mexico will not pay for any wall." Amid the spat, the draft of the travel ban order was beginning to make the rounds in other parts of the government, too—but not in the kind of formal way that was typical in previous administrations.

At the Justice Department, career lawyers finally got to see the order late in the week and were taken aback. "This is not legally defensible," one lawyer recalled saying. Attorneys in the Civil Division, which was responsible for defending presidential actions in court, scrambled—and failed—to get a written declaration from the State Department that the decision to keep out people from the countries listed was a necessary national security concern. On the basement level of the West Wing, where the president's top national security officials work, one of the aides ran into Josh Geltzer, the Obama-era holdover who had served as the senior NSC director for counterterrorism, and Chris Costa, the career civil servant who would eventually replace Geltzer. The aide was clutching the draft order. "We just got this," the aide said. "We were told we have forty-three minutes to offer comments." Among the offices that still hadn't yet signed off was NSC legal, the team of lawyers whose specialty was examining national security initiatives. But even if the career lawyers in the office had seen the document, it was not likely their concerns would have been heeded. In a meeting not long after, Flynn, the president's national security adviser, asked Keith Kellogg, Flynn's chief of staff, whether there had been any feedback about the travel ban. "Just some legacy comments," Kellogg said. "Nothing we care about."

At the offices of Customs and Border Protection, acting commissioner Kevin McAleenan also got a heads-up about what might be coming his way. But not from his own team. He learned about the order from several congressional staffers who had forwarded copies of the draft that had leaked out. (An internal review of who knew what at DHS would later conclude that McAleenan and the leadership at CBP learned most of what they knew about the executive order from "congressional staffers who apparently were better informed about the parameters of the EO than CBP itself.") A lawyer who had applied to the FBI after the 9/11 attacks, Mc-Aleenan had worked under Bush and Obama, rising through the ranks at the CBP. Married to a Salvadoran immigrant, he had never struck his colleagues as someone who would embrace something like Trump's travel ban, especially without enough notice for his agents.

On Thursday, Reince Priebus, the president's chief of staff, gathered about fifteen senior officials in his West Wing office so that Hamilton could brief them on the travel ban executive order. By then, it was clear to all present that this was something the president wanted, and they best not object; nobody did. But the next morning, hours before Trump was to sign the order, Rob Porter went to Priebus and Bannon with a warning. This thing is not ready to be signed—it's a bad idea, Porter told them. He had spent hours on the phone over the past few days with the Office of Legal Counsel lawyers trying to make edits that would satisfy their concerns and win their approval of the directive's "form and legality." They kept saying no. If he really turned up the heat on the staff over there and pressured them to bless this thing today, they might oblige, Porter said, but they wouldn't be happy about it. Neither would he, Porter added.

Bannon didn't want to hear it. Why can't you guys get this shit done? he kept demanding to know. Maybe we need better staff. Bannon and Miller had already told the president he was going to the Pentagon this afternoon to sign these orders, and he was damn well going to sign them. Priebus was nervous, too. There were clearly problems with the order, but of the dozen or so immigration directives that Miller was trying to push through—each one wilder than the next—the travel ban seemed like the least-bad. If it could pass the bare-minimum OLC form and legality test, Trump was going to sign it. The train simply couldn't be stopped at this point. Porter went back to OLC for another round of haggling, and later that day the staff there finally signed off. The fifty-four-word approval letter to Trump for his travel ban was sent to the White House hours before he was scheduled to sign the travel ban.

That same morning, Trump's effort to smooth over the diplomatic spat with Mexican president Peña Nieto began with a phone call at 9:35. In previous administrations, foreign leader calls were made in carefully controlled settings. But that day, close to twenty people came and went from the Oval Office during the call—Miller, Bannon, Spicer, Jared Kushner, the president's son-in-law and senior adviser, Flynn, and many others. It did not go well. In the course of the fifty-three-minute phone call, Trump insisted once again that the United States would build a wall across its border with Mexico. "We do not want people to come across the border. We do not want them coming across. We have enough people coming across. We want to stop it cold," Trump told Peña Nieto. He called New Hampshire a "drug-infested den" because of drugs coming from Mexico and insisted that he won the state because of his position on keeping out "tough hombres."

Trump was wound up, especially about his promise that Mexico would pay for the wall. "If you are going to say that Mexico is not going to pay for the wall, then I do not want to meet with you guys anymore, because I cannot live with that," Trump said, according to a transcript of the call that later leaked to *The Washington Post*. Peña Nieto, his translator's voice echoing from the speakerphone on the Resolute Desk, a 137-year-old gift to America from Britain's Queen Victoria, repeatedly tried to seem agreeable, but refused to accept Trump's terms. "My position has been and will continue to be very firm saying that Mexico cannot pay for that wall," he told the president. Trump did not disagree, but he implored Peña Nieto to keep quiet about it. "But you cannot say that to the press," Trump said. "The press is going to go with that, and I cannot live with that." The call was tense and resolved nothing. "I have the prime minister of Great Britain coming in in a little while," Trump told Peña Nieto as he brought the call to a close. "If you want, you can put out a statement saying that we had a great conversation." After the call ended and the group began to break up, Andrew Bremberg, the director of Trump's Domestic Policy Council, turned to a colleague sitting next to him. The colleague had one of the dark blue badges that indicated he had been part of Obama's administration, not the newer, light blue badges of the Trump White House. "Did you ever see anything like this?" Bremberg asked. No, the colleague said truthfully. The call had been a disaster. But Bremberg was positively giddy. "You just witnessed," he said, "the art of the deal."

Within hours, Trump began his closed-door lunch with British prime minister Theresa May with a familiar, disjointed series of subjects. He talked about his inauguration a week earlier and the size of the crowd, disputing press reports that more people had participated in the women's march than had watched him take the oath of office. The subject of women led Trump to talk about the issue of abortion. Some people think that abortion shouldn't be allowed under any circumstances, he told May, pointing to Vice President Mike Pence, an evangelical Christian, who was sitting a few seats away. "Mike believes this," he said. If a prisoner broke out of jail, snuck into his home, and raped and impregnated his daughter, even then, he doesn't believe his daughter should be able to get an abortion, Trump said. Isn't that right, Mike? Pence sat silently. May, whose top officials had been briefed about what to expect from Trump, had a vaguely horrified look on her face.

But soon Trump was on to the issue of immigration and German chancellor Angela Merkel's decision to admit one million refugees from Syria and other countries into Germany. Is Merkel going to win reelection? Trump asked. May said she would. "That surprises me," Trump responded, indicating that he thought Merkel would lose. May came to her German counterpart's defense. Merkel is the most accomplished politician on the continent, she said, and the most important in the European Union. Trump was unconvinced. The refugee debate would sink her, he said. Refugees were behind the rise of crime and violence in Europe, he said, and the German people weren't going to stand for it.

May tried to steer the conversation toward a new subject. She was deeply concerned about Trump's position on Russia and its dictator-president Vladimir Putin. Going into the luncheon meeting, she had wanted to remind the president about how important it was to hold the line on Ukraine. She was concerned about the Russian presence in the Baltics and how aggressive the Russians had become. You can't give the Russians any space, she said, because they will just keep taking more of it. Trump said that he was looking forward to talking with Putin.

Flynn piped up. Putin had already placed a call to Trump and they were trying to find the right time to call him back.

Trump whipped around to look at Flynn. Do you mean that Vladimir Putin called and you didn't put the call through? he snapped. Flynn stumbled for an answer, telling Trump that when calls from foreign leaders come in, they work on addressing them in a timely fashion. Don't worry, Flynn assured him, we are working on getting the call on your calendar. Trump looked at May. Can you believe that? he asked. Putin called me and I didn't know about it. My staff knew about it, but I didn't know about it. He looked back at Flynn. Russia is the only country in the world that can destroy us, and I can't speak to their president? May sat impassively, watching Trump lecture his staff. After she left, Trump laid into Flynn again, yelling at him for failing to put the call from Putin through immediately. "I can't believe you," the president said, shaking his head.

At 3:13 p.m. that Friday, Trump got into the presidential limousine for a brief ride to the Pentagon for the ceremonial swearing-in of James Mattis, his new defense secretary.

By that afternoon, details about the draft travel ban had found their way to a broader group of people inside the Department of Homeland Security. Hamilton already knew about it, of course. When Trump became president, he had appointed Hamilton to be Kelly's counselor at DHS. Kelly had been briefed multiple times by Hamilton on the broad outlines of the executive order, but it was not clear how much attention he had paid to the details as he raced against the clock to prepare for the early days of a chaotic administration. Kelly was out of town that Friday, flying back to Washington from Miami on a Coast Guard plane.

That afternoon, as Kelly headed home, the other top DHS officials gathered at what is affectionately called "the NAC," short for the Nebraska Avenue Complex, a reference to the fact that the department's headquarters was located a twenty-minute drive from downtown D.C., along Nebraska Avenue near American University. In a concrete-walled conference room across from Kelly's office on the fifth floor, more than a dozen people from the agency—immigration lawyers, refugee experts, management officials—assembled for what had been billed as a meeting to discuss the implications for the department of the president's draft travel ban. Kelly was dialed in from his flight, and he had dispatched Kirstjen Nielsen, then his chief of staff, and Alan Metzler, her deputy, to attend in person. McAleenan, whose border patrol agents at the ports of entry would be charged with implementing the ban, was on a video screen, attending the meeting remotely from his office in the Ronald Reagan Building downtown.

As Hamilton opened the discussion and passed out the draft executive order, he still was not certain when the president might sign it. No one had told him for certain when it was coming, and the first days of the Trump administration had been so frantic and disorganized that no one could predict what the president might do. The final draft had been so closely held that McAleenan, across town, hadn't gotten a formal copy. Neither had the congressional leaders, the senior lawmakers on committees that oversaw immigration and homeland security issues, or any of their staff, beyond those Hamilton had drafted to help write it. Inside the large conference room at the NAC, it was clear to those around the table that none of Kelly's top people had seen the document or knew what to expect from it. There were several heavy moments of silence as officials digested what they were reading, their eyes widening as they began to contemplate the implications. The conversation around the table grew louder and faster as they tried to make sense of the order, and what it might mean for their part of the agency. Some noted inconsistencies between what the executive order said in one section and what it said in another. A few raised a glaring issue: the ban seemed to apply to legal permanent residents, known as green card holders. Was that right? Others asked questions about the diplomatic impact of abruptly cutting off travel from countries that were allies of the United States. Several of the officials turned to Hamilton with a bottom-line question: How long do we have to get comments to the White House on this?

It was already too late. Before Hamilton had time to answer, Mc-Aleenan interrupted, the urgency in his voice from the video monitor cutting off discussion in the room.

Inside the DHS conference room, McAleenan's voice echoed through the silence. "I'm sitting here in my office," he said, sounding alarmed. "And CNN just reported this document has been signed by the president."

On television sets in McAleenan's office and across the country, news cameras showed Trump at the Pentagon, flanked by Mattis and Vice President Mike Pence, brandishing his Sharpie as he signed a leather-bound document. He proudly read the title of the travel ban executive order: "This is the protection of the nation from foreign terrorists' entry into the United States," he said. "That's big stuff."

— 5 —

"BRING OUT THE CRAZIES"

SALLY YATES HAD JUST left the White House and was in a car on her way to Reagan National Airport when her cell phone rang around the same time that the DHS officials sat stunned in their conference room.

Yates was in her eighth day as acting attorney general, an Obama holdover serving as the nation's top law enforcement official until Trump could get his team in place. It was her responsibility to lead the Justice Department as best she could until the Senate confirmed Senator Jeff Sessions for the job. Scarcely more than a week in, the task was already proving to be a messy and uncomfortable one. But the call that afternoon caught Yates off guard.

"You're not going to believe this," her assistant said when Yates answered the telephone. "I was just on the *New York Times* website, and it looks like the president has instituted some kind of travel ban." Yates was vaguely aware of reports that an executive order on vetting of immigrants might be coming; everyone remembered Trump's campaign pledge to impose a Muslim ban, and the press had been carrying reports for days of just such an action. But she and most of the other career lawyers at Justice had been cut out of its development. And even though she had just come from the White House, no one in the West Wing had bothered to give her a heads-up that the president was about to sign it.

Few people knew it at the time, but Yates was already engaged in another crisis. She had gone to the White House that afternoon for a second session with Donald F. McGahn II, the White House counsel, to discuss her concerns about Mike Flynn, the national security adviser. Law enforcement officials had caught Flynn lying to the FBI about his contact with Russian ambassador Sergey Kislyak, and she thought it was possible that the national security adviser might be compromised, vulnerable to blackmail by the Russians. It was an explosive and unprecedented development, coming just days after Trump's inauguration. In an interview months later, Yates laughed as she recalled predictions that holdover attorneys general rarely have anything to do while they keep the seat warm. "My chief of staff actually told me it would be so quiet there would be time for a lot of long, boozy lunches," Yates said. In fact, there had been no long lunches, boozy or otherwise, in the week since the inauguration. And now, the president's executive order banning travel from mostly Muslim countries threatened to become another all-consuming issue.

On its face, the travel ban seemed to Yates like an ugly extension of the president's rhetorical attacks on immigrants during the campaign. A veteran of the Justice Department for almost three decades, Yates speaks softly and with the southern drawl she developed in her native Georgia, where she was raised the daughter of a state appeals court judge and the granddaughter of a judge on the State Supreme Court. She went on to serve as a federal prosecutor under Democratic and Republican presidents, at one point leading the case against Eric Rudolph, who pled guilty to several bombings, including one in Atlanta during the 1996 Summer Olympic Games. Throughout her career, she had been one of the rare political appointees who had attracted bipartisan support. Her nomination by President Obama to be a U.S. attorney was confirmed unanimously, and when he promoted her to deputy attorney general, the Senate voted in favor, 84–12. After Trump was elected, Yates was determined to do what her predecessors had always done in the interests of law enforcement continuity: put personal politics aside, stay in place, and support the newly-elected president.

But Trump's travel ban was alarming. Even as she boarded her flight back home to Atlanta for the weekend, Yates knew that the legal challenges to the president's executive order would be filed in short order. That would draw Yates and her department's attorneys deeply into the furious debate about the policy that was just beginning to erupt around the country. Even though the Justice Department had played virtually no role in drafting the order—its National Security Division had neither been shown a draft, consulted formally or informally, nor given any sign-off—Yates knew that she had to start thinking about the inevitable question: How could they defend such an action?

And the more important one: Should they?

Trump's motorcade arrived back at the White House from the Pentagon at 5:02 p.m. on the evening of Friday, January 27. Eighty-eight minutes later, Trump walked into the Green Room on the main floor of the White House residence to begin what would later be revealed as the dinner with FBI director James B. Comey in which Trump demanded his loyalty. But even as the pair dined on shrimp scampi and chicken parmesan, the vast machinery of government began to feel the chaotic consequences of his decision to impose a travel ban.

The crown jewel of Trump's new, restrictionist immigration plans sparked immediate mayhem and confusion at airports throughout the United States as airline passengers who were already in the air when he signed it began arriving—only to find themselves blocked from entry or detained, with their status unclear. Consular officials at the airports frantically called their supervisors, seeking guidance that had not yet been distributed about who was permitted to enter the country. Journalists who phoned the White House Press Office, desperate for information about which countries were affected, found clueless aides at the other end of the line, frantically Googling to follow the legislative citation in the six-page document. Lawmakers began getting flooded with calls from constituents in their districts. House Speaker Paul Ryan picked up the phone and called John Kelly, looking for talking points that his members could use to explain what the president had done and why he had done it. Congress had been caught "totally flat-footed," Ryan complained. In the end, Ryan's staffers wrote their own talking points.

The American Civil Liberties Union had been preparing for this since the moment that Trump had been elected. Throughout his campaign, Trump had been brutally transparent about what he intended to do to immigrants if he was elected. Now, flooded with donations from concerned citizens, the ACLU had added a hundred people to its staff—a 10 percent hiring spree—in preparation for an onslaught of litigation against the new president. That Friday night at 7 p.m., Lee Gelernt, the group's top litigator, dialed into a conference call with leaders and lawyers from the National Immigration Law Center, Yale Law School's Immigrant Rights Clinic, and the International Refugee Assistance Project to plot strategy for challenging the order. After two and a half hours, there was a consensus: this was an urgent matter that called for an aggressive litigation timetable—maybe even as soon as ten days from now. But as soon as they hung up, Gelernt's cell phone began blowing up with text after emergency text. People were being held and detained at airports all over the country. His colleagues were getting the same urgent messages. They didn't have ten days to wait. They were going to have to sue right now.

On Saturday morning at 7:15 a.m., Charlie Dent, a Republican representative from Pennsylvania, got a text from his son, then an engineering student at Penn State. "Dad, I need to speak to you right away. It's important." Alarmed and worried, Dent called him. Relatives of his son's friend Joey Assali were being held at Philadelphia International Airport and refused entry to the country. Could he do something? Dent's son asked. Tell him we'll look into it on Monday, Dent said as he flipped on the television. Dent had gone to sleep early the night before and hadn't watched the news. But that morning, CNN was broadcasting live images of the chaos at the nation's airports and, within ten minutes, Dent had texted his son. Get me the number for your friend's mother. When he reached her, she was distraught. The Assalis were Syrian Christians who had settled years ago in Allentown's tight-knit Syrian community, one of the largest in the United States. Six of her relatives—two brothers, their wives, and two teenage children—had spent the last thirteen years applying to immigrate to the United States and had finally received their visas. A long and arduous trip from Damascus, Syria, through Beirut, Lebanon, and Doha, Qatar, had concluded when they landed that morning in Philadelphia. The Assalis had already bought them a house in nearby Allentown. Once they cleared customs, they would be permanent legal residents of the United States.

But Trump had signed the travel ban while they were in the air, blocking all entry from Syria. They were detained at the airport, not allowed to communicate with the Assalis. "They were going nuts," Dent said. At a loss, Dent called Kevin McCarthy, the Republican lawmaker from California who served as the majority leader. "Who the hell do I call?" Dent asked. McCarthy suggested Ben Howard, a former aide of his who had gone over to the White House to serve as a legislative liaison. When Dent reached him, he had no answers. "Was this run by Defense? State? Homeland? Justice?" Dent asked. "No," Howard responded. Dent gave Howard the names of the Assali family relatives, but it was too late. At 10:45 a.m., all six were put back on the plane they arrived on and sent to Damascus. It would take ten days and numerous calls to the State Department and DHS to get the family returned. Dent was furious. He became one of the first Republican lawmakers to denounce the president's travel ban. "This is ridiculous," he told *The Washington Post*. He called the new policy unacceptable. "I urge the administration to halt enforcement of this order until a more thoughtful and deliberate policy can be reinstated."

By Saturday afternoon, word of the travel ban—and anger about it—had also spread around the world. Boris Johnson, the British foreign secretary, called the State Department looking for answers, but he was directed to the White House switchboard and told to ask for Stephen Miller, a clear indication that America's diplomats were as unprepared to answer questions about the order as they were uninterested in defending it. In addition to banning travel from Iran, Iraq, Libya, Somalia, Sudan, Syria, and Yemen, the executive order halted all entry by refugees worldwide. But even the president's own ambassadors were in the dark. John Feeley, the American ambassador to Panama, was sitting in his office in Panama City when he saw news reports of the president's travel ban. He fired off a note to his consul general: Did we know this was coming? "No," she answered. In Washington, officials at the U.S. Chamber of Commerce started receiving panicked calls from their member companies, worried about how the president's order would affect their ability to hire foreign workers. With no answers, the business group referred calls to the ombudsman at the Department of Homeland Security. That office had no answers either.

As the travel ban chaos reached a crescendo Saturday evening, many of Trump's top White House aides were at the Capital Hilton, three blocks from the White House. Dressed in formal wear for the annual Alfalfa Club dinner were Sean Spicer, the White House press secretary, Reince Priebus, the chief of staff, Kellyanne Conway, the president's counselor, and Mike Pence, the vice president, who made a joke at the dinner about building a wall between the White House and the press and making *The New York Times* pay for it. Ivanka Trump and her husband, Jared Kushner, were also at the dinner; the president's daughter later posted a picture of herself in a shimmery silver Carolina Herrera gown and Kushner in a tuxedo for her 4.7 million Instagram followers. But behind the scenes, the atmosphere quickly grew ominous as the travel ban began to take hold and mayhem descended on major American airports. As the white-tie revelry continued, Priebus and the rest of the senior staff rushed backstage and got on secure phones to try to figure out what the hell was going on, and what they were going to do about it.

In Brooklyn that Saturday night, Gelernt showered, shaved, and told his wife and kids that he would be back shortly. "I don't think this is going to be a big deal," he said, even as his television showed images of chaos at the airports. Federal district court Judge Ann M. Donnelly had agreed to hold an emergency hearing that night on behalf of two Iraqi men who had been ensnared by the travel ban, and Gelernt and a lawyer for the International Refugee Assistance Project were going down to represent them. Hameed Khalid Darweesh was an interpreter and engineer who had earned a special visa to come to the United States in recognition of the work he had done for Americans in his country. Haider Sameer Abdulkhaleq Alshawi had been granted a visa to join his wife and son, who already lived in the United States. When Gelernt arrived at court, about forty people had gathered outside, some holding signs protesting the travel ban—an unusually lively showing for a hearing on a Saturday evening. Little did he know, as he disappeared into Judge Donnelly's soundproof courtroom, just how much national attention the case was drawing. Inside, the scene was dramatic—like something out of a television courtroom drama. At one point, an aide rushed over to Gelernt with a note saying that his client would be boarding a plane to Saudi Arabia in twenty minutes. "Your honor," Gelernt said. "You have to act RIGHT THIS SECOND." By nine that night, Donnelly had. In her ruling, the judge said that implementing Trump's order by sending the travelers home could cause them "irreparable harm." She said the government was "enjoined and restrained from, in any manner and by any means, removing individuals" who had arrived in the United States with valid visas or refugee status. When Gelernt emerged from the courthouse that night, the forty people had multiplied to thousands, and he took out his phone to dial his wife and alert her that it might take him a bit longer to get home than he had expected. "It's gotten a little bit bigger than I thought," he said, gazing out at the throng. I know, his wife replied. We're watching on MSNBC. The whole world was.

On Fox News moments after Judge Donnelly's ruling, Rudy Giuliani defended the president's travel order, telling host Jeanine Pirro that back in 2015, Trump had asked him how he could impose a "Muslim ban" legally. "He called me up. He said, 'Put a commission together. Show me the right way to do it legally.'" Giuliani claimed credit for the memo that congressman Michael McCaul had orchestrated during the campaign to walk Trump back from his call for a ban on Muslims. Speaking off the cuff, as he liked to do, Giuliani told Pirro that he had assembled a group of "very expert lawyers" to counsel the candidate. "We focused on, instead of religion, danger. The areas of the world that create danger for us. Which is a factual basis, not a religious basis. Perfectly legal, perfectly sensible." It didn't take long for the headlines to appear, suggesting that Trump had asked Giuliani for a legal way to ban Muslims from coming into the

United States. Oh, fuck, McCaul and the others thought. That's not at all what the purpose of that memo was. The administration's whole argument was that this order wasn't the Muslim ban dolled up to appear legal; Giuliani had just gone on TV and suggested that was precisely what it was.

For many in the administration, the travel ban episode was an early warning sign that Trump intended to rely on his gut instinct about immigration—and the advice of his hard-line advisers like Miller and Sessions—rather than the well-established, but often slow, procedures for developing immigration policies by the agencies that have to implement them. For Kelly, who ran the Department of Homeland Security, the ill-planned implementation of the travel ban was a professional humiliation that made his agents look unprepared and ill-informed. He shared Trump's views about threats from abroad, but he was nonetheless livid that the employees in his department were forced to act with no guidance or preparation. At the State Department, Kristie Kenney, an Obama holdover who served as one of the secretary's top foreign policy advisers, had gone home sick with the flu. But Tom Shannon, the acting secretary of state, called her back in on Saturday morning to prepare for an urgent White House meeting in the Situation Room scheduled for that evening.

When the meeting began, Stephen Miller was sitting at the head of the table, growing more annoyed by the minute.

It had been twenty-four hours since the president had issued his executive order, and now the officials in charge of implementation were all bitching about it. Kelly was there. K. T. McFarland, the deputy national security adviser, and Tom Bossert, the president's homeland security aide, were each seated in one of the oversized, black leather chairs around the table. Kenney represented the State Department, and Nikki Haley, the new ambassador to the United Nations, was on one of the room's big television screens, having called in on a secure video link. There were major issues with the executive order, they all said. Kenney noted that about a hundred refugees had left camps to travel to the United States but were now banned from entry and couldn't be safely returned to the camps. American embassies around the world also needed to be secured against possible violence, she said. Others around the table described confusion about whether people who already had green cards could still come back into the country. One official noted that the ban was blocking the families of Iraqis who had worked closely with the American military in their country. Kelly at times seemed annoyed at being quizzed by Miller; the decorated four-star Marine general was still wary of Trump's brash, thirty-one-year-old immigration whiz. But the officials were mostly respectful and tried to offer solutions to help ease the sense of crisis that was playing out on TV screens and newspaper front pages. Still, to Miller, it all sounded like whining.

"This is the new world order. You need to get on board," he said, seizing control of the meeting and repeating the message that he and Bannon had delivered to Trump earlier that day: everything is going according to plan. Long before the president signed the executive order, Miller and Bannon had talked about the reaction that it would generate. They chose to announce it abruptly on a Friday afternoon, believing that the outrage it would cause would play into their hands, showing Trump's critics to be bleeding-heart radicals. "The only way we win is, you got to bring out the crazies," Bannon would say. "The radical crazies. The open-borders crowd." So nothing that happened in the order's aftermath came as much of a surprise to either of them. Miller told the group assembled in the Situation Room that they should tune out the complaints. This is exactly what we wanted, he said—to turn on immigration enforcement in a big and noticeable way. The theatrics and hysterical overreaction at airports only proves that border patrol agents are following the president's new approach, Miller said, and that his critics have lost their minds opposing commonsense measures to protect the country. It's no longer a free ride to get into the United States.

It was barely a week into Trump's term and Miller had already moved to take control of a meeting that in any other administration would have been led by someone else. Kelly was a member of the president's cabinet but he wasn't at the head of the table. Neither was Bossert, who as Trump's homeland security adviser had to officially convene the Situation Room meeting on Miller's behalf. Miller had hinted at his plan to control the immigration agenda during the brief conversation with Cecilia Muñoz at the disaster drill a month earlier. Issues involving immigration had to be under his purview, even if that meant wresting control away from the National Security Council. The power play was obvious to everyone in the room that Saturday night. As the meeting ended and people started leaving, Kenney turned to one of the other attendees. A career foreign service officer who had served for twenty years at the State Department, including as one of George W. Bush's ambassadors, Kenney had been in countless Situation Room meetings.

"Well," she said to her colleague, "that's a new era."

Not everybody in the West Wing was on board with Bannon's and Miller's no-apologies approach. Ivanka Trump and Jared Kushner, a senior White House adviser, were livid about the Friday-afternoon debacle. For one thing, it unfolded just as they were beginning their observance of Shabbat. As observant Jews who routinely made a point of their adherence to the Orthodox rule against doing any work on the sabbath—including the use of electronic devices like cell phones—it was well known that they went offline on Friday afternoons and did not resurface until late Saturday, when the rest day was complete. They suspected the unfortunate timing was deliberate. Gary Cohn, the chairman of the National Economic Council, was also infuriated at what he considered a badly mishandled debut of an absurd policy. At a meeting Monday morning in the Roosevelt Room, Cohn and Kushner unloaded on Bannon and Miller, telling them the botched rollout had embarrassed the president, created a media firestorm, and tainted the administration's image at a key moment. Bannon and Miller were adamant that their strategy had worked perfectly. This is the way we stop any kind of terrorism problems, they said. We're 100 percent within our rights to do this, and it's absolutely necessary, they argued. The media firestorm, Bannon went on, was just an indication that the press was the "opposition party," and should be treated as such.

Kenney had just pulled into the State Department parking lot at about 7 a.m. Monday morning when her phone rang. It was Miller and he was agitated. For some reason, he complained, calls from angry foreign governments were being routed to him. In addition to the earlier, angry call from Boris Johnson over the weekend, he had gotten an urgent inquiry from the Canadians about their citizens who had been caught up in the travel ban. What was Kenney doing to fix this? he asked. "I'm tired of them all calling me." It suddenly dawned on Kenney: this was all new to Miller, who had never been held accountable for the consequences of the policies he advocated. "Welcome to the world of governing," she thought. But Kenney had been through transitions before, and she believed that presidents have the right to shift the direction of American diplomacy and policy. If this is what Trump wanted to do, it was up to the State Department to figure out the best way to accomplish it. She convened a meeting of senior officials in the seventh-floor conference room that morning to brief them on what she had learned in the Situation Room. The mood was somber. Officials who worked with refugees were heartbroken about the temporary ban. Others complained about the damage to relations with Iraq and other countries. Kenney was not unsympathetic to their desire to emote, but she chided her team. "You work in good times and bad," she told them. "Where do we go from here?"

Over at the Justice Department, Yates was confronting that same question.

As she expected, critics had moved quickly to file lawsuits challenging Trump's travel ban, forcing the government's lawyers into court unprepared. Gisela A. Westwater, a senior litigator in the civil division who had worked on immigration issues for more than a decade, had drawn the short straw to argue for the travel ban by phone from Washington during Saturday's hearing in Judge Donnelly's Brooklyn courtroom. When lawyers for the American Civil Liberties Union told the judge that an immigrant was being deported at that very moment, Westwater said she simply did not know if that was true. Throughout the weekend, Yates and her top lawyers in the national security and civil divisions at the Justice Department had pored over the executive order and the lawsuits. Hamilton and Miller had used national security as the primary justification for the travel ban, but to the career lawyers examining it, there didn't seem to be any real evidence of a threat from foreign travelers. The department's top litigators—the lawyers who were being asked to devise a strategy to defend the order in court—were beside themselves.

Yates knew she had to make a decision quickly. Her lawyers would soon need to appear in courtrooms defending the constitutionality of the order. They would have to tell judges that the order was not an assault on a particular religion. And yet, given everything that Trump had said, she didn't really believe that. Even if she had, there was another problem that Yates and her staff knew would be a major liability in court: the order asserted as a key rationale that "numerous foreign-born individuals have been convicted or implicated in terrorism-related crimes" since the terrorist attacks of September 11, 2001. But national security professionals at both the State Department and the Justice Department had no data showing that individuals from the countries covered by the order fit that description or posed any heightened risk to the United States. How, Yates asked herself, could she send her staff into court to defend something that simply was not borne out by any facts?

By Monday afternoon, Yates had sat down in front of her computer and typed out a four-paragraph, 325-word letter to all Justice Department lawyers. It was framed as a principled, legal argument against the travel ban, but it amounted to a remarkable rebuke to the sitting president, her boss. In the letter, Yates acknowledged that the Office of Legal Counsel had provided a cursory assessment that Trump's executive order was constitutional but argued that her role as the acting attorney general was broader than that. The review by the OLC "does not take account of statements made by an administration or its surrogates close in time to the issuance of an Executive Order that may bear on the order's purpose. And importantly, it does not address whether any policy choice embodied in an Executive Order is wise or just." Further, she argued, it was her responsibility to make sure that the Justice Department only took actions to promote justice and "stand for what is right." She wrote that she was not convinced that defending the president's executive order would be consistent with that responsibility. And she said she wasn't even sure it was legal.

"Consequently," she concluded, "for as long as I am the Acting Attorney General, the Department of Justice will not present arguments in defense of the Executive Order, unless and until I become convinced that it is appropriate to do so."

The letter was nearly unprecedented, and it threatened to precipitate something akin to the so-called Saturday Night Massacre in 1973, when President Nixon's attorney general and deputy attorney general resigned after being ordered to dismiss the special prosecutor in the Watergate case. For a brief moment, Yates harbored a sliver of hope that the letter might give Trump and Miller pause, and that they might pull the order back so that the rest of the government could provide the kind of input that didn't happen before the president signed it. "There was some part of me that thought, you know, maybe that'll happen," Yates recalled later. But she also understood the more likely repercussions that would flow from sending it. At 9:15 p.m., a letter signed by Johnny DeStefano, one of the president's aides, was hand-delivered to Yates at the Justice Department. "The president has removed you from the office of Deputy Attorney General of the United States." Moments later, Sean Spicer released a searing statement to the press on behalf of the president, accusing Yates of betraying the Justice Department by refusing to enforce a legal order.

"Ms. Yates is an Obama Administration appointee who is weak on borders and very weak on illegal immigration," Spicer said in the statement. "It is time to get serious about protecting our country. Calling for tougher vetting for individuals traveling from seven dangerous places is not extreme. It is reasonable and necessary to protect our country."

On Capitol Hill a week later, DHS head Kelly told angry lawmakers that responsibility for the rollout was "all on me." But privately, he was livid at Trump's team for shoddy work that had made his agents at airports around the country the face of a poorly thought-through, disastrously unplanned directive. "That's not going to happen again," he said. He established a new rule inside DHS: if anyone from the White House calls and tries to give you orders, you bring it straight to me.

"A FUCKING WATERED-DOWN VERSION"

H. R. McMASTER HAD barely settled into his West Wing office at the beginning of March when he gathered the president's foreign policy team around his desk for a lecture. Mike Flynn, the president's first national security adviser, had been pushed out after it was discovered that he had lied about his conversations with Sergey Kislyak, the Russian ambassador to the United States. McMaster's books had not even arrived at the White House yet, and the only picture in the room was of McMaster and Najim Abdullah al Jabouri, the onetime mayor of Tal Afar, an Iraqi city in northern Iraq near the Syrian border that McMaster's 3rd Armored Cavalry Regiment helped to liberate in 2005. A West Point graduate and decorated Army commander, Trump's second national security adviser had spent years in Iraq building the delicate relationships that allowed American troops to carefully navigate the sectarian crosscurrents in the dangerous civil war. Now, after just days in the White House, McMaster was not about to be part of an executive order that banned the country's Iraqi allies from traveling to the United States. Mattis was there, along with Sessions, Kelly, and Rex Tillerson, the secretary of state.

Iraq has to be excluded from the travel ban, McMaster told them. On a practical level, it will complicate cooperation with Iraqi allies still in the field fighting insurgents. Banning Iraqis will play into the hands of jihadists who want to portray America as waging a war against the Islamic religion. McMaster was blunt about his disdain for a policy that seemed to focus on the dangers posed by Muslims to the United States. That doesn't acknowledge the fact that the vast majority of victims of terror are Muslims themselves, he said.

Sessions was unmoved. "I'm not impressed," he told the group.

"Well, Mr. Attorney General, you should be impressed," McMaster snapped, grabbing the photo of himself and al Jabouri. The Iraqi mayor was a Sunni Arab who had worked side by side with McMaster and the Americans as they fought to defeat al Qaeda and create stability in Tal Afar. When it was over, and Shia militias targeted al Jabouri for death, McMaster sponsored green cards for al Jabouri and his family, who came to live in McMaster's home for six months, eventually buying a house and settling in Virginia. More recently, al Jabouri had been going back to Iraq to continue the fight against ISIS, returning frequently to his family in the United States. It was unthinkable, McMaster told Sessions and the others, that any new policy would bar al Jabouri from returning to his family.

Sessions backed down. "Okay, okay," he told McMaster, "we'll take Iraq off." McMaster was relieved and invited the group to go to the chief of staff's office to tell Reince Priebus of the decision. As they walked down the hall, McMaster put his arm around Sessions. "I'm really going to appreciate working with you," he told the attorney general.

But the warm feelings didn't last for long. Bannon and Miller were in Priebus's office, and they were not backing down on keeping Iraq in the order. What began as a discussion devolved into a heated argument. "They're not an ally. They're a fucking protectorate," Bannon yelled. "I don't want to hear this shit." Bannon did not want the president to take Iraq, or any country, off his travel ban list. Trump's over-the-top rhetoric had won him the presidency. Backing off now would just make him look weak and feckless to the people who supported him. And anyway, he insisted, the Iraqi government couldn't even vet the people coming to the United States. Who the hell knows what kind of terrorists might be coming to America from Iraq? Miller jumped in, citing statistics about the number of Iraqis who had stayed in the United States longer than their visas allowed. His voice rising into the usual rat-a-tat-tat as he threw out facts and figures, Miller railed about the Iraqi government's lack of the proper "chain of title" in determining the real identity of people applying for visas. Maybe, he told Mattis, McMaster, and Tillerson, the United States should just pull out of Iraq altogether.

McMaster was furious. "Iraqi boys are putting their lives on the line," he yelled. For years, the United States had granted Iraqis a Special Immigrant Visa, under a program signed into law by President George W. Bush and aimed specifically at recognizing Iraqi nationals who worked on behalf of the U.S. government. In the immediate aftermath of the president's travel ban, Iraqis with those visas had been told they were no longer eligible to enter the United States. It was an outrage, and must be reversed, McMaster said. Tillerson agreed. "The international community is going to go crazy," the secretary of state insisted. Mattis, normally taciturn, could hardly contain himself. Like McMaster, much of his military career had been spent working with the Iraqi people in the fight against terrorists. The Iraqis who were being blocked by Trump's order were the good guys, not the bad guys, and everyone around the world except the president and his White House aides seemed to know it. Mattis had gotten an earful about banning entry from Iraqis while he was at the Munich Security Conference in mid-February. Paul Wolfowitz, who was deputy secretary of defense during Bush's first term, had called Mattis to complain, too.

The pissing match was going nowhere. Trump needed to decide. The next morning, the group convened again in the Oval Office and reprised the fight for the president. Iraq is our ally, McMaster and Mattis told Trump, who was hearing none of it. "We shouldn't even be there." He asked Mattis how many American troops were in Iraq. "What the fuck? Why the fuck are we all over the place? This has got to stop. You generals just want to bomb everything," Trump said. Mattis, Kelly, McMaster, and Tillerson were rattled but unmoved, continuing to try to press the president to remove Iraq from the order. It was clear that Trump agreed with Miller and Bannon, but he always found it difficult to say no to "my generals," as he often referred to them. Iraq could come off the banned list, but the president wasn't going to be happy about it.

Opposition to the president's travel ban order was coming from everywhere. But nowhere was the reaction as fierce as it was inside the government itself.

Almost immediately after the president signed the executive order, the staff at the DHS intelligence office prepared an analysis of the travel ban. The three-page analysis that the office produced was completely off message. Its title was: "Citizenship Likely an Unreliable Indicator of Terrorist Threat to the United States." Using publicly available data, the report undercut the entire premise of the president's travel ban. Out of eighty-two people convicted of terrorism in the U.S. since the start of the Syrian War in 2011, it found, about half were native-born Americans. And the rest came from twenty-six different countries, most of which were not part of Trump's travel ban, including Pakistan, Bangladesh, Cuba, Ethiopia, and Uzbekistan. Hamilton and Miller were furious at the report's conclusions, saying it was flawed because it did not take into account classified intelligence data. When it became clear that the report was never going to be released, someone leaked it to the Associated Press and it generated headlines in newspapers across the country: "DHS Report Casts Doubt on Need for Trump Travel Ban," *The Washington Post* wrote.

At the Refugee Affairs offices, Barbara Strack was trying to console her staff. During an all-hands meeting in the lobby area of the program's eighth-floor headquarters at 111 Massachusetts Avenue, she delivered a just-the-facts speech about the impact the ban would have on their efforts to help refugees reach the United States. We didn't see this thing ahead of time, and we know there are a lot of questions, but we are coordinating with the State Department and we're trying to get it under control, she told her staff. But despite her efforts at reassurance, Strack recalled later, "There certainly was a sense of the program being under siege, and a sense of concern and unfairness." A short time later, Strack led another, more emotional meeting at a second office, which housed many of the circuit riders who had been grounded, along with several newly minted refugee corps officers. They had been part of a hiring and training spree under Obama, who had made a push late in his final term to ramp up the number of refugees, especially Syrians, admitted to the United States. Many of them were angry at the situation, and deeply worried.

From the back, a man had the question on everybody's mind. The travel ban executive order said that when the refugee program restarted, priority for admittance to the United States was to be given to religious minorities, which—given that the ban targeted majority-Muslim countries—was understood as a mandate to give preference to Christians. "If we're asked to discriminate in favor of Christians, what are we supposed to do?" the man said. "How can I, as a person of conscience, be a party to that?" Strack urged her staff not to panic. "We don't need to go to the darkest interpretation prematurely," she told them. "Don't assume the worst." But privately, she was glad that someone had had the guts to say out loud what everyone was thinking: this was a Muslim ban dolled up to look like a legitimate national security directive. They did not want to be instruments of a discriminatory policy.

Inside the State Department, career officials were just as amped up against the order. Foreign service officers circulated a "dissent channel" memo, a rarely used form of internal protest designed to give diplomats a safe and private way to express their frustration to the secretary of state. Officials in American embassies around the world started signing the five-page memo to Secretary Tillerson just days after Trump signed his order. "A policy which closes our doors to over 200 million legitimate travelers in the hopes of preventing a small number of travelers who intend to harm Americans from using the visa system to enter the United States will not achieve its aim of making our country safer," they wrote. "Moreover, such a policy runs counter to core American values of nondiscrimination, fair play and extending a warm welcome to foreign visitors and immigrants." The memo warned that the ban would sour relations with the Muslim world, increase anti-American sentiment around the globe, impose "terrible humanitarian burdens," and harm the economy. All while not preventing terror. The authors of the memo compared the travel ban to the internment of Japanese Americans during World War II. "We do not need to sacrifice our reputation as a nation which is open and welcoming to protect our families," the memo concluded.

For Miller, Bannon, and the others in the White House, the nearly open revolt was confirmation of what they had suspected even before the president took office. They were convinced that career bureaucrats, especially at Citizenship and Immigration Services and the State Department, were actively sabotaging the Trump agenda—slow-walking memos, leaking unflattering documents, refusing to implement the president's new policies. It was bad enough that lower court judges were blocking Trump's executive order by substituting their own judgments in place of the president's. And the liberal judges on the Ninth Circuit Court of Appeals had unsurprisingly upheld the lower courts. But the resistance inside the administration was even more infuriating. Elections were supposed to have consequences, and insubordinate actions by some of the bureaucrats were providing ammunition to Miller, Bannon, and other White House aides who insisted that nothing be shared widely out of a fear that it would leak to the press. "We were getting bled out by the leaks in DHS, Justice, etc.—the Obama crowd—I mean, it's unbelievable," Bannon said. "Guys are breaking scoops on us nonstop, and Trump's head is blowing up."

Trump was already in a rhetorical war with his intelligence and law enforcement community, and his early interactions with them added to the strains. On February 14, about a dozen officials, including the attorney general, the deputy director of the CIA, the FBI director, and the director of the National Counterterrorism Center, gathered in the Oval Office at about 4:15 in the afternoon to deliver their first briefing for Trump about the overall terror threat facing the country. Top White House officials were there, too: Bannon, Kushner, Priebus, and homeland security adviser Tom Bossert. When someone in the group mentioned the existence of about one thousand domestic terrorism investigations, Trump interrupted. "Well, why don't you just kick those people out of the country?" he asked. It was clear to everyone in the room that Trump assumed all of the people under investigation in those thousand cases were foreign-born nationals who could be deported. In fact, as the intelligence officials patiently explained, many of the subjects of those inquiries were native-born Americans or legal permanent residents—not foreign terrorists. For some of the officials in the room, the president's remark was a stark reminder about how little he understood the real threats from abroad, and how many erroneous assumptions he made about the dangers from immigrants. After the meeting ended, Trump asked James Comey, the FBI director, to stay behind. According to Comey's recollection in a contemporaneous memo, the president railed about leaks in his administration and urged Comey to drop the investigation of Mike Flynn.

The president's annoyance was on public display two days later, when he abruptly decided to hold his first news conference. Standing in front of golden curtains at one end of the East Room, Trump mounted a vigorous defense of the first three weeks of his presidency. The rollout of his travel ban, he said, had been "very smooth." He claimed that he had originally wanted to give people from the seven banned countries a month to prepare before the ban took effect, but that Kelly had told him that would allow "the bad ones" to come in. "Kelly said you can't do that. And he was right," Trump told the reporters. "As soon as he said it, I said, 'Wow, never thought of it.' I said, 'How about one week?' He said no good. You've got to do it immediately because if you do it immediately, they don't have time to come in. Now nobody ever reports that. But that's why we did it quickly." If he'd have allowed a month as he originally suggested, Trump said, "everything would've been perfect."

The problem, Trump insisted, was not with the travel ban itself, but with the courts that had blocked it with injunctions. Trump was furious that an appeals court had upheld the decisions of the lower courts, and even more furious that his lawyers were urging him to give up. Sessions and lawyers at the White House and Justice Department had decided that waging an uphill legal battle to defend the directive in the Supreme Court would fail. Instead, they wanted to devise a narrower travel ban that could pass legal muster. Earlier that same day, the Justice Department had informed the Ninth Circuit that the president planned to issue a new, modified order to take the place of his original travel ban. "Rather than continuing this litigation," the lawyers said in their brief, "the president intends in the near future to rescind the order and replace it with a new, substantially revised executive order to eliminate what the panel erroneously thought were constitutional concerns." Trump thought that it was a mistake to give up on the first one, repeatedly telling anyone who would listen that they should continue to fight for it. Publicly, though, the president appeared ready to move on.

"We're going to put in a new executive order next week sometime. But we had a bad decision," he said at his news conference. "The only problem that we had is we had a bad court. We had a court that gave us what I consider to be, with great respect, a very bad decision. Very bad for the safety and security of our country. The rollout was perfect."

"I don't want a fucking watered-down version!" the president yelled at his lawyer.

It was March 3, fifteen days after the president's news conference, and the people around Trump had rarely seen him angrier. A day earlier, the president had been touring the USS *Gerald R. Ford*, a 100,000-ton aircraft carrier, when news broke that Jeff Sessions had recused himself from overseeing the investigation into Russian election meddling. That sent Trump into a rage. This Friday morning, the already seething president was in the Oval Office, surrounded by his top advisers, as White House Counsel Don McGahn reminded Trump that he had to sign a new travel ban to replace the original one. The ban had never gone into effect, blocked by court actions that Trump saw as legal obstructionism on the part of Democratic judges and immigration advocates. Activists were crowing that they had thwarted the new president and Mr. Trump was furious about being forced to back down to politically correct adversaries. It was a familiar moment for his advisers. The president could sometimes accept being told no in private and would occasionally relent. But he couldn't abide a public turnabout, a retreat. "As long as he doesn't lose face publicly, he's okay," one former top adviser later recalled.

At the news conference, Trump had said he would abandon his original travel ban. But with Marine One waiting on the South Lawn that Friday so Trump could begin his weekend in Palm Beach, he refused. "I want to fight in court," he barked at McGahn as the confrontation escalated. Trump was seated at the Resolute Desk, surrounded by Bannon, Miller, Priebus, Kushner, Ivanka Trump, Spicer, and Mike Dubke, his new communications director. Outside the Oval Office, reporters waiting in the Rose Garden could see Trump's top aides yelling and waving their arms. Bannon was in Trump's face and McGahn refused to back down. We don't have a choice, the president's lawyer insisted. The Justice Department had already promised the court that Trump would issue a new order; we ran that by you, and you signed off! They had no choice but to follow through.

At the Justice Department, Sessions was trying in vain to get through to Trump on the telephone, hoping to make the case for the revised directive and persuade him to sign it. But Trump, livid about the recusal, refused to take Sessions's calls.

"This is bullshit," the president exclaimed repeatedly, ranting in the Oval Office surrounded by his staff. "I don't want a fucking watered-down version!" He lashed out at McGahn, calling him incompetent. You've fucked everything up! Rather than try to talk Trump down, Bannon got in his face and shouted back at him. You can't rewrite history here, Bannon said to the president. We all knew this recusal was coming, and it's done, we've got to move on. As Trump railed about the recusal and berated McGahn, Priebus was getting pings from the Secret Service. The president had to go. The helicopters had been idling for so long there was a risk they might run out of fuel. Neither the travel ban nor Sessions's recusal was going to be resolved right now. Priebus and Bannon said they would stay back, but the president had to get going. As Trump stormed out to Marine One at 10:45 for the ten-minute helicopter ride to Joint Base Andrews, Spicer tapped out a quick note of warning to one of his deputies who was waiting on Air Force One. Trump, he wrote, is "coming in hot!"

The next day, Bannon, McGahn, and Sessions boarded the attorney general's plane and headed to Palm Beach. They had no choice, Bannon told the attorney general. Trump was refusing to take calls from Sessions, but they had to convince Trump to sign the new order, and Sessions had to be the one to do it. The president was a bully and a coward, Bannon told Sessions, and you can't let his rage fester; you have to stand up to him right away and make your case. "You have to bring it today," Bannon told Sessions as the pair flew south to Florida, preparing for what both of them knew would be a difficult and contentious argument with the president. "You've got to stand up to this guy. You're executing his entire program. This is everything." Sessions agreed with Trump that the first version of the travel ban was stronger, and he thought it was ridiculous that courts were using what Trump said in speeches or on Twitter to claim that the order was unconstitutional. But he also understood the argument by the top lawyers at the department that a revised ban would strengthen their appeal. And they had already told the court they would submit one.

If there was any doubt about what the president's mood would be when Sessions and Bannon arrived, it was erased at 6:35 a.m. when Trump tweeted a stunning accusation against his predecessor. "Terrible! Just found out that Obama had my 'wires tapped' in Trump Tower just before the victory. Nothing found. This is McCarthyism!" In three more tweets over the next twenty-seven minutes, Trump repeated the unsubstantiated charge, compared former President Obama to Nixon during Watergate, and called Obama a "bad (or sick) guy!" That afternoon, as the rest of the world scrambled to try to understand the basis of Trump's accusation, Sessions, Bannon, McGahn, Miller, and Kelly met with the president in the enclosed sunroom at Mar-a-Lago. For five hours, Sessions led a painstaking discussion with Trump of everything his administration had planned on immigration, and how vital the travel ban was to the agenda. He explained why revisions were needed and swore that it would not weaken Trump's restrictions; if anything, Sessions argued, it would strengthen the president's hand. Trump was grumpy and angry, lashing out at Sessions repeatedly for the recusal, which he said was unnecessary. The session extended to dinner on the patio, and at one point Trump even took Sessions aside and asked him whether he could un-recuse himself—just take it back and say he would oversee the Russia investigations after all. By the end of the meeting, Trump had relented. He would sign the new order, even though he didn't want to.

On Monday, March 6, 2017, after returning to Washington, Trump signed the revised order in the Oval Office, with no press present. He left it to Sessions, Kelly, and Tillerson to make the announcement at the Customs and Border Protection headquarters later that day. One senior adviser later recalled never having seen a president so angry signing anything. It would take almost sixteen months and a third, modified version before the president's travel ban would go into full effect, winning the blessing of the Supreme Court. That version was based on specific risk factors for evaluating which countries should be barred. The final list included Chad, Iran, Libya, North Korea, Somalia, Syria, Venezuela, and Yemen. But in the meantime, Trump's anger about the resistance to his immigration agenda—from the courts, the Democrats, and his own bureaucracy—continued to fester.

— 7 —

SHACKLES OFF

ONCE A WEEK IN the Roosevelt Room down the hall from the Oval Office, Stephen Miller convened a team of loyalists and policy minds from across government to churn out radical new ideas about how to overhaul the immigration system in the United States. The working group had no formal name. Its creation was never announced in a news release, and White House officials were loath to even acknowledge its existence. But Miller's mysterious gathering had an ambitious mandate and broad influence. He was running a sort of secret immigration think tank out of the West Wing.

The group, which usually met on Fridays, was part of a quiet but methodical effort, overseen by Bannon but largely orchestrated and executed by Miller, to seize control of the machinery of government and use it to make good on the president's immigration agenda in ways large and small. It was also a way for Miller to cement his ownership of the immigration portfolio inside Trump's White House, where lanes of responsibility were ill-defined and turf wars over policy were the norm. Miller had the broad and amorphous title of senior policy adviser, one that he envisioned as a sort of uber-policy position that would allow him to reach into any issue and exert his influence. But his West Wing colleagues often chafed at Miller's tendency to horn in on their territory. McMaster hated when he inserted himself in national security debates, Cohn couldn't stand it when he intervened on economic issues, and Porter routinely batted down Miller's efforts to take control of trade discussions. So before long, they came to a sort of unspoken truce. Miller would mostly stay out of their hair on their core issues if he could dominate anything that had to do with immigration. He still enjoyed outsized influence with Trump, with whom he had developed a rapport during the campaign that was unmatched by any other senior official in the West Wing. And his involvement in writing the president's speeches gave him an important foothold in policy fights, allowing him a strong hand to shape Trump's decisions. But for the most part, Miller devoted himself to immigration, and expected everyone else to stay out of his way. So when Porter moved in June to streamline the policy process and put one person in charge of each issue, it was no surprise to anyone that Miller insisted on being put in charge of a broad portfolio that also incorporated refugee and international migration issues, previously the province of the NSC. McMaster, whose own relationship with the president was somewhat strained, was not about to get in the way of Trump's favorite immigration wunderkind.

Miller's Friday group was a way to exert his influence beyond the walls of the White House, bringing in players from the State Department, the Department of Homeland Security, and the Justice Department. The group was not unlike Hamilton's transition team, and it contained many of the same people. There was Hamilton, Miller's friend from his days in Sessions's office, who was by now a counselor at DHS. Francis Cissna, now the director of policy at DHS, came to some of the meetings, as did Dimple Shah, a lawyer at the department. Tracy Short, who became the top lawyer at Immigration and Customs Enforcement, attended the weekly meetings. So did Kathy Nuebel Kovarik, who started out in the Trump administration as an adviser to Kelly and would later become the chief policy adviser at Citizenship and Immigration Services, and Jon Feere, a onetime policy analyst at the right-wing Center for Immigration Studies who had left that post to volunteer with Trump's campaign and landed at Citizenship and Immigration Services once he took office. Andrew Veprek of the Domestic Policy Council was a regular attendee, along with a clique of young Miller acolytes in the office who seemed to follow Miller's every move and ideological cue. One senior official who attended the sessions referred to Veprek's clique collectively as the "young, foolish men." They often had the task of calling attendees in between meetings and delivering messages from Miller. Stephen thinks you should do x, y, z. Stephen wants to know why you haven't done x, y, z. Bannon popped in occasionally. And Miller made sure that two members of the White House counsel's office attended regularly to provide the legal expertise they would need. Julia Hahn, a twenty-five-year-old aide whom Bannon had brought over from Breitbart News, was also a fixture at the meetings, acting as an assistant to Miller and a pair of eyes for Bannon, briefing him regularly about what the task force was up to.

Like Miller, Hahn had grown up in a wealthy suburb of Los Angeles, raised in Beverly Hills, where she attended the exclusive Harvard-Westlake School. After college at the University of Chicago, she had become a producer for Laura Ingraham's show on Fox News and befriended conservative celebrities such as Ann Coulter. Her career at Breitbart had been made when she showed up at the Janesville, Wisconsin, home of Paul Ryan, the speaker of the house, and snapped photographs of the fence along the perimeter of his property, as part of a story hitting the Republican for failing to steer federal money to building a fortified border barrier seven hundred miles long. "PAUL RYAN BUILDS BORDER FENCE AROUND HIS MANSION, DOESN'T FUND BORDER FENCE IN OMNIBUS," her story's headline blared in December of 2015. "Upon even the slightest appearance of any unusual activity—such as a 5'2" female taking a photograph of the fence—Ryan's border agent will deploy into action to ensure the perimeter's sovereignty," Hahn wrote.

Over time, as White House officials started asking questions about the regular gathering, Miller moved his task force's meetings to his small office on the top floor of the West Wing, jamming fifteen or twenty people around a conference table as they developed a strategic plan to remake the nation's immigration policies, one step at a time. They scribbled their plans on large white flip charts, and the list of what they had to do grew longer and longer. They discussed overhauling the way the United States admits skilled workers, revamping ICE's enforcement priorities and strategies for enhancing visa security. One early assignment from Miller was for the group to scour the immigration statutes and look for grounds of inadmissibility that were not being enforced. Another target was an old but ill-defined standard that said the country did not have to admit anyone who was likely to become dependent on the government for survival. That one would ultimately become an obsession for Miller.

As much of a fan as he was of splashy public debates like the one that attended the travel ban, Miller also shared Bannon's belief that to bring about real, lasting changes in immigration policy, he would have to burrow deep inside the government bureaucracy—Bannon called it the "administrative state"—to dismantle existing policies plank by arcane plank. Miller compared the government's immigration system to ancient sedimentary rock—layer upon accumulated layer of policy decisions, executive memoranda, legal interpretations, and day-to-day practice that made it all but impossible to understand what the law actually said. And there were precious few government bureaucrats with that knowledge who shared his ideology. While Trump would speak in broad strokes about getting tough and cracking down, Miller was learning that it was through the painstaking, often extremely wonky work of rule-making and policy-memo-drafting that he could push past the resistance of civil servants and the pro-immigration lobbyists who served the interests of both parties and enact the president's agenda. During meetings of his group, Miller often quizzed them about obscure points of immigration law: Why does it take two hours or two days to deport a Mexican, but forty days to deport a single adult from Central America? He played a different part than Bannon, who relished the attention he drew from making over-the-top pronouncements. But Bannon encouraged Miller's brain trust, which he believed was doing the real work of Trump's immigration takeover. Bannon thought it was brilliant. "A work of art," he marveled later.

The chaos of the travel ban had done little to convince Miller and his group to put on the brakes. On the contrary, the race was on to translate Trump's immigration vision into policy, as his rhetoric intensified. During a speech to hard-core activists at the Conservative Public Action Conference three weeks after becoming president, Trump repeated his campaign promises: "As we speak today, immigration officers are finding the gang members, the drug dealers and the criminal aliens, and throwing them the hell out of our country. And we will not let them back in. They're not coming back in, folks. If they do, they're going to have bigger problems than they ever dreamt of."

In the first days of his presidency, ICE agents rounded up more than six hundred undocumented immigrants in raids in eleven states that sent waves of fear through immigrant communities. In Alexandria, Virginia, ICE agents arrested two men coming out of a hypothermia shelter at the Rising Hope Mission Church. After an Arizona woman who had regularly checked in with immigration officials was abruptly deported, the Mexican government issued a statement warning of a "more severe application of immigration control measures" in the United States and urging Mexican immigrants to "take precautions and keep in touch with the nearest consulate." The raids and deportations made Trump happy. "The crackdown on illegal criminals is merely the keeping of my campaign promise," he tweeted. "Gang members, drug dealers & others are being removed!"

At the end of January, Kelly announced that Trump was appointing Thomas D. Homan, a former New York cop and more than thirty-year veteran of the Border Patrol and ICE, to be the acting head of ICE. Burly and tough-looking, with a thick neck and a crew cut, Homan had won a Presidential Rank Award, the government's highest civil service honor, during the Obama administration for overseeing a record number of deportations and handling a migration surge from Central America. But he had chafed under Obama's restrictive enforcement policies, which dictated that his agents ignore undocumented immigrants if they stumbled across them during the course of other investigations. It felt like the agents were shackled, and he longed to let them do what they were trained to do. "All I wanted to do was enforce the law and not apologize for that," Homan told anyone who would listen. That's just what Trump and Miller wanted, too.

On February 20, the one-month anniversary of Trump's inauguration, DHS head Kelly issued new directives for ICE agents, freeing them from the Obama-era rules that prevented agents from arresting immigrants whose only violation was their immigration status. In a pair of memoranda, Kelly revealed the broad scope of the president's ambitions: to publicize crimes by undocumented immigrants; strip immigrants of privacy protections; enlist local police officers as enforcers; erect new detention facilities; discourage asylum seekers; and, ultimately, speed up deportations. The crackdown was being heard around the world. In February, Kelly and Tillerson were at the InterContinental Hotel in Mexico City, preparing for a meeting with President Peña Nieto, when Trump began boasting about how aggressively his administration was moving to stop immigrants at the border with Mexico. "It's a military operation," he said during an appearance with manufacturing CEOs. As Tillerson and Kelly headed to the motorcade in Mexico City, Tillerson was informed of Trump's comments and told Kelly. "Holy shit!" Kelly said as the pair disappeared back into the hotel suite to strategize. The president's comment blew up the talks and forced Kelly to publicly disagree with his boss. "I repeat: There will be no use of military in this," he told Mexican and American reporters.

In an on-camera briefing on February 21, Sean Spicer, the White House press secretary, made clear what the goal was for the government's immigration agents: "You have a mission, there are laws that need to be followed; you should do your mission and follow the law," Spicer said to reporters at the White House.

In a nutshell, Spicer said, Trump wanted to "take the shackles off."

Inside his new, second-floor West Wing office, Miller wanted to erase any doubt about what Spicer meant as he began crafting the president's first address to Congress, a nationally televised event that would be Trump's first major speech since the inauguration. Miller thought it should send a message to the public about the president's priorities. But it would also serve as a stark reminder to career bureaucrats inside Trump's own government that he was charting a new and different course, especially when it came to immigration. Miller's speech included bold phrases that could hardly be ignored: He described "an environment of lawless chaos" at the nation's borders and warned that drug dealers and criminals "prey on our very innocent citizens." He wrote that America's leaders cannot allow a "beachhead of terrorism" to exist inside the country or accept laws that provide "a sanctuary for extremists." Watching the speech from the gallery would be family members of people who had been killed by illegal immigrants. "Your loved ones will never, ever be forgotten," Trump would pledge.

The speech quickly became a tug-of-war between Miller and Obama-era holdovers in the government. At Miller's request, the Department of Justice scrambled to compile a spreadsheet that listed all terrorism convictions since the September 11, 2001, attacks. On February 10, George Toscas, a lawyer in the department's National Security Division, sent over the list, but with caveats: the data excluded cases related solely to domestic terrorism, he wrote in an email to the White House, and only supported the general idea that "convictions have been obtained against hundreds of defendants for terrorism or terrorism-related charges." A few days later James E. Rybicki, the chief of staff at the FBI, wrote that the frequent use of aliases by terrorists and conflicting information in the data made it hard to accurately identify where people were born. The list provided to the White House "likely contains gaps or errors" when it came to the nationalities of the people involved in terror cases, he said.

The White House paid little attention to the caveats. In drafts of Miller's speech that made their way back to the Justice Department, officials there learned that Trump planned to say that their data showed that "the vast majority of individuals convicted of terrorism and terrorism-related offenses since 9/11 came here from outside of our country." They were aghast. It wasn't true. Their statistics showed just the opposite. "There was unanimity from career people that the data doesn't support this," one former official at the department recalled. Several top officials appealed to change the sentence in the president's speech. Their pleas fell on deaf ears; the false claim stayed in the address.

Miller also wanted the speech to be a high-profile moment for Trump to make good on his promise to call out the threat from "radical Islamic terrorism," underscoring the president's view of the dangers from certain countries that formed the basis for his travel ban. During the campaign,

Trump had repeatedly mocked Obama for shying away from the phrase and choosing instead to condemn "violent extremism." In a campaign event in the summer of 2016, Trump had lashed out at Obama and other Democrats, saying that "anyone who cannot name our enemy is not fit to lead this country. Anyone who cannot condemn the hatred, oppression and violence of radical Islam lacks the moral clarity to serve as our president." Now that Trump was in office, Miller believed it was critical for Trump to follow through; in early drafts of the address to Congress, Miller included the phrase numerous times.

Miller was paranoid about leaks as he wrote the speech, refusing to use email to distribute it to colleagues for input. But as printed copies circulated in the White House, McMaster objected. Repeatedly suggesting that all of Islam was responsible for terrorism would not be helpful, McMaster told Miller as he crossed out the multiple mentions of "radical Islamic terrorism." Miller put them back in. Mike Dubke, who had just started days before as the White House communications director, agreed with Miller that Trump had to use the phrase. But he also thought McMaster was right that the phrase didn't have to be in every paragraph of the speech.

By the time Trump began speaking from the House lectern at 9:09 p.m. on the 28th of February, his speech contained only one reference to "radical Islamic terrorism." On that point at least, Miller had largely caved.

For Trump, immigration, like every other issue, was about winners and losers, who was up and who was down. And the president measured the success of his immigration agenda in large part by a simple scorecard: how many people were crossing the border illegally. By that metric, Trump's policies seemed to be working when he met with his cabinet for the first time in mid-March.

With Defense Secretary James Mattis sitting on his left, and Secretary of State Rex Tillerson to his right, Trump boasted that in the wake of his January executive orders, illegal immigration on the nation's southern border had fallen "by an unprecedented 40 percent" during his first full month in office. He was right. Total apprehensions at the southwest border with Mexico had dropped from 42,463 in January to 23,555 in February—a 44 percent decrease. Homan, the president's acting ICE director, believed it was the happy result of the huge enforcement effort that his agents had unleashed in the early days of the administration.

Even better, the number of families and unaccompanied children from Central America who were trying to cross into the United States had gone way down. More than 16,000 families and 7,000 unaccompanied children had been caught trying to cross the border in December of 2016, part of what officials believed was an attempt to seek refuge ahead of what the migrants expected would be a Trump crackdown once he became president. And now that Trump was in office—and clamping down as promised with very public policies like the travel ban—the message was being received. In March, Border Patrol agents arrested barely more than 1,000 families and another 1,000 children, a plunge of more than 90 percent. The Obama administration had faced a crisis in 2014 and again in 2016 about what to do with the families and children, and had encountered legal challenges from immigrant rights advocates when they tried to detain them for long periods of time. But with Trump in office, that problem had largely evaporated.

For months, Trump bragged that his tough rhetoric and policies were having the intended effect of discouraging illegal border crossings. "Look at this, in 100 days, that's down to the lowest in 17 years and it's going lower," Trump told the Associated Press. "Now, people aren't coming because they know they're not going to get through, and there isn't crime." At a rally in Kentucky in March, Trump hailed the numbers. "Since the day of my election, we've already cut illegal immigration at the southern border by 61 percent—think of that, 61 percent!—and we haven't started."

The White House dubbed it the "Trump Effect."

But if Trump was crowing about the effects of his crackdown, lawmakers on Capitol Hill were growing angry. On St. Patrick's Day, John Kelly accepted an invitation from Democratic House members to a luncheon on Capitol Hill to discuss the president's policies. Michelle Lujan Grisham, who represented an immigrant-heavy district in Albuquerque, New Mexico, and chaired the Congressional Hispanic Caucus, laid into Kelly. Your agents have created panic and fear in our communities. They have reduced, not increased public safety, she said. Judy Chu, whose district northeast of Los Angeles is one of the nation's most diverse, piled on, accusing ICE and Border Patrol agents of targeting Hispanics for enforcement. What is needed, she demanded, is greater oversight of the agents so they do not act on their personal prejudice and bias.

Kelly couldn't contain himself.

"I reject almost everything you've said about our officers," he shot back, complaining about what he called "wild reporting" about his department and the people who worked there. "I've never experienced a level of reporting so inaccurate," he said. "I don't deport anyone. ICE doesn't deport anyone. DHS doesn't. Laws do. Judges do. If you don't like the law, change it."

Kelly was a decorated military commander, but he thought of himself as a political operator who understood how Congress worked. As a one-star general in the mid-2000s, Kelly had run the Marine Corps' legislative team, building relationships with lawmakers as a way to safeguard support for the military's funding. Later, as the top military aide to Secretary of Defense Leon Panetta during Obama's administration, Kelly was frequently on the Hill, interacting with members and earning goodwill. "He took the approach of: 'Let's have a relationship here. How can we build that?'" recalled one colleague from that era. But Kelly was also a quintessential Marine, whose exacting work ethic and relentless sense of patriotic duty often came across to lawmakers as dismissiveness or disdain. As secretary of homeland security, Kelly was the personal embodiment of Trump's hard-core immigration agenda, and that put a target on his back.

Despite Kelly's reputation as nonideological and coldly rational, there were some early indications that he shared the president's tendency to hype the threat from immigrants. Before he started the job, Kelly would often tell people that he wanted to focus on tracking down and deporting the three to four million violent criminal aliens who were living in America. In fact, the number of criminal immigrants was a fraction of that, somewhere around 200,000. In an interview with CNN's Wolf Blitzer in early March, Kelly said that, at the president's urging, he was weighing a policy of separating children from their parents who crossed the border illegally, "in order to deter more movement along this terribly dangerous network. I am considering exactly that. They will be well cared for as we deal with their parents." The public blowback to Kelly's comments was swift, and the idea soon faded from public discussion, but internal conversations continued, and members of Congress took notice.

At a similar meeting with the Congressional Hispanic Caucus in early April, lawmakers demanded to know what the secretary was doing to control what they called "rogue" immigration agents who were inspired by Trump's tough rhetoric to round up illegal immigrants whether they had committed serious crimes or not. "The 99 percent of the agents are not the problem," Ruben Gallego of Arizona told Kelly. "It's the 1 percent we are concerned about," he said. Within ICE, "there are some that go rogue." Senator Catherine Cortez Masto of Nevada chimed in, saying that agents needed to make choices about who to arrest and who to ignore. "Where is the discretion?" she said. Kelly pushed back. Questions about discretion have to be made by prosecutors or judges. Agents can't make those determinations in the field. "At the front door, at 4 a.m., they don't have the discretion to investigate those questions," he said.

The meeting ended when Lujan Grisham handed Kelly a letter that she said contained questions about immigration enforcement that she would like answered. She asked whether Kelly would be willing to meet with the caucus every six weeks. "We want to get to a place where we can work together," she said.

Notes of the meeting from one member recorded the following: "Secretary Kelly did not say yes or no."

Trump and Miller were growing increasingly impatient. The travel ban was stuck in litigation, blocked by judges who they felt had no business telling the president who could and couldn't come into the country. There weren't enough immigration judges. The president wanted to hire more

ICE agents, more quickly. And inside the sprawling agencies that were supposed to be implementing Trump's new immigration agenda, they felt there was still too much resistance from Obama and Bush appointees who didn't share the president's philosophy or his urgency.

At the Executive Office for Immigration Review, which runs the nation's immigration courts, Obama-era holdovers resisted Miller's demands to speed more judges to the border, explaining that the physical courtroom infrastructure didn't yet exist for so many judges, and neither did the caseloads. Miller got his way in the end; a call from the deputy attorney general to Juan Osuna, the head of EOIR, saw to that. But the abrupt order led to an absurd scramble for courtroom space for the new judges in which desperate EOIR officials even entertained the idea of using inflatable car garages designed for auto shows to provide temporary, blow-up courtrooms for the immigration judges. (Osuna's staff ultimately rejected the idea of what they were calling "bouncy-house courts.")

Miller continued to be frustrated that everything was taking so long. His irritation was evident at a White House meeting on a Friday in early March attended by officials from Justice, DHS, and the Domestic Policy Council. Miller led the meeting. The president was angry, he said, that more had not been done to punish so-called "sanctuary cities" for the refusal by local officials to help federal officials deport people whose only crime was being in the United States illegally. In the view of the president, liberal politicians were flouting long-standing federal immigration laws. At the meeting, Miller urged the group to come up with legislative proposals that could tighten the screws on the cities and counties that were refusing to comply. Miller gave them four days to come up with text that could generate legislative proposals. What was needed by Tuesday, he told them, was very tough language.

There should be, he demanded, "no wiggle room" for local jurisdictions.

During the meeting, Miller also insisted that the group must do more to publicize the brutal consequences of crimes committed by illegal immigrants. Their public affairs departments needed to make people aware of cases in which immigrants who were released by sanctuary cities later went on to commit heinous acts, he told them. It was a favorite subject for Miller, who was convinced that the more they knew about crimes perpetuated by undocumented immigrants, the more they would rebel against politicians who refused to treat the immigrants harshly. Never mind that statistics routinely showed that immigrants were far less likely to commit violent crimes than native-born Americans; in Miller's view, even one crime perpetrated by a person who was not authorized to be in the United States was too many. Miller told the group that they needed to portray immigrant crime as a crisis, and to demonstrate muscular action showing that the government was taking it seriously. It had to be made "highly visible," he said.

In case there was any doubt of who would be watching, Miller said that Trump was "very interested in seeing those reports." Every time the Justice Department prosecuted a case against MS-13, the brutal transnational criminal gang with roots in El Salvador, they were under strict orders to send an email to Miller and Julia Hahn.

No one escaped Trump's rage about the resistance to his immigration agenda, least of all Jeff Sessions. Yet despite the president's anger at him over the Russia investigation, Sessions was pushing harder than just about anybody else in the administration to institute changes he had been advocating for years—and please Trump in the process.

At just after 1:30 p.m. on a Monday at the end of March, the attorney general made a surprise appearance in the White House briefing room, introduced by Sean Spicer for an "announcement regarding immigration enforcement with respect to sanctuary cities." Sessions looked into the bank of television cameras and delivered a six-minute warning to state and local politicians whose cities had failed to hand over illegal immigrants to federal authorities. Speaking in his slow but deliberate Alabama drawl, Sessions assailed what he called the willful violation by local authorities of section 1373 of the federal code. By refusing to detain illegal immigrants at the request of federal agents, Sessions said, the local and state governments were putting dangerous criminals on the streets. He cited a Denver case in which an illegal immigrant from Mexico named Ever Valles had been charged at the end of 2016 with murder and robbery. Sessions said he had been released from a Denver jail despite a request by Immigration and Customs Enforcement to detain him on their behalf.

"The President has rightly said disregard for the law must end," Sessions declared. To drive home that point, the attorney general announced that the Justice Department would no longer provide public safety grants to communities that do not adhere to the letter of the law. A failure to remedy violations, he said, "could result in withholding grants, termination of grants, and disbarment or ineligibility for future grants." Sessions also cited a just-issued report by ICE that sought to "name and shame" jurisdictions by listing more than two hundred cases in which local and state governments had refused to honor an ICE request to hold an illegal immigrant, a decision known as a "declined detainer." ICE promised that the report would be published weekly until the governments abandoned their sanctuary policies. "Such policies cannot continue," Sessions insisted. "They make our nation less safe."

What Sessions didn't acknowledge publicly was the anger that had been generated by the ICE report and the threat of withholding grants. Mayors, sheriffs, and police chiefs around the country were furious at being publicly accused of breaking federal laws. In a heated meeting in the attorney general's conference room at the Justice Department, leaders of the nation's law enforcement associations hammered Sessions over the sanctuary city issue. Richard Stanek, the sheriff in Hennepin County, Minnesota, ripped into the attorney general for the ICE report, which had accused Stanek's jail of refusing to cooperate with immigration agents. It wasn't true, Stanek yelled. "He was hot," one of the participants in the meeting said later. "He gave the AG an earful."

Days later, sixteen mayors, police chiefs, and sheriffs met for a similar venting session over breakfast with John Kelly, the secretary of homeland security, in a meeting room at an Embassy Suites in Washington. Kelly opened the meeting with a long and boastful soliloquy about the virtues of the department he led. "It's a great organization with great people," Kelly told the local officials. They do "everything according to the law." Federal agents are not conducting random sweeps, Kelly insisted, but are targeting criminal illegal immigrants for deportation. He blamed Congress for being unable or unwilling to confront the issue of illegal immigration, but said it was the responsibility of those in the room to enforce the nation's laws.

The reaction was blunt and unsparing. J. Thomas Manger, the veteran police chief of Montgomery County, Maryland, a wealthy Washington suburb, was sitting next to Kelly on his left. Manger told the secretary that he didn't appreciate that his department was publicly shamed and labeled as a sanctuary county—it wasn't. Manger was also offended by the punitive threats of funding denials hanging over their heads. "It's not helping our relationship," he said. Police officials respect federal immigration authorities, Manger told Kelly, but local governments don't have the police or jail resources to be immigration police. The secretary was polite and somewhat contrite, pledging that his department would work with local law enforcement to resolve their issues. After the meeting broke up, Manger turned to Kelly and thanked him for listening and for sounding reasonable.

"What you said here this morning is so encouraging. When I hear what the president says, when I hear what the attorney general says, and then I listen to you—you all aren't on the same page," Manger said.

"Chief," Kelly responded, "you don't want me on the same page as the president."

The anger among law enforcement officials across the country continued for days. On Capitol Hill, Manger ran into ICE acting director Tom Homan. Manger complained again that the agency's report named Montgomery County as an offender. "It's not good for either one of our agencies to be doing that stuff," Manger told him. Homan shook his head. "You're right," he said. "We've got to support each other." Within days, Homan went to Kelly to warn him that the report was a problem. "This is a blue-on-blue report," Homan told the secretary, using law enforcement lingo to describe an intra-police dispute. "It's going to hurt the sheriffs who are cooperating with us." Soon, the federal government had abandoned the weekly ICE reports. In a short statement on the agency's website, ICE officials said they remained committed to publishing "the most accurate information available" but that the agency was continuing to analyze and refine its reporting methodologies. But the notice added: "While this analysis is ongoing, the publication of the Declined Detainer Outcomes Report will be temporarily suspended," it said.

Nearly two years later, that brief statement was still on the website.

— 8 —

ANGELS AND DEMONS

AT DAWN ON THE morning of January 31, 2015, five months before Donald Trump would announce his candidacy for president, Julie Golvach was in bed in her Houston, Texas, home when she was awoken by a knock at her front door. She opened it to find two police officers standing on her stoop, there to inform her that her twenty-five-year-old son, Spencer, had been fatally shot in the wee hours of that morning.

Spencer, who had his own guitar shop and a job as a forklift operator at a local warehouse, had been in his white Toyota pickup when it happened. He had just dropped off his girlfriend—it was her birthday—and was waiting at a red light to turn left and head home to his apartment when he was fatally shot in the head. In the days that followed, Golvach learned about the man who had murdered her son. He was a Mexican man by the name of Victor Reyes with a long rap sheet including burglary, assault, and multiple illegal entries into the United States, who had been in and out of federal prison and had been deported four times. Each time, Reyes would simply walk across the border again. The bullet that took Spencer's life was part of a shooting spree that had begun earlier that night when Reyes shot another man in the face. After Spencer, he killed another two people and wounded three, before dying himself in a shootout with police.

The pain of losing her son was unimaginable. But for Golvach, the tragedy was all the more bitter because it should never have been allowed to happen in the first place. Reyes should not have been in the United States to begin with, she thought. Her son had not only been a victim of a convicted felon's bullet; he had also been a victim of a badly broken immigration system that allowed people like the man who murdered him to sneak into the country and wreak havoc in communities like hers. Everybody knew it was a problem, she thought, and nobody did a thing about it.

So Golvach was thrilled in June of 2015 as she watched TV news coverage of Trump's campaign announcement, listening to him talk about criminals who come to the United States from Mexico. "When I heard what he said, I said 'It finally looks like somebody gets it, and cares about us,'" Golvach said.

A short time later, Golvach was contacted by Maria Espinoza, a conservative activist who ran an organization called the Remembrance Project, which describes itself as "a voice for victims killed by illegal aliens," often called "Angel Families." The group receives substantial funding from U.S. Inc., another group, founded by John Tanton, that pushes for tougher immigration enforcement and less immigration into the United States overall. Espinoza told Golvach that she had been reaching out to each of the presidential campaigns asking what they planned to do for families like hers. Few responded—until Trump. His campaign wanted to meet Angel Families and invite them to his arena-style campaign rallies.

Trump instantly understood the power of the Angel Families. Weeks after he announced his candidacy, thirty-two-year-old Kate Steinle had been shot and killed by Jose Ines Garcia Zarate, an undocumented immigrant, while walking along San Francisco's Embarcadero. The case generated national headlines and became a frequent topic of discussion on Fox News. One day as he watched *Fox & Friends*, the morning program he rarely missed, Trump saw an interview on the subject with a man named Jamiel Shaw, whose seventeen-year-old son, with whom he shared a name, had been killed by an undocumented immigrant in Los Angeles in 2008. Trump was so taken with Shaw's story that he called the Fox control room to ask to be put in touch with him.

By November, Trump had announced plans to hold a rally in Beaumont, Texas, about an hour and a half east of Houston, and Golvach was told that he wanted to meet between eight and ten Angel Moms and Dads. She and several others gathered backstage at the Ford Park Arena to wait for Trump, many of them holding banners and wearing T-shirts emblazoned with the names and photographs of their loved ones. Trump was late, but when he arrived, Golvach recalled later, he seemed captivated by their experiences, listening intently to the horror stories about how their sons and daughters died, and the parents' grief and sense of powerlessness.

This is important stuff, Trump said. People need to know about this. Trump turned to his campaign staff and told them he wanted the families to join him onstage. During the rally, he interrupted his own comments to call up the parents, one by one, to talk about their loved ones. Golvach felt seen for the first time.

Trump stayed close to the Angel Families, who Miller called the emotional spine of his campaign, invoking their names often in his speeches as proof that his immigration agenda was compassionate. Once he won the presidency, Trump created an office within DHS to help them and named it Voice, or Victims of Immigration Crime Engagement. He regularly invited Angel Families to the White House to call attention to their plight, using them as a political counterpoint whenever he was accused of pushing immigration policies that tore families apart.

"When I sit here and listen to somebody talking about families being separated, no one has any compassion for what I'm feeling, except President Trump," said Golvach, who visited the White House in July 2017 along with other Angel Families. "He's looked all of us in the face, and he knows our stories, and understands the human tragedy of this."

The Angel Families provided a powerful anecdotal rationale for Trump's restrictive immigration policies, but data shows that their tragic stories were the exception, not the rule. Numerous studies have found that immigrants are less likely than native-born Americans to commit crimes or to be behind bars, and there is no evidence that higher levels of immigration lead to higher crime rates; in fact, reputable analyses have shown just the opposite.

In a 2015 report published by the American Immigration Council, a team of researchers wrote, "For more than a century, innumerable studies have confirmed two simple yet powerful truths about the relationship between immigration and crime: immigrants are less likely to commit serious crimes or be behind bars than the native-born, and high rates of immigration are associated with lower rates of violent crime and property crime. This holds true for both legal immigrants and the unauthorized, regardless of their country of origin or level of education. In other words, the overwhelming majority of immigrants are not 'criminals' by any commonly accepted definition of the term."

But there was another group of Americans whose misfortunes Trump often invoked when speaking about the evils of immigration, whose plight resonated with voters across the country. They were the "forgotten men and women" who Trump often said had seen their livelihoods devastated by large-scale immigration, and there was plenty of evidence and scholarly research to suggest their plight—that of low-skilled workers who had seen their wages fall and job prospects dwindle because of large-scale immigration—was real.

"Decades of record immigration have produced lower wages and higher unemployment for our citizens, especially for African American and Latino workers," he said at the Republican National Convention, in a speech that cited the Harvard economist George Borjas and his research. Trump was oversimplifying; most scholars believe there are economic upsides and downsides to immigration, with the potential depressing of wages for some natives offset by the growth in wealth to the country overall. But Trump was not wrong altogether.

A study prepared in 2016 by the National Academies of Sciences, Engineering, and Medicine, which looked at immigration trends over the previous two decades, found that immigration had a net-positive impact on the United States economy, a conclusion that would seem to be at odds with what Trump was claiming. But when the analysis examined wages, it found a more complicated dynamic at play. "When measured over a period of more than 10 years, the impact of immigration on the wages of natives overall is very small," it said. But there was an important asterisk that Trump would exploit to great effect during his campaign. "To the extent that negative wage effects are found," the study reported, "prior immigrants—who are often the closest substitutes for new immigrants—are most likely to experience them, followed by native-born high school dropouts, who share job qualifications similar to the large share of low-skilled workers among immigrants to the United States."

In other words, while immigration was positive for the U.S. economy overall, there were clear winners and losers. It benefited employers who had access to a much larger, and therefore cheaper, pool of labor, but could be a threat to workers of similar educational and skill levels. Perhaps not surprisingly, Trump's candidacy held strong appeal for many of those Americans. In 2016, he won 66 percent of white voters who lacked a college education.

NO LEGAL BASIS

NEARLY ONE HUNDRED YEARS before Trump's inauguration, lawmakers in Washington put in place the roots of the country's modern system of border controls. The cruel science of eugenics had gained credence after the turn of the century, propelled by leading scientific institutions and embraced by politicians eager to justify their xenophobic beliefs with "biological laws." Motivated by a fear that the "American identity" was slipping away, Congress passed the Immigration Act of 1924, establishing quotas based on an immigrant's national origin and restricting the entry of southern Europeans, Italians, Japanese, Chinese, and others. The reluctance to welcome foreigners continued through World War II, as the United States turned away Jews fleeing Adolf Hitler's Nazi Germany and politicians warned that the United States was in danger of being "overrun, perverted, contaminated or destroyed" by immigrants.

The anti-immigrant sentiment of the 1920s was just one of many such surges of racism and hatred in America, described by Daniel Okrent in *The Guarded Gate* as "a perfect sine wave, periods of welcoming inclusiveness alternating with years of scowling antipathy." Nearly forty years earlier, the hostility of native-born Americans to Chinese laborers who poured into the United States to work on the booming railroads gave rise to the

Chinese Exclusion Act of 1882. By the 1950s, anxiety about the spread of communism fueled efforts by lawmakers to wall off the United States from ideological threats around the globe. The 1952 McCarran-Walter Act granted the president new powers to "suspend the entry of all aliens or any class of aliens as immigrants or nonimmigrants, or impose on the entry of aliens any restrictions he may deem to be appropriate." It wasn't until the mid-1960s, during the political convulsions of the civil rights movement, that Congress began debating the Immigration and Nationality Act, to eliminate quotas based on national origin and replace them with preferences based on skills and family connections. That law, signed by President Lyndon Johnson in 1965 in the shadow of the Statue of Liberty, opened the door to waves of migrants from new parts of the world. In 1960, nearly 75 percent of the immigration into the United States was from Europe. By 2010, more than 80 percent came from Central or Latin America or Asia.

But the changes that Johnson unleashed reinflamed racial resentments that would simmer for a half century before Trump seized upon them to get elected. He was not the first to do so; his campaign rhetoric bore the echoes of previous politicians who rose to power by stoking fear, anger, and anxiety. More than sixty years before Trump's call for a border wall to stop an invasion from Mexico, Nevada senator Pat McCarran warned that "today, as never before, untold millions are storming our gates for admission and those gates are cracking under the strain." But in 2016, at a moment when his party had concluded it had to embrace the country's growing diversity, Trump yanked it back, winning the presidency with a nativist appeal to struggling white Americans at a time when immigration levels were near their lowest in two decades. Once in office, Trump and Miller invoked remnants of the immigration laws of the 1920s and 1950s to empower their crackdown. Defending the travel ban, Miller repeatedly cited the language of the McCarran Act to insist that Trump had the power to act unilaterally, a claim that was later upheld by the Supreme Court. The administration invoked the same authority in 2018 to defend the president's attempt to bar asylum seekers who crossed the border illegally.

It didn't take long for the impact of Trump's crackdown to be felt in immigrant communities across the country as ICE agents began enforcing immigration laws more aggressively.

For eight years, Meldy Lumangkun had made regular visits to the Boston offices of Immigration and Customs Enforcement, checking in annually like clockwork. An Indonesian Christian who had fled religious persecution in his country, Lumangkun had entered the United States illegally. But since September of 2010, he had lived and worked openly under an ICE program known as Operation Indonesian Surrender, a compromise of sorts worked out during the Obama administration that was designed to allow Lumangkun and others like him to remain in the Boston area without fear of deportation. He and his wife, Eva Grasje, had done just that, along with their three children, two of whom are American citizens. The arrangement seemed to work for both sides. As long as Lumangkun and his family stayed out of trouble and checked in with ICE, they could avoid being deported back to Indonesia, where Christians routinely face torture and persecution from the Muslim majority. For their part, ICE agents could move on to more important cases involving serious criminals and the Lumangkun family could become productive, tax-paying members of the community.

Then Trump arrived. On February 28, 2017, a week after Sean Spicer told reporters in the briefing room that the president wanted to liberate immigration agents from their shackles, Lumangkun received a Denial of Stay, signed by Chris Cronen, the field office director for ICE's Enforcement and Removal Operations division. The document ordered Lumangkun, an elder in the Rochester Indonesian Seventh Day Adventist church, to report to an ICE office on October 6, 2017.

The directive was a result of the executive order that Trump had signed days after taking office the previous month, and an indication of the way in which Miller and the rest of his administration were determined to carry it out—quickly, aggressively, and without exception or apology. One key provision in that order targeted what the president called "removable aliens," who—like Lumangkun—were living in the United States illegally, often because of a fear of persecution or because their home countries refused to take them back. "The presence of such individuals in the United States, and the practices of foreign nations that refuse the repatriation of their nationals, are contrary to the national interest," the president's order said. "We cannot faithfully execute the immigration laws of the United States if we exempt classes or categories of removable aliens from potential enforcement."

It took only weeks for law enforcement agents to put the legalistic language into practice on the ground. Rather than continue to look the other way when it came to Lumangkun and his family, the president's new approach meant that they and other Indonesian Christians like them would be summarily sent back home.

By the time Lee Gelernt, the ACLU lawyer, began hearing about the plight of the Indonesian Christians in Boston, he was already trying to block the immediate deportation of a group of Iraqis in Detroit. After the travel ban, Gelernt, one of the nation's best-known immigrant rights lawyers, had expected that things would calm down for him and the team of attorneys that had swung into action for the frenzied legal battle to beat back that first executive order. Instead, his workload was growing with each passing week, as Trump pushed the boundaries of the law, seemingly on every front, to carry out his immigration agenda. There were no days off, and multiple cross-country flights, as Gelernt flitted from courtroom to courtroom acting out the equivalent of a legal game of immigration whack-a-mole with the Trump administration. "Every month, week, he's doing something that's really novel and dramatic," said Gelernt, a soft-spoken New Yorker who lectures at Columbia Law School, where he received his law degree in 1988. "The whole thing is just so extreme that we have to sue on everything." So by the time the Indonesians came along, Gelernt knew exactly what he was up against.

Like the Indonesians, the Iraqis living in Michigan's largest city—many of them Chaldean Christians—were at risk of deportation. They had arrived in the United States decades ago after fleeing Saddam Hussein's autocratic rule, and some had committed crimes that caused immigration judges to order them sent home. But for years, Iraq refused to accept them back, making it diplomatically impossible for the United States to deport them. As a result, immigration officials had assured the Iraqis that they could raise their families without looking over their shoulders. But that changed in the summer of 2017. ICE agents descended on the community and rounded up 114 of the Iraqis in a single raid. Among them was Usama Jamil Hamama, an Iraqi known as "Sam" who had entered the United States legally in 1974, but was ordered deported in 1994 after he was convicted of assault and possession of a firearm in 1988. Hamama had served his time and settled in West Bloomfield, Michigan, where he had married a U.S. citizen. The couple had four children, including two who went on to attend the University of Michigan. On June 11, 2017, ICE agents arrived at Hamama's home and arrested him. He was going back to Iraq, they said.

The president's directive translated into orders for ICE to round up everyone. No group was exempt from deportation. But the Iraqis were also vulnerable because of the travel ban. The first version of the ban had included Iraq, but when Mattis and McMaster convinced the president to take Iraq off the list of banned countries, officials cut a deal with Iraq to allow the United States to finally send immigrants like Hamama back to their country. It was the final straw for nearly 1,400 Iraqis around the country who were in similar situations—subject to deportation at any moment even though they had built lives in the United States over years and even decades.

Hamama became the lead plaintiff in Gelernt's case to stop the Iraqi deportations, at least until people like Hamama had a chance to make their argument that they would face persecution, torture, and even death if they returned to their country. "They are all American. They lived here. They've grown up here. It's been twenty years," Gelernt said. "We rushed to court and said you can't deport them without giving them a chance to show that circumstances have changed and they will be killed if they go back to Iraq, because they're Christian." For the ACLU, Hamama's case became the first in a series of urgent legal efforts to protect small pockets of immigrant communities around the country. In addition to the Indonesian Christians in New England and 1,400 Iraqis throughout the United States, ICE began rounding up Somalis in Miami, Cambodians in Los Angeles, and scores of Mauritanians in Ohio. During hearings in court-rooms across the country, ICE lawyers bluntly explained that they were just carrying out Trump's orders. "It's against the law for them to remain in the United States. They no longer have a legal basis to be in this country," Jennifer Newby, a government lawyer, told Judge Mark A. Goldsmith of federal court in Michigan. "It is ICE's job to enforce those orders."

Judge Goldsmith seemed unmoved, asserting in a ruling in June of 2017 that there was no reason why the deportations should not be delayed until Hamama and the others like him could have an opportunity to pres-ent information about what they would face in Iraq. In a ruling that day, Goldsmith issued a nationwide injunction preventing ICE from deporting Hamama and the other Iraqis. It was another blow to Trump and Miller and their theory of the executive's vast power when it comes to immigra-tion. Once again, a judge was sending Trump a message: there are limits to the actions you can take, even against those without the protection of citi-zenship. The judge's ruling added to the seething anger in the West Wing. Similar rulings delayed—at least temporarily—the immediate deportation of other groups of Christian immigrants.

Six months later, in January of 2018, Gelernt would be back in federal court, this time before Chief Judge Patti B. Saris in Massachusetts, who was hearing the ACLU's case involving the Indonesian Christians. In long exchanges with Vinita Andrapalliyal, the government's lawyer, Judge Saris became more and more exasperated. Why, she kept asking, is the govern-ment insisting on deporting the Indonesians so quickly? What's the rush? Why send them on a plane back to Indonesia—where they could face danger—before the immigration courts have a chance to fully evaluate their case? "You know, it's that old song, 'Slow down, you move too fast,'" Judge Saris told the lawyer, quoting from the lyrics to "The 59th Street Bridge Song" by Simon and Garfunkel. "I mean, you're moving so fast to get them out of here that a court hasn't even had a chance to read it."

Andrapalliyal tried to make the case that Judge Saris shouldn't have jurisdiction in the case, arguing the technicality that the proper venue is an immigration court, not a federal district court. But the more the lawyer pressed her case, the more the judge seemed to push back. From everything that she could see, Judge Saris said, the government was refusing to guarantee that the Indonesian Christians would get a hearing on their predictions of persecution before they were put on planes. How in the world could they appeal their case after they've already been sent home? And worse, if they did suffer persecution, torture, or death when they got back to Indonesia, it would make a mockery of laws in the United States that are supposed to prevent the government from deporting people into exactly that situation.

About halfway through the hearing, Judge Saris asked Andrapalliyal whether she had seen a recent article in *The New Yorker* about immigration and ICE. The article, titled "When Deportation Is a Death Sentence," had mentioned the 1951 Convention on Refugees, which enshrined international norms that prohibit asylum seekers and refugees from being turned away if they might be tortured or killed in their home countries. The article also referenced the *St. Louis*, a German ship filled with more than nine hundred Jewish refugees fleeing the Holocaust that was turned away by the United States and other nations. More than two hundred of the Jews were killed when they returned to Germany.

"The country said, 'Never again are we going to do that,' those shipments of people," Judge Saris told Andrapalliyal and the other lawyers in the courtroom that day. " 'We are not going to do that ever again.' And so I think that's the law they're talking about—is this one. Am I right? I think that's the convention against torture.

"So you know," she continued, "we're not going to be that country. So I think we don't want to put them on the ship back unless somebody has had a chance to look at whether there's a really bad situation for them. That's the concern I have."

Judge Saris barred the government from deporting the Christians back to Indonesia without giving them a chance to make their case to an immigration judge. Across the country, other judges did the same for the

Somalis, the Mauritanians, the Iraqis, and others. The legal battles would continue for months. Trump's government was on notice: it had to give persecuted minorities their day in court.

But the long-term impact of the legal setbacks was unclear. The president vowed to fight in court, condemning the judges as tools of a political establishment unwilling to protect native-born Americans from an immigrant invasion. Almost single-handedly, Trump had given birth to an era of anti-immigrant sentiment that rivaled those of decades past. The idea that a handful of judges might get in the way of his agenda made him furious and more determined than ever to push forward.

— 10 —

THE TRUMP EFFECT FADES

BY SUMMER, THE TRUMP Effect had already begun to evaporate.

Despite Trump's repeated claims that his mere presence in the Oval Office had helped reduce illegal immigration, border crossings had begun to increase again in May 2017, and continued rising in June and July. By August, the number of people attempting to enter the United States from Mexico illegally had grown by nearly 20 percent from Trump's first full month in office. In public, Trump largely ignored the upturn, continuing to brag for months about decreases from previous years. But privately, he was furious. And among the aides most responsible for his immigration policies—Miller, Hamilton, Sessions, and Kelly—the turnabout created a sense of panic as they sought to find new and more aggressive ways to reduce the flow of immigrants.

Hamilton, who was a senior adviser at DHS and a key advocate for Miller's agenda in the department, tried to light a fire under his colleagues. He gathered the department's top leadership for an urgent brainstorming session in the conference room at the Nebraska Avenue headquarters. To Hamilton, it was no different from what executives at a widget-making company might do to find better ways to make widgets. The government needed to do more to stop the flow of immigrants, Hamilton told them.

He directed them to come up with a memo for the secretary detailing ten new things the government could do to discourage illegal crossings by Mexicans and Central American migrants and enforce the rule of law. The list included many of the hard-line ideas that Trump had long advocated: zero tolerance at the border, restricting asylum claims, detaining families, sending Central American migrants to Mexico. Take forty-eight hours, Hamilton told them. One participant described Hamilton as seizing the meeting "by the scruff of the neck."

Calling a meeting was one thing. Forcing action was another, and Hamilton quickly ran into obstacles. Among the top officials at the table for the meeting was Jim Nealon, the assistant secretary for international affairs and the acting head of the department's office of policy. Nealon was a lifelong diplomat who had served as the ambassador to Honduras in Obama's administration. But he was also a friend of Kelly's, having served as his deputy and foreign policy adviser when Kelly was the commander of forces at the U.S. Southern Command. When Kelly became DHS secretary, he had asked Nealon to join him. Philosophically, Nealon was anything but a true Trump believer. And when Hamilton demanded that his office quickly draw up proposals for limiting the flow of immigrants into the country, Nealon balked.

He thought some of the ideas that Hamilton was proposing were illegal and others were unethical or immoral. In some cases, as Nealon's staff began contacting experts throughout other parts of the government, there were practical concerns. Nealon's policy office refused to sign off on some of the memos. Others were sent to other offices at DHS for approval and never returned. Days stretched into weeks and Hamilton's fury deepened. It was exactly the kind of resistance that the White House suspected was at work to frustrate the president's agenda—a "deep state" comprised of bureaucrats from previous administrations who were working secretly behind the scenes to frustrate the new president's agenda and embarrass Trump. To Hamilton, the lack of urgent action from Nealon and the other bureaucrats at DHS was outright obstinance that bordered on insubordination. But there was little that he could do to force the issue, even with Miller calling repeatedly from the White House, demanding to know what more could be done at DHS to turn the numbers around.

One of the items on the list that Nealon opposed was a proposal to routinely separate all adults from their children when they crossed the border illegally. It had been considered, and rejected, long before Trump was elected. Top Obama officials held similarly urgent meetings during migrant border surges in 2014 and 2016. Migrants were increasingly exploiting existing immigration laws and court rulings and using children as a way to get adults into the country, on the theory that families were being treated differently from single people. In a meeting in the Situation Room with Obama, Jeh Johnson, the secretary of homeland security, had presented some of the more extreme options, including building detention facilities to hold teenage children. But he warned that options like that carried risks. Obama's legacy could be building "Gitmo for kids," Johnson warned, referring to the infamous prison for terrorists at Guantánamo Bay. Johnson and Cecilia Muñoz, the domestic policy adviser, knew that cleaving families might discourage migrants from trying to enter the United States. But they told Obama that having law enforcement agents separate families would become a logistical nightmare and a certain political disaster. "I do remember looking at each other like, 'We're not going to do this, are we?'" Muñoz recalled later. "We spent five minutes thinking it through and concluded that it was a bad idea. The morality of it was clear—that's not who we are."

The feeling had been shared across the bureaucracy, including by those who would have been charged with carrying out the family separations. During one White House meeting in 2014, officials pressed ICE's Homan to order his agents to round up unaccompanied children who had exhausted their appeals and been ordered deported by a judge. "You realize what you're asking me to do?" he said to the officials seated around the table. "You are asking me go to a home in the United States and remove a child from the home. You want me to buy a bunch of car seats and transport children?" Later, Homan told colleagues that he never wanted to be in the position of having to outfit his ICE vehicles with toddler seats.

Three years later inside the Trump administration, officials had similar concerns, but the pressure was mounting to do something dramatic. Despite what Kelly had told lawmakers on Capitol Hill, the Trump administration continued to actively consider the idea. But given the resistance inside DHS, little happened quickly.

Only one thing made Trump feel a little better about the pace of his immigration agenda: a rally. On June 21, the president boarded Air Force One at 4:39 p.m. for the two-hour flight to Cedar Rapids, Iowa, and another campaign-style rally at the U.S. Cellular Center arena. Trump slipped past the Planned Parenthood protesters and was greeted with chants of "USA! USA!" as he entered to Lee Greenwood's "God Bless the USA." Large blue signs behind the stage declared "Promises Made. Promises Kept."

"Yes, we will build the wall. We've already started planning. It will be built," Trump told the enthusiastic crowd, which roared to life: "Build the wall! Build the wall!" they chanted, just as they had during the campaign. Two days earlier, Gary Cohn, Trump's top economic adviser, had mentioned an offbeat proposal by a company that said it could finance part of a border wall if it included solar panels. At the rally, Trump decided to take credit, calling it "an idea that nobody has heard about yet." He went on to add that "we're talking about the southern border, lots of sun, lots of heat" and patted himself on the back for the idea. "Pretty good imagination, right? Good? My idea." After an extended rant about the dangers of gangs like MS-13, Trump returned to his favorite topic. "When they're gone, our now very strong borders, especially with the wall, will never allow them back in. So, we're doing a lot of things. We're very proud of what we've done."

The applause got even louder.

Trump knew the truth, whether he was willing to admit it to himself or not. Almost none of his wall had been built yet, and the money for it was at that point mostly a pipe dream. The Mexican president continued to insist that his country would never pay for it and the United States Congress, even under Republican control, had not yet been willing to provide the $25 billion that it would cost to build the wall across the entire two-thousand-mile southern border. In fact, Congress had added language to its spending bills barring any money from being spent for the construction of a brand-new border barrier of the kind the president talked about. The wall that he had promised again that night was largely stalled.

The same could be said about other parts of his immigration agenda. At the rally, he talked about legislation to prohibit immigrants from using public welfare services for five years after they enter the United States. But no such legislation had yet been proposed. The "extreme vetting" that Trump had announced five months earlier was still stalled in the courts, blocked by judges even after the president gave in to demands for what he considered a watered-down version of the travel ban. Sanctuary cities were still operating across the country, largely with impunity. The new judges on the border had made little dent in the backlog of asylum cases. And perhaps worst of all in his eyes, the numbers of apprehensions of illegal immigrants at the southern border—which he continued to brag were historically low—were increasing again. The number of families and children arrested trying to cross the border illegally had more than doubled since March. Overall, more than 20,000 migrants had been arrested at the border in June, up from the low of about 16,000 in March.

Two days after the rally, Miller visited Trump for a private moment at the residence early in the morning. He told the president that members of his own administration and Obama holdovers were conspiring to thwart the "extreme vetting" Trump had promised. Trump's demands for a tough immigration enforcement were being ignored. He showed the president the documentation—a country-by-country breakdown of foreign entrants that were still flooding into the United States.

They're making a fool of you, Mr. President, Miller said.

"They all have AIDS!" Donald Trump bellowed.

The president was sitting at the Resolute Desk and screaming at his top advisers as he clutched a sheaf of papers that Miller had given him in the residence that same morning. The documents made clear that despite the recent declines in illegal immigration, tens of thousands of immigrants were still streaming into the United States. Many of them, in Trump's mind, were terrorists and criminals.

The June 23 meeting had been listed on the president's public schedule as a routine, 10 a.m. briefing, and the officials who had been summoned were told only that they were being brought into the Oval Office to discuss "immigration." But by the time he arrived, Trump was already furious. Ticking down Miller's list of visa entry numbers since his inauguration, Trump unleashed a racist, nativist rant. Look at all these Afghans—they were terrorists, he said. Forty thousand Nigerians? the president scoffed. "You're telling me they are going to come to the United States, see all this, and go back to their huts?" Trump questioned, making a spectacularly uneducated reference to the population of the wealthiest country on the African continent. "They're not going back to their huts!" And if we aren't careful, he yelled at his aides, we'll become just like Brussels—overrun with Muslims. It used to be a great place, he said ruefully, but look what had happened since foreigners had immigrated en masse: It had become, he said, a "fucking hellhole."

Sitting in chairs before Trump on the gold-hued carpet were some of the men charged with carrying out his immigration crackdown. Miller, his top domestic policy adviser, nodded in agreement at the emotional outburst he had engineered. Kelly, the homeland security secretary, sat stoically, listening to the president vent. Rex Tillerson, the secretary of state, fumed in his seat, feeling unfairly blamed. H. R. McMaster and Tom Bossert, the soft-spoken but loyal homeland security adviser, took in the president's racially charged rant in stunned silence, as did several aides who were seated on the floral couches behind them. Kelly's deputy Kirstjen Nielsen sat with other aides on a couch behind the more senior advisers.

As his team sat, slack-jawed, Trump singled out Haiti, the island nation that had been devastated by earthquakes and floods during the last ten years. The document Miller had given him showed that 15,000 Haitians had obtained visas to enter the United States. As he blurted out that Haitians had AIDS, staffers looked at their shoes and surreptitiously exchanged incredulous looks. Trump was apparently harking back to a widely discredited theory from the 1980s that Haitians were responsible for the spread of HIV. Back then, the belief led the Food and Drug Administration to ban blood donations from Haitian immigrants, but the policy was decried as racist and unscientific, and abandoned in 1990. But Haiti was not all bad, Trump said to his aides, his mood apparently brightening suddenly. "I love that island," he said. "They all voted for me anyway."

His aides were baffled. Haiti is a sovereign country in the Caribbean and its citizens—95 percent of them black descendants of African slaves—could no more vote for Donald Trump than Russia's could. Was he thinking of Haitian Americans? He had campaigned in Miami's Little Haiti in September of 2016 and told Haitian Americans he wanted to be "your greatest champion," but they did not see him that way. He lost the Haitian American vote that year.

By now, Trump's inner circle had become accustomed to hearing him speak in crude ways about immigrants. He had done it during his presidential campaign, tapping into the anger and grievances of white working-class voters. He had done it in the months since he became president, defending his travel ban by invoking fears of uncontrolled migration. Here, though, was a moment of clarity about the new commander in chief. He understood virtually nothing about how foreigners came and went from the United States, and yet he had a visceral antipathy toward them. In his mind, they were a teeming mass of infiltrators that was changing the face of the country for the worse. Trump was not a policy expert, nor an ideologue with well-formed views. He was a real estate executive and reality TV star who spoke and acted from his gut, and his outburst revealed the racially tinged stereotypes that moved him. He had surrounded himself with people like Miller, who were singularly focused on the evils of immigration and had learned to play to the ego and instinct of a president who could not bear to be seen as weak. And although he was the privileged grandson of a German immigrant and husband of a Slovenian one, Trump understood keenly the political power of blaming migrants for the ills and dangers facing the country.

No aide or adviser spoke up to the new president to tell him he was wrong. It was futile, they knew, and potentially dangerous to their careers

to challenge the president on immigration. Miller turned his ire on Tillerson, blaming him for the influx of foreigners and prompting the secretary
of state to throw up his arms in frustration. The whole meeting had been
an ambush. Tillerson objected to the numbers that Miller had presented
to the president. If he was so bad at his job, maybe he should stop issuing
visas altogether, Tillerson said. Tempers flared, and Kelly asked that the
room be cleared of the more junior staff members. Even after they left the
Oval Office, the junior aides could still hear the president loudly berating
his most senior advisers through the heavy, closed door. Afterward, Kelly
complained to Bannon that the meeting was a "shit show" and an "ambush." You can't have all those people in there when Trump is over-the-top
like that, Kelly said. It's like "Grand fucking Central Station" in there.

Inside the room, the president's eye found the line for the number of
arrivals into the United States from Mexico, the country that, more than
any other, had come to symbolize Trump's opposition to immigration. He
veered off topic, regaling his advisers with a description of the rally two
days earlier in Cedar Rapids. The crowd was chanting "Build The Wall!"
and roaring with adulation, he recalled with pride.

Now he demanded to know when he could give the people what they
had chanted for, and he had repeatedly promised he would deliver.

"Where is the goddamned wall?"

THE ADMIRAL'S ALMANAC

ONE MORNING IN JUNE 2017, President Trump's top White House adviser on refugee issues made a heartfelt request to Catholic leaders who were gathered for a World Refugee Day event a few blocks from the West Wing: Pray for me. "The more I'm educated," Garry Hall, the senior director at the NSC in charge of refugees, told the Catholic activists, "the more I can educate others."

Hall, many of them thought, was badly in need of a tutorial. A retired Navy rear admiral with no experience on issues of human rights or refugee policy, he had quietly been installed two months earlier at the NSC, and his appointment reflected how low a priority the Trump White House placed on refugees. Tall, white-haired, and kind-faced, Hall liked to tell corny jokes and regale colleagues with lengthy yarns and folksy sayings. An avid viewer of Fox News, he could often be found in a leather armchair in his office, watching the president's favorite channel or reading the newspaper. Like many in the Trump White House, he had come to the job almost by accident, as a favor to Steve Bannon. Hall was an old friend of the Bannon family, having flown helicopters with Bannon's brother, Chris, in the 1980s. Hall had been an informal national security adviser to Bannon for years, and soon after Trump won, he received a text from his old buddy. "We need you on the team," Bannon wrote. Hall ignored the looks of shock and distaste from people he respected, including his priest, and agreed to sign on. "The humanitarian portfolio is kind of the Catholic portfolio," Hall, a late-in-life convert to Catholicism, would tell them. It was his duty to serve, he said.

Even before Hall arrived, Trump's team had made it clear that the president was not looking for a robust voice for refugees in the White House. In the Obama NSC, there had been a special assistant to the president for multilateral affairs and human rights. Samantha Power, the author of a definitive work on genocide, had held that post, and after her it was Stephen Pomper, a specialist on international humanitarian and human rights law. But under Trump, the words "human rights" were excised from the title. The job was to be known as special assistant to the president for international organizations and alliances. And Hall had little experience with any of it. Despite a thirty-five-year career in the Navy, which earned him two stars and included a stint as the Navy adviser to NATO, he was an unusual choice for the job, having never been involved in the kind of detailed policy discussions that NSC runs. But as a Catholic, Hall thought of himself as a passionate humanitarian. He was an adviser to the archbishop of the military service on child and youth protection, and served on the National Review Board advising the U.S. Council of Catholic Bishops on Child and Youth Protection. While in the Navy, he had participated in disaster relief and humanitarian assistance operations. Bannon affectionately referred to him privately as a "bleeding heart," a "globalist," and a "squish." Inside of Trump's NSC, though, some of his colleagues thought Hall was in over his head.

Veterans of his office would wince silently when Hall would refer to the U.N. Security Council as the "U.N. National Security Council." (The National Security Council, where Hall worked, is the group within the White House that advises the president on national security and foreign policy matters, while the U.N. Security Council is the fifteen-nation body that has primary responsibility for maintaining peace and security around the globe. Hall could not seem to keep the two straight.) Hall rarely sent emails, a liability in a White House that leans heavily on electronic communication. It was next to impossible for aides to get his approval on urgent matters, and routine requests seemed to languish, untended and unanswered, in his inbox. When he did email, he liked to begin his messages with military slang. "BLUF:" he would begin, using an acronym favored by military professionals for "bottom line up front."

Hall was a happy warrior who seemed to enjoy his job immensely. He took full advantage of the perks of working in the West Wing. He was a frequent visitor to the White House Mess, the exclusive basement eatery run by the Navy, which is open to White House officials and their invited guests. (His other favorite dining haunt was the Army-Navy Club, a short stroll from the White House, where he enjoyed long lunches.) Hall often brought family members and friends through the White House on tours, and when it came time for the annual rituals of White House life—the Easter Egg Roll, the tours of the elaborate gardens in springtime—Hall was always among the first to request tickets.

He also thought of himself as something of a leadership guru, and he was eager to share what he knew with the masses. For three decades, Hall had been giving a version of the same lecture on leadership to audiences around the world, and in 2017 he had become interested in podcasting, purchasing professional equipment and deciding he was going to broadcast his pearls of wisdom over the internet. Several months into his White House tenure, he launched his own podcast, *The Admiral's Almanac*, in which he said he would share lessons in leadership and management that he had learned over his long military career. He created a website topped with a photograph of him wearing his dress uniform, with a leather bomber jacket slung over the chair in the background. The site greeted visitors with a hearty "Welcome Aboard!" and promised that those who heeded "the wit and wisdom of retired Rear Admiral Garry Hall" might "improve your personal and professional life." The first episode was called "Leadership, Fitness and Sex," a title Hall admitted within the first few minutes was mere clickbait for prospective listeners to his twenty-three-minute monologue on the importance of responsibility, vision, and commitment. "To think about commitment, take your average breakfast," Hall said at one point, launching into one of his signature convoluted analogies. "A farmer participated, and he provided the potatoes for hash browns. A baker contributed and participated by providing bread for toast. And a chicken participated, providing the eggs for those scrambled eggs. Now the pig. The pig is committed. He provided the bacon.

"So if you're gonna be a leader," Hall concluded, "we need you to be committed. We need you to be the pig in that breakfast."

The podcast earned Hall an unflattering story in *Politico*, in which former White House officials marveled on the record at how a senior NSC director had the time to devote to such frivolity. At the White House, things were even worse. Hall got a scolding from Keith Kellogg, the NSC chief of staff and executive secretary, and a barrage of incredulous calls from officials in the press office. "What is this about?" they wanted to know. Hall took down the podcast almost immediately. But the episode fed an intense debate that had begun among NSC officials months since Hall had first arrived: Had Bannon pitched Hall for his post strategically, knowing that he would be little more than a figurehead, without the wherewithal to speak up for refugees? Or had he merely lucked into the situation?

Whether by design or otherwise, Hall was outgunned when it came to making a case for refugees—and he knew it. The affable admiral was no match for Stephen Miller, who had decided that as the White House's unofficial immigration czar, he should be in charge of refugees, too. Hall would routinely complain to McMaster that the unwieldy format of the NSC, a 320-person behemoth that existed in a carefully prescribed world of meetings and memoranda, made it impossible for him and his staff to provide Trump with the full picture about refugee resettlement in the United States, while Miller had a lean staff of a dozen at the Domestic Policy Council and could pop into the Oval Office anytime he wanted to get his points across. "General, we're getting run around, we're not getting out our message," Hall would tell McMaster.

As unschooled and uninterested as he was in the hand-to-hand combat of West Wing policy debates, Hall relished being the administration's face on refugee issues. He often took meetings with humanitarian groups, and Catholic organizations in particular, in which he would talk about the importance of human rights as an American value. He would spend the first twenty minutes of his meetings regaling visitors with war stories, and jokes, and then shower them with vague reassurances. "Yes, we know refugees aren't a real risk. We know that it's in our interest to bring them here. Of course!" Hall told them. Human rights activists came away mystified but pleasantly surprised. "Our national values are all about human rights," he told the Catholic leaders on that World Refugee Day in 2017. "Those values are a compass that always points in the right direction," he said. He said that the vast majority of refugees—87 percent—were fully employed and off of government aid within six months of their arrival in the United States, and said that since 1980, there had not been an attack or threat from any of the millions of refugees who had been resettled in the United States. Those arguments, factual as they were, were the exact opposite of what Stephen Miller was pressing government officials to say about refugees, as he plotted to slash the program devoted to resettling them in the United States.

To the activists, Hall made it sound like Trump's position on refugees might not be as bad as they feared, despite the president's divisive rhetoric and the actions he had already taken. Maybe Hall was a potential ally in the West Wing, someone who would advocate on behalf of refugees and be a moderating force on Trump, Miller, and the other hard-liners in the White House. But in reality, Hall was no match for Miller. "You left no chips on the table, no cards unplayed," he would tell his dejected staff when they would lament what was happening to refugees under Trump. "There's nothing more you can do. It's out of our hands."

— 12 —

REFUGEES NOT WELCOME

WHEN STEPHEN MILLER CONVENED the government's foremost experts on refugees in the Roosevelt Room one afternoon in March of 2017, not long after the president's Oval Office tirade about not wanting to water down his travel ban, he brought a message directly from Trump.

"The president believes refugees cost too much," Miller declared as he looked around the room at White House aides and career officials who had built their professional lives around resettling persecuted people in the United States. It came as no surprise to anyone seated around the table that Trump was taking aim at refugees. His travel ban had capped their admissions at 50,000—less than half the number Barack Obama set out to admit the previous year. But now, Miller told the group, he wanted economic data that justified rejecting refugees. The meeting in the Roosevelt Room had been called to seek input for a report mandated by the travel ban that would tally the long-term costs of the U.S. refugee program. But from the moment it got started, Miller made it clear that he and Trump had already reached their conclusions, and that everyone there was expected to follow suit.

Gathering data about the dangers and costs of immigration was something of a fetish for Miller, one he honed during his years on Capitol Hill,

where a potent statistic or killer anecdote could change the tenor of an entire debate and sway blocs of votes. In late-night emails to journalists and
fellow aides, Miller would circulate study after alarming study purporting
to prove what in fact were dubious or sometimes downright false claims.
As a congressional aide, he had repeatedly pushed the idea that migrants
were too expensive and not worth the risk for the nation. Now, as an influential White House adviser, Miller made it his mission to inject data
that supported those beliefs into official policy statements and records of
decision making, in the hopes of bolstering his case for turning refugees
away from American shores.

He had a strategic reason for doing so. Despite his brash claim that the
travel ban rollout had gone precisely as planned, Miller had been chastened
by the experience. Keeping it secret from the bureaucrats had meant cutting corners, which left the order vulnerable to legal challenges. This time,
Miller, who was obsessed with wielding power effectively from the West
Wing, wanted a paper trail that would provide a clear rationale for blocking refugees. "We need a process to implement all of this stuff," Miller
said. After months of being frustrated by the "deep state" bureaucrats who
had tried to short-circuit the president's policies, Miller seemed interested
in embracing their process. But he also made clear that he meant to keep
a tight rein on the results.

In the meeting, Miller laid out his argument. Refugees are disproportionately likely to be uneducated and to be dependent on public benefit
programs like federal food aid, cash assistance, and Medicaid, he told the
group. They are a drain on the country's resources. Miller cited a 2015
report released by the hard-line Center for Immigration Studies, which
argued for scaling back immigration. The group's study estimated the
costs of resettling a refugee from the Middle East—including welfare and
educational costs—but ignored their contributions through taxes or other
means. CIS claimed that it was 12 times more costly to admit a refugee to
the United States than to help that same refugee in, or near, his or her own
country. Miller wanted the State Department's report to embrace those
conclusions.

Larry Bartlett, the veteran career official who oversaw refugee admissions at the State Department, knew the study was flawed. Bartlett, a quietly intense man with a shock of fine white hair and beard to match, was a fierce defender of the refugee program who had spent ample time correcting misperceptions about it, and seemed eager to set the record straight for Miller. There's another study out of Cleveland, Bartlett said, showing that refugees, over time, were actually positive economic contributors.

"That's not what we're going for," Miller snapped. It's not what Trump believes. We're going to need to see a draft of your report before you release it so that we can make sure that we don't embarrass the president, he said.

As he left the meeting, Miller briefly huddled with Domestic Policy Council aides and asked if anyone knew the name of the civil servant who had dared to challenge him. "Who was that guy?" Miller wanted to know, nodding toward Bartlett as he gathered his things to leave. "Oh, you mean Larry Bartlett?" somebody answered.

"He's not with us," Miller said ominously. They would have to keep an eye on him.

A career civil servant who had more than twenty-five years of experience in the field, Bartlett had won a Presidential Rank Award in 2015 for having directed efforts to resettle hundreds of thousands of refugees in the United States. But he arrived at the meeting a marked man. Weeks after Trump's inauguration, Bartlett was featured in an article on the conservative Breitbart website headlined, "Top 10 Holdover Obama Bureaucrats President Trump Can Fire or Remove Today." At No. 9, Bartlett was referred to in the piece as "an active apologist for the refugee resettlement industry for many years." That wasn't far from the truth. For years, as part of his role at the State Department's Bureau of Population, Refugees, and Migration, Bartlett had traveled the country explaining the ins and outs of the refugee program and fielding questions from reporters, elected officials, and citizens about how it would impact American communities.

It often fell to Bartlett to answer the jeers and boos of attendees at public forums who wondered aloud whether they were putting themselves and their families at risk to accept refugees into their towns. "Do I get all the hard questions?" he quipped sarcastically at one such event in Twin Falls, Idaho, when asked whether communities were consulted before refugees were resettled there. Sitting on a stage in front of an audience of more than seven hundred people in an auditorium at the College of Southern Idaho, Bartlett tried desperately to counter the fears that many people had about refugees. "They're not terrorists," Bartlett said. "They are people fleeing terrorism."

The challenge only got more difficult as the 2016 presidential race heated up. In the fall of 2015, Trump warned darkly that Syrian refugees could be a huge terrorist army in disguise. "They're all men, and they're all strong-looking guys," Trump told a high school gymnasium full of voters in Keene, New Hampshire. "They could be ISIS—I don't know," Trump said, adding that he had heard 200,000 refugees could be headed for the United States. His number was wildly inflated, and his portrayal of the refugees was a lie; most were women and children. But that did not stop Trump from spinning his fear-soaked tale. "This could be one of the great tactical ploys of all time. A 200,000-man army, maybe. Or if they sent 50,000, or 80,000, or 100,000, we've got problems, and that could be possible. I don't know that it is, but it could be possible."

Trump went even further a month later in the wake of a shooting and foiled bomb attack in San Bernardino, California, carried out by a Pakistani American man and his Pakistani-born wife, both of whom had pledged allegiance to ISIS. The next day, Trump released his written state-ment calling for a Muslim ban, which he read for dramatic effect at a rally in South Carolina, referring to himself in the third person: "Donald J. Trump is calling for a total and complete shutdown of Muslims enter-ing the United States until our country's representatives can figure out what the hell is going on. We have no choice. We have no choice."

Bartlett's message about refugees could not have been more dissonant from Trump's campaign-trail rhetoric. He was an unapologetic cheerleader for the refugee program, which he argued was part of what made the na-tion exceptional. "The United States Refugee Admissions Program reflects the United States' highest values and aspirations of compassion, generosity and leadership," Bartlett testified at a Senate hearing the day after Trump had warned that Syrian refugees could be a Trojan horse for a terrorist onslaught. At the time, Obama was making an aggressive push to respond to the crush of people fleeing the brutal Syrian civil war by setting a goal of taking in as many as 10,000 Syrians and a total of 85,000 refugees in 2016—a 21 percent increase over the previous year. "With the continued support of Congress and the American people, refugee resettlement will remain a proud tradition for many years to come," Bartlett said. It was Jeff Sessions, then still a senator, who presided over the hearing, flanked from behind by his two top aides—Miller on his left and Hamilton on his right. The young pair prompted Sessions with documents, scribbled notes, and occasionally a covert whisper as the senator grilled Bartlett and others with pointed questions about the economic costs and security risks of refugees.

"We must be cautious," Sessions insisted, rattling off statistics compiled by Miller listing the high percentages of refugees who received food stamps, free health care, and cash assistance. "Once here with refugee status, those individuals can claim any job and collect any federal welfare benefit," he warned. Over two hours, Bartlett and the other officials defended the refugee program, but it was clear that Sessions thought it was misguided. "We're entitled to have our officials protect our interests, the people's interests," the senator said. His public remarks that day left little doubt about what he would do to the refugee program if he were ever in charge. And in private, Sessions had been even more direct, telling State Department officials that he was concerned that Muslim refugees would not fit into American society. During one briefing in the Capitol, Senator Sessions vented his concern about boosting the number of Syrian refugees. "We are a Christian nation," he told Anne Richard, the top official for refugees at the State Department. "No, senator," Richard answered. "The founders gave us religious freedom." Sessions was unmoved, shaking his head gently. "I mean culturally," he said, "and if you don't understand that, then you're not as smart as I think you are."

In the Roosevelt Room eighteen months later, Bartlett was witnessing the worst-case scenario unfold. Now, the candidate who had called for banning Syrian refugees was a president who had the power to do so.

The senator who had grilled him at a subcommittee hearing in public and privately warned against accepting Muslims was now the attorney general, with a seat at the table for deciding how many refugees to accept. And the staff aide in a back-row chair at a subcommittee hearing on Capitol Hill was now a senior adviser to the president, running a meeting in the West Wing.

And Miller did not like being challenged by a bureaucrat.

Miller knew from his experience in Congress that Trump had the power to change course from Obama's priorities with the stroke of a pen. Under federal law, the president must consult with Congress each fall about how many refugees could be admitted, setting the maximum for the coming year. Obama had used the power to set ambitious goals for refugee resettlement during his last two years in office, leaving behind a ceiling for 2017 of 110,000 refugees, an unprecedented high. Now, as an October deadline to set the 2018 refugee cap approached, Miller was determined to push the number to historically low levels that would starve the refugee resettlement program virtually out of existence. He told colleagues that if he had his way, there would be no refugees arriving in the United States at all on Trump's watch. And he wasn't the only powerful person in the White House who felt that way. At the end of July, Trump chose John Kelly to be his second chief of staff, replacing Reince Priebus. Kelly had reluctantly accepted, telling confidants that he had no choice but to accede to the president's request that he come and straighten out what he had privately complained was a woefully dysfunctional White House. Before he left the Department of Homeland Security, Kelly had told Hamilton that he wanted to keep the refugee number very low for 2018. One day near the beginning of the deliberations, Miller and Bossert had crossed the driveway outside the West Wing to personally deliver the message to NSC and agency officials at their offices in the Eisenhower Executive Office Building next door to the White House. There's no daylight between the president and Kelly on refugee resettlement, they said. You guys do your work. We don't need a lot of paper. But at the end of the day, there's a big backlog of asylum seekers and people pouring across our southern border, so the refugee program does not have to be as large or robust as it has been in the past. The message was as clear as it was shocking to the subject-matter experts who heard it as a directive to inject bias into their work: We want a low number.

Miller had already seen to it that his argument about the costs of the refugee program were reflected in some of the administration's official policy statements. Trump's budget declared that first-generation immigrants cost the country nearly $147 billion more than they paid in taxes, and that refugees were a big part of the problem. "Each refugee admitted into the United States comes at the expense of helping a potentially greater number out of country," the budget said. But Miller was irate to learn that the draft report he wanted about the cost of refugees said the opposite. At the Department of Health and Human Services, career officials had drawn up a fifty-five-page report entitled "The Fiscal Costs of the U.S. Refugee Admissions Program at the Federal, State, and Local Levels, from 2005–2014." It showed that the net economic impact of resettling refugees in the United States over a decade was overwhelmingly positive. "Overall, this report estimated that the net fiscal impact of refugees was positive over the ten-year period, at $63 billion, meaning they contributed more in revenue than they cost in expenditures." The study said that refugees had about the same fiscal impact as the rest of the U.S. population. In other words, the argument that Miller had been repeatedly making about the soaring costs of resettling refugees in the United States was invalid.

Miller was livid. This was the work of politically motivated, "deep state" bureaucrats and Obama administration holdovers who were pushing their own agenda and trying to hurt the president, he believed. He had his staff request a meeting to discuss the report. What were the assumptions made in the report? he wanted to know. They must be the wrong assumptions. This was not, he said, what the president had asked for, and not what he had put in his budget. He intervened and the HHS report was shelved. It was never forwarded to the White House and never surfaced again in discussions about the refugee program. Instead, HHS submitted another, much slimmer report. That three-page document detailed how much the department spent on refugees over a decade, and concluded that in an "average year," the per-capita cost totaled $3,300, about $800 more than the per-person cost for the U.S. population. It made no mention of tax revenues or any other contribution made by refugees over their lifetimes.

Despite Miller's best efforts, the refugee resettlement program had powerful advocates in the senior ranks of Trump's national security team. At the Pentagon, Mattis was determined to keep the flow of refugees as robust as possible, seeing it as a national security imperative. It was one way to protect Iraqis, Afghans, and those in other countries who risked their lives to help the U.S. military carry out dangerous missions, acting as translators, security guards, engineers, and sometimes fighting alongside American soldiers. It was part of the military's commitment to leave no individual behind, and a critical way of maintaining credibility with foreign partners in the region. If the U.S. turned its back on refugees, Mattis feared, it would be harder to establish good relationships in areas where the U.S. military was engaged. Mattis liked to tell the story of the time an Iraqi professor was taken into custody for planting an explosive device. During his interrogation, Mattis gave the man a cigarette and got him talking. Eventually, the Iraqi asked whether it would be possible to emigrate to the United States after he got out of prison. Mattis thought the story showed the power of America to inspire, even for those gripped by hatred. "Think about that," Mattis once told cadets at Virginia Military Institute. "The hatred he felt was so much that he would go out and try to put a bomb in the road to kill us, but the example of America was so strong that if he could be sitting where you are today or have his son and daughter in that audience, he'd have given his eyes or teeth." When it came to the refugee cap, Mattis wanted to keep the number at 50,000. The Joint Chiefs of Staff agreed. Nikki Haley was on board, too, as was Rex Tillerson. Lowering the ceiling below 50,000, State argued, would make it harder for the United States to persuade other countries to take their fair share of refugees.

A quiet but intense battle over the number began brewing inside the West Wing as aides at the National Security Council prepared a discussion paper laying out the basics of the refugee resettlement program, in which they noted that refugees were extremely well vetted—screened more thoroughly than any other immigrant or traveler to the United States. The early drafts of the paper included the government's intelligence assessment that refugees posed no greater risk of terrorism than any other group and that resettling them in the United States had clear national security benefits. But soon, NSC officials began to notice a pattern. Anything positive they would say about refugees—including stating what they saw as the basic facts of the resettlement program—would be met with an objection: "We can't say that." Officials who were in charge of putting together options for Trump were exasperated and upset. "How do you make the case for a robust ceiling if you are not allowed to make any arguments in favor of it?" one distraught aide asked.

As it turned out, you couldn't.

Andrew Veprek at DPC, working on Miller's behalf, objected to many of the standard assertions about refugee resettlement that had been accepted for decades, calling them unsubstantiated. Who says that the United States has to take a leadership role in resettling refugees, so that other countries will follow suit? There's no proof of that, he said. Take it out. Were refugees actually the best-vetted of any traveler into the United States? Veprek thought not; can't say that. And when discussion documents referred to refugee resettlement as a "humanitarian program" and stated that 80 percent of those resettled were women and children, officials from the Domestic Policy Council crossed it out. Experts on the program from the NSC defended the passage. "It's a fact," one said. But Veprek and his colleagues scoffed. "It's a heartstrings fact," one responded. John Zadrozny, another Miller ally at the Domestic Policy Council, said the statistic sounded great, but it was misleading. "When you say women and children, children can be up to age eighteen, and they're very capable of being terrorists," Zadrozny said. Leaning across the table, he singled out Jennifer Arangio, a senior director at the NSC, and pointed at her, his voice rising. "And you used to know that, Jennifer!" Arangio was no bleeding-heart liberal; she was a national security expert with top secret clearance who had been a senior counsel on the House Homeland Security

Committee, and she was fiercely loyal to Trump, having worked on his campaign as the director of women engagement and staffed his daughter Ivanka on the campaign trail. But lately, she had been resisting Miller's efforts to slam the door shut on refugees, arguing that the changes he and his allies were advocating were unfounded and ill-advised, and worse yet, went way beyond what the president would want if he were presented with the relevant facts. Her reluctance enraged Miller's DPC crew, who saw Arangio as a turncoat who was undermining Trump's agenda.

"Yeah, I did used to think that the refugee program was vulnerable to terrorist infiltration," Arangio answered. "But then I got here and made it my business to learn the facts about the program, and now I know that refugees are the most vetted category of any immigrant. You'd be crazy to come if you were a terrorist. This is the last way you would try to get into this country." Nor was she going to stand for being portrayed as some sort of saboteur of Trump's agenda. "Don't tell me about the president's agenda," Arangio said, looking around the room. "I left my three kids in Washington to move up to Trump Tower and get the president elected, and I don't recall seeing any of you there."

Miller and his allies in the White House used legal arguments to prevent anything positive about refugees from being documented. Lawyers at the White House counsel's office and the Justice Department insisted that anything that promoted the benefits of refugees ran counter to what the government was arguing in its defense of the travel ban, which had been enjoined by federal judges as illegally motivated by racial animus—not national security considerations. There would be a "litigation risk" of saying anything positive about the refugee program, the lawyers advised the national security aides, so those points could not possibly be allowed to appear in discussion papers. "No, it's just a fact—it's not related to the litigation," one NSC aide said when confronted about the issue during a phone call with a colleague in the counsel's office. "At some point, we won't be able to write anything in this discussion paper if everything comes under this litigation. We'd have to take out everything." That seemed to be the point. As he did in the Senate, Sessions also weighed in at key moments to undercut the refugee program. At one pivotal meeting, as a representative of the National Counterterrorism Center was briefing about an interagency report that asserted there were essentially no known instances of terrorists having infiltrated refugee flows since the September 11, 2001, attacks, Rachel Brand, a top Justice Department official, interrupted the presentation. The attorney general has read that report, she said, and he doesn't agree with its findings.

Even as Miller inserted unfounded claims about the dangers and costs of refugees, administration officials who had long experience with the program pushed back. They repeatedly removed the assertions from the documents to ensure that the presidential record would be accurate. At one point, Chris Munn, who handled national security vetting and screening issues at the NSC, interrupted a meeting on the matter to try to pull Miller back. "I just want to remind everyone that this is the presidential record. It's not a matter of campaign rhetoric. Everything that is put in this paper has to be based in fact." Munn, a large and commanding man who had a decade of experience at the Defense Department in intelligence and watch-listing, would routinely brush aside Miller's assertions, saying things like, "That's just not true, and we can't put that in the presidential record." But it became a sort of macabre game: Miller would insert his talking points into the discussion paper, the staff would remove them, and the cycle would keep repeating itself.

One day in September, a junior aide in the Border and Transportation Security Directorate at NSC was surprised to receive a telephone call from Air Force One. It was Miller, enraged. "You let IOA commandeer this paper!" Miller said, using the acronym for International Organizations and Alliances, the office where Garry Hall and Arangio worked. He was angry that his edits had been stricken.

Miller refused to give up. Mattis and Haley were a lost cause. But Tillerson was another matter. He had initially endorsed a limit of 50,000. But in mid-September, the secretary of state was part of the entourage, including Miller, that traveled to the United Nations General Assembly in New York for several intense days of huddling privately with the president. By the time they returned, Tillerson had moved a little in Miller's direction. Under pressure from the White House, the secretary of state now said he wanted a maximum of 45,000 refugees. For Miller, it was progress. But Elaine Duke, the acting secretary of homeland security, who had replaced Kelly when Trump picked him to be White House chief of staff, was the big unknown. Career DHS officials had assumed Duke would support a level of 50,000 refugees—in line with the limit set earlier in the year by the travel ban. But ahead of a National Security Council meeting to discuss the subject, she had yet to weigh in.

Hamilton, who was Duke's senior counselor, saw an opportunity to push his boss to a much lower number. He told staff at the U.S. Citizenship and Immigration Service, which screens refugees, to prepare a variety of projections for how many they could process, from the current level on down to zero. If the bureaucrats concluded that they didn't have the resources to process 50,000 refugees, Hamilton reasoned, it wouldn't make sense to set the cap that high. The request made Barbara Strack, the head of the Refugee Affairs Division at USCIS, nervous. The very fact that there was discussion of a ceiling below 50,000 was alarming, she thought. In her mind, the United States should set an ambitious goal for admitting refugees and try to reach it. Strack's office completed a series of projections of how many refugees they could process. At the high end, her staff estimated they could handle about 40,000 in the coming year, maybe a few more.

Hamilton looked at the USCIS analysis and decided the real capability was at the low end of Strack's projections—somewhere between 12,000 and 20,000. On the Friday night before a scheduled Tuesday meeting at the White House to discuss the number, Hamilton informed the NSC that the Department of Homeland Security was prepared to recommend a maximum refugee cap of just 26,000—a dramatically low number that would represent a huge victory for Miller. NSC aides were taken aback. Arangio told Hamilton that there were important foreign policy objectives in play and humanitarian reasons to keep the number as high as possible. "I don't know who you're listening to," Hamilton told her. "But that's not what the president thinks." Maybe so, she answered, but that's probably because he's unaware of the humanitarian and foreign policy arguments that the Defense and State Departments are trying to make. Hamilton asked that the White House hold off on formally including the 26,000 number in final discussion documents for the meeting. The request was an odd one, but Hamilton had a good reason for being cagey: Duke had neither seen nor signed off on it.

When Duke found out that Hamilton had told the White House that DHS supported such a paltry figure, she was annoyed. And once she was briefed, she objected to the lower number. If Homeland Security officials had projected that they had the capacity to screen about 40,000 refugees in the coming year, she told Hamilton, that was the number the department should propose. Miller was not pleased. When the group finally met to make a decision that Tuesday, the president's top officials unanimously backed a minor trim rather than endorsing the massive cut to the refugee program Miller had envisioned. They split the difference, placing the cap at 45,000. Even more frustrating for Miller, his attempts to justify deep cuts by arguing that refugees were a threat to the country and a sap on the economy had fallen flat, leaving the decision to be based strictly on how much capacity the government had to resettle refugees.

That did not stop Miller from drafting a press release asserting that security was the chief reason for curbing the program and resurrecting his debunked arguments for shutting out refugees. "President Donald J. Trump has established the annual cap for refugees coming into the United States at a level that upholds the safety of the American people," Miller's release said. "Some refugees who have been admitted to the United States have posed threats to national security and public safety," it added, citing statistics about the numbers of refugees who had been investigated, arrested, or convicted on terrorism-related charges. The draft press release also resurrected the cost argument, asserting that "refugee resettlement increases financial strain on Americans," and quoting the CIS claim that a dozen times as many refugees could be helped in or near their own countries as in the United States.

NSC officials who had worked on the process were furious when they saw it. "We fought day after day to get the stuff out, but what was the point of it, if at the end of the day, this is what they go out and tell the American public—that we're keeping you safe from these horrible refugees?" one of them told a coworker. They tried marking up Miller's press release and sending it back to him with the offending passages stricken. They had just spent three months pushing back against what they considered misinformation on the refugee resettlement program only to see it now being used as a justification to the American public for why the number was so low.

Miller's original version had referenced the San Bernardino shooting attack, which NSC aides had to point out had been carried out not by refugees, but by a U.S. citizen and his wife, who had entered the United States on a visa. The release said that refugees in some states had been a threat to national security, and contained an alarming—and false— statistic that refugees were 30 times more likely to be involved in domestic terrorism than the general population. Those lines came out of the news release, but the rest of it went out largely as Miller wanted, hailing Trump's "America First Refugee Program." And while the number of refugees had landed substantially higher than he had hoped, Miller took steps to ensure that his efforts to dismantle the program would not be undercut by career officials again. It started with a change at the State Department.

In the weeks after Trump announced his decision on the refugee ceiling, the word came from the White House through Christine Ciccone, Tillerson's deputy chief of staff: Larry Bartlett, the State Department official who had dared to mention a study that ran counter to Miller's view, had to go. Simon Henshaw, the top diplomat for refugees, tried to intervene, apologizing on Bartlett's behalf for whatever he might have done to draw the wrath of the West Wing. But Ciccone said the decision had been made. Bartlett was abruptly removed from the Bureau of Population, Refugees, and Migration at the State Department and assigned to a job in the office that handles Freedom of Information Act requests, sitting next to low-level civil servants entering keywords into a computer. He went to Puerto Rico for several weeks to assist in the federal response to Hurricane Maria, and later took a temporary assignment in Ankara, Turkey, with the Bureau of Near Eastern Affairs, assisting with the response to the crisis in Syria. At his farewell party at Tonic, a pub near the State Department filled with wooden tables and adorned with exposed brick, colleagues and refugee advocates wept, not just because they were sorry to see Bartlett go, but because his departure seemed to say so much about the dangers of standing up for refugees in an administration determined to shun them.

Bartlett's exit seemed to be the end of an era of refugee resettlement in the United States, and it wasn't clear what would come next. But within months, two senior House Democrats, Eliot Engel of New York and Elijah Cummings of Maryland, asked the State Department's inspector general to look into whether Bartlett's unceremonious dismissal had been politically motivated. They said agency whistle-blowers had provided "credible allegations that the State Department has required high-level career civil servants, with distinguished records serving administrations of both parties, to move to performing tasks outside of their area of substantive expertise."

Elaine Duke remained in Miller's crosshairs. In October, as she flew back from a G7 ministerial meeting in Italy, Duke received an in-flight call from Miller, who berated her over what he characterized as lax security screening for refugees, saying she had not been doing her job as laid out in the president's executive order. He insisted that Duke should permanently shut off refugee flows from eleven countries the administration had identified as high-risk, and was especially insistent about banning people from Somalia. Trump had complained loudly as a candidate about the large numbers of Somali refugees who had settled in the United States, and the threats he claimed that they posed, and had raged at Duke during a briefing at his Bedminster golf club several weeks earlier, asking why he could not ban refugees from "fucking Somalia." Both he and Miller seemed to have a particular dislike for Somalia, often citing it or its nationals when they spoke of the potential dangers of refugees and other immigrants. But Duke refused to do what Miller was asking. She was all for stepping up vetting of refugees from countries that presented elevated security risks, she said, but we're not going to say that we're just shutting it down. No way.

In a call with homeland security adviser Tom Bossert shortly afterward, the two commiserated about Miller. Bossert sympathized, he told Duke. Miller's tendency to insert himself into low-level NSC debates was counterproductive and demonstrated his inexperience in the policymaking process, he told her. But he wasn't malicious, Bossert said. "I don't think Stephen is a bad person—I did at first—I just think he's an immature person," he told Duke. "But he got exalted into this position." Besides, Bossert said, Miller was only doing what Trump wanted him to.

The impulse to block refugees was coming from the very top of the White House, from a president who had campaigned on keeping them out of the country. There was little that anyone could do to stand in the way.

— 13 —

A NOT-SO-GLOBAL COMPACT

"STEPHEN WON'T ACCEPT THAT," Andrew Veprek, an immigration adviser at the Domestic Policy Council and a Miller loyalist, would often say.

In the spring of 2017, as White House officials began negotiating the joint statements—known as communiqués—that Trump and other world leaders would issue at the conclusion of the Group of 7 and Group of 20 summits later that year, Miller tried to seize control of the talks. He ruled out what had previously been considered boilerplate references to global cooperation and the benefits of migration. When officials began circulating drafts with their counterparts in the other six countries, Veprek weighed in to remind everyone of the unmentionable items, calling them "red lines" that Miller had said must not be crossed. Immigration policy is a matter of national sovereignty, he would say, and not subject to negotiation or review. Besides, he would argue, these are just veiled references to the Global Compact for Migration.

The compact was an agreement that world leaders had committed to develop and adopt as part of a historic United Nations declaration reached in New York weeks before Trump was elected. As one of his last acts as president, Obama had hosted a meeting on the global refugee crisis at the United Nations General Assembly in September 2016. He had called for world leaders to come together to address the refugee and migration crisis facing the world by doubling the number of refugees they resettled and providing them more aid, jobs, and educational opportunities. Obama never mentioned Trump in his speech, but his words were laden with references to the then-Republican presidential nominee. The outgoing president rejected the idea of turning refugees away because they were Muslim and called the refugee crisis "a test of our common humanity—whether we give in to suspicion and fear and build walls, or whether we see ourselves in another.

"Just as failure to act in the past—for example, by turning away Jews fleeing Nazi Germany—is a stain on our collective conscience, I believe history will judge us harshly if we do not rise to this moment," Obama said. He had ended his speech with a counterpoint to the callousness of Trump's suggestion that the United States bar Syrian refugees. Obama quoted from a letter he had received from a six-year-old New York boy named Alex who had seen a viral video taken in Aleppo of Omran Daqneesh, a five-year-old boy sitting bloodied and stunned in an ambulance following a bombing of his war-torn city. "We will give him a family, and he will be our brother," Alex had written. By the end of Obama's meeting, the assembled nations had signed on to the New York Declaration, pledging that the international community would step up its efforts on behalf of refugees and meet again in 2018 to develop and ratify a global migration agreement. The declaration was a worldwide statement of support for the rights of refugees and migrants, a promise to treat them humanely, and a reaffirmation that refugees have the right to seek asylum and would not be forced to return to countries where they would face persecution.

But with Trump in office, the United States was sending a very different message to the rest of the world. On Air Force One in May, as the president returned to Washington from a G7 meeting in Taormina, Italy, Miller bragged that American negotiators had successfully infused Trump's "America First" philosophy into the communiqué. "This is language we fought really hard for: 'We affirm the sovereign rights of states, individually and collectively, to control their own borders and establish policies in their own national interests and national security.' Now, that's a major statement inside the G7 communiqué that America pushed for and was successful in getting into it," Miller said as he briefed reporters in the section of the plane reserved for journalists. "It shows the influence that the president of the United States is having on the global dialogue in a very profound way."

In Washington, Miller told White House officials, and indeed representatives of governments throughout the world, that the United States was not even willing to mention the Global Compact, or the New York Declaration that paved the way for it.

It was one early indication that what was once standard procedure for multilateral diplomacy at the United Nations was often seen by Miller and Veprek as a politically motivated affront to Trump and his agenda. One afternoon in early spring, Veprek stormed angrily into Garry Hall's directorate, enraged to have learned that administration officials had been asked to prepare an extensive report on racism in America for the Committee on the Elimination of Racial Discrimination, an international body of human rights experts. How dare they question us on this? Veprek demanded to know. The report was going to be an anti-American screed and a hit job against Trump, he said, sputtering with anger, and it would consume the valuable time of senior administration lawyers who would have to spend precious hours responding to it, hosting a visit from the committee, and consulting with outside groups. Instead, Veprek wanted the White House to skip all those steps and produce a terse report. Hall's staff explained that participating in the effort was part of the normal functioning of the U.N. It was important for the United States to be seen as taking part, they explained, so that when it came time for a similar international bodies to investigate bad behavior by rogue regimes like Iran and North Korea— work that was often the foundation of U.N. resolutions to hold countries accountable—the process had credibility. Well, we don't have to open our doors to them, Veprek said. It's nothing more than a kabuki show designed to tag us as racist. The committee can just read our Constitution and the Thirteenth, Fourteenth, and Fifteenth Amendments as well as our civil rights laws to see that we've addressed racism in our society, he said. Hall's staff was shocked. Ian Moss, an NSC lawyer who was one of the few remaining African Americans at the White House, launched into a lengthy history of racial discrimination in the United States, and all of the ways in which it was still alive and well. Veprek did not want to hear it. The American people voted for this president, he said, and they explicitly rejected this internationalist approach.

"Is there anyone here who *really believes* that the Global Compact for Migration serves the interests of the United States?" Miller demanded one November afternoon in the Situation Room, where H. R. McMaster, the national security adviser, was presiding over a meeting that included top officials from the State Department, DHS, and the Justice Department, as well as Nikki Haley, the U.N. ambassador, who was joining by teleconference. Everyone fell silent. "Speak up!"

For weeks, Miller and Veprek had been quietly laying the groundwork for pulling the United States out of negotiations on the compact, which were set to begin in a couple of weeks in Puerto Vallarta, Mexico. Under normal circumstances, it was common practice for American officials to take their seat at the table for talks on such documents, even if the United States later decided not to sign. But these were not normal times. Miller was determined that American diplomats not have any role in shaping a document that ran so counter to Trump's agenda. The very concept of the agreement—the nations of the world banding together to take on a global refugee crisis by mapping out an ambitious collective response—offended Trump's sensibilities. It oozed globalism, and was the polar opposite of the "America First" posture the president was putting forward.

If they were going to prevail in pulling the United States out of the talks, Miller and his allies knew they needed a policy reason for doing so. Veprek found one in an obscure article posted on the blog of the *Harvard Law Review*, in which the author argued that even though the Global Compact would be nonbinding, it could shape the behavior of the countries that signed on, "which will create new norms that will eventually become entrenched as international law." With Hamilton's help, Veprek and Miller argued that the essay proved that the migration compact could take on the weight of "soft law" and be invoked by individual litigants who could then claim protections under the agreement that the United States would be forced to provide. If that happened, they argued, the United States could be forced to accept waves of migrants from around the globe. Legal scholars and national security experts considered the possibility so remote as to be almost laughable, and in any case, argued that the government would have all sorts of means to beat back any such legal challenge. But Miller and Veprek, repeatedly citing the essay that made their case, insisted on the point. Eventually, Hamilton conceded that it was highly unlikely that the United States could be successfully sued to enforce the terms of a nonbinding international agreement, but he insisted that the mere possibility that the Department of Justice might have to expend resources to defend against such litigation was too much to tolerate.

In the Situation Room that day, Jeff Sessions bolstered Miller's case. "In my forty-year career, I've never seen anything like this," he said of the compact. "It will open the floodgates to our courts!"

The compact didn't even exist yet. Negotiating teams hadn't so much as put pen to paper on what was called their "zero draft," the baseline for developing what would ultimately be a painstakingly negotiated document. And yet here was the attorney general of the United States warning grimly about a possible onslaught of litigation. As evidence that the agreement ran counter to the president's policy, Veprek had even added to the discussion paper a copy of the president's immigration principles, which had been hastily compiled by Miller the month before, calling for stricter asylum standards and fewer refugees in the United States. "Limit the number of refugees to prevent abuse of the generous U.S. Refugee Admissions Program and allow for effective assimilation of admitted refugees into the fabric of our society," was the final recommendation.

Nikki Haley, the U.N. ambassador, who had joined from New York via videoconference, was the sole voice in the meeting pushing back against Miller and Sessions. She argued that the United States should at the very least attend the negotiations on the compact, present its views, and try to shape the outcome. If the end result wasn't acceptable, they could always walk away and refuse to sign on. This is what we do at the U.N., Haley said. We take on tough problems all day long, we represent the national interest. So I'm all for engaging, I'm all for seeing what this thing looks like. "We can handle this," she insisted. "It's not the end of the republic as we know it."

This had been the State Department's position at a meeting earlier that month, when John Sullivan, the deputy secretary of state, had argued that negotiators should go to Mexico and see what came of the talks. But now Brian Hook, the head of the State Department's policy office, who was attending the meeting in Tillerson's place, sided with Miller, and others around the table were mostly silent. Jennifer Arangio made a brief attempt to challenge him, saying that the United States could better influence the outcome of the agreement by sitting at the negotiating table than by shunning it outright. But Miller was hearing none of it. This compact would be disastrous for the United States, he said, and the Trump administration wanted no part of even talking about it.

His dramatic words hung in the air inside the Situation Room as Haley could be seen on the videoconference screen rising and walking out. It was clear the meeting had come to an abrupt end, and Miller had gotten his way.

"Well," McMaster quipped from his seat at the head of the table. "That was fun."

— 14 —

BLIND SPOT

STEVE BANNON WAS DETERMINED to save Donald Trump from himself.

The president's take-no-prisoners approach on immigration, his un-apologetically ugly rhetoric on the issue, and his refusal to back down even in the face of public revulsion were the core elements of his appeal to his ardent supporters. They were the ultimate source of his political power, his chief strategist believed, and Trump's unique form of genius was in instinctively understanding and finding ways to stoke that dynamic. But Trump had a blind spot, and it terrified Bannon. Trump had a weakness for the Dreamers, Bannon knew, and if he gave in to it, it could ruin him. Brought into the United States as children by their parents, this particular group of undocumented immigrants had tugged at Trump's heartstrings since he first found out they existed during his meeting with several of them at Trump Tower in 2013. Raised in American schools and churches and towns, they were high school valedictorians and military enlistees—promising young people who epitomized the American dream. When Trump made sweeping generalizations about immigrants bringing filth and poverty and crime into the country, he didn't mean *them*.

As a presidential candidate, Trump had denounced Barack Obama for ignoring Congress and acting on his own to protect the Dreamers from deportation, vowing that if he won the presidency, he would end what he branded an "illegal amnesty." On Day One, Trump promised, he would scrap Deferred Action for Childhood Arrivals, the program known as DACA that Obama created in 2012 to shield the Dreamers from deportation and allow them to work legally in the United States. But Bannon knew that Trump didn't really want to do it, and he was surrounded by people who were telling him he shouldn't. Ivanka was among them. "You can't let this happen," she would say, deploying a potent blend of plaintiveness and melodrama that she had honed for maximum effect over the years in conversations with her father. You have to figure out a way for the Dreamers to stay.

What was worse, Bannon believed that supporters of the Dreamers were scheming to lure Trump into a disastrous deal to legalize the recipients of DACA protections by trading it for his border wall. Senator Lindsey Graham, the conservative South Carolina Republican who had been at the center of bipartisan efforts to overhaul immigration policies for years, approached Bannon one day with just that idea. "How about this?" Graham said to the president's chief strategist, sitting in Bannon's West Wing war room, which was filled with whiteboards displaying Trump's campaign promises. "DACA. We do the DACA thing, because that's got to get done—and he's soft on it anyway—for your crazy wall. You can build your wall!"

Bannon was incredulous. "Lindsey," he said. "DACA is amnesty. We will never do amnesty for a wall. We'll build a hundred miles of wall, and then you'll stop funding it!" Besides, he told the senator, the wall is "not the paramount thing"—it wasn't enough, in and of itself, to compensate for a move that would undermine Trump's entire immigration message. A deal like that would destroy Trump's credibility with his hard-core base, trashing his central promise—that illegal immigration would never be tolerated or forgiven—and with it any chance of a successful presidency. But Bannon was nervous. Trump was extremely persuadable, especially on this issue. The president loved to make a good deal, and he was desperate for a way to avoid hurting the Dreamers. Bannon needed a way to get the decision off of the president's plate, a forcing mechanism that would allow him to see that ending DACA was the only option.

Bannon called in Kris Kobach, the Kansas secretary of state who had built a national profile around defending hard-line immigration policies in court, to help devise a strategy for killing DACA. Kobach, an archconservative with a bachelor's degree from Harvard, a doctorate from Oxford, and a law degree from Yale, was the architect of his state's strict voter ID law that required proof of American citizenship to vote. But his influence extended far beyond Kansas; he had helped draft, and then defend in court, an Arizona law that allows local law enforcement officers the right to check the immigration status of people they suspect are in the country illegally. He had also pushed, without success, for a measure to bar undocumented immigrants from receiving in-state college tuition. More recently, Kobach, who had met Donald Trump Jr. through a mutual hunting buddy and then befriended his father during the New Hampshire primary, had become a favored adviser to Trump during his campaign and transition.

Kobach had an encyclopedic knowledge of immigration law, often spewing out statutory citations down to the letter-heading subsection of the United States Code where they could be found. He had represented a group of Immigration and Customs Enforcement agents and the state of Mississippi in 2012 when they had challenged DACA in federal court, trying to block its implementation. They were unsuccessful; a judge ruled in 2015 that neither the agents nor the state had standing to contest the program. But Bannon was certain that Kobach would have a legal strategy for figuring out how to eviscerate the program, or at least for getting the decision out of the White House and over to the Justice Department, where Attorney General Jeff Sessions was eager to end it.

As it happened, Kobach was already working with a coalition of like-minded attorneys general from around the country who were looking for an opportunity to challenge DACA, and he told Bannon about them. Kobach still held out hope that Trump would listen to reason and act on his own to end the program, and had spoken to the president several times about his belief that DACA was illegal and had to be terminated at once.

But he was dismayed to find that Trump seemed to be listening to the conflicting advice he was getting from DACA advocates inside the White House, including his daughter and son-in-law. I don't have to end DACA, Trump would say, parroting the arguments of those who wanted to save the program or delay its termination. Kobach and Bannon knew that they had to make sure that Trump understood that from a legal perspective, there was only one right answer: DACA had to go, and go quickly.

Kobach came up with a plan to make that clear. The group of attorneys general would threaten to bring a lawsuit calling the program unconstitutional, in an effort to strike it down. The courts had already blocked a similar executive action Obama had taken in 2014 to extend DACA to more Dreamers and grant legal status to their parents. All Sessions would have to do was decline to defend DACA against the promised legal challenge, and it would be clear the program was dead. Trump would have no choice but to end it.

From the start, Trump was being pulled in opposite directions by vying members of his inner circle and other influential voices.

On the morning of November 10, two days after Trump won the election, he traveled to Washington for a face-to-face meeting with Barack Obama in the Oval Office, which was planned as a short meet-and-greet to fulfill a long-standing tradition in which a sitting president makes a public gesture of welcoming his newly elected successor. Instead, the meeting lasted ninety minutes, and Obama later told a confidant that much of that time had been taken up discussing DACA and the Dreamers. While he had Trump's attention, Obama made the case for preserving the program and the protections it extended, explaining that DACA recipients were as American as any native-born kids and should be treated as such. Trump was sympathetic and gave Obama the impression that he was not inclined to abruptly yank their protections.

But ten days later, Trump invited Kobach to his Bedminster, New Jersey, golf resort, where the president-elect was auditioning candidates for cabinet positions and beginning to formulate his agenda. On a long list of restrictionist immigration proposals that Kobach brought with him to give to Trump—and flashed, perhaps inadvertently and perhaps not, within view of the phalanx of news photographers there to document the parade of transition visitors—was the immediate ending of DACA. It's a promise you can't afford to break, Kobach told the president-elect. A few weeks after that, Trump was once again tugged in the other direction during a meeting in the famous boardroom at Trump Tower with technology titans including Sheryl Sandberg of Facebook, Tim Cook of Apple, Jeff Bezos of Amazon, and Satya Nadella of Microsoft. It would be insane for you to end this program, they told Trump. A huge self-inflicted wound. Your presidency would be over before it even began. Don't worry, the president-elect assured them, in an answer he would repeat often in the coming months. We're not going to do that.

But no one really knew what Trump would do. As the clock ticked down on his final days in office, Obama and his aides were anxious that Trump would, in fact, follow through with his vow to end DACA as soon as he took office. Lawmakers and outside immigrant rights groups lobbied Obama to take aggressive measures, urging him to issue pardons to hundreds of thousands of Dreamers to shield them preemptively from deportation. Cecilia Muñoz, the outgoing director of Obama's Domestic Policy Council, and others inside the White House concluded that was impossible, both legally and politically. If Trump was going to end the program, officials concluded ruefully, there was little they could do on their way out the door to stop him. The one thing they could and would do, they decided, was to help as many Dreamers as they could for as long as they could. At USCIS, the agency responsible for administering the DACA program, León Rodríguez, the director, ordered his staff to speed up approvals for Dreamers who had applied, so that officials could process as many as possible before Trump took over. Obama, who had made it clear he would largely refrain from criticizing his successor, issued a stern, public warning that all bets were off if Trump targeted the Dreamers. "The notion that we would just arbitrarily, or because of politics, punish those kids, when they didn't do anything wrong themselves, I think would be something that would merit me speaking out," Obama told reporters in the White House briefing room on his third-to-last day in office.

The matter came up again two days later, moments after Trump took his oath of office on the West Front of the Capitol. Inside, at the luncheon in Trump's honor with congressional leaders, Senator Dick Durbin of Illinois, the senior Democrat who had first sponsored legislation to protect Dreamers sixteen years earlier, grabbed a chance to plead their case with the new president. You simply cannot deport these young people, Durbin told him. They could be forced to leave the only home they had ever known if Trump followed through on his threats. Trump assured the senator that he needn't worry. "We don't want to hurt your kids," he said. Hamilton's group had prepared an executive order ending DACA, but the president did not act on it, and his top aides seemed to be downplaying the chances that he would quickly do so.

The day after Trump was sworn in, as he left the presidential inaugural prayer service at the National Cathedral, Chief of Staff Reince Priebus paused on the stone steps to pull out his cell phone and call Paul Ryan, the speaker of the house, about a possible deal to save DACA. "How much money do you think we can get for a deal on the Dreamers?" Priebus asked Ryan. It was clear to both men that DACA could be a key piece of leverage to extract funding for Trump's wall. In an appearance on *Fox News Sunday* the following day, Priebus said that Trump wanted to work with congressional leaders to find a "long-term solution" to the issue. Sean Spicer, Trump's spokesman, told reporters at the White House that ending the program was not a priority for the president.

Trump continued to muse publicly about being generous to DACA recipients, telling *Time* magazine in mid-December that "we're going to work something out that's going to make people happy and proud." But his statements infuriated immigration restrictionists, who accused him of betrayal for failing to end the program. From his office near Reagan National Airport in Virginia, Roy Beck of NumbersUSA typed up a blog post to blast out to his millions of members asking them to join a campaign to urge Trump to keep his DACA campaign promise. A suggested tweet read, "Candidate @realDonaldTrump said he would 'immediately' end #DACA—@POTUS should end it NOW!" But weeks went by, and Trump seemed no closer to doing so. Privately, Paul Ryan was advising Trump that destroying DACA was a horrible idea, arguing that if the new president picked a fight over the program, it could swamp the party's entire agenda, costing Trump vital political capital and creating a mess from which it would be difficult for him to recover. "Don't get into this DACA fight," Ryan told Trump. "Don't pull the plug, or you will risk our entire agenda. You pull the plug now, and we're stuck."

Back and forth it went. The president, who hated to display even a shred of doubt about most issues, talked openly about his dilemma. "To me, it's one of the most difficult subjects I have, because you have these incredible kids," Mr. Trump told reporters at the White House when questioned about it. He said he would address the matter with "great heart," but noted that there were tricky politics involved. "I have to deal with a lot of politicians, don't forget. And I have to convince them that what I'm saying is right." Inside the West Wing, Bannon and Miller winced. Trump shouldn't be referring to them as kids, they told Spicer. They may have come to the United States as children, but some of these people are in their thirties, Miller would say. If the president insisted on referring to them as "kids," the idea of revoking their legal status, already deeply unpopular, would be even less appealing to the public. And bottom line, giving them special legal protections was just the kind of amnesty that Trump had promised not to embrace.

Even as Bannon put his plan to kill DACA into motion, Kelly, the DHS secretary, was on Capitol Hill reassuring lawmakers that he would handle the issue humanely. At his first meeting with Durbin in the senator's office on the third floor of the Capitol, Kelly said, "I care about the Dreamers as much, if not more, than you do." At a gathering with members of the Congressional Hispanic Caucus, Kelly described himself as the chief protector of the Dreamers, their "best friend" in the Trump administration. "I'm the best thing for DACA that you've ever seen," he told them.

"Nobody," he added, "has done more for the Dreamers than me." That was galling to hear for a roomful of Hispanic members of Congress who had been working for years to win protections for the group. Luis Gutiérrez, the loudmouthed Democratic congressman from Chicago, asked Kelly how he could say such a thing, given that Sessions had said he wanted to end the program and Trump had promised to do just that. Kelly told the lawmakers that most legal experts believed the program was unconstitutional, but that he was sympathetic to the Dreamers, and wanted to help them. "That's not true of everybody in this administration," Kelly told the lawmakers ominously. "I'm the best advocate they have."

In fact, Dreamers had other allies in the West Wing. Without telling Kelly or Bannon, Ivanka Trump and Jared Kushner had launched a covert effort save the program, and were quietly working with Graham and Durbin on a potential deal. In conversations in the senators' offices on Capitol Hill and in the West Wing of the White House, the group had begun exploring what it would take to get Republicans and Democrats to embrace a legislative solution for the Dreamers along the lines that Graham had pitched to Bannon. The Dreamers would get legal status and Trump would get his wall and other immigration restrictions. A win-win. Even Durbin was optimistic.

Kushner was supremely confident in his own negotiating prowess despite the fact that he was unfamiliar with the many nuances of the issue. As a Manhattan real estate developer and entrepreneur, he had never cracked open an immigration statute, never paid the slightest bit of attention to the raucous debates in Washington around the topic, and certainly never attempted to navigate the political crosscurrents dividing both parties that had scuttled efforts to fix the system for the better part of his lifetime. Still, Kushner believed this lack of experience was in fact a virtue, and he envisioned ultimately going even further than Durbin and Graham suggested. He began meeting with business executives, lawmakers, and immigration advocates to prepare the ground for what he was calling "*our* version of comprehensive immigration reform." In one gathering in his office in April with Dina Powell, a deputy national security adviser who had served in George W. Bush's White House, and a few outside advocates, Kushner laid out the kind of deal he was hoping for: a bevy of strict immigration enforcement measures, including more money for detaining and deporting illegal entrants, paired with a pathway to legal status—but not citizenship—for the millions of undocumented immigrants already living in the United States, and a shift to a merit-based immigration system for the future, which would prioritize skills over family ties. True, Sessions is pretty conservative on this stuff, but we can work with him, he said. In fact, Sessions had always insisted on slashing legal immigration and imposing tough new enforcement measures—the kinds of restrictions that had always doomed a broad, bipartisan immigration overhaul. One meeting attendee, experienced in the ins and outs of the bitterly partisan immigration fights of years past, told Kushner how far they were from a compromise that could actually pass Congress. To be honest, that's not remotely in the ballpark of what we're talking about here, the attendee said. Kushner shrugged off the skepticism. He wasn't a politician, Trump's son-in-law insisted. He wasn't bound by the silly rules that had divided Republicans and Democrats before. He could get it done.

When Bannon caught wind of Kushner's DACA rescue mission, he saw it as the perfect pretext for sidelining the president's son-in-law, whom he viewed as a mortal enemy who was tainting Trump's instincts and becoming an increasingly bothersome adversary inside the West Wing. He and Miller went to Priebus with an idea: We tell Trump that Jared is going over Kelly's head on DACA, and say he has to go. Bannon knew that at that moment, Trump adored Kelly, with his military bearing and his good-soldier demeanor. In the disastrous aftermath of the travel ban, despite his private griping about having been ill-informed about what was in the order and how it was to be rolled out, Kelly had gone on television and sought to calm the chaos, telling the public that any problems were his own fault, basically throwing his own body on the grenade that was the botched order. If Trump believed Kushner was getting in Kelly's way, Bannon thought, he would push aside his son-in-law. "This is the kill shot, man!" Bannon exalted to Priebus. "Jared will forever be in the doghouse."

Priebus was incredulous. This is crazy, he said. I'm not going to go in and try to take out the president's son-in-law over a policy dispute. If anybody's going anywhere, he told Bannon, it's you. Priebus was sympathetic; Kushner's constant meddling in any issue he took an interest in was a pain in the ass. (Rex Tillerson would later tell the story of the time that he was eating at a Washington restaurant and ran into Kushner having dinner with Luis Videgaray, the Mexican foreign secretary. "Welcome to Washington," Tillerson said dryly to the pair as the color drained from Videgaray's face. "I don't want to interrupt what y'all are doing. Give me a call next time you're coming to town.") But to think that Trump would turn on his own family was preposterous, Priebus knew. Besides, everyone understood that the president had a soft spot for the Dreamers; the notion that Kushner was trying to cut a deal to save them wasn't going to provoke the president's anger. We're all going to be gone before Jared, Priebus said ruefully.

The rift was inevitable. The truth was that Trump's White House was at war with itself on immigration issues, with Bannon and Miller, hard-right immigration restrictionists, just steps away in the West Wing from Jared and Ivanka, progressives at heart who were constantly trying to prod the president to soften his stance, and Gary Cohn, the former Goldman Sachs investment banker, who believed that immigration was an economic imperative. Cohn had been an unlikely choice for the Trump White House, a Democrat who believed in free trade and was often referred to derisively at the White House as "Globalist Gary." When Trump summoned him for an interview in Trump Tower shortly after having won election in 2016, Cohn had made it clear that he broke with the president-elect on immigration. We have to continue to have robust immigration in this country, he told Trump then, because there are a lot of jobs in the United States that Americans won't do. Like Dina Powell, Priebus and Spicer were establishment Republicans who never bought into Trump's hard-line stance. And the president was caught in the middle. While Trump's impulses hewed to the Bannon-Miller-Sessions way of thinking, he was a man untethered from any particular policy vision and untroubled by the idea of ideological inconsistency. Trump would do whatever was politically expedient, publicly marketable, and personally satisfying in the moment, and it was when those things came into conflict—as in the case of the Dreamers, who tugged at many Americans' heartstrings, including his own—that Trump was most likely to stray from his restrictionist bent. Bannon often said privately that Trump "doesn't give a shit about his agenda." Most days, he had little patience for hearing about the ways in which it was being carried out. "I don't give a fuck," the president would say. Or, "I don't care about that shit."

Bannon had failed to push Kushner aside, but he was determined to insert Miller into the negotiations, to be his eyes and ears and to shape the outcome. When Jared and Ivanka hosted a dinner at their mansion in D.C.'s tony Kalorama neighborhood with Graham and Durbin to discuss DACA, they invited Miller. "They're going to try to co-opt you," Bannon told Miller. "Just sit there and take it in." As Durbin walked into the Trump-Kushner residence and saw Miller there, his heart sank. We're never going to be able to do a deal if he's a part of it, Durbin thought. He was mostly right. Briefing Bannon in the White House days later, Miller said that Jared and Ivanka were discussing just the kind of deal that Graham had described: a bill that would grant legal status not just to DACA recipients but to up to a million additional people who were eligible for the program but had never applied. In return, Trump would get funding for his wall. It was a total nonstarter, Miller said. Bannon agreed.

Even as Bannon and Miller plotted to make sure that Trump didn't agree to what they saw as a terrible DACA deal, Kelly was trying to avoid being saddled with the responsibility for ending it. The program had been put in place by Jeh Johnson, Kelly's predecessor, and as the homeland security secretary, getting rid of it would require his signature. "Why are they sticking me with this? This shouldn't be my decision to make," he confided to a colleague. "Only Congress can solve these issues. We're getting this out of here, and it's going to Congress, and we're going to play chicken and get Congress to act."

Behind closed doors, Kelly told lawmakers that he had no intention of targeting Dreamers for deportation. He made it official in a mid-June 2017 memo, in which he formally rescinded Obama's 2014 directive extending the program to Dreamers' parents, but also said that the DACA program itself would continue. The announcement generated mass confusion about Trump's true intentions; while Kelly's memo stated flatly that DACA "will remain in effect," department spokespeople and White House officials scrambled to clarify that Trump had made no long-term decisions about the fate of the program and was still considering ending it outright. "There has been no final determination made about the DACA program, which the president has stressed needs to be handled with compassion and with heart," Jonathan Hoffman, the assistant secretary for public affairs at DHS, said in a statement. Kelly, he added, "has noted that Congress is the only entity that can provide a long-term solution to this issue."

Thanks to Bannon's clandestine strategizing with Kobach, there would soon be a deadline to force the issue. By late June, with Kobach's prodding, ten Republican attorneys general, led by Ken Paxton of Texas, wrote a letter to Sessions at the Justice Department threatening to challenge DACA in federal court if DHS did not move within months—by September 5—to get rid of it. Like the 2014 order covering parents of Dreamers that had been struck down, they wrote, "DACA unilaterally confers eligibility for work authorization and lawful presence without any statutory authorization from Congress. . . . We respectfully request that the Secretary of Homeland Security phase out the DACA program."

Advocacy groups that had been obsessively tracking Trump's twists and turns on the issue began to raise red flags. One well-connected immigration operative went to the White House in early August to warn DACA proponents in the West Wing—including Dina Powell and Jeremy Katz, Cohn's deputy at the National Economic Council—that they had to do something dramatic if they wanted to stop the program from being eliminated. "You are going to get rid of DACA," he told them. "You are trapped." The officials swore that was not going to happen. The president doesn't want to touch it, they said; we just can't say that publicly. "It doesn't matter," the operative said, shaking his head. "You're jammed." Either the president calls Ken Paxton and tells him to call off the lawsuit, or this program is dead.

Thanks to his feuding advisers, Trump was boxed in and whipsawed by conflicting advice. Bannon and Kobach's plan had pushed him to the brink of canceling a program that even he didn't really seem to want to kill. His daughter and son-in-law, along with Cohn and deputy national security adviser Dina Powell, were tugging him in the other direction but offering no real solution for saving DACA. And Miller was pressing for him to endorse even further-reaching immigration changes that Trump barely understood. The president was, in many ways, at the mercy of his staff on immigration, unschooled in the details and surrounded by people who had competing agendas on the issue that he did not always share.

In early August, Trump held an event in the White House Roosevelt Room to announce that he was endorsing the RAISE Act, a Republican bill that aimed to shift the American immigration system from one based primarily on family ties to one based on "merit." The bill made large cuts to family immigration levels and gave priority for employment-based green cards to those with specialized skills or other desirable qualities like educational attainment. Minutes before the president's speech, an immigration advocate who had been visiting the West Wing told Trump's advisers that the president, who had in the past said that he did not want to cut legal immigration, was being deeply inconsistent in endorsing legislation that would slash it by nearly half over a decade. No, Trump's aides answered. That can't be right. They had just come from a briefing with the president where Trump had asked this exact question, and Miller assured him in front of everyone in the room that the RAISE Act did not cut legal immigration. Senator Tom Cotton of Arkansas, one of the measure's authors, was there, too. Maybe you have an outdated version of the bill, they said hopefully. The visitor assured his hosts that he did not. The president was going to endorse the bill in front of the whole world in twenty minutes, and the officials started to panic. One aide rushed out of the room to investigate, returning minutes later to report that the legislation did not touch legal immigration levels. At about the same time, the White House was sending out a fact sheet to reporters that acknowledged that the RAISE Act "reduces overall immigration numbers." And not long after Trump endorsed the bill, Miller appeared in the White House briefing room to tell the press that the legislation would make "a major, historic change to U.S. immigration policy" that would, in fact, "cut net migration in half."

Trump had just called for a massive cut to legal immigration, and some of his top advisers didn't even seem to know it. Trump would later claim that he had always opposed the idea.

NO WAY OUT

ON AUGUST 24, 2017, Elaine Duke, the acting DHS secretary, arrived at the White House for a meeting of the Domestic Policy Council, where she had been summoned to discuss the way forward on the DACA program. A career civil servant who had worked in the Bush and Obama administrations and was widely respected in the department, Duke was a procurement and acquisition expert who had been chosen to serve in the top echelons of DHS primarily to deal with the wall and operational issues. She wore her long brown hair loose and tucked behind an ear, and had an earthy way about her, with a wide smile and a gentle demeanor. Duke was the furthest thing imaginable from a political operator. She was not a Trump loyalist and not one for the public spotlight, and she had never expected to tackle high-profile decisions with giant political ramifications—certainly nothing as controversial and emotionally charged as the fate of hundreds of thousands of young immigrants. She was utterly unprepared for the lion's den she was about to enter.

When Duke arrived in the Roosevelt Room that day, it was clear that she had misjudged the situation entirely. This was not a routine meeting to discuss policy options; it was something of a procedural ambush. Miller and Sessions came into the room determined to drive a stake through the heart of the DACA program, but they needed her to acquiesce in order to carry out the plan.

As Duke sat at the large, wooden table opposite the twentieth-century bronze sculpture of a bison holding off a trio of menacing wolves, Miller and Sessions laid out the situation. The president wanted to end DACA, they said, and Duke was going to be the one to issue a memo killing it. The attorney general reiterated what he had said publicly about the program being illegal and unconstitutional. Even Obama had created it only reluctantly, after initially having said that he could not do so because he was not "king." Don McGahn, the White House counsel, was there to back up the legal arguments, saying that given the attorney general's conclusion that the program was unconstitutional, the Trump administration would look "foolish" if they tried to defend it. Hamilton and several other DHS officials piled on as well, siding with Miller and Sessions.

Duke was surprised and taken aback. During her stints outside of government, Duke volunteered at Hogar Immigrant Services in Virginia, an organization led by Catholic Charities, tutoring immigrants on civic education and American history to help them pass their citizenship tests. She wanted to follow the law, but she also wanted to do the right thing. She was deeply resistant to the idea of putting hundreds of thousands of undocumented immigrants at risk of deportation, and effectively telling them that the country they considered their own did not return the sentiment.

From the start, Duke had known that Trump's most important advisers wanted to end DACA. And she shared their view that the program was problematic and probably illegal. She was aware of the threat of a lawsuit from the Republican attorneys general, and of Sessions's position that the program was legally indefensible. Lawyers at DHS and the Justice Department liked to say that they couldn't find a single lawyer who thought the program was legal. Hamilton and other DHS officials had advised her that the department could not continue issuing permits for a program that the Justice Department considered unconstitutional. It had to go, they told her. But there had to be a way to salvage some measure of protection for this one group of immigrants, Duke thought. She had spent hours huddling with her staff in the days before this meeting, discussing the fate of the program.

But in the Roosevelt Room that day, Miller and everyone else around the table was acting like this was a done deal. As far as they were concerned, DHS was already on board, and here Duke was, acting like this was still a live discussion. It was like she was on a different planet, the others thought, going on and on about what alternatives there were to ending DACA, when the reality was that there was no alternative. Duke became defensive. She was not about to be bullied into something she wasn't sure was the right thing. You can't tell me what to do, she said. She may not have been nominated by the president or confirmed by Congress, but she was the acting secretary, and she was not going to be rushed or intimidated into making this decision. Kelly, still bent on punting the issue to Capitol Hill, raised the issue of potentially delaying the end of the program with a six-month grace period, both to avoid an abrupt termination and to pressure lawmakers with a date-certain by which they needed to act if they wanted to preserve the protections. But some officials said the program should be gone immediately. If we are saying it's unconstitutional and illegal, they argued, how can we continue to administer it? The session ended with no resolution.

Miller had conveniently scheduled the meeting when one key player was missing; Kushner had been out of town. Once he got back, he set to work trying to slow the process. Maybe there's a more gradual way to do things, Kushner argued. It doesn't have to be here today, gone tomorrow. Kushner's intervention threw more sand in the gears that Miller and Sessions had put in motion. About a week later, officials gathered in the Roosevelt Room again for another DACA meeting, this one billed as the forum for a final decision to be reached. But as they sat and waited for the session to begin, one of Kelly's aides entered and told everyone it was off.

With scarcely more than a week to go before the deadline set by the attorneys general, DACA proponents on Capitol Hill and in Washington's powerful lobbying circles were staging a last-ditch rescue mission for the program. Speaker Ryan called Kelly to beg him to reconsider. "Please don't do this," Ryan told Kelly. "It will derail tax reform, and we can't afford to have that happen." Kirstjen Nielsen, Kelly's deputy when he was DHS secretary, had just gone over to join him in the same role at the White House, and several leaders of the U.S. Chamber of Commerce organized a dinner to introduce her to some of the capital's most influential business lobbyists. At the dinner, they delivered the same message about DACA. You are creating an artificial deadline in the middle of tax reform, and it is going to blow up in your face, said members of the group, which included Neil Bradley, the Chamber's executive vice president, as well as Brett Loper, the top lobbyist for American Express, and Marc Lampkin, the managing partner of one of the district's top lobbying firms. We could end up in a shutdown over immigration, with tax cuts as the collateral damage. They discussed Republicans' failed efforts to repeal Obamacare and explained that the president and the party badly needed to put some accomplishments on the board. "Don't roll this hand grenade into the middle of tax reform," Bradley implored Nielsen. But she did not appear to understand the power of the White House to chart a course on a controversial issue. If the administration doesn't act, she said, the state attorneys general will sue and do it for us, she insisted. Well, then you should convince them to delay, the group replied. Yet Nielsen also appeared to have great confidence in Kelly's idea for a six-month wind-down. An artificial deadline would give Trump leverage to get the wall in exchange for legislation extending DACA protections. It would be a slam dunk, she said. The lobbyists were incredulous. You think this is a great issue, they told Nielsen. Actually, it's a terrible issue politically. The White House, they concluded, had absolutely no idea what the termination of DACA was about to unleash.

Inside the West Wing, Trump was still conflicted, and DACA supporters secretly hoped they could appeal to him to preserve the program. On the Friday before Labor Day, with only days before the legal deadline and speculation rampant about the president's intentions, Ryan tried one last tactic to get Trump to back down. In an interview with WCLO, his hometown radio station in Janesville, Wisconsin, Ryan said that the president should not terminate DACA. "I actually don't think he should do that," Ryan told the station. "I believe that this is something that Congress has to fix." The White House was incensed. Trump still had to make the decision, and he seemed to change his mind by the hour about what he wanted to do. Exasperated, the president kept demanding that his aides find him "a way out of this." Trump reluctantly told advisers that he would accept Kelly's idea, ending DACA with a six-month delay that would put pressure on Congress to save it or let it die. But he felt torn, trapped, and unsatisfied with the decision.

Duke had quietly agonized, too. She did not want to terminate DACA, but she knew there was no avoiding it given the inclinations of Trump and his team. She was deeply disappointed that the Dreamers would only have six months of protections, counting it as a personal failure that she hadn't been able to buy them more time. And there were limits to what Duke was willing to do to help the White House accomplish something she viewed as inhumane. She would issue the memo rescinding the DACA program, but she refused to sign on to the policy reasons Miller and Sessions were pushing for doing so. There would be no mention of the claim that the program encouraged illegal entry and disrupted the normal, legal channels for immigrating to the United States. In other words, no policy rationale would be given for ending the program. Duke would simply refer to prior court decisions and Sessions's assertion that it was unconstitutional. Nor did she want to be the public face of announcing DACA's demise. Sessions stepped up to do so instead. Duke would later tell people that she was grateful to Sessions for agreeing to be the face of the DACA decision, saying he was "good to me" on an issue that tore her up inside.

By Sunday of a frenzied Labor Day holiday weekend, Ryan received a call at his home in Janesville from Kelly, who was phoning to tell him that Trump would soon announce that he was terminating DACA with a six-month delay, to give Congress time to act on legislation that would address the Dreamers' situation. Ryan was disappointed but resigned to the outcome, and hopeful that the move might actually spark a new phase of legislative negotiations in what had, up until then, been directionless behind-the-scenes talks about what would become of DACA. Ryan only had one request, one that his staff had shared with Marc Short, Trump's legislative chief, a few days before: if Trump is going to do this, he needs to make an on-camera announcement, personally calling on members of Congress to act to codify the program's protections. It would put the presidential imprimatur on the idea of legalizing the Dreamers, and give Republican lawmakers the political cover they needed to embrace a measure that was certain to be condemned as "amnesty" by their core supporters. That was the plan as of noon on Labor Day, when White House officials told Ryan's office that Trump and Sessions planned to announce the termination the following day.

But in the Oval Office, Trump was still hesitating. He detested the press coverage of his impending decision, which painted him as conflicted and portrayed ending DACA as a coldhearted, shortsighted move. In general, Trump relished his reputation as a tough guy who was willing to hit back at his opponents and insult his critics, but he could not stand the thought of being seen as mean to defenseless kids. Neither could he tolerate the idea of backing down from a promise he had made his supporters, particularly on immigration, the issue that defined his brand. In the dining room off the Oval Office where he passed much of his time watching television and reading news clips, the president spent his Labor Day huddling with Miller and Hope Hicks, his director of strategic communications, making edit after tortured edit to his brief remarks.

Like a student with a particularly ominous homework deadline looming, Trump felt trapped by the September 5 deadline, much as Bannon and Kobach had intended. The "way out" that his advisers had offered him—ending the program, but not doing so right away—was a middle ground that somewhat softened the blow of taking away protections from hundreds of thousands of young immigrants with promising futures, but it was also in some ways the worst of all worlds. Trump would get some credit from his hard-core base for terminating the program but be criticized by many on the right for failing to switch it off immediately. And advocates of the Dreamers, including the immigrants themselves, would be outraged that he was wiping away the protections—despite the brief delay—and thereby opening hundreds of thousands of people once again to deportation. Instead of the kind of black-versus-white, good-versus-evil message that Trump liked to deliver, he was having to prepare a nuanced statement he feared would please no one, least of all himself.

"As president, my highest duty is to defend the American people and the Constitution of the United States of America," Trump's statement began. "At the same time, I do not favor punishing children, most of whom are now adults, for the actions of their parents. But we must also recognize that we are a nation of opportunity because we are a nation of laws." On the one hand, on the other hand. Forget it, Trump finally decided. He wasn't going to make any remarks at all. Let Sessions do it. He would put out a written statement instead. At nine that evening, Ryan's office got the call: the attorney general will be announcing this tomorrow, not Trump. By now, the speaker had become accustomed to the fact that Trump was not a president who understood or cared much about giving his Republican brethren any political cover. But he was still annoyed by the last-minute change, and fearful of what it portended. If Trump wasn't willing to speak about the DACA termination publicly, would he be willing to step up and use his influence to help lawmakers cut a deal to fix the problem he was creating? Or would Republican lawmakers be left holding the bag for a decision the president had made unilaterally?

In his written statement, Trump called DACA an "amnesty-first" approach and emphasized that he felt sympathy for those it was designed to protect, but argued that the program was illegal and misguided. He laid out the complicated consequences for those currently protected under the program—their permits would not begin to expire for six months, and some would last as long as two years—and said they would not be targeted for deportation unless they were criminals. "I am not going to just cut DACA off, but rather provide a window of opportunity for Congress to finally act," Trump said. But he also made it clear that that opportunity would not come for free. In the eleventh paragraph of the tortured, sixteen-paragraph statement, the president laid out his priorities for immigration reform. "Before we ask what is fair to illegal immigrants, we must also ask what is fair to American families, students, taxpayers, and jobseekers," he said. That meant overhauling the nation's green card system and building a skills-based immigration process, he said. These were the kinds of changes Miller and the serious immigration restrictionists saw as enduring and crucial.

The threat of a lawsuit from the states opposed to DACA had vanished when Trump ended the program, but now he faced legal challenges from the other side. Within days, immigrant rights advocates launched a legal assault on Trump's decision to end DACA. Fifteen states and the District of Columbia filed a lawsuit in New York the day after Trump's announcement. Janet Napolitano, the president of the University of California, who as Obama's first DHS secretary created the DACA program, filed suit on behalf of the California colleges two days later. The NAACP sued, too. The challenges were not unexpected; Miller and Sessions knew they were coming. But inside the White House, they added to Trump's deepening anger about judges and the courts. Trump was also right about the political reaction; there was little praise for his decision from hard-core restrictionists, but plenty of outrage from Democrats and advocates of the Dreamers. The day after the announcement, Representative Luis Gutiérrez of Chicago lashed out at Kelly, calling him a "hypocrite who is a disgrace to the uniform he used to wear. He has no honor and should be drummed out of the White House along with the white supremacists and those enabling the president's actions by 'just following orders.'" The criticism was especially stinging for a Marine general who had lost his son in Afghanistan seven years before. Gutiérrez had been unaware that Kelly was a Gold Star father, and when the chief of staff arrived in the Capitol later that afternoon for a closed-door meeting with members of the Congressional Hispanic Caucus, the congressman apologized, saying his comment had been inappropriate and he should never have allowed his criticism to become personal. Kelly was gracious, shaking Gutiérrez's hand and telling the congressman, "Apology accepted." But his visit left a bitter taste anyway.

In a roomful of lawmakers who were immigrants themselves or had parents who were, Kelly said Trump did not want people to come to the United States poor and unable to support themselves or their families; he wanted well-educated immigrants, able to speak English and contribute to society. The lawmakers held their tongues, but many were offended and worried. If this is what the White House chief of staff really thinks of immigrants—really thinks of us—they wondered, what will become of the Dreamers?

"What's in it for me?" Trump wanted to know.

It was a week after his decision to end the DACA program, and the president had invited Senator Chuck Schumer of New York and Representative Nancy Pelosi of California, the Democratic congressional leaders, to dinner in the oval Blue Room of the White House, with the lit-up obelisk of the Washington Monument visible out the window in the distance.

Trump was in deal-making mode that night. He had ordered up a Chinese-themed meal from the White House chef—crispy honey sesame beef and sticky rice—as a nod to Schumer's fondness for the cuisine as well as their shared hard-line views on China. The pie for dessert was chocolate, a Pelosi favorite. He had seated himself at the head of a rectangular wooden table between the two leaders he had recently dubbed "Chuck and Nancy," a chummy moniker that had for the moment taken the place of "Cryin' Chuck," the president's go-to Twitter insult of the Senate minority leader. After a discussion of trade issues and China, Schumer steered the conversation to DACA. Trump had ended the program and was calling on Congress to act, and Democrats had a proposal, the senator said. If Trump would support the Dream Act, which would permanently protect undocumented immigrants brought to the United States as children, Schumer said, Democrats would be willing to negotiate with him over a package of strong border security measures—although they would not embrace his call for a wall on the border with Mexico. The president seemed intrigued, as much for what the deal would mean for him as for how it might help the hundreds of thousands of DACA recipients whose fate he had just placed at risk.

Schumer, a schmoozer by nature who sensed an opening, had a ready answer for Trump's question. The president had spent the summer alienating people both at home and abroad, he said. He thumbed his nose at

America's allies with his decision to pull out of the Paris Climate Accord, then sparked outrage with remarks after the racial unrest in Charlottesville, Virginia, that seemed to condone white supremacy and neo-Nazism. Now was his chance, Schumer said, to prove that he could do more than just divide people. Now was the time for Trump to show that he could be the dealmaker he always claimed to be. The president, never one to hold his tongue when criticized, took in the senator's argument, even chuckling at one point.

But at the other end of the table, his aides were panicking, fearful that Trump was about to give away the store. When the president called on Kelly to weigh in, the chief of staff rose from his seat to make an impassioned argument for fortifying the border, including with stronger barriers. He said that Mexico was descending into crime and chaos, almost as bad as Venezuela under Hugo Chávez. Such a collapse on the southern border could be devastating to the United States, Kelly said, and Congress needed to step up aggressively to address the threat. Marc Short, the White House legislative chief, warned Trump about what the Democrats were actually suggesting. Let's just slow down for a second, he cautioned. You know they're talking about the Dream Act here? Unlike DACA, which granted temporary permits to about 800,000 people but did not give permanent legal residency or citizenship, the Dream Act would cover at least a million more—some estimates put the total at well over three million—and ultimately allow its beneficiaries to become American citizens. Trump gestured vaguely with one hand, as if to brush off Short's concern, and urged the Democrats to keep talking. Wilbur Ross, the seventy-nine-year-old secretary of commerce, repeated the president's initial question: What does he get out of this? Pelosi tried to answer, only to have her voice drowned out by others at the table, all men. "Do the women get to talk around here?" she said wryly, drawing nervous laughter and then silence. What Trump would get, she said once the room had fallen quiet, was the cooperation of Democrats to achieve other elements of his agenda, which he would no doubt need in the months and years to come.

Dinner ended on a positive note. Not only were they willing to work together to cut the deal that Trump had discussed with the Democrats, but they had agreed that each side would put out a statement reflecting a shared desire to craft legislation that would give Dreamers a pathway to citizenship, and at the same time hammer out a deal on border security measures. Trump had one request for the wording of the statements: he did not want anyone to use the term "Dreamers," he said. Native-born Americans have dreams, too, Trump said, and he didn't like the impression that the DACA population would be getting special treatment. Ever the salesman, Trump thought it would be better for marketing purposes to use the program's acronym, DACA. His Democratic guests agreed to the condition.

But sensing that they had outmaneuvered Trump, Pelosi and Schumer were not about to allow the aftermath of the dinner to unfold entirely on his terms. Minutes after they left the White House, the Democrats—well aware of Trump's penchant for changing his mind and going back on his word—issued a brief joint statement calling the dinner "very productive" and making clear that the president had endorsed the idea of legislation that would pair help for the Dreamers with border security, but leave out the wall. "We agreed to enshrine the protections of DACA into law quickly, and to work out a package of border security, excluding the wall, that's acceptable to both sides," their statement said.

The reaction from Trump's base was as swift as it was bitter. "AMNESTY DON" blared the headline on Breitbart, coining a phrase that quickly went viral in the conservative Twittersphere. "TRUMP CAVES ON DACA." Miller was frustrated and angry, feeling partially responsible for allowing Trump—always thin on the specifics, ever in search of a deal—to stray so far, in essence undercutting his own negotiating position in the coming talks over DACA and making it more difficult for Republicans to find a workable middle ground. Ryan had advised Trump in a call earlier in the day that he should aim for a DACA-for-wall deal, not the all-out Dream Act Democrats were demanding or the other restrictions that Miller was hoping to tack on. With a few plates of sesame beef, that plan seemed to have evaporated.

Trump had been outhustled by Chuck and Nancy, and he knew it. But the president still did not seem to comprehend how to salvage his leverage. In private conversations, Trump told senior Republican lawmakers that he would not insist that a wall be in the DACA bill, but he would insist on having it funded eventually. The president did not understand that if he was going to have a crack at securing his wall, the DACA legislation was the only way to do it. The morning after the dinner, it fell to Ryan to help Trump save face. On Capitol Hill, the speaker held a news conference to try to clean up the mess. Trump hadn't agreed to anything, Ryan said, and any bill that he would accept would have to include border security. "These were discussions, not negotiations," Ryan said. "There isn't an agreement. And it's very clear—and I want to make this clear over and over again—if we don't fix the problems we have with border security and enforcement, and we would only fix DACA, we're going to have another DACA problem a decade from now. That's the symptom of the problem, so let's fix both."

Ryan dispatched Casey Higgins, his top immigration aide, to begin private talks with Miller about what a potential deal might look like. But the distrust on both sides was profound. As a congressional staffer, Miller used to routinely savage Ryan as an open-borders enthusiast and amnesty apologist. He would feed unflattering information about Ryan to reporters at Breitbart and other hard-right outlets, and then blast out the resulting stories to an email distribution list that went to scores of congressional offices. (Despite repeated entreaties, Ryan's staff could never get Miller to include them on his immigration news clips list.) One such article was the wall exposé from Ryan's front yard in Janesville by Julia Hahn, who now worked alongside Miller at the White House. For Miller, the prospect of collaborating with Ryan's staff on a compromise was risky, given the speaker's long-established enthusiasm for a business-minded immigration overhaul. But the path to an eventual bill that could clear Congress and land on the president's desk ran through his office. So the odd coupling commenced.

Ryan also put together a Republican working group to try to build consensus on what that would look like. It drew from all over the spectrum, from leaders Ryan and Kevin McCarthy, the No. 2 in the House, who had developed a rapport with Trump; to hard-liners like Bob Goodlatte of Virginia, the Judiciary Committee chairman; Raúl Labrador of Idaho and Jim Sensenbrenner of Wisconsin; to more moderate voices including Mike McCaul, the Homeland Security Committee chairman; Martha McSally of Arizona; as well as Will Hurd of Texas and Mario Diaz-Balart, both of whom had been at the forefront of trying to forge bipartisan immigration deals in the past. But the group could hardly agree on anything, and without clear guidance from the White House about what the president would or would not accept, their efforts floundered. The messages from the White House about the elements of a DACA deal were mixed at best. One day, the RAISE Act—which slashed legal immigration by up to 50 percent—seemed to be the priority; the next, it was ending chain migration. Trump kept inviting different groups of lawmakers to the White House, seeming to cast about for possible solutions.

As he tried to figure out the contours of a deal, Miller stayed in close touch with the Freedom Caucus, the ultraconservative group that had forged a tight alliance with Trump and was deeply hostile to Ryan, speaking almost daily and sometimes more with its chairman, Representative Mark Meadows of North Carolina. Miller began developing a draft of immigration principles that would put the focus back on enforcement, restrictions, and reducing the number of people admitted to the United States, where he believed it belonged. Miller told colleagues that he was increasingly convinced that the idea of ending chain migration was the key to any agreement, both because it would make enduring changes to the existing immigration system and because it "polls through the roof." In other words, it would put Democrats in a tricky political position, forcing them to explain to the public why awarding green cards based merely on family ties was better than doing so based on skills and accomplishments.

But Miller was also convinced that this was his chance—maybe his last—to win all sorts of immigration concessions in return for addressing the fate of the Dreamers. So he enlisted the Department of Homeland Security to help draw up an elaborate wish list. One Saturday evening in

October, Duke frantically summoned her senior staff to an office at the Reagan Building. "Right now, I need a list of everything we could trade for DACA," a distraught Duke told them. It was clear she had been upbraided by the White House and was desperate to deliver as big an ask as she could put together in exchange for protecting the Dreamers. The resulting four-page list would serve as the raw material for a lengthy menu of immigration demands Trump would issue the following week, each of which he said "must be included" in any DACA deal. "It was terrible government," said an official involved at the time. "It was just a list of every single thing that everyone around the table wanted that could be immigration-related. And we just threw it together."

The Tuesday after Duke's frenzied brainstorming session, Ryan's immigration working group gathered in the small Ways and Means Committee room on the first floor of the Capitol for a briefing on the laundry list, which was chock-full of measures that Democrats—and even some Republicans—regarded as poison pills with the potential to kill any DACA deal. It included the wall and more money for border enforcement, but also cuts to legal immigration, which Ryan had made clear he opposed, and dozens of other proposals meant to block migrants from entering the United States. New restrictions would make it easier to remove unaccompanied children who arrived at the border and make it more difficult for people to claim asylum. The country would accept fewer refugees fleeing war and persecution. The immigration system would be based on skills, rather than family ties, and the diversity visa lottery eliminated. Lawmakers wanted to ask practical questions about what the administration needed to make the immigration system workable, but Francis Cissna of USCIS spent much of his time hammering on the idea of ending chain migration, repeatedly making the political case for basing immigration priority on employment skills, rather than family members whose relatives happen to reside in the United States. Miller took a hard line as well, making it clear to lawmakers that the White House was going to insist on all of these measures as part of any DACA deal. Their rhetoric grew heated as they previewed what the public case would be for Trump's position. As lawmakers peppered Miller with questions about how a proposal like this could possibly ever make it through the Senate—even if it could pass the House—Miller seemed to have no answers.

Only Duke appeared to acknowledge the political realities. She conceded that some of the measures Trump was demanding were politically difficult and potentially unachievable. While the wall was the top item on Trump's list, when lawmakers pressed her on it, Duke would not say the wall or even border fencing was a top priority; while DHS had identified some areas where it was needed, she said, the bigger gap was in technology, an item that had been omitted from the document altogether. Ron Vitiello of Customs and Border Protection said he shared that assessment.

But even as Miller pressed for a wide-ranging immigration measure full of new restrictions, Trump was musing about a far different plan. During a Columbus Day golf game at the president's club in Sterling, Virginia, Lindsey Graham chatted up Trump about the same sort of deal he had been discussing with Kushner months earlier: legalize the Dreamers and give their parents work permits in exchange for strong border security measures, including a wall component. In a nod to the goal of limiting chain migration, Graham proposed barring Dreamers from sponsoring the parents who brought them to the United States illegally. And they would do away with the diversity visa lottery, which Trump viewed as the most egregious aspect of an immigration system that seemed to allow people in almost at random.

Trump seemed intrigued. I want to fix this, he told Graham, and I'm willing to sit down with Democrats and get it done. They met again for golf the following Saturday. "He wants to make a deal," the South Carolina Republican told *The New York Times* a few weeks later. The senator said that Trump was even entertaining the idea of a second phase of immigration changes after DACA had been dealt with, in which he would grant legal status to the nation's 11 million undocumented immigrants—those who were not felons. But Graham wasn't the only one trying to get Trump to endorse an ambitious plan.

For weeks, as a year-end deadline loomed to reach a deal on federal spending, groups of Republicans would make pilgrimages to the White House to try to get the president's stamp of approval for their wildly divergent immigration ideas. They thought they were racing against a clock; Democrats had said that legislation to address the plight of the Dreamers should be part of any year-end spending legislation, raising the specter of a government shutdown to cap off Trump's first year in office if no agreement could be reached. But they could not get a clear read from the White House. Trump was desperate to get his wall, but Miller was instead fixated on broader immigration changes. At a meeting at the White House, Miller told the heads of the leading immigration restrictionist groups that if they were ever going to win his main goal and theirs—making major cuts to the number of immigrants allowed into the United States—an amnesty for the Dreamers was the only way to do it. They're not going anywhere anyway, Miller acknowledged. And this is the only chance we're going to have to cut legal immigration. If we don't do it now, who will? He implored the anti-immigration leaders not to oppose the idea.

Pressure was beginning to mount in Republican ranks to address the issue. Just after Thanksgiving, Mark Amodei, a four-term congressman and the only Republican in Nevada's House delegation, became the first in his party to sign on to an insurgent effort to force a vote on legislation to protect the Dreamers. The so-called "discharge petition" was an arcane but potentially potent parliamentary tactic that would essentially compel Ryan to schedule action on a DACA bill if a majority of the House—218 members—signed on. Thirty-four House Republicans signed a letter to Ryan calling for such a measure. With his working group in shambles, the speaker was increasingly worried that more of his members would take the same position as Carlos Curbelo of Florida, another contrarian Republican lawmaker, had: that they would not vote for any more spending bills until there was a deal to save DACA.

But Democrats were not going to force a shutdown over the Dreamers—at least not yet. In late December, Schumer decided he would allow a stopgap spending measure without a fix for DACA to pass, thus punting the issue to January and averting a shutdown. Rank-and-file

Democrats were furious, and members of the Congressional Hispanic Caucus gathered off the House floor and marched across the Capitol to Schumer's office to demand an audience with him. During a tense meeting in the Senate Democratic leader's suite, Gutiérrez unloaded on Schumer, accusing him and other Democratic senators of ignoring the plight of the Dreamers and "throwing them under the bus." The argument got heated, as Schumer chided Gutiérrez for speaking ill of members of his own party. But in the end, when Republicans muscled a month-long spending bill through the House, Senate Democrats refrained from trying to block it. Privately, Democratic leaders explained their rationale for forgoing a year-end fight with Trump over DACA. They simply did not want to be blamed for a government shutdown.

LIFE IN TWO-YEAR INCREMENTS

WITH INERTIA SETTING IN in Washington, the real-world consequences of DACA's demise were being felt around the country by hundreds of thousands of young immigrants. Itzel Guillen Maganda was one of them.

As a young girl growing up in San Diego, Guillen lived in constant fear that the secret of her birthplace would get out. Born in Mexico City in 1994, Guillen had crossed illegally into the United States at age five, accompanied by her twelve-year-old brother, in a car driven by a man she did not know. Her mother, terrified that she would never see her children again but desperate to get them out of Mexico, followed a few weeks later with Guillen's aunt and cousin. Guillen's earliest memories of America in the weeks before they arrived were of the numbing heartache of not being with her mother or even knowing where she was—along with the sheer joy of trying McDonald's for the first time.

It was delicious. Guillen was terrified.

The anxiety never really subsided, even after her family was reunited and they settled into life in San Diego, ten people to a three-bedroom apartment where Guillen crowded into one bed with her mother, aunt, brother, and cousin. She would often stay up after midnight worrying that her mother, who usually returned at 2 a.m. from her job cleaning offices, might not actually make it home safely. When her mother was late, Guillen would worry that she had been caught and deported. She slept fitfully until she heard the familiar click of her mother's key in the door.

Growing up, Guillen became adept at hiding where she was from. From her mother, she learned to fear law enforcement; when a police officer was around, Guillen knew to stand up straight, be polite, and not call attention to herself. The look on her mother's face and the way her body tensed when any uniformed official was nearby were unspoken signals to Guillen that she had to be on her guard. From her friends at school, she learned never to mention that she had been born elsewhere, or how she came to live in the neighborhood. At the age of twelve she discovered what "undocumented" was when she joined protests in San Diego against legislation to take harsh measures against the roughly 11 million immigrants, like her and her family, living undocumented in the United States. Around the same time, Guillen confided in a friend at school that she was from Mexico and had snuck into San Diego as a child. She was heartbroken when the girl responded by calling her an "illegal alien." As a teen, she was in the car when her mother mistakenly blew through a stop sign and was pulled over by a police officer. Guillen's mother did not have a driver's license, and as the officer slowly walked to his car to call in the infraction, the two exchanged horrified expressions. "If I have to go, we go together," her mother said. Guillen nodded silently, then texted her brother to say they might never see him again. After what seemed like an eternity, the officer returned. They were free to go, he said amiably, with a warning.

But for every near miss, there was another panic-inducing risk around the corner. When she took the SATs, Guillen hesitated before filling in the bubble indicating that, "NO," she was not a United States citizen. She shielded her paper with a hand, worried that someone would see. But when Guillen turned eighteen, everything changed. Barack Obama signed a directive creating the Deferred Action for Childhood Arrivals program, or DACA. It was for people like Guillen, whose parents had brought them to the United States as kids and who had grown up, in almost every way, as Americans. She applied, and within a few months Guillen received a permit, which gave her legal status for two years. She would be able to get a job. She enrolled at San Diego State University and studied political science. Guillen still lived in fear of what might happen to her mother, who remained undocumented, living and working in the shadows. But for the first time she could remember, she stopped worrying about being deported herself.

That all changed the night that Donald Trump was elected. Guillen knew in an instant that DACA was doomed—that it was only a matter of time until he would end the program. Trump's public waffling on the issue, his musing aloud about what a tough decision it was for him to consider hurting "these incredible kids," only made things worse. "The dangling," she would say later, "that was torture." Even though Trump was hesitating, she took matters into her own hands. Guillen applied to renew her DACA permit in July 2017, a year early, just to be certain that she would be safe if the president ended the program. But she went further. As a DACA recipient, Guillen was shielded from deportation and had legal status to work or go to school. But the program could not fix the problem of her initial illegal entry into the United States. She would never be able to adjust her legal status to become a permanent resident until she had left the country and reentered legally.

So Guillen decided to attempt the second-riskiest journey of her life. She hired an immigration lawyer and applied for emergency permission to travel to Mexico and return to the United States afterward. When she received it, her colleagues told her there was no time to waste—she had to go *right now.* Nobody knew when Trump would decide to end DACA, and what might happen to people in the program when he did. So on a sunny day in late August, with a duffel bag slung over her shoulder and butterflies in her stomach, Itzel left her home in San Diego in a car driven by a friend and they made the short drive across the border into Mexico. She stayed five days in Tijuana, visiting migrant shelters and deported veterans, and talking about her own experience growing up undocumented in the shadow of the border wall. She walked on the beach near the hulking structure, taking in the colorful slats of the wall and the Customs and Border Protection vehicle just beyond on the U.S. side. She ate tacos stuffed with meat and hugged the deported parents of Dreamers, people just like her mother—except they had gotten unlucky instead of lucky when it mattered most. When it came time to return to the United States, the trip back was harrowing. Once again in a car approaching the border, Guillen flashed back to her five-year-old self, uncertain and afraid. Only back then, she did not know enough to have been worried about being detained by an agent at the border. This time, her heart was in her throat for the entire hour-long wait to approach the port of entry. Once there, as she sat waiting to be processed, Guillen had a moment of panic when a border agent called her forward by name. But he was only making conversation; seeing her surname, he wanted to know if she was of Filipino descent. Guillen didn't fully exhale until the car she was riding in had crossed the border and she was safely back in the United States.

Days later, Trump announced he was, indeed, ending DACA. Guillen helped organized an evening rally at Waterfront Park in downtown San Diego, where crowds of people protesting the decision held signs that said, "We Are All Immigrants," "Dreams Don't Have Borders," and "Defend DACA." Standing in front of the crowd that night, Guillen delivered a message of hope and optimism for the Dreamers, saying that Trump's actions had galvanized a powerful movement that was showing its determination to stand strong against his agenda. It was only after she stepped down from the stage and hugged a colleague, the mother of another Dreamer whose future was now uncertain, that Guillen broke down in tears. She was back to living in fear for her future. She took up running to ease her anxiety and postponed a decision about whether to go back to school and pursue an advanced degree.

"It's just really hard," Guillen said, "to make decisions in two-year increments."

FORCED REMOVAL

ELAINE DUKE WAS IN agony again.

It was November 5, 2017, the first Sunday of the month, and on Monday she would have to decide the fate of more than 300,000 immigrants who had been living and working legally in the United States, some for more than two decades, under a program known as Temporary Protected Status. They had homes, families, jobs. And yet the White House was putting enormous pressure on Duke to terminate TPS and send them home, essentially declaring that the United States would no longer be a refuge from the natural disasters and violence that had forced them to flee their homes in Haiti, Honduras, Nicaragua, and El Salvador. The law said that as acting secretary of homeland security, Duke had to decide what to do, but she just didn't feel right about it. Sitting in front of a laptop computer at her townhouse overlooking the Occoquan River a half hour south of Washington, Duke typed out a memo to herself, recording her doubts for posterity. She documented the intense campaign that Miller and others had waged for weeks to impose what she termed an "America First view of the TPS decision" and noted that Secretary of State Rex Tillerson and the National Security Council had sent her reports urging termination.

And yet, she wrote, most of the evidence supported the idea that there would be serious negative consequences if she ended TPS. "Most notably, the Department of State recommendation states that neither El Salvador or Honduras have the current capacity to accept and assimilate the TPS individuals back to their country without major disruption," Duke wrote in the memo, which she classified as *CONFIDENTIAL/NOFORN/LAW ENFORCEMENT SENSITIVE* to ensure that it would not be released to the public or distributed to foreign nationals. (The memo, and hundreds of other documents, would later be released as part of a lawsuit challenging the administration's TPS policies.) Duke knew that Miller and Sessions were obsessed with reducing illegal immigration, yet Duke noted in her memo that reports from the DHS Office of Intelligence and Analysis and the Customs and Border Protection's intelligence officials had determined that ending Temporary Protected Status would make the situation at the southern border worse, not better. "A CBP Intelligence Note stated that the termination of TPS for Haiti, Honduras or El Salvador will likely cause an increase in migrants crossing illegally from the United States to Canada and claiming refugee status," Duke wrote. In the end, she lamented, "I do not have all the necessary information to make this determination in an appropriately deliberative manner prior to the time specified."

Earlier in the day, two of Trump's top aides had called to lean on her. Tom Bossert, the president's homeland security adviser, and Zach Fuentes, the deputy White House chief of staff, stressed that the decision would be criticized no matter what she did. And they insisted the conditions that led to the TPS designations no longer existed. "Gutless fed bureaucrats have extended" TPS in the past, they said, according to notes that Duke scribbled on the back of a five-page printout of section 244 of the Immigration and Nationality Act. Three and a half weeks earlier, around the same time that Duke had frantically called a meeting of her aides to brainstorm about legislative proposals that could be traded for a DACA bill, Trump had nominated Kirstjen Nielsen, Kelly's top aide at the White House, to be the next homeland security secretary. Now, with only hours to go before the TPS deadline, the White House was not letting up. Bossert and Fuentes told Duke that they didn't want Nielsen to have to deal with the issue so soon after being confirmed. "Extremely disappointed if kick into lap of next sec," Duke jotted down. But she stood her ground, telling them the same thing she later wrote in her memo.

"I have concluded that additional time is necessary for me to gather further information and further evaluate it," she wrote. She was more comfortable with terminating TPS for Haiti, Nicaragua, and El Salvador. She agreed in principle that Congress never intended for the program to be permanent. But she had all but decided to put off the decision for Honduras, triggering an automatic six-month extension of the TPS protections for tens of thousands of immigrants.

It would not, she knew, be a popular decision inside the White House.

Nearly thirty years earlier, when President George H. W. Bush signed the law that created Temporary Protected Status on November 29, 1990, the civil war in El Salvador had been raging for a decade. Death squads and massacres had led to the killing of more than 75,000 Salvadorans, many of whom simply disappeared amid the violence and chaos. Under the new American immigration law, refugees from the war who had fled to the United States were granted legal status, given the opportunity to apply for work permits, and told they could stay for almost two years. In the twenty-eight years that followed, the United States government granted similar protections to citizens of twenty-two countries, as America sought to help Liberians fleeing a civil war in 1991, Nicaraguans and Hondurans seeking safety from Hurricane Mitch in 1998, and Haitians displaced by a massive earthquake in 2010 that killed more than 100,000 people. Unlike some other immigration programs, TPS offered only the most basic benefits: the right to be in the United States legally and work permits for those who registered with the government and did not commit crimes. Beneficiaries had no opportunity to become permanent residents or American citizens. And they generally did not qualify for public benefits like food stamps or housing vouchers.

Over time, some countries dropped off the list as natural disasters ebbed, wars ended, and conditions improved. Still, in some places, recovery was slow or nonexistent. Rather than send the refugees back to countries still wracked by poverty, war, hunger, and crime, Democratic and Republican presidents repeatedly extended TPS, turning the temporary protections into a kind of quasi-permanent status. Citizens from El Salvador, Honduras, Haiti, and other places put down roots. They married, had children, started businesses, attended college, bought houses, and paid taxes. By the end of 2016, about 85,000 Hondurans had been living in the United States for nearly twenty years. More than 250,000 Salvadorans had spread throughout the country, many of them protected by TPS after a second designation following a 2001 earthquake that destroyed 100,000 homes. Haitians fleeing the earthquake in 2010 had settled down in the United States as their country struggled to recover.

There had always been some in the government who tried to end the program, arguing that TPS was creating a sense of entitlement. If the United States wasn't careful, they argued, the country would find itself with hundreds of thousands of people who would never leave. Others believed that TPS was a useful tool to help countries in severe crisis, many of which had partnered with the United States in fights against communism or terror. In their view, TPS was part of a larger diplomatic relationship that helped prop up struggling allies and advance American interests. Over the years, that view won out, and with it, any appetite for taking the politically unappealing step of ending the status waned. Successive administrations, with the support of Republicans and Democrats in Congress, repeatedly extended TPS.

Then Trump came along. Egged on by Miller and Sessions, he was determined to transform the nation's immigration system from one based on family ties and humanitarian considerations into one that was singularly focused on attracting skilled workers and those with advanced educations. Refugees who had been admitted to the United States because of political strife or natural disasters didn't meet the test. At his meeting with Trump at Bedminster during the transition, Kobach had urged the president to end the TPS grants, which he viewed as an egregious abuse of a program intended to offer short-term, temporary help to people from countries in distress.

"You've got to move on that," Kobach told Trump.

The administration's first TPS decision came in the spring of 2017, seven months before Duke sat in her house agonizing. At the time, John Kelly was still secretary of homeland security and he knew that Trump and Miller were primed to end the status. But the social and economic conditions in Haiti continued to be grim. Even for Kelly, who agreed that the program needed to be terminated, it was hard to argue with the American ambassador to Haiti and others at the State Department who were insisting that Haiti was in no condition to accept all of its citizens back. As the former commander of U.S. forces in the Southern Hemisphere during the Obama administration, Kelly was familiar with the ongoing strife in Haiti, and he knew things had not improved much since.

But inside DHS, officials responsible for evaluating Haiti's TPS designation were feeling immense pressure from the White House to recommend terminating the program. The first Haiti decision memorandum drafted by DHS officials on March 2 strongly urged Kelly to extend Haiti's TPS designation for eighteen months, writing that there remain "continued extraordinary and temporary conditions in Haiti that prevent Haitian nationals from safely returning to Haiti." That began to change as Miller's allies in the White House weighed in. In an April 17 email from Gene Hamilton to David Lapan, Kelly's communications director, Hamilton wrote that "African countries are toast" when it comes to continuing TPS, and told Lapan that "Haiti is up next." In the weeks that followed, DHS bureaucrats were directed to rewrite the decision memo for Kelly, changing the conclusions to suggest that the devastation from the 2010 earthquake had "been largely ameliorated."

Conflicted and under pressure from the White House, Kelly cast about for more information that might help justify doing what the president and Miller wanted. In an email to Nielsen about Haiti, Kelly directed her to gather "details on how many are on public and private relief, how many school aged kids in school, how many convicted of crimes of any kind." His directive quickly got sent down the chain, where it stunned the veteran civil servants. Never before had anyone asked for that kind of information about TPS recipients. They didn't qualify for public benefits, and there was nothing in the law that made any of that relevant to whether Haitians in the United States should remain protected by TPS. More to the point, that data didn't exist. In a series of emails to the political appointees at DHS, the experts said that no one had collected information about criminal acts or welfare use among Haitians living in the United States under the TPS program.

Kelly was also getting pressure from another member of the White House staff. Omarosa Manigault Newman, the director of communications for the Office of Public Liaison at the White House, had taken it upon herself to become the unofficial liaison to the Haitian government. Newman was a friend of Trump's from his NBC reality show *The Apprentice*, where television viewers got to know her as a ruthless and combative drama queen who specialized in sowing conflict and who, as the only African American on the show, often injected race into the conversation. She had an odd and somewhat ill-defined role in the White House, popping up at meetings on a wide variety of topics, and always when the president had African American visitors. She had been part of the delegation sent to Haiti to attend the inauguration of Haitian president Jovenel Moïse just days after Trump took office. After she returned, she kept in frequent contact with Haitian officials, telling them that she had the ear of the president and would make sure that TPS was renewed. One day, Newman went up to Kelly and introduced herself, saying, "I'm Omarosa, and I'm in charge of Haiti." Kelly had never seen her before. "What's an Omarosa?" he said. "And I don't see it that way."

In the end, Kelly reluctantly agreed to extend TPS for Haiti for six months. In a statement, he said that "conditions in Haiti supporting its designation continue to be met at this time." (Newman issued her own statement bragging about having talked to Trump about the issue after she returned from Haiti.) Still, Kelly made it clear that the reprieve for Haiti's TPS population would be short-lived.

At a meeting with the Congressional Hispanic Caucus, Kelly responded to sharp questions about his decision. Ending TPS is "a difficult choice because these individuals are living their lives legally," he told the lawmakers.

But he warned them that his decision to renew TPS for Haitians was not likely to be repeated. "It is a temporary status and it has gone beyond what it was intended to be," Kelly told the group. In his formal announcement, Kelly issued a public warning to Haitians who were allowed to live and work in the United States because of the TPS law.

"Beneficiaries are encouraged to prepare for their return to Haiti," Kelly urged, "in the event Haiti's designation is not extended again."

Another TPS debate rolled around in late summer. About 1,000 refugees from Sudan, a poor country in northeast Africa beset by its third civil war, had been living legally in the United States since 1997, thanks to TPS. Trump's political appointees were determined to bring that to an end. But there was a problem. The 1990 law that created the status required that the decision about whether to extend TPS for up to eighteen months be based on extensive assessments by State Department experts about whether the conditions in the country had improved enough to send the refugees home. And the veteran diplomats in the State Department hadn't yet embraced the "end TPS" message. They were still documenting the dire conditions that existed in places like Sudan.

That problem became obvious in late August, when Francis Cissna, then the director of immigration policy at DHS, received a twenty-five-page draft memo for Duke ending TPS for Sudan. Cissna had been part of Hamilton's tightly knit group that helped to draft immigration executive orders during the transition. The son of a Peruvian immigrant and the husband of a woman whose mother was a Palestinian refugee, Cissna was an unlikely ideological ally for Miller. He spoke only Spanish to his children at home, and he often spoke warmly about immigrants. "Our family is literally a product of our nation's legal immigration system," he told lawmakers during his confirmation hearing in May of 2017 to become director of U.S. Citizenship and Immigration Services. He noted that his testimony would probably be the longest stretch that his children had ever heard him speak English. But nearly two decades of work at the State Department, DHS, and on Capitol Hill had instilled in him a fierce determination to ensure that the nation's immigration laws were enforced and obeyed. Shortly after taking over at USCIS, Cissna changed its mission statement, eliminating the previous pledge to "secure America's promise as a nation of immigrants," replacing it with one that said the agency "administers the nation's lawful immigration system." He thought of himself as different from Miller, and resented that his zeal for law and order was too often confused with being a hard-ass, malicious, or racist. But Cissna was a true believer in Trump's agenda of blowing up the immigration system to make it fairer to American workers and more faithful to the law, and he volunteered for his campaign. He fully supported the idea that TPS should be ended.

But as Cissna read through the Sudan draft, he grew increasingly annoyed. Paragraph after paragraph drew on work from State Department diplomats, who described the ongoing crisis in Sudan that justified keeping the TPS program in place. "Because the conditions supporting Sudan's TPS designation persist, termination does not appear to be warranted," the USCIS draft said. And yet, on page 5, the memo concluded with the following: "USCIS recommends termination."

"This memo reads like one person who strongly supports extending TPS for Sudan wrote everything up to the recommendation section," Cissna wrote in an email to his colleagues at DHS. "And then someone who opposes extension snuck up behind the first guy, clubbed him over the head, pushed his senseless body out of the way, and finished the memo. Am I missing something?"

Just after noon the next day, Kathy Nuebel Kovarik, the chief at the USCIS Office of Policy and Strategy and another member of Hamilton's secret transition group, sent an urgent note to her staff. "We're getting questions about the Sudan TPS notice and how the rationale for termination reads," she wrote. "We're going to need to cut/redraft that section." The response that she got back from Brandon Prelogar, one of her staffers, offered a blunt choice: they could include only the "country conditions" that supported terminating TPS, but that might open them up to charges that they were cherry-picking the evidence. Or, Prelogar said, they could simply eliminate all mentions of "country conditions."

"The country conditions are what they are," Prelogar wrote. "If they're uncomfortable with the termination conclusion following from them, and they want to stick with that conclusion, we propose paring down that section."

Two weeks later, at Duke's urging, Hamilton himself cut the memo further, removing examples of human rights violations by the Sudanese government that State Department officials had included in their analysis. Duke had told Hamilton that inclusion of human rights violations in the memo was not relevant to whether or not TPS should be extended. But Prelogar was exasperated. "Based on what we've seen to date, State would likely object to the removal of examples of human rights violations— pared down as the language already was—that was in there," he wrote about Hamilton's edits. Prelogar, a career diplomat, said in the email what others at the State Department and DHS were thinking.

"This could be read as taking another step toward providing an incomplete and lopsided country conditions presentation to support termination," he wrote, "which may increase the likelihood of criticism from external stakeholders to that effect."

Tom Shannon was one of the State Department diplomats who was objecting to what the White House had in mind.

A thirty-four-year veteran diplomat who had for years managed America's relationship with Latin America, Shannon was the most senior official who had served in the State Department under Obama to continue working there after Trump's inauguration. For the twelve days before Rex Tillerson was confirmed, Shannon served as the acting secretary of state, and then returned to his post as undersecretary of state for political affairs. It came as no surprise to Shannon that TPS would be under assault from the new regime. He had watched Trump's campaign with alarm, and understood that the TPS program already had a target on its back. Saving the biggest of the TPS programs—for Honduras, El Salvador, and Haiti— would require building a strong case that the United States couldn't afford to send the immigrants home. He directed the ambassadors in the affected countries to begin preparing their analyses of the "country conditions" that would determine whether TPS continued.

On June 29, Heide B. Fulton, the chargé d'affaires in Tegucigalpa, made her case in a cable to Tillerson for extending TPS for Hondurans. "Honduras continues to suffer from the same serious security and economic challenges that have led many recipients of TPS to remain in the United States," she wrote, noting that Honduras had one of the highest murder rates in the world. "Adding tens of thousands of deportees to an economy that is not prepared to integrate them will only exacerbate the principal cause of irregular migration." She did not mince words: Giving the government of Honduras more time before canceling TPS is "directly in the U.S. national interests." Jean Elizabeth Manes, the ambassador in El Salvador, sent her cable a week later, and echoed her colleague. She cited a "climate of fear and hopelessness" in the country, complicated by intense violence, a 2016 drought that devastated the sugarcane industry, and a government that "cannot provide basic services." And the gang violence is overwhelming, Manes wrote. "Many parents in El Salvador refuse to even send their children to school out of fear of the gangs."

Even before the ambassadors in El Salvador and Honduras weighed in, the two State Department agencies responsible for evaluating the TPS program were pursuing two very different strategies to preserve it. At the Bureau of Population, Refugees, and Migration, Simon Henshaw, a veteran diplomat, wanted to take the straightforward approach, arguing that the conditions hadn't changed in either country and there was no reason to put the fate of hundreds of thousands of people at risk. But Henshaw's friend and counterpart in the Bureau of Western Hemisphere Affairs, Francisco "Paco" Palmieri, wanted to try a more subtle play. His team drafted up a memo recommending that TPS be ended, just as Trump's team wanted. But they advised that the termination for the three big countries be delayed for thirty-six months—almost until the end of Trump's term in office. (The Nicaragua TPS program, which protected just a few thousand people, could be ended more quickly, they said.) It was never stated plainly, but the idea was obvious: Embrace the president's goal but move slowly enough on it that it would never actually be achieved. Henshaw signed onto the idea, even though both men and their staffs understood what that conclusion could mean for the countries involved. When the reports landed on Shannon's desk, he called Henshaw and Palmieri into his office on the seventh floor and shut the door. No one else was in the room. It was just the three of them.

"Do you guys really believe this?" Shannon demanded.

Both men tried to explain. Yes, they understood the arguments being made by the ambassadors. But senior officials in the Office of Policy Planning, who were close to Miller, had argued strenuously that TPS should be handled in the same way that Trump had treated the DACA program. Terminating it would put pressure on Congress to finally find a better, more permanent solution. There was also the legal argument. State Department lawyers, with the blessing of the Policy Planning staff, had taken a literal reading of the 1990 law. If the conditions that originally gave rise to the TPS designation—a hurricane, earthquake, or civil war—no longer existed, then TPS must be terminated, they told Palmieri and Henshaw. At least if we wind it down over thirty-six months, there will be ample time for the political process to work and enact legislation to preserve some status for TPS beneficiaries, they argued.

"Listen," Shannon told them that day in his office. "Our job is not to implement the dictates of the Domestic Policy Council. Our job is to give the Secretary of State the best foreign policy advice possible." For nearly twenty years, the State Department had concluded that TPS was justified given the conditions in each of these countries. What could possibly have changed in the last eighteen months to justify a different conclusion?

"Go back," he said. "I want you to sit down with your staff, and I want you to reflect on this and come back to me with what you really believe."

Henshaw's team reversed course, reverting to his original instinct and rewriting its report to recommend that TPS be extended for El Salvador, Honduras, Haiti, and Nicaragua. The Bureau of Western Hemisphere Affairs, under Palmieri, stuck to its original conclusion, betting on the idea of a long delay in the implementation. Instead of reaching the usual consensus, their reports would be sent to Tillerson as a rare "split memo." For Shannon, it was a moment of truth. He rarely tried to tip the scales himself, but this was a special case. The human cost of lifting TPS weighed on him. Sitting in his office, Shannon typed up a two-page memo for Tillerson's eyes only.

During World War II, about 120,000 Japanese Americans were sent to internment camps in what would become a painful and ugly stain on the country's history. Ending TPS for all four countries, Shannon wrote in his memo to Tillerson, would directly affect almost four times as many people. When you add spouses and children, the number could rise to as many as 800,000 people. Those immigrants were living legally in the United States as productive members of their communities. They posed no national security risk. His message to Tillerson about the impact on those immigrants was unsparing: This would be one of the largest forced removals in American history, Shannon wrote.

He also made the diplomatic case against ending TPS. The United States had long and complicated relationships with the countries, he wrote. America partners with them to address migration issues, drug trafficking, and transnational crime. Rescinding TPS would be a step backward. It would undermine confidence in the United States as a diplomatic partner and it would put an impossible strain on their economies. Sending the TPS recipients home would put an end to millions of dollars in remittances that they send home to families. And there was no way the countries could produce jobs for tens of thousands of returning migrants. Keep in mind, Shannon concluded in his memo, that the law gives the decision about TPS to the secretary of homeland security, not the secretary of state. The department's only role is to make a foreign policy assessment. On that score, Shannon wrote, the record is clear.

Eyes-only memos were often hand-carried to the secretary, but Shannon wanted this one in the official record. He instructed his chief of staff to put it into Everest, the State Department computer system that gives documents tracking numbers. The idea was to have a historical record of his message to the secretary. After he sent the memo, Shannon went to see Margaret Peterlin, Tillerson's chief of staff. The secretary of state should be careful, Shannon told her. Those urging him to support a termination of TPS were using him to do the work of Miller's Domestic Policy Council. "The secretary should not permit himself or his staff to be used this way," he said. In fact, along with the memos from Shannon, Henshaw, and Palmieri, Tillerson also received one from Brian Hook, the department's policy chief, which argued to end TPS for Honduras, Haiti, and El Salvador on a much shorter timeline.

For weeks, Shannon heard nothing. Then, as Tillerson concluded one of his regular Monday morning staff meetings in the secure conference room on the seventh floor, he abruptly raised the issue. There's going to be some press about a decision I made, Tillerson told the group of assistant secretaries and others in the room. I have decided to rescind Temporary Protected Status, he said. It was a law that had been misused for years. That might be the kind of sloppiness that other administrations would tolerate, Tillerson said, but not anymore.

Shannon was stunned. Tillerson had not come to him first, a breach of protocol and basic decency. Shannon spoke up. "Sir, you do realize that this is a decision for DHS? All we are doing is making a determination on country conditions." Yes, Tillerson replied, echoing the arguments of the Policy Planning staff about how the country conditions no longer supported extending the TPS protections. He had accepted their recommendation for a shorter delay in ending the program. Later in the day, at a smaller gathering of undersecretaries in a smaller conference room, Tillerson asked Shannon to work with the Policy Planning office to devise a way for Congress to regularize the status of people on TPS after the programs were ended. Shannon was dismayed. "Sir, that's not a State Department responsibility or authority," he told his boss. "That lies with DHS and the White House." Tillerson was unmoved. In a formal letter to Duke that he sent on Halloween, the secretary of state acknowledged the likelihood of diplomatic disruption, but nonetheless urged her to end TPS for all four countries.

"The fact remains that the conditions in these countries do not—in the State Department's judgment—meet the legal requirements for extension," he wrote. Tillerson followed up with a call to Duke. The conditions in these countries are what they are, he told her. But this is the way it has to be. This is politics in Washington right now.

Shannon had worked in Democratic and Republican administrations for more than three decades, and he understood that policy approaches often shifted under different presidents. But he considered the TPS decision a grave diplomatic mistake and a human rights tragedy. The sense of failure that he felt prompted a grim gallows humor. He jokingly told people who asked about that period in his life that he had contemplated whether to hang himself in his closet. In the last weeks before he retired, Shannon held town hall meetings with State Department employees under his supervision, some of whom openly wept about Trump's assault on migrants.

— 18 —

"JUST BITE THE BULLET"

THREE DAYS AFTER HALLOWEEN, the White House convened a Principals Committee meeting, which brings together the government's most senior officials, in an attempt to ratchet up the pressure on Elaine Duke. Jim Nealon, the DHS assistant secretary who had infuriated Miller and Hamilton by dragging his feet months earlier, had pleaded with Duke in a memo to extend TPS for Honduras, El Salvador, and Haiti, arguing that eliminating the program would force 300,000 people "into the shadows" by taking away their legal right to live and work in the United States. But this time, Nealon was outflanked. Tillerson had sent his recommendation to end the TPS programs on the same day. And Duke was on the hot seat again to make a decision.

The agenda for the meeting at 9:15 a.m. in the White House Situation Room was distributed by Keith Kellogg, the retired Army lieutenant general who served as the executive secretary for the National Security Council. But there was little doubt that Miller was the driving force behind it. In previous administrations, similar meetings provided a neutral forum for the president's top advisers to debate pressing issues. There was nothing neutral about Friday's gathering. The first two sentences of the agenda's two-page memo bluntly described the purpose of the discussion:

"To coordinate the conditions and process for terminating temporary protected status (TPS) for aliens from El Salvador, Honduras, Nicaragua, and Haiti. The Acting Secretary of Homeland Security must make a decision by Monday, November 6, 2017." Three days from now. After two paragraphs of background, the memo made it clear what Miller and the others thought. "Extending TPS for any or all of the four countries would prolong the distortion between the temporary protections that TPS was designed to provide and current circumstances."

Duke arrived at the Situation Room braced for what she knew was coming. It would be like the DACA debate all over again. The Trump loyalists saw her as an obstructionist standing in the way of the immigration policies that the president wanted to put in place. And they still thought she was an easy mark, someone who could be rolled. John Sullivan, the deputy secretary of state, was there in Tillerson's place, and he made the case for ending the program. "Conditions do not warrant TPS extension," Sullivan said, according to notes that Duke took of the meeting. Mercedes Schlapp, the White House strategic communications director, focused on the political impact of the decision. Termination of the TPS protections would put pressure on Congress to decide who gets to come into the United States based on the skills they bring, she said. Schlapp was also concerned about the impact that the decision could have on the midterm elections in 2018, according to Duke's notes.

Then it was the attorney general's turn. The law is clear, Sessions insisted. The administration "can't keep certifying." Duke told the group that she did not feel like she had enough time to make a decision, especially on Honduras. "Just bite the bullet," the attorney general told her, suggesting that it would be legally suspect to make a different decision for each of the four countries. Think about what the American people would say if Duke extended the TPS programs, certifying the aliens to remain in the United States rather than be sent home, the attorney general pressed. The American people would want to know: "How did you let this happen?" That had been the case for years in previous administrations. "No one has the guts to pull the trigger," Sessions said. Duke's notes underlined the attorney general's next comment two times: "Cannot certify."

The intense discussion shifted to how Congress might react to the end of the TPS programs, which had broad, bipartisan support among lawmakers. On that point, Sessions was firm. The administration should pressure House Speaker Paul Ryan to pass a strong immigration bill that would include a more permanent solution for allowing many of the people from the four countries to stay in the United States, he said. But nothing will happen in Congress until the TPS program is ended, he told Duke. "Until we end the eligibility, amnesty vote is non-starter," he said, according to Duke's notes.

As she left the meeting, Duke was noncommittal, saying that she appreciated the input. She agreed that Nicaragua could easily handle the return of about 2,500 citizens who had been living in the United States. But it was clear to everyone around the table that Duke was still uncertain about the 85,000 Hondurans that would be sent home if she ended the TPS designation for that country.

Feeling under pressure like never before, she headed home to weigh her choices.

On Monday morning, Duke attended her usual intelligence briefing in the department's SCIF, or Sensitive Compartmented Information Facility, where top secret material could be safely discussed. At the end of the meeting, she asked a top aide to stay behind. "I just can't deal with this administration anymore," she said, breaking down in tears. "What these people want to do is just wrong, and they're pressuring me to do things I think are wrong, and I'm not going to do it the way they want me to." Duke said she did not think ending TPS for Honduras abruptly was the right thing to do, and she expressed frustration with "the echo chamber in the White House and everyone being scared of the president." Distraught and stressed, she told her aide: "I don't know how long I can stay in this administration."

By then, word of Duke's indecision on Honduras had traveled across the globe, to Japan, where Kelly was traveling with Trump for meetings with Emperor Akihito and Prime Minister Shinzō Abe. It was thirteen hours later there—the middle of the night. Kelly had been woken up by an aide, who described Duke as having refused to make a decision about Honduras. Kelly was furious. Not only should it have been clear to Duke what Trump wanted, but refusing to make a decision would saddle Nielsen, his close ally, with a controversial decision as one of her first acts after being confirmed as the secretary of homeland security. With the clock ticking toward the deadline at the end of the day on the East Coast, Kelly called Duke.

Just make a decision, he barked on the call, which included Zach Fuentes, Kelly's deputy, and Tom Bossert, the president's homeland security adviser. Kelly told Duke that she would be criticized no matter what she decided—it came with the job. No one knew that better than Kelly. He knew what it meant to be a cabinet secretary, and he was careful not to tell Duke what to do. But it was clear to Duke what "make a decision" meant. Kelly and the rest of the administration wanted the programs to be terminated, with a final date set for the immigrants to be sent back to their countries of origin. She was refusing to toe the line.

Just before 3:30 Monday afternoon, Duke sent an email to Kelly informing him of her TPS decisions. The deadlines for El Salvador and Haiti were still a few weeks away, so the fate of those programs did not have to be decided yet. She would terminate TPS for Nicaragua, she told Kelly, giving people in that country twelve months to return home. But Honduras was different. TPS for that country would be extended for six months under a formal "no decision" that she would issue that day. "Much of the documentation I received within the last 5 days is conflicting and I have not had sufficient time to deconflict it," she wrote to Kelly. Duke insisted that even her "no decision" would send a tough message to the Hondurans that the program would eventually be terminated, but with a clear plan about how to deal with the consequences. "By not affirmatively extending, I'm stating that I'm not satisfied that the country conditions remain— but not yet sure how to best end TPS for this country," she wrote. Taken together, she argued in the email, her decisions "will send a clear signal that TPS in general is coming to a close. I believe it is consistent with the President's position on immigration." In a news release, the Department of

Homeland Security explained that Duke believed "additional information is necessary regarding the TPS designation for Honduras, and therefore has made no determination regarding Honduras at this time. As a result of the inability to make a determination, the TPS designation for Honduras will be automatically extended for six months."

Duke had stood her ground on Honduras, refusing to make what she considered a rushed judgment. But when word leaked a few days later about the call from Japan, Kelly was furious all over again. The news stories suggested that Kelly had pressured Duke to terminate TPS for Honduras. At 3:14 a.m., he took out his iPad and sent an email to the senior staff. "The reporting on my phone call with Secretary (Acting) Duke is foolishness," he wrote. "The conversation revolved around 'make a decision.' That the decision on TPS was entirely hers." He was clearly frustrated that the conversation had leaked out. "Only Elaine can set the record straight. I hope she does." He added: "I will be calling the Honduran president today to correct this poorly sourced article."

Duke was contrite. In a response to Kelly a few hours later, she apologized for all "this noise" about the telephone call. "Unfortunately, I think you are getting inaccurate information on me and positions," she wrote in an email to Kelly, alluding to the description of her as refusing to make a decision, "which is probably why you were woken up in the first place." Kelly responded quickly, sending a short note back, this time from Da Nang, Vietnam, where Trump was by then. "Am with you. I think it's best if you set the record straight." Sarah Sanders agreed and advised Duke to paper over any internal discord. In an email to Duke, she wrote, "if you are willing, I think best way to end it is for you to go on record saying what took place on call and that you and gen Kelly as well as rest of administration working together, etc."

In a statement that evening, Duke called the press reports "seriously flawed," and said that Kelly had "consistently reiterated that, as the Acting Secretary, the current decisions were mine to make and should be done in accordance with the existing law. At no time did he pressure me to terminate TPS for Nicaragua, Honduras or El Salvador." And she denied reports that she had offered to resign.

"I have no plans to go anywhere and reports to the contrary are untrue," Duke said.

But Duke's resistance was effectively over, and she soon informed Kelly that she intended to resign once Nielsen was confirmed to replace her.

On November 20, Duke announced that she had decided to terminate the TPS program for Haiti, doing what Kelly had hesitated to do six months earlier. "Acting Secretary Duke determined that those extraordinary but temporary conditions caused by the 2010 earthquake no longer exist. Thus, under the applicable statute, the current TPS designation must be terminated," DHS wrote in its announcement. On December 5, the Senate confirmed Nielsen to lead the department permanently, handing responsibility for the future TPS decisions to her.

Days later, the new secretary received a call from Jim McGovern, a twenty-one-year Democratic congressman from central Massachusetts. McGovern had worked for longtime Democratic representative Joe Moakley in the late 1980s. At Moakley's request in 1989, he had traveled to El Salvador to lead a congressional inquiry into the killings of six Jesuit priests by the U.S.-backed Salvadoran military. A framed copy of an honorary degree from Central American University in San Salvador is on display in McGovern's office. In 1990, McGovern had helped write the original TPS legislation providing protection for Salvadorans fleeing the violence in their country, and in the years since, the Massachusetts congressman had become the leading advocate for the program.

In a letter to Duke in mid-September signed by 115 of his colleagues, McGovern had argued that terminating TPS would "needlessly tear apart families" and would "likely bring destabilizing consequences throughout the region." When he placed the phone call to Nielsen from his office in the Cannon House Office Building, McGovern was hopeful that he might convince her to change her mind. But the conversation did not start off well.

Nielsen told McGovern that the devastating 2001 earthquake in El Salvador no longer justified extending TPS for that country. The department's lawyers, she said, had concluded that the program must be terminated. "That's ridiculous," McGovern said, demanding to see her legal analysis. The law was written to give the secretary wide latitude to consider the overall conditions in the countries, he said. And the drug and gang violence in El Salvador has made the country even more dangerous than it was during its long and brutal war in the 1980s. Nielsen was unmoved, echoing the line that other Trump officials had repeatedly seized on: "You know, Temporary Protected Status means temporary," she told McGovern. "The key word in that is 'protected,'" responded McGovern, who later recalled his frustration with Nielsen as the call went on. She was pleasant and polite, but unmoved by McGovern's arguments. "Clearly she had no idea about the statute. There was not a lot of familiarity with the law, let me put it that way. It was frustrating. I said, 'This is crazy, this is cruel.'" McGovern tried to explain the potential impact on Salvadorans who had lived in the United States for years, recalling one man who told him he could never take his thirteen-year-old daughter, an American citizen, back to El Salvador if he was deported. Ending TPS for El Salvador would mean many families would be separated.

"I thought maybe there was room for some reconsideration," McGovern recalled later. "But clearly there wasn't."

On January 8, 2018, Nielsen ended TPS for the 200,000 Salvadorans living in the United States. The official announcement said that she based the decision on "careful consideration of available information" and had concluded that "under the applicable statute, the current TPS designation must be terminated." Nielsen made a virtually identical announcement about Honduras on May 4, finally satisfying the administration's desire to declare an end to TPS for all four of the major countries. In the months that followed, the administration made no effort to reach out to Congress to put in place new legislation to permanently protect the recipients of TPS. "If they really wanted us to legislate or remedy this, maybe they would work with us," McGovern said during an interview in his office in early 2019. "Maybe they wouldn't end TPS until we had something in place. How do you treat human beings like this?"

Duke announced her intention to retire from government on Febru-

ary 23, 2018, even as the beneficiaries of TPS and their children began su-
ing the department. One lawsuit alleged that the decision to end TPS for
Haiti violated the due process clause of the Constitution's Fifth Amendment by discriminating against Haitian immigrants on the basis of race
and ethnicity. Another lawsuit argued that the government's reasons for
ending TPS were little more than "pretext for invidious discrimination
and belied by well-established facts." A third cited Trump's remarks that
"all Haitians have AIDS" as evidence that the TPS decisions were based
on an underlying racial animus. Still a fourth claimed that the administration's interpretation of the TPS statute for El Salvador, Haiti, Nicaragua, and Sudan was arbitrary and capricious. Before 2018 ended, a federal
judge overseeing the fourth case imposed a nationwide injunction, forcing
the Trump administration to put the termination of TPS on hold until the
legal issues were resolved.

The plaintiffs "have presented a substantial record supporting their
claim that the Acting Secretary or Secretary of DHS, in deciding to terminate the TPS status of Haiti, El Salvador, Nicaragua and Sudan, changed
the criteria applied by the prior administrations, and did so without any
explanation or justification in violation of the Administrative Procedure
Act," wrote Judge Edward M. Chen, an Obama appointee on the federal
bench in Northern California. It was clear from his ruling that Judge Chen
was receptive to the argument that the TPS decisions had been marred by
the same kind of political agenda that had caused judges to order a halt to
other Trump immigration policies.

"There is also evidence that this may have been done in order to implement and justify a pre-ordained result desired by the White House," he
wrote. "Plaintiffs have also raised serious questions whether the actions
taken by the Acting Secretary or Secretary were influenced by the White
House and based on animus against non-white, non-European immigrants in violation of Equal Protection guaranteed by the Constitution."
He said the issues "are at least serious enough to preserve the status quo."

To the top officials at the Justice Department and DHS, the rulings
were nonsensical. The TPS statute literally had the word *temporary* in its
title. Lawyers in the department were certain that the Supreme Court

would never uphold the lower court rulings. It was, they told the White House, another example of judges imposing their own ideology about immigration on a straightforward legal question. Still, it was infuriating to have to tell Trump that the courts had once again stepped in to prevent him from following through on his promises. Devin O'Malley, a spokesman for Sessions, issued a blistering statement, saying that the judge's ruling "usurps the role of the executive branch in our constitutional order" and promising to "fight for the integrity of our immigration laws and our national security."

"SHITHOLE COUNTRIES"

A FEW DAYS AFTER New Year's 2018, most of the Republican congressional leadership assembled at Fort McNair, the U.S. Army base that sits on a small peninsula between the Anacostia and Potomac Rivers in Washington, D.C., to make their way to a weekend retreat with the president. Paul Ryan, the House speaker; Kevin McCarthy, the majority leader; Steve Scalise, the House whip; and John Cornyn, the second-ranking Republican in the Senate, along with members of their senior staff, boarded V-22 Ospreys—hulking military aircraft that are essentially a cross between a helicopter and a turboprop airplane—and strapped themselves in, bright orange earplugs and all, for a brief and extremely noisy flight to Camp David, the presidential getaway in the Catoctin Mountains of northern Maryland. Mitch McConnell, the majority leader, was traveling up by car for the weekend, which was to include a series of strategy sessions on the year's agenda.

Trump and his guests had traded their business suits and ties for jeans and fleeces or chinos and sport coats for the occasion, set among the comfortably appointed but rustic-looking cabins of the sprawling complex. At a long wooden table in the wood-paneled conference room at the Laurel Lodge, they held a series of discussions about the legislative agenda for the year. There was a detailed briefing on infrastructure from Gary Cohn and an evening screening of *The Greatest Showman*—McCarthy's choice—in the movie theater in Hickory Lodge. Early on, McConnell and McCarthy teamed up for a presentation about the Senate and House perspective on the midterm congressional elections. They argued that Republicans should push a positive message that highlighted economic growth and credited Trump's large tax cuts and aggressive moves to gut federal regulations. They warned of dark clouds on the horizon for their party, which was facing both the headwinds of history—for decades, the party that won the White House had suffered defeat in the midterm congressional contests two years later—and their own set of specific challenges. McCarthy had prepared a detailed overview of polling data, and some of it was sobering. Polls were showing a potentially disastrous year for Republicans, with voters far more inclined to vote for Democrats for Congress and the president's approval rating hovering under 40 percent. Trump jumped in when he heard that. That's not what my guys are telling me—right, Bill? he said, turning to Bill Stepien, his political director. As if on cue, Stepien, paging through a set of thick briefing binders he had arrayed in front of him, began describing a much rosier scenario, in which Trump's numbers were solid and voters were far more likely to vote for a Republican come November. Perplexed, an aide seated nearby peered over to see what data Stepien could possibly be quoting from. He was reading Trump the results for Republicans, the aide later told colleagues, not voters overall.

There was no individual session on immigration, but the Republican leaders recognized they would soon need to deal with the unfinished business of what to do about DACA. The stopgap spending deal they had reached in December would only hold them for a few more weeks before they would again face the possibility of a government shutdown. On top of that, federal spending caps that constrained everything Congress did had to be renegotiated and would need the support of both Republicans and Democrats to pass. Everyone understood that an agreement on the Dreamers was the key to unlocking both deals.

The problem, which had become all too familiar to Republicans, was that it was impossible to figure out what Trump was willing to sign—and they were too divided among themselves to lead the way. Ryan's immigration working group had all but disbanded amid bitter rifts about how to proceed, and the speaker believed that Republicans did not have the votes to push a DACA bill through the House. Some conservative lawmakers wanted to try to muscle through a hard-line bill that tacked Trump's entire immigration wish list onto limited protections for the Dreamers. The House Freedom Caucus privately blamed Ryan for failing to do so, saying he was unwilling to strong-arm enough Republicans to get it done. But moderate Republicans who were nervous about their reelection prospects knew that voting for a measure like that would be a political death sentence. It would almost certainly die in the Senate anyway. The moderates were focusing instead on how they could build an agreement that would be embraced by at least some Democrats and have a prayer of reaching the president's desk and becoming law. As the leaders hunkered down at Camp David that weekend, Ryan insisted to his colleagues that the House simply was not in a position yet to advance the legislation.

McConnell said the Senate would be willing to move first on a potential solution. But they first had to know what the president would support. Days before, Trump had unveiled a ten-year, $18 billion plan to build a wall. But Stephen Miller, who was at the retreat, had been quietly telling lawmakers that the White House would insist on ambitious changes to legal immigration, including limiting how many family members could get green cards and ending the diversity visa lottery. Nielsen, who would announce her decision to end TPS for El Salvador the following Monday, was at Camp David, too. She told the lawmakers that her priorities were funding for the wall and changing the law to vastly expand her department's authority to quickly remove immigrants from the United States, including unaccompanied children and adults claiming asylum. In other words, the White House was all over the map. Senate Republicans and Democrats were scheduled to visit with Trump in a matter of days for a discussion about immigration, and the leaders desperately wanted to be on the same page going in, to maximize their chances of striking a workable deal. But they left Camp David with no clear sense of what Trump's bottom line was.

When the lawmakers arrived at the White House the following Tuesday, it got murkier still.

Trump was in a gregarious mood that morning, seated at the long, rectangular wooden table in the Cabinet Room flanked by senators and representatives from both parties. He invited the presidential press pool in for what was scheduled as a brief glimpse of the meeting—known in the parlance of White House correspondents as a "spray"—and then proceeded to host an hour-long reality show of sorts on the making of an immigration bill. The first audience surprise came in the first few minutes, when Trump said he was thrilled to have Democrats in the room to discuss a DACA deal because he wanted to sign "a bill of love." Keen watchers of his 2016 presidential campaign recalled the phrase, because it echoed language that his archrival Jeb Bush once used to describe illegal immigration—not a crime, Bush had said, but an "act of love." At the time, Trump's campaign had used Bush's words as a cudgel against him, running an advertisement that blared, "Forget love. It's time to get tough!" Now the same message was coming out of Trump's own mouth.

But he was just getting started. After endorsing the idea of a DACA deal that paired legal status for the Dreamers with border security measures, Trump said he would be open to comprehensive immigration reform— a phrase considered toxic to restrictionists, who consider it synonymous with granting "amnesty" to millions of people who have flouted American immigration laws. But as his aides looked on in stunned silence and the cameras continued to roll, Trump went even further, saying he could even support a bill that would create a pathway to citizenship for the rest of the 11 million undocumented immigrants living in the United States. "I'll take the heat," Trump declared.

The president, relishing the spectacle he was staging, barreled on, seemingly in no rush to dismiss the reporters. He careened wildly between policy positions, first declaring that any DACA deal must include measures to end chain migration and eliminate the diversity visa lottery, and then indicating that he would accept any DACA deal that lawmakers brought him. Sensing an opening, Senator Dianne Feinstein, the California Democrat, asked whether the president might be willing to accept a "clean" DACA bill—legislative code-speak for a bill that dealt with one thing only, in this case legal status for the Dreamers. Border security and other immigration changes could come later, Feinstein suggested. "I have no problem," Trump answered. "I think a lot of people would like to see that, but I think we have to do DACA first." At that, McCarthy jumped in to steer Trump away from the precipice from which he appeared ready to leap. "Mr. President, you need to be clear though," McCarthy said. "We have to have security, as the secretary would tell you." Senator John Cornyn, the Republican whip, said what was on everyone's mind. "Part of my job is to count votes in the Senate," he told the president. He reminded Trump that over the weekend at Camp David, both Ryan and McConnell had "made crystal clear that they would not proceed with a bill on the floor of the Senate or the House unless it had your support, unless you would sign it. The lens we need to be looking through is not only what could we agree to among ourselves on a bipartisan basis," Cornyn said, "but what will you sign into law."

Over fifty-five remarkable minutes, Trump had raised more questions about his intentions than he had answered. And when the journalists were ushered out, things got even weirder. Once the cameras had left, Nielsen handed out a four-page list of "must-have" items for any DACA deal—the Miller-designed wish list derived in part from the frenzied brainstorming session that Elaine Duke had convened a few months earlier. The list included $18 billion for the wall, cuts to family-based immigration, and the elimination of the diversity visa, among other conservative demands. It was a far cry from the DACA-first approach Trump had seemed to endorse just moments before, and Durbin said so. The president seemed agitated and caught off guard. "I don't know what this is," Trump erupted. I've never seen it before, and it doesn't represent all of my positions, he said. Just ignore it, he told the lawmakers. In an effort to move toward some consensus, they agreed to deputize McCarthy, Cornyn, and their Democratic counterparts—the "Number Twos," as they were called, as the second-ranking leaders in their parties—to try to forge an agreement on DACA that both sides could accept. But they left the White House as confused as ever about what Trump was willing to sign.

Later that night, a federal judge in California complicated the issue still further. Ruling in the case brought by Janet Napolitano and the University of California, Judge William Alsup ordered the Trump administration to partially restart the DACA program, saying it was unclear whether officials had followed the proper procedures to end it. If Trump's decision were allowed to stand, Judge Alsup wrote, the result would be "hundreds of thousands of individuals losing their work authorizations and deferred action status. This would tear authorized workers from our nation's economy and would prejudice their being able to support themselves and their families, not to mention paying taxes to support our nation." For the moment, DACA was still alive.

On the morning of Thursday, January 11, 2018, Durbin was sitting in a Judiciary Committee meeting when word came from the White House that the president was trying to reach him. In between committee votes, Durbin ducked into the committee's anteroom, one of the few places on Capitol Hill that still boasts a row of old-school telephone booths with folding-glass doors and wooden benches. He wedged himself into a cubicle and found himself patched through to the president. Trump had heard that Durbin and Lindsey Graham had a DACA deal for him, the president told Durbin, and it sounded good—like just what he was looking for. Could he come down to the White House so the three of them could go over the details? Durbin could hardly believe his ears. "Wow," he told a top aide as he emerged from the booth. "I think we may actually have a deal." Durbin punched up Graham's number on his cell phone and told his negotiating partner that he had just had a great conversation with Trump, and they needed to follow up. Graham hung up and dialed the White House. When he reached Trump, the president sounded upbeat. The deal sounds great, Trump said. Come to the White House and tell me more. Graham was elated.

Durbin and Graham had been toiling behind the scenes for months to reach a deal to extend DACA protections, and that week they had finally come up with what they thought was a workable solution. Their plan would give legal status to the DACA recipients and include enough border security measures and other immigration changes to make it palatable to Trump and Republicans. It had not been easy. Durbin had drawn the wrath of progressive groups for including Trump's wall in the proposal, and bitter criticism from the Congressional Black Caucus for proposing to cancel the diversity visa lottery—which granted more than 40 percent of its visas to immigrants from African countries. That very morning, before the president called and summoned him to the Oval Office, Durbin had been scheduled to meet with a group of Asian Pacific American lawmakers and activists who were angry that the proposal he and Graham were working on would eliminate some categories of family-based visas, scaling back one of the primary ways that people from their communities immigrated legally to the United States.

Graham, too, had endured his share of anger from his right flank. He had worked intensively to keep negotiations on track among a small but determined group of senators that included four other Republicans—Jeff Flake of Arizona, Cory Gardner of Colorado, Thom Tillis of North Carolina, and Jim Lankford of Oklahoma—as well as two Democrats, Michael Bennet of Colorado and Robert Menendez of New Jersey. But the group had its issues. Tillis and Lankford were in close touch with the White House and had been quietly but persistently holding out for stricter immigration measures. One day in December, after the group had arrived at a tentative agreement, one of Lankford's aides sent around a lengthy list of additional items—major provisions on enforcement, immigration court proceedings, and sanctuary cities—that would have to be considered to draw the senator's support. Then when the group met just before Christmas to discuss their emerging deal, Lankford and Tillis did not show up. Graham had kicked them out after that. At last, Graham and Durbin felt they had the right mix of hard-edged changes and protections for Dreamers to win the president's support and push the measure through Congress. Now Trump seemed to agree.

Durbin, as the No. 2 Senate Democrat, had a security detail that included a chauffeur-driven Suburban. He sent an aide to meet with the Asian Pacific American group, while he and Graham hopped in the SUV to head for their audience with the president. The car made its way through a pair of black iron gates and up West Executive Avenue, the short drive separating the White House from the Eisenhower Executive Office Building, and deposited the two senators at the awning-covered entrance to the West Wing. They strode in and climbed the stairs to the carpeted lobby, where they took seats to wait for their meeting with Trump. Both men were somewhat giddy with excitement. Gazing around the reception room waiting for Trump to invite them into the Oval Office, Durbin turned to Graham. "This is pretty heady stuff!"

Their mood changed when the door to the lobby swung open and Senator David Perdue appeared. Perdue was a true hard-liner who, along with Senator Tom Cotton, was spearheading the effort to slash legal immigration. Perdue was on the record saying that he would never allow a Dreamer "amnesty" unless it came with deep cuts to family-based immigration. Cotton was next to come through the door, followed by Chuck Grassley and Bob Goodlatte, immigration restrictionists who were the chairmen of the Senate and House Judiciary Committees, and after them, McCarthy, the House majority leader. Before long, Stephen Miller and John Kelly arrived. Graham and Durbin had expected a private briefing with Trump in the Oval Office to seal their deal. Who had invited these guys? Durbin turned to an aide with a grim look on his face. "I think the fix is in."

It was exactly what Graham had been hoping to avoid. For months—on golf courses, on the telephone, and in person—he had been whispering in Trump's ear about this potential deal, hoping to ice out Miller, who Graham viewed as unreasonably hard-line and impossible to work with. But Miller quickly got wind that Graham was trying to go around him. The optics of a meeting between Trump, Graham, and Durbin would be disastrous, Miller thought. And the risks were very real. This was a president who loved to cut any deal, and he was particularly keen to be seen as sympathetic to the Dreamers. Graham was crafty, and would tell Trump what he wanted to hear, using the buzzwords "chain migration" and "diversity visa" that he was listening for. But as Miller saw it, this was an agreement that gave away the store—amnesty in exchange for nothing substantial. The proposal to limit chain migration was a sleight of hand, he thought. It would end it only for undocumented parents of DACA recipients who weren't eligible to bring family members into the United States anyway. Miller wasn't about to let the president be railroaded.

Kelly, too, bristled at the idea of a senator making an end run around him to sell a bad deal to Trump. It was his job to keep order in the West Wing, and that included intervening when the president was being led astray, he thought. It didn't take long for the calls to go out from the White House to Capitol Hill, summoning the half dozen Republicans to come to the Oval Office. One of them, Mario Diaz-Balart, had been casting a vote on the House floor when he was pulled aside without warning by an aide and hustled into a motorcade to the White House. When he entered the West Wing lobby, he went over to Durbin and Graham and the three exchanged quizzical glances and silent shrugs, wondering what was about to unfold. In her office at the DHS complex on Nebraska Avenue, Nielsen got the call. She and Chad Wolf, her chief of staff, jumped into a car and raced to the White House.

Inside the Oval Office, Graham made his best effort to pitch the proposal as a balanced one. The Dreamers would get a pathway to citizenship, he told Trump, but as part of the deal, the diversity visa lottery would end, and chain migration would be scaled back. Once they got permanent legal status, the Dreamers would not be able to sponsor the parents who had brought them unlawfully into the United States, Graham explained, essentially breaking the chain. Some of the roughly 50,000 visas now granted through the lottery would instead be given to people who had Temporary Protected Status, like those from Haiti, who had come to the United States after a natural disaster or other catastrophe and been living here for many years.

The president interrupted. "Wait a minute—why do we want people from Haiti here?" he demanded. Graham hesitated, trying to explain that TPS covered hundreds of thousands of people from several countries, some of whom had been living in the United States for decades. But Trump was not liking what he was hearing. Can't we just leave Haiti out? Graham tried moving on to one of Trump's favorite topics: merit-based immigration. The rest of the diversity visas would be given out according to merit, the senator explained, which would preserve diversity from places like Africa, which sent many higher-skilled workers to the United States through the program. "Why would we want all these people from shithole countries?" Trump asked, stunning Graham into silence. The United States should take more people from Europe, from places like Norway, Trump declared, naming a country whose prime minister, Erna Solberg, he had just hosted at the White House the day before, and whose country is more than 80 percent white. Solberg had made a big impression on Trump, regaling him with stories about how Norway was the happiest country in the world, with barely any unemployment, crime, or debt. Everyone loves everyone, she had told Trump, and we are becoming an economic powerhouse. Now the president of the United States wanted to know why his country couldn't be more like that. Those people work hard, Trump said, and there's very little crime there!

Durbin could hardly believe his ears; his face turned ashen as he gazed around the Oval Office and tried to comprehend what he had just heard coming out of the mouth of the leader of the free world. Graham, who had been so optimistic about his deal only minutes before, was watching it all unravel in front of his eyes. He had spent months trying to build a relationship with Trump so that he could be in a position to influence him on issues like immigration. But he wasn't about to sit quietly and listen to Trump's racist rant without giving him a piece of his mind. "America is an idea, not a race," Graham told Trump, his face growing flushed as he spoke. Diversity was a strength, not a weakness. And by the way, if you want to talk about immigrants from poor countries coming here with no education, Graham added, you're describing my family. I'm descended from immigrants from "shithole countries with no skills." Graham, who grew up poor in South Carolina, the son of bar owners and the first in his family to attend college, lectured the president while the rest of the lawmakers said nothing. My parents weren't educated, Graham said, but they were good people, and that's what America's all about. Trump seemed unfazed by the scolding and unaware of the impact of his own words. Just give me $20 billion, the president said, moving on to one of his favorite topics, and I'll build the wall in a year.

When the senators emerged, they were grim-faced and quiet. In the West Wing lobby, Graham opened his mouth to say something, but Durbin cut him off. "Let's wait until we get in the car," he muttered. Sitting in the backseat of the Suburban, Durbin turned to Graham. "I never thought that I would be in a situation where the president of the United States would show himself to be an open racist in the Oval Office." Durbin shook his head and thanked Graham for speaking up during the meeting. It had made him proud, he said, to see Graham stand up to the president that way. As they headed back to Capitol Hill to brief their colleagues, both men had tears in their eyes as they took stock of what Trump had just said, and what it might mean for the last, best chance to help the Dreamers.

Word of Trump's comments leaked quickly and drew swift condemnation on both sides of the political aisle in the United States, and from countries around the globe. Jim Nealon, who had lost the battle to save TPS months earlier, was sitting in Mexico City working on trade and border issues with his Mexican counterparts, when a cacophony of iPhone alerts cascaded through the room, heralding news alerts about the president's outrageous comments. There was quite a bit of cursing in Spanish, Nealon later told colleagues. In Washington, Republicans and Democrats rushed to distance themselves from the ugly sentiment: Republican senator Ron Johnson of Wisconsin called the comment "totally inappropriate" and urged Trump to apologize. Other Republicans used words like "wrong and indefensible," "insulting and distracting," "unacceptable," and "abhorrent and repulsive." The human rights spokesman at the United Nations bluntly declared that "there is no other word one can use but racist." Haiti's largest newspaper called the remark "racist and disgraceful."

But at the White House, the president was mystified. Sure, he had used some harsh words, but was it really such a big deal? Had he even used the word "shithole"? Nielsen told her colleagues at DHS that she hadn't actually heard the president say it, having arrived late to the Oval Office meeting, which was more like a noisy cocktail party than a subdued policy discussion. Numerous different conversations had been going on at the same time, and people were filing in and out of the room. While the president was talking with Durbin and Graham at his desk, Nielsen had been on the other side of the room, listening to a rapid-fire immigration commentary from Miller. Nielsen's first indication that Trump had said something awful was when she heard Durbin, across the room, say something about the Statue of Liberty.

Even the president told some of his staff he wasn't sure that he had made the offending remark. Some of Trump's staunchest allies swore that they heard him say "shithouse," not "shithole," and urged him to claim he had never uttered the offending phrase. The president was more than happy to seize on the technicality. "The language used by me at the DACA meeting was tough, but this was not the language used," he finally tweeted. "What was really tough was the outlandish proposal made—a big setback for DACA!"

Kirstjen Nielsen sat at a long wooden table in a cavernous Hart Building hearing room paneled with white marble slabs and faced a phalanx of stern-faced senators. Days after the president had launched into his racist, expletive-laced outburst about immigrants in the Oval Office, they wanted to see her squirm.

What "strong language" had Trump used? Durbin asked Nielsen over the whir of the camera shutters of the scores of photographers crouched on the floor in front of her. The Senate Judiciary Committee hearing, complete with Nielsen raising her right hand to swear to tell the truth, was being broadcast live on television. "Let's see, 'strong language,'" Nielsen responded, visibly uncomfortable. "There was—I—apologies, I don't remember a specific word."

Graham, who knew that Trump watched television obsessively and was preoccupied with his own image, addressed his questions to Nielsen, but his remarks were unmistakably aimed at the president. What had happened last Thursday, he wanted to know, between 10 a.m., when a DACA deal seemed imminent, and 12 p.m., when Trump ranted from his big chair behind the Resolute Desk about rejecting immigrants from "shit-hole" countries? How could Trump's behavior behind closed doors be so different from the performance he had given a few days earlier, when he had talked in front of TV cameras about wanting a "bill of love" to pre-serve DACA. "Tuesday, we had a president that I was proud to golf with, call my friend, who understood immigration had to be bipartisan," Gra-ham said. "You had to have border security as essential—you have border security with a wall. But he also understood the idea that we had to do it with compassion. Now, I don't know where that guy went." Graham threw his arms open in a gesture of desperation. "I want him back."

Graham believed that Trump was in the thrall of Miller and other ad-visers like Kelly, who were preventing him from reaching the kind of deal he instinctively wanted. Left to his own devices, Graham believed, Trump would take their DACA agreement in a heartbeat. He just had to be per-suaded to overrule his staff—and that meant stroking Trump's ego. The president had been thrilled with the media coverage the week before, when he had turned his immigration meeting in the cabinet room into an hour-long reality show. He detested the reports about the "shithole" meeting two days later and blamed his staff for failing to negotiate more effectively on his behalf.

But publicly, as a shutdown loomed and a DACA deal teetered on the precipice of collapse, Trump blamed Democrats. On his way into his West Palm Beach golf club for dinner with Representative Kevin McCarthy, who had flown down to join him, the president declared "I am not a rac-ist," and said that if a DACA deal failed, it would be because Democrats didn't want one. After the federal judge in California ruled that Trump's decision to end DACA had probably been unlawful, he ordered DHS to resume issuing permit renewals for those who had already applied for and been granted protection under the program, effectively freezing Trump's effort to wind it down while a legal challenge continued. It was a tem-porary victory for proponents of the program, but White House officials were beginning to worry that it was easing the pressure on Democrats to strike a deal to preserve the protections.

On Capitol Hill, Kelly sought to calm tempers among Democrats and present himself as the reasonable adult at the White House, as well as the person responsible for talking sense into a misguided president when it came to the border wall. In a private meeting with members of the Congressional Hispanic Caucus, Kelly said he had single-handedly saved DACA from certain death, pressing for the six-month wind-down to give Congress the time to enshrine the protections in legislation. If you want to save the program, he told the Hispanic lawmakers, you have to pass a bill. Kelly also urged them to take Trump's insistence on a border wall with a grain of salt. That was just an "uninformed" proposal the president seized on during the campaign, he said. Since then, in his travels to the border and in conversations with Customs and Border Protection, Kelly said he had been "educated" about how to secure the border and had, in turn, "educated" Trump, managing to talk the president out of his silly fixation with a concrete wall along the entire southwestern border, from sea to shining sea. The president has "evolved" on this. Some shook their head silently, thinking, "He is not going to like that one bit." They were right. By the next morning, Trump lashed out at Kelly in a series of tweets. "The Wall is the Wall," he wrote. "It has never changed or evolved from the first day I conceived of it."

ASH AND TRASH

IT WAS THE MIDDLE of January 2018. Time was running out for a DACA deal, and Trump could feel the walls closing in.

Democrats were under mounting pressure from their core supporters to shut down the government over protecting the Dreamers. A group of former Obama aides who had gained a national following for their podcast, "Pod Save America," were spoiling for just such a fight on their website Crooked.com. Jon Favreau, Tommy Vietor, Jon Lovett, and Dan Pfeiffer were known as the "pod bros," a nickname that reflected the all-male, towel-snapping, and exceedingly hipster-feeling vibe of their popular audio stream. They had decided to grade Senate Democrats on their willingness to wage war with Trump over DACA. Democrats who they believed would side with Republicans to prevent a shutdown were listed as members of "Waffle House," while those who had declared they would not vote for any funding bill without a DACA deal were admiringly listed as part of "Fight Club." It was the progressive answer to the Freedom Caucus, the ultraconservative group of Republicans who would brook no compromise. Trump was feeling the pressure from his right flank as well. Mark Meadows, the Freedom Caucus chairman from North Carolina, called to advise him to stand strong and insist on major concessions on immigration, including the wall and the wish list of restrictions his staff had drawn up. The president wanted to, he told Meadows, but he also desperately wanted to avoid a shutdown. He wanted to cut a deal.

On a Friday morning in January, with less than twenty-four hours to go before government funding would lapse, Trump called Schumer. He gave his staff little notice, and Kelly and Miller immediately began having flashbacks to the "Chuck and Nancy" dinner a couple of months earlier, worried that the president was about to cut a bad deal with Democrats who would be only too willing to grab whatever concessions they could get. Over the phone, the two New Yorkers got down to business. Schumer insisted that they work on a long-term spending deal rather than the temporary one that was being negotiated—so far without much success—on Capitol Hill. Trump agreed, and invited Schumer to the White House to hammer out the details. Over cheeseburgers in the president's study next to the Oval Office, at the same table where Trump had agonized several weeks earlier over his statement announcing an end to DACA, they outlined a plan. With their chiefs of staff looking on, Schumer said he would support a large increase in military spending and consider full funding for Trump's border wall—"pick a number," he told Trump—and the president said he would back legal protections for the Dreamers. To sweeten the deal, the measure would include disaster funding and a reauthorization of the Children's Health Insurance Program, CHIP. To give everyone time to finalize the broader package without the government shutting down, lawmakers would first pass a short, three-day stopgap bill, Schumer said, and then vote on the broader agreement the following week. Trump said he was on board.

But no sooner had Schumer arrived back on Capitol Hill than the idea began to unravel. McConnell had gotten word of the cheeseburger summit and called Kelly. The president should not give in to the Democrats' demands, the Senate Republican leader said. Republican lawmakers would have trouble voting for the kind of deal Trump seemed to be entertaining. Soon Trump was on the phone to Schumer, walking back the plan they had discussed over lunch. He feigned ignorance; we discussed a three-week stopgap bill, not three days, right? Absolutely not, Schumer said. With the Democratic grass roots agitated and spoiling for a shutdown fight, it was getting increasingly difficult for Democrats to vote for any spending measure without a DACA fix included. They would swallow a few days to allow time for a broader deal to be finalized, but they would never go for three weeks. Trump said Schumer should call McConnell to hash out the details of any short-term deal. Soon after, Kelly called Schumer to make clear what the president had left unclear: There was to be no deal. The proposal Democrats had offered was too generous in its treatment of the Dreamers—it helped too many of them and granted a path to citizenship—and too stingy with hard-line immigration changes that were important to the president, Kelly told Schumer.

"Not looking good for our great Military or Safety & Security on the very dangerous Southern Border," Mr. Trump wrote on Twitter less than three hours before the clock ran out on a shutdown. "Dems want a Shutdown in order to help diminish the great success of the Tax Cuts, and what they are doing for our booming economy."

Schumer said the president had abruptly reversed himself and walked away from a perfectly reasonable compromise. "In my heart, I thought we might have a deal tonight," he said in the Capitol, after the shutdown took hold at midnight. "Negotiating with President Trump," he said the next day on the Senate floor, "is like negotiating with Jell-O."

The government was officially closed. That weekend, as congressional leaders and White House officials scrambled to find a way out of the shutdown, Trump stewed and sulked as he watched TV. It was the one-year anniversary of his inauguration, and instead of flying to his Mar-a-Lago retreat in Palm Beach to golf and attend a lavish $100,000-per-couple fundraiser celebrating his first year in office, the president was cloistered inside the White House, unsure of how to navigate his way out of a government shutdown. He spent his Saturday toggling between coverage of the shutdown, including a clip that seemed to play on an endless loop of him criticizing Obama for allowing the government to shut down in 2013, and images of women with anti-Trump signs clogging the National Mall for the Women's March. From the residence, Trump began rage-tweeting before dawn. "This is the One Year Anniversary of my Presidency and the

Democrats wanted to give me a nice present," he wrote, with the hashtag #DemocratShutdown.

On Capitol Hill, a group of Republican and Democratic senators calling themselves the Common Sense Coalition met to search for a way out of the impasse. In a marathon set of weekend talks, passing around a traditional African Masai talking stick wrapped in colorful beads to indicate which member was recognized for a chance to speak, they hashed out a plan in which Democrats would agree to support a three-week spending measure in exchange for a commitment from McConnell to put DACA legislation on the floor in the near future. But Graham, a key member of the group, worried aloud that Trump's aides would make an agreement on such a bill impossible.

"His heart is right on this issue; I think he's got a good understanding of what will sell," Graham told reporters in the Capitol. "Every time we have a proposal, it is only yanked back by staff members. As long as Stephen Miller is in charge of negotiating immigration, we are going nowhere. He's been an outlier for years."

The shutdown was short-lived; before long, Schumer caved and agreed to a spending agreement, and McConnell committed to holding a series of votes in the coming days on legislation to codify DACA. But there was still no consensus on what that bill should look like.

The Number Twos negotiations were at a standstill, and everyone was frustrated—the lawmakers, their aides, the White House officials who were sitting in listening to the same conversations over and over. One afternoon in McCarthy's office, John Kelly broke the monotony. The chief of staff had said little in most of these sessions, but on that Tuesday, he chimed in as Durbin made the case that they should help as many Dreamers as possible with whatever plan they came up with. A pathway to citizenship should be available not just to the 690,000 people who had DACA permits, Durbin said, but also for the more than one million others who were eligible but had never received them. "Because they were too lazy to get off their asses and apply," Kelly groused from his end of the table. Durbin was taken aback. Steny Hoyer, the House Democratic whip, took exception. That's no way to talk about these kids, he said. Besides, the Democrats told him, Kelly was wrong. The reason many eligible people did not have DACA protections was because when the program was created they were too young to receive a permit. It had nothing to do with being lazy. The spat was yet another reminder, as if it were needed, that a compromise was not in the offing. Kelly left the session and repeated the "lazy" comment to reporters waiting outside, drawing outrage from Democrats and immigrant advocacy groups.

As the date McConnell had set for a DACA debate approached, Trump appeared to be backing away from a bipartisan deal. He was insisting on his "four pillars"—DACA protections, wall funding, eliminating the diversity visa lottery, and ending chain migration—and Chuck Grassley, the Republican chairman of the Senate Judiciary Committee, produced a bill that mirrored the wish list. The Common Sense Coalition was toiling quietly to finalize its own plan, which would pair $25 billion in border wall funding with a path to citizenship for 1.8 million Dreamers. It was a fragile compromise—one that demanded that Democrats embrace a wall their core supporters detested and Republicans accept an amnesty their base reviled—but after weeks of negotiations, the group believed they had the sixty votes necessary to push it through the Senate, even over the president's objections.

All that changed late on the night of Valentine's Day, the eve of the Senate vote, when the Common Sense Coalition unveiled its final legislative language. At around 10 p.m., top officials at DHS who were running a legislative war room from the department's office in the Ronald Reagan Building several blocks from the Capitol received the text of the Coalition's bill—what was being called the "Schumer-Collins-Rounds" measure, named for three of the lead sponsors, including the Senate Democratic leader, the moderate Maine Republican Susan Collins, and Senator Mike Rounds, another centrist Republican, from South Dakota. The DHS aides, who were allied with Miller and keeping in touch with him, read through it and immediately knew: they could never in a million years support this. Over the next five hours, rushing against a self-imposed early-morning deadline to register the administration's deep opposition to the bill before senators made up their minds to support it, they composed a scathing, over-the-top takedown of the legislation. "Schumer-Rounds-Collins Destroys Ability of DHS to Enforce Immigration Laws, Creating a Mass Amnesty for Over 10 Million Illegal Aliens, Including Criminals," was the statement's headline.

What followed was a lengthy rundown of the administration's objections to the bill, including what it characterized as overly generous grants of legal status to large populations of Dreamers and other undocumented immigrants and a failure to end chain migration, secure the border, or end the diversity visa lottery—all items that Trump had demanded. The most damning talking point against the measure claimed that a late addition to the bill, a provision to codify enforcement priorities so that ICE would focus on criminals, national security threats, and people who had entered the United States most recently, was in fact an enforcement "holiday" that would bar the deportation of anyone who arrived before June of 2018. Collins had inserted the provision in an effort to toughen the measure's enforcement measures, but DHS officials portrayed it as a backdoor amnesty. With Milleresque flourishes of hyperbole, their statement was unsparing in its assessment of the legislation. "It would be the end of immigration enforcement in America and only serve to draw millions more illegal aliens with no way to remove them," it said.

The statement went out the following morning and had its intended effect. The sixty votes the group had assembled behind the bipartisan proposal evaporated, even as the White House put out its own statement saying flatly that the proposal, "if enacted, would be the end of immigration enforcement in America." Trump said he would veto the measure. Later that day, the bill failed in a vote on the Senate floor, as did Chuck Grassley's Republican-only plan that reflected Miller's wish list and another bipartisan alternative. Democrats said the Republican bill was draconian, while conservatives rejected it as amnesty for the Dreamers. Not only did Grassley's measure fail to reach a sixty-vote threshold it would have needed to advance; it fell well short of even a simple majority. The vote was 39–60. DACA had officially stalled in the Senate.

The experience left a bitter taste for Republicans and Democrats who had worked to find a middle ground. In a meeting with Nielsen in a hearing room in the Russell Senate Office Building the following month, Democratic senators complained bitterly about the statement her staff had issued about the Common Sense Coalition plan, saying that it was nothing more than a campaign press release masquerading as an official government document, and that it willfully distorted their plan. I stand by every word of that statement, Nielsen responded. Tim Kaine, a Democrat from Virginia, pulled it up on his phone and went through the document point by point. "That's not true," he would say after reading each bullet point. "That's not true." Here was a group of Democrats that had held their noses and agreed to support the president's wall as well as his immigration enforcement priorities, drawing the ire of immigration advocacy groups and their progressive base, only to see their chance to help the Dreamers vanish with the issuance of a press release. You will never get us to agree to these numbers again, they told Nielsen.

Few on Capitol Hill were motivated to keep trying for a DACA deal. In late February, the Supreme Court had rejected an unusual request by Sessions to immediately overrule the lower court rulings from January and strike down DACA. The refusal by the justices to act sent the decision back to the lower courts and delayed it for months, effectively letting existing DACA recipients keep their protections while the legal battle unfolded. Without the immediate threat of heartrending headlines about Dreamers being uprooted from their lives and deported, much of the pressure to act was off Congress. And there was far less incentive on either side to strike a compromise.

Even so, aides to Paul Ryan were still working to find a solution, however crude or imperfect, to allow DACA recipients to keep their status. They began discussing creating a sort of temporary fix for the program, by tucking a measure into a mammoth, "omnibus" spending bill that Congress had to pass in March. Senior Republicans quietly began private talks with Marc Short, the White House legislative affairs director, about a possible, scaled-back "DACA-for-wall" deal that could give Dreamers three years of protection in return for three years of wall funding. It wouldn't be a permanent solution to the DACA problem, but it would solve two looming political problems, pushing the issue well past the 2020 elections and giving Trump some of the wall money he had been demanding. But when word leaked to *The Washington Post* and *Politico* that the president was considering a "three for three" deal, conservatives were up in arms, calling it amnesty for a paltry amount of wall funding. The White House publicly panned the idea, dispatching a spokesman to deny that it was under consideration.

On a Sunday afternoon at three, aides to the "Big Four" congressional leaders—Ryan, Pelosi, McConnell, and Schumer—gathered in an ornate room in the speaker's suite to hash out what would be in the omnibus spending bill. Short was present, and the idea of DACA-for-wall was up for discussion. But when Short outlined the proposal, it had changed considerably from what Ryan's staff had initially proposed. There would be a three-year extension of DACA protections, but in exchange Trump would get all of the wall and border security money he was seeking—the full $25 billion—and several of his demands for stricter enforcement. The Democrats balked. Schumer's staff said there was no way they could accept that.

When Ryan heard how the session had gone, he phoned Pelosi and Schumer separately and implored them to work with him to find a better solution. Republicans were willing to negotiate on this, he said, and if they couldn't find an agreement, they would miss a ripe opportunity to help the Dreamers. In spite of the fact that the White House had publicly rejected the idea, Ryan's staff revived the three-for-three proposal, quietly sending it to senior Democratic aides in hopes of sparking a negotiation. A top aide to Pelosi explained why the proposal could never work. Democrats wanted to extend the protections to all 1.8 million Dreamers who were eligible for DACA, not just the 690,000 who had applied. And Democrats wanted to move the effective date so that more immigrants could qualify. But Ryan's aides feared that doing so would blow up the fragile consensus that had emerged around a simple extension of the program. Still, they said they were open to talking about the number of beneficiaries who could be included, and potentially to dropping some of the enforcement measures—maybe even all of them. In other words, they begged: Make us an offer.

But as the hours ticked by and staff negotiated the other elements of the huge spending measure, Democrats never sent a counteroffer. Short on time, Ryan's aides sent Democrats yet another proposal: they would drop some of the enforcement provisions and expand the population of Dreamers who could apply, effectively capturing around 120,000 people who had aged into the program since Trump had rescinded it. There was still no response. That night, negotiations on the omnibus spending measure closed with no deal on extending DACA. The next day, as senior congressional officials ticked through the customary list of final legislative odds and ends to agree on which should be attached to the catch-all spending bill—a process known as "ash and trash"—DACA came up a final time. Schumer's staff weighed in: No.

— 21 —

"NO MORE DACA DEAL!"

IT WAS THE FIRST day of spring, and a giant nor'easter—the fourth in three weeks—had covered Washington with a thick blanket of snow. With schools closed, a throng of sledding children dotted the hulking slope of Capitol Hill, and the streets of the District were mostly empty as federal workers enjoyed a day off and commuters mostly stayed home. But congressional leaders were hard at work putting the finishing touches on the omnibus agreement, a $1.3 trillion spending bill to fund the government through September that was more than 2,200 pages long. It contained massive increases in military and domestic spending and was the product of painstaking negotiations between Democrats and Republicans. What it did not include was any money for the president's border wall, and conservatives were up in arms, calling it a big-spending betrayal of their agenda. By mid-morning, Trump's team notified Ryan's aides that the speaker had better get himself down to the White House. The president is pissed about this bill, they were told, and he's threatening not to sign it.

It was well after 11 a.m. by the time Ryan's black Suburban rolled through the White House gates on Wednesday, March 21, but Trump, who often arrived in the Oval Office at midday, had not yet left the residence. The president was seated behind Abraham Lincoln's large old wooden desk in the Treaty Room, and he was swearing up a storm. Vice President Mike Pence was there, as were Kelly, Nielsen, and Marc Short, the legislative affairs director, and McConnell joined by telephone from the Capitol. They took turns trying to quell Trump's anger. Ryan noted that the bill actually contained precisely the amount Trump had requested for border security: $1.6 billion. "Well, who the fuck asked for that?" Trump thundered. The figure had been in the president's own budget submission, someone mumbled quietly, but Trump seemed utterly unaware of it—nor did he care. Trump screamed at Short, who made the case for signing the bill. The president hated the situation in which he found himself, facing an all-or-nothing choice between rejecting the legislation and forcing a shutdown or swallowing what he considered a debacle of a compromise. McConnell, listening to the president's expletive-filled tirade, said little. When he did speak, he told Trump in his dour, slightly twangy monotone, that it would be disastrous to veto the bill. It simply needs to get done, he said. Ryan told Trump he could understand his frustration; this was no way to handle government spending, and in the future, he promised, Congress would not send him another gigantic take-it-or-leave-it bill. They would pass individual spending bills in turn, Ryan said, and Trump would have another crack at securing more money for the wall. That seemed to satisfy the president. By the end of the session, he was still grumbling, but he seemed willing to accept the measure and live to fight another day on his wall.

But that night, Trump came in for an absolute grilling on Fox News. "This is a president who is being mocked by Chuck Schumer and Nancy Pelosi and the Democrats as well as Paul Ryan and Mitch McConnell," Lou Dobbs told his viewers. "And there's no other way to put it. He's being mocked. Five percent on the border wall and he has to eat that?" Laura Ingraham said Trump had allowed himself to be played, and abandoned his principles in the process. "It pains me to say this, but the president is buying a pig in a poke here," Ingraham said. "He won on calling out the establishment, on naming names—yes, even when it made things uncomfortable. So, I have a question: Where did that Donald Trump go?"

What really stuck in Trump's craw was a point Mark Meadows had made to him. Chuck Schumer got his tunnel, the North Carolina con-

gressman kept saying, but Trump didn't get his wall. Meadows was refer-
ring to Gateway, a multi-billion-dollar rail tunnel project underneath the
Hudson River between New York and New Jersey that had long been a
top priority for Schumer, and the subject of intensive haggling on Capitol
Hill. Trump saw the project as a means of gaining leverage over the Senate
Democratic leader from New York. Following a meeting about it at the
White House the previous fall, the president had taken Schumer aside and
put it to him this way: If you give me my wall, I'll give you your tunnel.
Schumer had rejected the idea, but Trump never dropped it. If he couldn't
have a big, beautiful wall, Trump figured, Schumer couldn't have his Gateway. Now he was being told that the Democrat had gotten the better of
him. Not only did he have to swallow a giant spending bill he didn't like,
and that his supporters detested, but he was facing humiliation at the
hands of Schumer. If he was going to sign this thing, he was at least going
to let the world know he was not happy about it.

At 8:55 on that Friday morning, Trump fired off an angry tweet that
sent Washington reeling. "I am considering a VETO of the Omnibus
Spending Bill based on the fact that the 800,000 plus DACA recipients
have been totally abandoned by the Democrats (not even mentioned in
Bill) and the BORDER WALL, which is desperately needed for our National Defense, is not fully funded."

Ryan placed an emergency call to the White House to try to reason
with Trump. You have your facts wrong, Mr. President, and Meadows
does, too. There's no money for Gateway in this bill, the speaker said.
Trump was grumpy and unconvinced. For the past twenty-four hours,
the Fox News airwaves had been saturated by critics of the bill repeating
the mantra: Trump promised a wall, not a tunnel. How could he sign a
bill that made him look like a loser? The president was not entirely wrong.
While the bill didn't explicitly provide money for Gateway, it did include
$540 million in transportation funding that could be used for the project
and others like it, much of which could be accessed without express approval from Trump's administration. Ryan conveniently omitted any mention of those details, and finally succeeded in persuading Trump that the
spending bill did not, in fact, fund Schumer's beloved tunnel project. As

for the wall, Ryan told Trump again, we can come back later in the year and secure additional funding for that. It's not worth shutting down the government today, he pleaded, when we can take what's in this bill and fight it out again later. Trump grudgingly said he was willing to sign the bill. Before he hung up, though, Trump had a demand: Don't tell anyone I've agreed to sign it. I want to keep up the drama until the very last second. The reality show had to go on.

Ryan agreed, and hung up, convinced that Trump would not veto the bill. But over the next several hours, Trump made a public show of having second thoughts. Ryan called Jim Mattis, the secretary of defense, and asked him to hurry to the White House and brief Trump on all the military funding that was at stake if he vetoed the bill. All Trump seemed to want to talk about was the prospect of using Pentagon money, rather than the Department of Homeland Security, to build the wall, a prospect that Mattis told him could only be possible if Congress voted to reprogram the funds. Cable news was saturated with "will-he-or-won't-he" coverage, and White House officials caveated their predictions to reporters with the familiar caution: Nobody really knows what he will do. By midday, Trump decided to end the suspense. White House officials gathered reporters in the Diplomatic Reception Room to hear from Trump, who said he had signed the bill and lamented the "ridiculous situation" in which he found himself.

"There are a lot of things that I'm unhappy about in this bill," Mr. Trump said. "There are a lot of things that we shouldn't have had in this bill. But we were, in a sense, forced—if we want to build our military—we were forced to have. There are some things that we should have in the bill."

Then he issued a warning that foreshadowed future fights. "I will never sign another bill like this again," Trump said. "I'm not going to do it again."

The backlash from Trump's base was swift, and it was vicious.

Amy Kremer, a Tea Party activist who had helped found the group Women for Trump, assailed the president on Twitter, writing "I'm done." She predicted that Democrats would win the midterm congressional elections in November and said she wouldn't waste her time trying to prevent it. In a column dripping with snark that sarcastically attributed Trump's retreat on the wall to "3-D chess," Ann Coulter called the president "the Worst Negotiator God Ever Created," and suggested that he add a chapter to his book *The Art of the Deal* entitled, "How to Give Up Everything in Return for Nothing." Trump was enraged by the coverage and grasping for ways to show his core supporters that he was still committed to the wall, and willing to do whatever was necessary to build it.

Trump became more insistent about the idea of having the Department of Defense pay for the wall, arguing that he could do so by calling illegal immigration across the border with Mexico a national security issue. Privately, he told aides that he deeply regretted having signed the funding bill. Miller, Kelly, and the rest of the president's top aides in the West Wing were in a frenzy as they tried to find ways to address Trump's anger about the border. It was bad enough that the number of migrants crossing into the United States was increasing. But now Trump was watching every day as Fox News tracked the movement of about 1,000 Hondurans heading on foot toward the United States. The pressure to do something—anything—was intense. Every day, Kelly made calls to Hamilton, Nielsen, and others and his message could not have been more clear: "If you're not spending every waking minute thinking about securing the border, you're not doing your job," he told them.

The message came directly from Trump, too. The president had a habit of calling Nielsen many mornings, often well before six thirty as he watched Fox and digested stories clipped from right-wing websites. Frequently, Nielsen, who was not a morning person, would still be asleep when the president called. She would awake to an ominous message from the department's National Operations Center: "President Calls. Tries to Reach Secretary. Secretary Unreachable." Often, after seeing images in news reports of the wall along the southern border, Trump would unleash on Nielsen about its design. "Kirstjen, what the fuck are you doing building that ugly, ugly wall?" Trump demanded on more than one occasion. In late March, Nielsen went to Mexico to meet with President Enrique Peña Nieto for trade and security talks. When she returned and went to the

White House to brief Trump on the trip, he became even angrier about the caravan, demanding she do something to stop it. Nielsen explained—for the umpteenth time—the way in which immigration and asylum laws worked, that DHS had limited legal means of barring people from streaming north if they were determined to do so. Mexico had bolstered security at its southern border, but there were limits to its ability to control the flow as well, she explained.

Trump lambasted Nielsen for not doing enough to secure the border. There were too many ways for illegal immigrants to flood into the United States, he complained. Why wasn't she doing more to block them? In a particularly brutal series of calls, Trump berated her for failing to be tougher on the migrants crossing the border illegally in order to send a message to the Central Americans that they shouldn't even try to come. Nielsen tried to describe the actions her department was already taking to stem the flow of migrants while underscoring the complexities that make the problem difficult to solve. Trump did not want to hear excuses. He yelled at Nielsen to be more aggressive. Trump flew down to Mar-a-Lago for the Easter weekend, with Miller in tow, preoccupied with the caravan and feeling powerless to address it.

Miller had spent the past several months trying to drive home to Trump the importance of toughening the country's immigration laws—not just building a wall, but fundamentally overhauling the way the United States treated people who sought to enter. The caravan gave him a powerful bit of evidence to press his case in conversations with Trump at his Palm Beach resort. Because of the dysfunctional way in which our laws work, Miller explained to the president, migrants know that if they show up at the border and say certain magic words—that they have been persecuted, are afraid for their life and safety, or otherwise have legitimate reasons to fear returning to their home country—American immigration agents have to allow them in as asylum seekers with a "credible fear," and can only hold them for a short period of time before releasing them into the interior to await adjudication of their claims. It was known as "catch and release," and it made a mockery of any attempt at real enforcement. What was even

Kris Kobach, the Kansas secretary of state, is greeted by president-elect Trump at the Trump National Golf Club in Bedminster, N.J., on November 20, 2016. Kobach helped lead the legal assault on the Obama-era DACA protections for young immigrants.

A loyal campaign surrogate, Jeff Sessions used his position as Trump's first attorney general to supercharge the president's immigration crackdown, including the "zero tolerance" policy that led to family separations.

Steve Bannon, President Trump's chief strategist (right), and Reince Priebus, the White House chief of staff. Bannon helped shape Trump's hard-line positions and incendiary rhetoric. Priebus toiled to manage a chaotic West Wing marked by a disdain for policy process.

Stephen Miller, a senior adviser for policy, answers questions in the White House briefing room. Miller was the main driver behind Trump's immigration agenda, advocating for the president's most controversial policies.

Protesters gather at John F. Kennedy International Airport on January 28, 2017, after President Trump's ban on travel from predominantly Muslim countries. The directive was typical of the legally dubious and politically incendiary actions Trump took early in his tenure.

Donald F. "Don" McGahn II (center), the president's first White House counsel, listens to Trump during a Cabinet meeting. Trump raged at McGahn over having to sign a "watered-down" version of his travel ban executive order after the original version was blocked by a judge.

Elaine Duke, the acting secretary of homeland security, testifies before a Senate committee. Duke often found herself under siege by Stephen Miller and others at the White House who pushed her to end programs that gave legal status to immigrants.

John F. Kelly, the second White House chief of staff, with his successor at Homeland Security, Kirstjen M. Nielsen. A former Marine general who shared many of Trump's hardline views, Kelly often clashed with Democratic lawmakers and fiercely defended Nielsen from the president's anger.

President Trump is flanked by members of his national security team in the Cabinet Room. From left: National Security Adviser H. R. McMaster, Defense Secretary Jim Mattis, Vice President Mike Pence, and Secretary of State Rex Tillerson. McMaster, Mattis, and Tillerson sometimes broke with Trump on immigration issues.

A caravan from Central America makes its way toward the United States on Saturday, October 27, 2018. The formation of the caravans in the spring and fall of 2018 enraged President Trump and prompted him to demand an escalating list of extreme measures to deter immigration.

11

DHS Secretary Kirstjen M. Nielsen sits beside President Trump in the Roosevelt Room. Nielsen became the face of Trump's plan to separate migrant families and a frequent target of the president's rage about the border.

An image of a border wall tweeted by President Trump on December 21, 2018. Nielsen had asked her staff to develop the mock-up after the president described it in detail. It quickly became a meme and was roundly ridiculed online.

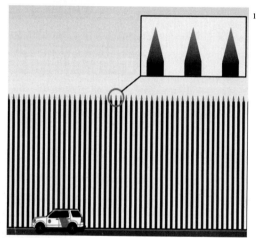

12

13

Jared Kushner, President Trump's son-in-law. A voice of moderation on immigration issues, Kushner held private discussions with key Democrats and Republicans to try to save DACA.

Vice President Mike Pence (center), Acting White House Chief of Staff Mick Mulvaney (far left), and Senior Adviser Jared Kushner (rear, left) cross the Capitol Rotunda on December 21, 2018, a few hours before a government shutdown. The trio was sardonically branded the "three wise men."

President Trump tells House Speaker Nancy Pelosi, Democrat of California, and Senator Chuck Schumer of New York, the minority leader, that he would be "proud" to shut down the government over his border wall during an Oval Office meeting on December 11, 2018, ten days before government funding was to expire.

Migrants massed in a makeshift encampment in McAllen, Texas, on May 15, 2019. The surge of migrants at the southwestern border, many of them families traveling with children, overwhelmed government authorities and nonprofit organizations.

The bodies of a Salvadoran migrant and his 23-month-old daughter were found on the Mexican side of the Rio Grande in June 2019 after they drowned trying to cross into Texas. The image crystallized the human tragedy at the border and fueled debate over Trump's efforts to prevent asylum seekers from entering the U.S.

worse, a more than two-decade-old court-ordered consent decree known as the Flores settlement placed a twenty-day limit on the time that children could be held in immigration detention, essentially guaranteeing that any parent of a minor child could not be held for longer than that unless the two were to be separated. The machinations over potentially codifying DACA, Miller argued to Trump, had made the situation even worse. Migrants had received the message, via smugglers who had a financial interest in stoking the rumor mill, that the United States was about to issue a mass amnesty and were therefore streaming north in the hopes of arriving in time to take advantage.

Trump was incensed by what he heard, even if he did not follow all the details. He spent Easter Sunday morning watching Fox and rage-tweeting about the migrants. "These big flows of people are all trying to take advantage of DACA," the president tweeted, misinterpreting what Miller had told him "They want in on the act!" He threatened to rip up the NAFTA trade deal if Mexico did not do more to stop migrants from getting near the United States, punctuating his message with, "NEED WALL!"

"Border Patrol Agents are not allowed to properly do their job at the Border because of ridiculous liberal (Democrat) laws like Catch & Release. Getting more dangerous. 'Caravans' coming," Trump wrote. "NO MORE DACA DEAL!"

By the time he returned to Washington, Trump was on the warpath, and his aides scrambled to translate his tweets into something resembling policy. In a meeting chaired by Bossert, the homeland security adviser, in one of the small secure rooms off the main Situation Room, Sessions made a radical suggestion: they should simply ignore Flores and start holding families for longer periods of time. Let the judge come after us, the attorney general told the others in the room, including Nielsen, Andy McCabe, the acting FBI director, and Don McGahn. The comment drew a tart response from McGahn, who seemed unable to believe that Sessions was proposing violating a consent decree. This wasn't some lower-court ruling that could be challenged and potentially overturned; these were a judge's direct orders, McGahn said as the conversation became heated. There were other ways to attack Flores, the White House counsel argued—they could promulgate a regulation or send Congress legislation—but they couldn't just pretend it didn't exist.

But Trump wanted a quick fix. Even when the president wandered out to the South Lawn of the White House to make the traditional presidential appearance at the Easter Egg Roll, he did not let go of the issue. Surrounded by young children making drawings to send to American service members stationed overseas, Trump responded to a reporter's shouted question about the Dreamers, saying that Democrats had "really let them down," and that, "now, people are taking advantage of DACA." That afternoon, Miller rushed to put together a conference call to answer the many questions the president had raised with his comments and tweets. Did the president actually think that the caravan was full of people trying to get DACA protections? Was he going to tear up NAFTA? When he blasted out, "ACT CONGRESS," what exactly was Trump asking them to do?

During the call, three senior administration officials outlined an elaborate package of immigration legislation they said Trump planned to push in the weeks to come. It would make it more difficult to apply for or be granted asylum in the United States, strip protections for children arriving illegally without their parents, so they could be turned back at the border or quickly removed. It would overturn Flores and allow families to be detained for longer periods while they awaited decisions from immigration authorities about their fate. In other words, it looked a lot like the list of demands Miller had produced as trade-offs for legalizing the Dreamers. Only now, Trump seemed to be suggesting that he was no longer willing to help the Dreamers. One aide told reporters on the call what Miller had told Trump over the weekend, that the debate in Congress over granting legal status to the Dreamers—which he called a "generous immigration benefit"—had created a "major pull factor" for new waves of illegal immigrants.

The next day, during a meeting with the leaders of Estonia, Latvia, and Lithuania, Trump surprised his staff and his cabinet with a declaration. "We are preparing for the military to secure our border between Mexico and the United States," the president said, with Jim Mattis, the defense secretary, seated next to him. If Congress wouldn't fund his wall and Nielsen wouldn't do what was necessary to block migrants from entering the country, Trump thought, he was still the commander in chief of the most powerful military in the world. He could use American troops to do what nobody else seemed to be willing to. Mattis was taken aback, although his dour expression betrayed no emotion. Under a late-nineteenth-century law known as the Posse Comitatus Act, much of the military was barred from performing domestic law enforcement duties, such as policing a border, and the principle had long been seen as sacrosanct. Beyond that, administration officials knew it was a horrible idea to amass troops at the southwestern border with a close ally, Mexico, whose cooperation they badly needed. All it would take would be an innocent blunder or misunderstanding and American troops could be engaged in hostilities with the Mexican military. Trump might have been willing to publicly dangle the idea of trashing NAFTA and closing the border, but his advisers knew that would be disastrous, too.

After the Baltic leaders left, Trump convened a meeting with Mattis, Sessions, Nielsen, Kelly, and General Joseph F. Dunford Jr., the chairman of the Joint Chiefs of Staff, to figure out what to do. Mattis made it crystal clear to Trump: he could not support sending active-duty troops to police the border, but if Trump wanted to send the National Guard to support immigration agents at the border, as other presidents before him had done, that would be acceptable. Don McGahn, the White House counsel, sprang into action to explore the legal dimensions of what Trump was asking for. The president had the authority to defend the border—there was no question about that—but he had to comply with international and domestic laws. In the space of a few hours, McGahn made himself an expert on the use of American troops to handle domestic crises, reaching all the way back to the late eighteenth century to analyze Trump's options.

In a briefing for the president in the Oval Office, McGahn pulled out centuries-old statutes and read from them verbatim, going all the way back to Thomas Jefferson's use of the Navy to deal with the Barbary pirates in

1802, and George Washington's putting down the Whiskey Rebellion in 1794, when the nation's first president used the military to quell an insurrection over a tax on whiskey that had been imposed to help pay off the government debt incurred during the Revolutionary War. A president's powers under the Insurrection Act are quite broad, McGahn told Trump, and they essentially provided a carve-out from Posse Comitatus. President George H. W. Bush had invoked the law in 1992 to deploy the military to restore order during the Los Angeles riots. That didn't mean it was a great idea, and the authority had never been used to deal with immigration, but if his advisers couldn't come up with a better idea, McGahn said, this avenue was available to Trump. By nightfall, the White House had massaged Trump's impromptu pronouncement into an actual policy: the president would be working with governors to send guardsmen to the border to assist DHS officials. But since Trump had sprung the announcement on his administration, officials could not say how many troops would go, or when. When reporters pressed the Pentagon for more details, it was clear that Mattis was not interested in owning this particular policy. Call the White House, they were told.

In early April, during a visit to White Sulphur Springs, West Virginia, where he was supposed to be touting the $1.5 trillion tax cut, Trump found himself distracted. Sitting on an elevated stage in a crowded auditorium adorned with standard royal blue pipe-and-drape and American flags typical of a presidential visit, Trump focused on his remarks for all of a few minutes, dutifully reciting his talking points. "America is open for business," he declared, flanked by local elected officials and West Virginians who had been invited to speak about what the tax cut had meant to them and their families. But soon, the president tired of his talking points, and delivered a lengthy rant against immigrants and the country's immigration laws, in which Trump accused Democrats of pushing tax policies because they wanted immigrant votes.

"We're toughening up at the border," Trump said. "We cannot let people enter our country—we have no idea who they are, what they do, where they came from. We don't know if they're murderers, if they're killers, if they're MS-13. We're throwing them out by the hundreds."

Going off-script clearly thrilled the president. "This was going to be my remarks," he told the audience, waving a sheet of paper in the air, "but what the hell? That would have been a little boring." He tossed the paper into the audience and told them he would rather riff. "I'm reading off the first paragraph, I said, 'This is boring.' Come on. We have to tell it like it is."

Flying back to Washington on Air Force One a short time later, Trump visited the cramped press cabin at the back of the plane and told the reporters traveling with him that there would be somewhere between 2,000 and 4,000 National Guardsmen deployed to the border. The president asked members of the press pool what they had thought of his off-message performance. Met with silence, Trump answered his own question: "Thought it was really great," he said.

The last thing Republican leaders wanted to do was make another run at fixing DACA. But throughout the spring, a group of moderates who had been pressing for action on the issue began ratcheting up their demands for a vote. Jeff Denham of California and Carlos Curbelo of Florida, whose districts had voted for Hillary Clinton in 2016, were leaders of the effort, but they were hardly the only Republicans to defy their leaders. One by one, more moderates added their names to the discharge petition, the list of lawmakers demanding a floor vote on a bipartisan bill to protect the Dreamers, and with each passing day, they moved closer to having enough signatures to force action.

Republican leaders considered this possibility disastrous. If the bipartisan bill reached the floor, they knew, it would easily win the support of the vast majority of Democrats and enough centrists in their party to pass the House, producing a humiliating result and dividing the party as it braced for midterm elections that could cost Republicans control of the chamber. There was only one way to stop that from happening, Ryan and McCarthy agreed: they had to come up with their own Republican alternative, a compromise that melded what the moderates wanted with what conservatives were insisting on, something that their members could be for without handing Nancy Pelosi control of the floor. The White House was initially cool to the idea. This was the speaker's problem—a "floor management issue"—not Trump's, they said. Miller was sick of trying to cut a DACA deal that was clearly not coming together. Short, the legislative affairs director, assumed Republicans would lose the House in the fall and the issue would remain unaddressed, giving Trump and Republicans an issue to run on in 2020.

But Ryan knew there was no avoiding a DACA vote; his moderates, who were toiling to hold their seats in districts where more moderate voters held sway, would not allow it. With the White House mostly on the sidelines, Ryan's staff began an intensive behind-the-scenes effort to mediate a compromise. The talks were exhaustive and often emotional. At one point, Ryan's staff asked the White House for a list of the top ten enforcement measures they wanted in exchange for legal status for the Dreamers; when the moderates agreed to accept all ten, members of the Freedom Caucus still said they couldn't sign on to a deal. After weeks of negotiations, the negotiators came up with a measure they believed reflected a fragile kind of consensus among Republicans, and something that Trump could sign. Miller even called members of the restrictionist groups to ask them to support it—or at least not try to kill the deal.

But Trump's ambivalence was palpable. Days before the scheduled votes, Trump strode out on the White House driveway for an interview with Steve Doocy of Fox News and distanced himself from the compromise bill. "I certainly wouldn't sign the more moderate one," he said, suggesting that he preferred a different, more conservative version instead. After a day of confusion and mixed signals, White House aides insisted that he had misspoken, and he really did back the bill. But privately, they acknowledged the reality: Trump did not want to be on the record enthusiastically endorsing something that might not pass—particularly a measure that could be tarred by his core supporters as "amnesty" for illegal immigrants.

A few days later, the president went to Capitol Hill to offer his personal reassurance to Republican lawmakers who were deeply nervous about backing the compromise that they would have political cover from him for voting yes. They were desperate for Trump to explicitly bless the compromise, to sell lawmakers on the Ryan-engineered DACA measure, and to make it clear he wanted Republicans to vote for it. He would thank lawmakers who had worked tirelessly in the backroom negotiations—both the moderates and conservatives—for sticking with a difficult process and coming up with a consensus. He even had a list of people to name-check. But when Trump got up to speak in the basement conference room under the Capitol Crypt on Tuesday evening, June 19, he didn't do any of that.

"I'm with you 1,000 percent!" Trump told the roomful of Republican lawmakers. The problem was, nobody knew what he meant. Trump gave a meandering stump speech touting his own success as president and boasting of his popularity, resurrecting his campaign-trail hyperbole to drive home his point. He could shoot someone on Fifth Avenue and not lose support, the president said. He flitted from topic to topic, from his trade war with China to his great relationship with Kim Jong-un. He regaled the group with a lengthy yarn—one of Trump's favorites—claiming that he had single-handedly negotiated down the price of the F-35 fighter jet. In true Trumpian style, the president teased and attacked members of his audience with varying degrees of cruelty. He drew laughs for a wisecrack about Trey Gowdy's hair and more chuckles when he mused aloud about whose idea a DACA-for-wall deal had been. When the members reminded him it was Mario Diaz-Balart, Trump quipped, "I like him more than his brother." (Diaz-Balart's brother José was a journalist.) There were muted boos from rank-and-file Republicans when Trump singled out Mark Sanford, who had just lost his primary to a Trump-friendly opponent, and called the vanquished congressman a "nasty guy." The president remembered to thank conservative members of the Freedom Caucus—Louie Gohmert of Texas, Meadows, and Ohio's Jim Jordan—and praised them for defending him in the face of the investigation by Robert S. Mueller III, the special counsel, into Russia's interference in the 2016 election. But then Trump was off on a tangent about the "Russia hoax" and how his adversaries were grasping for ways to bring him down. He never got around to thanking the moderates whose political careers were on the line.

As he treated the Republicans to his stream-of-consciousness narration, the president touched on immigration only glancingly. He slammed the Democrats, saying they only wanted more immigrants because they wanted more voters for themselves. I'm with you all the way, Trump told the Republicans. He paused to recall the first time he had addressed them as a group, and said he had thought to himself, "Who are these people?" Now, the president said, I know these people. And with that, he walked out, applause echoing behind him.

It was hardly the heartfelt presidential pitch Republican leaders had been hoping for. This was the worst performance they'd ever seen from Trump, some of them said. Republican leaders begged White House officials to clarify the president's position after he left. He had never actually said he supported the leadership's DACA bill, they said. But no clarification came. This was the very scenario Republican leaders had tried to avoid. They feared they were in for a replay of the disaster they had lived through the year before with their ill-fated effort to repeal the Affordable Care Act. Trump had never made clear which bill he supported, and after the House finally muscled one through and he held a ceremony in the Rose Garden hailing the measure, he turned around and pronounced it "mean," yanking the political cover they needed. Now, staring down a politically risky DACA vote, Ryan's staff asked White House officials to issue a formal policy statement declaring that Trump would sign the compromise measure. There was one drafted, they were told, but it was never sent out.

The day before the June 27 vote, Trump invited undecided lawmakers to the White House for lunch in the Cabinet Room, where Republican leaders hoped he would make the hard sell he had failed to deliver a few days before in the Capitol. Trump sat in the middle of the large wooden conference table, flanked by lawmakers, with Kelly, Short, and Nielsen joining him for the session. As the discussion unfolded, lawmakers worried aloud about how a vote to legalize DACA recipients would play in their districts, complaining that the issue was politically perilous and could cost them reelection. That's okay, Trump kept telling them. You don't have to vote for it. It was the opposite of the message a president is supposed to transmit on the eve of a difficult vote.

Later, Ryan's staff got word from the White House that Trump planned to tweet something "nice" about the DACA bill in a last-ditch effort to get Republicans to vote yes. They sent back word to the White House: Tell him not to bother. They had already done their informal nose-count, and they knew it wasn't going to pass. A presidential tweet would be too little, too late. Trump tried it anyway, blasting out an all-caps endorsement of the "STRONG BUT FAIR IMMIGRATION BILL."

It failed spectacularly, 121–301, with Republicans almost evenly split and Democrats unanimously voting no.

ZERO TOLERANCE

THE MEMO SEEKING KIRSTJEN Nielsen's approval to separate migrant children from their parents had been sitting on her desk for weeks.

The five-page document laid out in blunt terms the roots of President Trump's growing fury. Illegal immigration was still increasing, with crossings of single adults at the southwest border "averaging over 1,000 aliens" every day, the authors wrote. Even worse, the number of families trying to cross illegally with children had peaked in mid-April to its highest levels since 2016, with almost 700 families trying to cross in one two-day period. That was nearly as many families as were crossing in an entire month when Trump first took office. The memo was signed by three of the department's top officials: Kevin McAleenan, the president's top border official; Francis Cissna, the head of USCIS; and Tom Homan, the acting director of ICE. "Without statutory changes and additional policy and operational intervention," it concluded, "U.S. Customs and Border Protection (CBP) anticipates the number of apprehensions and inadmissible aliens will continue to rise in April and May."

Among the possible courses of action they offered Nielsen for fixing the problem was a nuclear option that had been uniformly rejected by prior administrations as impractical and morally questionable, not to mention politically suicidal. She could "direct the separation of parents or legal guardians and minors held in immigration detention so that the parent or legal guardian can be prosecuted," the memo said.

The idea had been under consideration inside the administration for more than a year, although most officials had been careful to mention it only in private. The one exception had been John Kelly, who had been questioned weeks into his tenure as homeland security secretary by Wolf Blitzer of CNN about whether he was considering separating children from parents caught crossing the border illegally. Kelly's answer—that he was, indeed, weighing the tactic as a deterrent—drew swift condemnation from lawmakers and an almost instant public retreat by the new secretary. But privately, some tough-minded immigration enforcement officials had told Kelly they thought the government should go even further and adopt a policy in which immigrant children were routinely separated from their parents even when they were apprehended deep in the interior of the country, far from the border.

Inside the administration, discussions about family separation quietly continued, and soon the Trump administration launched a secret pilot program to test its effectiveness. For about five months between July and November of 2017, the Justice Department and Border Patrol officials ran an unannounced experiment in the El Paso sector, which stretched from New Mexico to western Texas. Border agents who encountered families during that time were instructed to detain and refer them for criminal prosecution for illegal border crossing, even if that meant that the children would have to be sent to shelters for months while their parents were detained elsewhere. For decades, it had been common practice for Customs and Border Protection to exempt migrants traveling with minor children from such criminal prosecution unless they were suspected of another crime or of not being related to the children they were transporting. Within months, Justice and DHS had their results, and they were impressive: the number of families crossing the border illegally in the sector had dropped 64 percent.

In late 2017, a discussion document titled "Policy Options to Respond to Border Surge of Illegal Immigration" circulated inside of DHS, suggesting separating children from their parents to accommodate increased adult prosecutions. Under a list of things that could be done within thirty days, number one was titled "Increase Prosecution of Family Unit Parents" and said: "The parents would be prosecuted for illegal entry (misdemeanor) or illegal entry (felony) and the minors present with them would be placed in HHS custody. . . . The increase in prosecutions would be reported by the media and it would have a substantial deterrent effect." A second option on the document noted that separation of families would immediately draw a legal challenge. "Advocacy groups are aware that this policy shift may occur and therefore are seeking to identify families who have been separated in order to bring a class action lawsuit. Hence, close coordination with DOJ will also be required." The memo noted that the status of the family separation idea was "currently under consideration" and added: "Secretarial memo needed for full implementation."

Trump's immigration brain trust, including Sessions, Hamilton, and Miller, was convinced that Central American migrants were using children to exploit a loophole in American immigration law that prohibited minors from being detained in jail with adults. Because of that restriction, if a migrant arrived with his or her kids, the entire family would be released into the United States to wait for an immigration hearing. But that could take months or years, giving them a chance to skip out on their court appearance and disappear into the shadows. Trump's advisers thought that routinely separating all children from their parents when they crossed illegally would close the loophole for good. It was an explosive policy option, but one designed to send a powerful message of deterrence to any migrant who was even considering traveling toward the United States border. It was one of the many ideas Jim Nealon, the DHS assistant secretary, had refused to sign off on in mid-2017, and when it resurfaced, Duke, the acting secretary, had shelved it.

By April of 2018, the formal policy memo had landed on Nielsen's desk calling for a broad adoption of family separations all along the southern border. The memo hailed the success of the El Paso trial, noting the steep drop in border crossings that had resulted, and adding that the pace only picked up again "after the initiative was paused." Now it was time to expand the effort across the entire southern border, the memo argued. Just days earlier, on April 6, Trump had issued a presidential directive titled "Ending 'Catch and Release' at the Border of the United States." It was designed to be a swift kick in the pants for the president's top immigration officials—a reminder of the president's frustration, in case any of them had missed his tweets. In the directive, Trump demanded that "more must be done to enforce our laws and to protect our country from the dangers of releasing detained aliens into our communities." Within hours, Attorney General Jeff Sessions took action, sending his own letter to federal prosecutors along the country's southwest border. Sessions announced a policy of zero tolerance for illegal border crossings. The Justice Department would prosecute 100 percent of the cases referred by DHS officials at the border, he wrote. No exceptions. Sessions described the decision in military terms, saying that "those seeking to further an illegal goal constantly alter their tactics to take advantage of weak points." Prosecutors on the border are "on the front lines of this battle," Sessions wrote. "Remember, our goal is not simply more cases. It is to end the illegality in our immigration system."

For Sessions, the idea was also a matter of survival. Trump had begun to lash out at him routinely for failing to send enough judges to the border to prosecute illegal crossers or winning enough cases against them. So the attorney general had contacted every single United States attorney who covered a border state, either by telephone or in a meeting at the main Justice building on Constitution Avenue, and seen to it that there was a border coordinator in each of their offices. Crossing the border illegally was a misdemeanor, Sessions told them, and they were to prosecute every case that the Department of Homeland Security brought to them. But it soon became clear that there was a flaw in the strategy: in keeping with long-standing policy that dated back decades, DHS was not referring parents arriving with minor children—a group that had increased almost sevenfold since 2013.

It was obvious to Sessions that there was a breach in the wall: that if you came with children, nobody was detained. Migrants who came with a child were all released immediately on bail, given a date to come back for a hearing, which might be weeks or months away, and would disappear into Los Angeles or Houston or someplace and not come back. It was simply unacceptable, Sessions argued. The administration was not going to give immunity to adults who brought children across a dangerous border. Not on his watch.

Gene Hamilton met with McAleenan, Cissna, Homan, and Carla Provost, the acting Border Patrol chief, to drive home Sessions's message. We want Nielsen to start referring people for prosecution, Hamilton told them during a meeting in a small conference room at the headquarters of Customs and Border Protection. "You want me to refer *everybody*? That's several thousand people a week," Provost replied. "Yes," Hamilton said, nodding vigorously. "We're ready. We've got the judges ready—it'll be no problem." For Provost, a no-nonsense former cop from Kansas who had served in the Border Patrol for more than twenty years before rising to its helm, it simply didn't compute. How were her agents supposed to refer this many people? It would be a logistical impossibility. Maybe we'll start slow, and try referring a few hundred a week, she suggested. Just start referring people, Hamilton answered, clearly eager to see zero tolerance become a reality.

In the end, it was up to Nielsen. A former George W. Bush official, she had been a little-known part of the Homeland Security bureaucracy whose consulting company did work for the Obama administration before Kelly picked her to become his top aide, first at DHS and then briefly in the White House. Her loyalty to Kelly had earned her the job replacing him at the helm of the 240,000-person agency. But Trump had always viewed her with suspicion, telling aides she was "a Bushie," and part of the "deep state" who served his predecessors. Nielsen, a lawyer who graduated from Georgetown's School of Foreign Service, had mostly avoided politics, but in 2015, she contributed to a group backing Jeb Bush's presidential campaign, a deed that Trump's base viewed as an unforgivable offense. Her public denials, including under oath before Congress, that she had heard the president use the term "shithole" to describe African countries months earlier had earned her some grudging admiration in the Oval Office. Sessions had explained to Nielsen in a meeting in the conference room across from his office at the Justice Department that prosecutors could only bring charges once cases were referred to them. By signing the DHS memo, Nielsen would be ordering Border Patrol agents to refer all illegal border crossers to the Justice Department, even if it meant separating them from their children. Hamilton had met with Homeland Security, Customs and Border Protection, and Health and Human Services officials who would be responsible for all aspects of the process of separating the families and reuniting them once each prosecution was complete, and had been assured that they could handle it. If it was done right, Sessions assured Nielsen, it would be manageable. The children would be separated briefly, but reunited with their parents quickly. The memo from the department's top officials laid out three options, two of which would have limited prosecutions to adults traveling without children. But Nielsen's advisers made clear what they thought she should do. "We recommend Option 3 as the most effective method to achieve operational objectives and the Administration's goal to end 'catch and release,'" they wrote.

"This initiative would pursue prosecution of all amenable adults who cross our border illegally, including those presenting with a family unit."

For months before Nielsen received the memo, officials at the Office of Refugee Resettlement had been noticing a distinct uptick in the number of separated children. An agency within the Department of Health and Human Services, ORR oversees a network of facilities that temporarily house migrant children, many of whom arrive at the border alone, without an adult. But since about the fall of 2017, the agency had begun tracking an increasing number of children who had arrived in the United States with a parent but were separated at the border before being placed in ORR care. Throughout the fall, there were about one hundred more each month than usual. Jonathan White, the deputy director for children's programs at the agency, began sending notes to his boss, and to officials at DHS. Is there some change we should be aware of? Are children being purposely separated from their parents? The answer White got back was misleading. "There is no official policy that was going to result in family separation," White was told, according to testimony he later gave in a Senate hearing.

Officials did not reveal the existence of the El Paso pilot program, and they did not mention that they were considering vastly expanding it to apply along the entire southwestern border.

White was frustrated. A lifelong advocate for families and children with a master's degree in social work from Catholic University, he was supposed to be ensuring that the government always acted in the best interests of the children in its care. Separating children from their parents was a drastic move that would have severe consequences. In White's mind, such a policy would cause harm to the children, including the significant potential for traumatic psychological injury. He was also worried about the growing strain on ORR resources. There were a limited number of available beds at the agency's facilities around the country. If DHS kept sending more kids at such a relentless rate, White wasn't sure that there would be anywhere to put them. But there was little that he could do. Officials at DHS, and even Scott Lloyd, his boss at ORR, were telling him that what he was witnessing with his eyes was not actually happening. No one had decided to split families apart at the border, they kept saying.

"During the deliberative process over the previous year, we raised a number of concerns in the ORR program about any policy which would result in family separation," White said during his Senate testimony. He was largely ignored.

Scott Shuchart was equally horrified.

As a senior adviser in the DHS Office for Civil Rights and Civil Liberties, Shuchart was part of the small team of bureaucrats whose job was to safeguard civil rights in a department whose mission sometimes entails impinging on people's freedoms in the interests of security. A soft-spoken lawyer with a bachelor's degree from Harvard, a law degree from Yale, and a Bachelor of Philosophy from Oxford, Shuchart had been laboring in the obscure office for more than seven years. CRCL, as it was known inside DHS, was a tiny piece of the sprawling homeland security apparatus. With a budget of about $20 million a year and eighty-six full-time staff, part of the office's job was to provide the secretary with private advice and counsel on difficult policy issues. But since Trump had taken office, the team was routinely cut out of the department's work, making it hard to know what was really going on. In April, Shuchart and his colleagues started hearing reports that children were being separated from their parents when they entered the United States and sought asylum. The office fielded calls from people who felt mistreated by DHS employees, and some of them were coming from parents with harrowing stories of children being seized at the border and whisked away with no explanation.

Was there an El Paso pilot program to separate children? Shuchart asked, having heard rumors about the existence of the trial. He got the same nonanswer that White did. Senior DHS officials deflected, insisting that there had been no decision to routinely take migrant children from their parents. And yet, Shuchart and his colleagues kept hearing horror stories about parents at the border weeping as they watched their children being taken away. Sitting at computer consoles equipped to show the picture that accompanied the case they were handling, they gazed at snapshots of little boys and girls, often smiling with gap-toothed grins as if in a school photo, as the officials tried unsuccessfully to console distraught parents who had called to say that their child had been taken. Some wept at their desks. If children were routinely being separated from their parents, Shuchart knew, the policy presented serious humanitarian concerns, affecting the fundamental rights of people covered by U.S. law and a variety of international treaties and agreements about refugees and asylum seekers. In addition, it was a huge breach of department protocol to pursue such a policy without having consulted the civil rights office.

Shuchart and others tried desperately to convince the top official in the office to demand answers. Cameron Quinn, a Trump appointee, was a longtime election law professor who once served as the top election official in Fairfax County, Virginia. Before moving over to DHS, she had worked in a similar role at the Department of Justice. But she had little interest in challenging Nielsen or her allies in the White House, even in the face of press reports that more than seven hundred children had already been separated from their parents as part of the El Paso program. Throughout April, Shuchart and other members of Quinn's staff repeatedly pressed her to challenge the idea of separating children from their parents. "She just doesn't appreciate what we are trying to tell her, or the gravity of it," a former colleague in the office recalled.

Finally, on May 12, Shuchart sent a stinging, six-page memo to Quinn, signed by the rest of the senior staff of the department. "The apprehension, custody and transportation of alien children raises serious humanitarian concerns," he wrote. In the memo, Shuchart said Quinn should not relinquish her office's authority to be part of serious policy debates. For example, he said, the civil rights office was aware of rumors that Nielsen had been given a decision memo on separating children. But neither Quinn nor anyone in the office had been given the opportunity to review and comment on it. It was an outrage that threatened to undermine the whole point of the civil rights office, which was supposed to be integrated into deliberations on serious issues and included in the review of new departmental policies. "In this instance, neither of these things happened," he wrote.

Shuchart saved his toughest language for his substantive concerns. The decision to separate children from their parents to deter future migration raises "civil and human rights" issues, he said. Using italics to underscore his points for Quinn, Shuchart said that the *use of seizure and ensuing trauma for general deterrence* would only be effective because a reasonable parent would not want to be forcibly separated from their child. "That is, *harm to children is being deliberately used for its deterrent effect.*" He cited Article 31 of the Refugee Protocol, part of global United Nations agreements from 1951 and 1967. He raised the likelihood that the department's actions could violate the United States Constitution. And he urged Quinn to consider the practical problems: a surge of children will overwhelm a system that is not capable of adequately caring for young children.

"In short," he concluded, "family separation and 'zero tolerance' prosecution of border crossers is likely to lead to a chaotic crisis this summer, in part, of the Department's own creation. We are concerned that the operational and human consequences of the family separation policy have not been fully considered or planned for."

The plea fell on deaf ears.

Nielsen didn't know what to do.

She shared the belief that something needed to be done to stop the increasing number of migrants flowing across the remote parts of the border. Most were relying on dangerous smugglers, known in the region as "coyotes," who took advantage of their clients' desperate hopes of escaping into the United States. Many migrants grew sick on the journey, were sexually abused or beaten. And almost all arrived tired and destitute. If separating families who crossed illegally succeeded in diverting those families to official ports of entry, where they could make legitimate asylum claims in safety, that would be a good thing, she thought. And providing a deterrent to something that was clearly against the law—crossing the border without authorization—didn't strike her as a such a bad idea either.

But as the White House and her colleagues at DHS pressed her to hurry up and approve the policy—"Do it! Do it! Do it!" was their constant refrain, she told confidants—Nielsen worried that the plan was half-baked. It was unclear to Nielsen whether Trump understood that families would be separated. But he viewed her as an obstacle to a decision to prosecute everyone who broke the law. "Just do it!" he yelled at her again and again. Nielsen worried that there was already a huge backlog in immigration cases and there wouldn't be the resources to handle the families when they were arrested at the border.

"Do you have all the facilities for the children, should we need them?" she asked officials at the Department of Health and Human Services. HHS already had a well-established process for dealing with unaccompanied children who arrived at the border with no parent at all, they assured her; they could handle it. Nielsen quizzed Rod Rosenstein, the deputy attorney general, about whether the Justice Department had the resources to prosecute all the people she would send their way. Did they have courtrooms for the judges? Metal detectors? Enough lawyers for all the new cases? When her staff raised doubts about whether Justice was ready, Nielsen went back to Rosenstein again to express her concerns. Rosenstein, Sessions, and several of her own top border officials predicted that the separations would taper off quickly once word got down to Central America that children were being taken at the border. That's what had happened during the El Paso trial, they said, and there was no reason to think it wouldn't happen that way again.

During a contentious congressional hearing on April 11, Nielsen had publicly rejected the idea of separating children for deterrence. "When we separate, we separate because the law tells us to, and that is in the interest of the child," she told members of the House Homeland Security Appropriations Subcommittee. She knew full well that there was a decision memo languishing on her desk that proposed a very different approach. But she hadn't signed it yet, and wasn't sure if she would. On April 26, the document was leaked to *The Washington Post*, which ran a story with the headline: "Top Homeland Security Officials Urge Criminal Prosecution of Parents Crossing Border with Children." Nielsen believed the leak was an effort by advocates of the idea to force her to sign the memo. If she didn't, she knew that Trump would see it as yet more evidence that she wasn't a team player and wasn't doing enough to secure the border. But the urgency baffled her. "Why is this suddenly the most important thing that has to be decided?" she thought. "We have Russians about to attack our election again. Why now?" The day of the *Post* story, Nielsen's spokeswoman issued a press release saying that "DHS does not have a policy of separating families at the border for deterrence purposes."

Nielsen finally gave in at the beginning of May, after a morning of relentless calls from McAleenan, Homan, and others. "You have to make a decision," they told her. The president wanted this done and the longer Nielsen waited, the more he would view her as an impediment. "Your ass is hanging out there. Sessions is doing zero tolerance. You have to sign this," they told her. She finally agreed, telling top aides that she would put her faith in the memo's three authors that they knew what they were doing and could reunite the kids quickly after the parents were prosecuted. Her decision codified the separations. Across the southern border with Mexico, adults crossing without authorization were forcibly separated from their children and jailed while they waited for prosecution. Their children were reclassified by border agents as "unaccompanied" minors, as if they had crossed the border without an adult, and sent to facilities run by the Department of Health and Human Services.

Once Nielsen signed the memo, it was clear that someone would have to announce the new policy publicly and frame it in the best possible light. But Nielsen's advisers at DHS argued strongly that it should not be her. "Let Sessions own this," Jonathan Hoffman, the department's top communications official, told Nielsen. "It's not something we can control. You do not want to be the face of this." This is a shit storm, her staff kept telling her. We cannot own any of this. Kelly, in particular, believed that whoever was seen as responsible for the policy would be savaged by the press and the public, vilified and tarnished in Trump's eyes. But Nielsen was conflicted. On one hand, she had no desire to be the public face of a draconian policy, but she also did not want Sessions to get the credit from the president for a tough measure that could work. What if this goes according to plan, she said, and the border crossing numbers do come down? People will be reunited quickly and everything will improve, and then Sessions will get credit and I'm going to be fired! She wanted Trump, who was constantly castigating her as incompetent, to see her as a critical player in delivering the results he demanded.

Nielsen's press team had warily prepared a rollout of the new policy with a conference call for reporters and talking points to provide background about its complex implications. But when Justice Department officials notified their DHS counterparts that Sessions had scheduled a major speech on immigration for May 7, Nielsen's staff seized the opportunity to let Sessions own the spotlight—and the public scrutiny. The conference call with reporters was canceled, the talking points scrapped. When Hoffman saw a copy of the prepared remarks that Sessions intended to give, he was concerned. The attorney general planned to openly declare that children could be separated from their parents as part of the initiative to prosecute all adults. Hoffman sent a note to his counterpart at the Justice Department, urging the removal of that language. The response he got back: Absolutely not. That's our money line.

"Today we are here to send a message to the world: we are not going to let this country be overwhelmed," Sessions declared on May 7, standing near a section of fence along the border with Tijuana, Mexico, in Border Field State Park, on the outskirts of San Diego. "That's why the Department of Homeland Security is now referring 100 percent of illegal Southwest Border crossings to the Department of Justice for prosecution. And the Department of Justice will take up those cases." If there was any doubt what the consequences of that change would be, Sessions unapologetically made them clear by delivering the line that DHS had urged him to remove: "If you are smuggling a child, then we will prosecute you, and that child will be separated from you as required by law."

ICE acting director Homan stood beside Sessions that day, appearing to put the DHS stamp of approval on the move even as he previewed a line that Nielsen would repeat incessantly in the months to come to justify the new family separation tactics. "Every law enforcement agency in this country separates parents from children when they're arrested for a crime," Homan said. "There is no new policy. This has always been the policy." But even Homan framed the approach as a Jeff Sessions initiative. "Now," he said, "you will see more prosecutions because of the attorney general's commitment to zero tolerance."

Sessions was a true believer. He fully agreed with the family separation policy; after all, he had helped to design it. But his aides were convinced that Nielsen and Kelly were setting him up to be the heavy, to take the public criticism that was already ramping up. The canceled press rollout by DHS was further evidence that Nielsen was trying to have it both ways. She wanted to dampen Trump's rage by assuring him in private that her department was doing everything possible to prevent migrants from crossing into the country illegally. But she also wanted to avoid being the public face of a plainly brutal policy. In the hours after Sessions delivered his San Diego remarks, his chief immigration spokesman, Devin O'Malley, was back in Washington helping to prepare judicial nominees for the Ninth

Circuit Court of Appeals ahead of their confirmation hearings the next day. Suddenly, his phone started ringing with urgent calls from reporters seeking information about the new family separation policy.

Having scrapped their own media plan, public affairs officials at DHS were referring all calls to him.

The decision was made, but it had yet to produce the kind of results that would assuage the president's frustration. The numbers of illegal border crossers was still rising. Two days after Sessions delivered his speech in San Diego, Trump was in another one of his rages.

On May 9, the president was scheduled to host an 11:30 a.m. meeting of his cabinet at the White House. Hours before, Hamilton and others at the Justice Department began to hear that Kelly wanted the cabinet meeting to focus almost entirely on immigration, and in particular on the Justice Department's failure to deal with the crisis at the border. The message from Kelly was that the president wanted to know why immigration judges couldn't get cases decided faster. The attorney general is going to have to explain that to the president, Kelly said.

Hamilton swiftly assembled a strike team of lawyers in the attorney general's conference room on the fifth floor to arm Sessions for what they saw as an orchestrated attack. They quickly gathered up charts and graphs showing the number of judges that had been sent to the border. And they prepared Sessions to fight back more broadly, to talk about the systemic issues at the border that caused problems long before cases were ever referred to the Justice Department and its immigration judges. The department was on the receiving end of a hose that was flooding them with cases from DHS. And Sessions didn't control the hose. To Hamilton and the rest of Sessions's team, the ambush that was about to take place was all about Kelly trying to deflect blame from Nielsen and shift it to Sessions. Everyone knew how much Trump disliked Sessions because of his decision to recuse himself from the Russia investigation. He was an easy target, already damaged goods in the president's eyes. But this was a low blow, they thought, even for Kelly.

At the start of the cabinet meeting, with reporters present and cameras rolling, Trump looked angry. "The laws in this country for immigration and illegal immigration are absolutely horrible. And we have to do something about it," the president fumed. After the reporters were asked to leave, Trump continued to rage about the border. Sessions defended his department and tried to deflect the president's ire. His aides had prepared him to tell Trump that the government could control the flow of migrants at the border, especially at the ports of entry, where the Border Patrol can determine how quickly they process people trying to enter the country. But the message that Trump and others around the table heard that afternoon from Sessions was simpler and far less nuanced. "You can control this," Sessions said to the president citing a written opinion from the Justice Department's Office of Legal Counsel that the president had authority to stop immigrants at the border. The problem isn't really with the judges or the immigration prosecutions, he said. "You've got to not let people in in the first place. Just turn them away." In other words, don't look at me. It's Kirstjen's fault.

Sessions's blame-shifting worked. For the better part of the next half hour, Trump turned on his DHS secretary, dressing her down relentlessly in front of her cabinet-level peers. His voice raised and his face red, Trump demanded that Nielsen "close down" the border. Mexico was not doing enough to prevent migrants from crossing through their country on their way to the United States, Trump said. And when the migrants get here, the laws are too weak to keep them out. He directed some of his anger at other members of the cabinet sitting around the table. But he focused most of his rage on his homeland security secretary. "Why don't you have solutions? How is this still happening?" he demanded.

Nielsen began arguing back. What Sessions had said was completely wrong, she told the president. There is no way to just "turn them away" when migrants arrive at the border. What does that even mean, anyway? International law, not to mention decades-old statutes, require the United States to consider all requests for asylum when immigrants arrive at the border, legally or illegally. For the thousandth time, she tried to explain that to the president. The argument dragged on as Trump repeatedly expressed his fury about what he saw as the Mexican government's un-willingness to stop migrants before they get to the United States. Nielsen challenged the president on that, too, though she could see Jared Kushner, who was sitting across from her, shaking his head quietly as he caught her eye, as if to say: "It's a lost cause. Just stop fighting."

Nielsen was exasperated. There were limits on what her department could do, she insisted. But Trump was not satisfied. "I don't want to hear it. Fix the problem!" The president yelled that if the borders couldn't be adequately defended then "we need to shut it down. We're closed." And he issued a blunt warning to Nielsen. "If I lose the election," he bellowed, "it's because of you!"

It was an extraordinary performance, even for Trump, and it severely rattled Nielsen. She often told friends privately that she was miserable in her job, where she was under immense pressure to carry out a policy she had little say in crafting, and was a slave to the whims of an unreasonable president who had no regard for the complexity of the things he was de-manding. Now, after being the target of his fury once again, Nielsen was unsure whether she could continue in her post. "I guess I'm not doing my job, so I can just quit," she told her colleagues. She canceled the rest of her meetings for the day and returned to her satellite office at the Ronald Reagan Building on 14th Street, two blocks from the White House.

Kelly was deeply offended by the way Trump had spoken to Nielsen that day and told her she should quit. "Why would you stay? That's ri-diculous. He's telling you to break the law." Unsure what to do, Nielsen went to see Vice President Mike Pence and his chief of staff, Nick Ayers, in Pence's West Wing office. "The president's really frustrated. It's not you, specifically," Pence told her. "I don't think you should quit." Several hours later, Kelly called back. He had changed his mind and urged her to stay. Other top White House aides tried to console her, too. I need to make sure I can be effective in the job, she told them. If it's widely perceived that I can't do it, that would be problematic, she said. By evening, word of her explosive confrontation with Trump and her threats to resign had leaked out to the press. In a carefully worded statement the next day, she said that she intended to "continue to direct the department to do all we can to implement the president's security-focused agenda." She did not comment explicitly on the irrational fit of rage that had been directed against her. Instead, she offered an explanation of sorts for it, and purported to identify with Trump's anger.

"The president is rightly frustrated that existing loopholes and the lack of Congressional action have prevented this administration from fully securing the border and protecting the American people," she wrote. "I share his frustration."

— 23 —

REVERSE BOOMERANG

THE IMAGES OF SOBBING children, forcibly separated from their mothers and fathers at the border, were seemingly everywhere on the muggy Thursday afternoon in June when Stephen Miller sat down for an interview in his third-floor suite of offices in the West Wing.

That morning, *The New York Times* had published the story of a five-year-old boy named José, who had been separated from his father at the Mexican border in El Paso and flown to live temporarily with an American family in Michigan. "The first few nights, he cried himself to sleep," the article said of José, quoting his foster mother. Then it turned into "just moaning and moaning." In another news report that day, an immigration advocate told the story of a seven-year-old girl and her older brother who had been separated months ago from their mother, and "cried and begged" to be reunited. At a rally in Chicago, protesters, including some young children, held signs that said: "Separating parents and children is a crime against humanity." A day earlier, on CNN, Senator Jeff Merkley, a Democrat from Oregon, described his visit to a border detention facility in Texas. "What you have is cyclone fencing and fence posts that look like cages," Merkley said that morning. "They look like the way you would construct a dog kennel."

In the interview, Miller was defiant and defensive, insisting that the zero tolerance policy would continue. He never expressed regret for the plight of children and their parents. Privately, he had told his colleagues in no uncertain terms that these families needed to be punished to deter others like them from coming to the United States. Miller's public posture was more carefully articulated—but no less absolute. Democrats, he repeatedly insisted over the course of a 90-minute discussion, were to blame for the children who were being separated at the border, because they refused to allow the Trump administration to make changes to long-standing laws and legal precedents. He spoke quickly with his trademark intensity about how the government must be able to indefinitely detain anyone who crosses the border illegally—even if they are children or families. And he fumed about what he called the "radical left of the Democratic Party," which he said believed in simply releasing everyone that came into the United States.

"The laws exist for a reason, and in an environment of lawlessness and chaos, innocent people are needlessly hurt," Miller said. Publicly, other Trump officials, including Nielsen, had tried to dodge the question of whether the family separation policy was intended to be a deterrent for the surge of migrants from Central America. But Miller went on at length about what he said was the biggest "pull factor" luring Central Americans to make the dangerous trek across Mexico. It wasn't American jobs and the prospect of a more affluent life, he insisted. It was the belief that immigration laws in the United States were easily evaded once they got here. The only way to send a different message back to Central America—to prevent illegal immigration—was to implement a crackdown. To do otherwise would be to continue offering what he called "an extraordinarily perverse incentive" to the migrants.

"But I do want to say this," Miller said as he turned to rifle through papers on a table next to his couch. He was looking for a document he had printed out so he could have it for reference—a list of arrests that federal immigration officials had made during a recent raid in Philadelphia. He had chosen Philadelphia because the city's Democratic mayor, Jim Kenney, had mounted and won a legal challenge in federal court to Trump's bid to deny federal grant money to cities that limit their cooperation with ICE. Kenney had called the president a "bully," and singled out Sessions for criticism, saying, "federal grant dollars cannot be used for a political shakedown," and he had been captured on video doing a jig in his office after he got word of the favorable ruling. "It is impossible to take moral lectures from people like the mayor of Philadelphia, who dance in jubilant celebration over sanctuary cities, when you had innocent Americans, U.S.-born and foreign, who are victimized on a daily basis because of illegal immigration," Miller said as he proceeded to read from the list. "We arrested an illegal alien who conducted lewd and lascivious acts with a minor. We arrested someone who had been convicted of murder, child neglect," Miller said, reading from the list. "May 25, 2017," he said, continuing. "Negligent manslaughter, stolen vehicle. Prostitution, racketeering, rape."

The sheaf of papers encapsulated how Miller thought about immigrants, not as part of the fundamental fabric of the country so much as a group of dangerous, uninvited guests who threatened native-born Americans. Three weeks earlier, Trump had sparked another round of outrage by calling immigrant gang members "animals," a fact that Miller thought was indisputable. "These aren't people, these are animals," Trump had said, referring to members of the brutal transnational gang MS-13 as he made the case for treating all undocumented immigrants more harshly. Several major news organizations covered Trump's remark, some of them suggesting that he had called all immigrants "animals." To Miller, the coverage highlighted how unwilling the media and both political parties had been to call illegal immigration by its name, and to enforce the nation's immigration laws to prevent grave harm to Americans. In Miller's world, there was no room for the niceties of asylum or refugee programs if they enabled the entry of even one person who would commit a crime.

As the conversation continued, Miller tried to steer away from the political implications of separating families, but he could hardly contain himself. He predicted that Americans would resoundingly side with the political party that secured the borders. "And not—not by a little bit. Not 55–45, 60–40, 70–30, 80–20. I'm talking 90–10 on that," he insisted. He lashed out at the Democrats again, arguing that the American public would reject what he called the "open-borders extremism" of the Democratic Party. He paused for effect and then ratcheted up his attack. "I would go one step further and say the current position of the Democratic Party is open-borders nihilism. They've adopted a point of view so radical that it can really only be described as absolute nihilism," he said.

Still, the images of the small children separated from their families were politically powerful. Is there any chance that Trump will back down in the face of those pictures? Could the White House really sustain this policy with condemnation coming from everywhere? His answer was classic Miller.

"The United States government has a sacred, solemn, inviolable obligation to enforce the laws of the United States to stop illegal immigration and secure and protect our borders," he declared as the interview came to a conclusion. "And there's no straying from that mission."

Eleven days after the Miller interview, ProPublica, an investigative news cooperative, posted a chilling audio clip online that had been secretly recorded by an employee inside a Customs and Border Protection detention facility and later provided to a Texas civil rights attorney. For almost eight excruciating minutes, children could be heard crying and wailing in Spanish for "Mami" and "Papá" and begging border agents to see their parents. "Well, we have an orchestra here, right?" a border agent could be heard joking about the chaotic noise of the children inside the facility. "What we're missing is a conductor." One little boy continued uncontrollably, in between sobs: "Papá. Papá. Papá."

As the heartrending sounds continued, one six-year-old girl from El Salvador, Alison Jimena Valencia Madrid, tried to reason with a female consular official at the detention facility. "Are you going to call my aunt so that when I'm done eating, she can pick me up?" Alison asked in Spanish. "I have her number memorized," she continued, rattling off her aunt's number: "Three, four, seven, two . . ." After a few more minutes, Alison tried again. "Are you going to call my aunt so she can come pick me up? And then so my mom can come as soon as possible?" The consular official did not tell Alison that her mother had been arrested and was not coming anytime soon. But the official told a colleague that she planned to call Alison's aunt. Alison explained what her mother told her before they were separated by Border Patrol agents. "My mommy says I'll go with my aunt and that she'll come to pick me up there as quickly as possible so I can go with her," she said.

The recording was difficult to listen to. And within hours, it was everywhere—broadcast in a seemingly endless loop on CNN and MSNBC; delivered on demand by every news website; played on the radio news programs during the morning and evening commutes. On Capitol Hill, Representative Ted Lieu, a Democrat from California, stood at a lectern on the floor of the House, reached into a pocket in his suit jacket, and pressed play on a small audio device. The sounds of the wailing children echoed through the largely empty chamber with the C-SPAN cameras running. "The gentleman will suspend," demanded Representative Karen Handel, a Georgia Republican who was serving as the speaker that afternoon. Lieu refused. "Why are you trying to prevent the American people from listening to what it sounds like in a detention facility," he declared, letting the sounds of the children crying continue to play. Handel grew frustrated and slammed the gavel. "Rule 17 prohibits the use of an electronic device to make sounds in the chamber," Handel insisted. "The gentleman will suspend!" Lieu refused to relent. "We have 2,300 babies and kids in detention facilities who were ripped away from their parents. I think the American people need to hear this." The sounds of the children from Lieu's recorder continued for another two minutes and thirteen seconds as he stood, stone-faced toward the cameras and Handel conferred with the House floor staff. Lieu finally turned off the recording only after Handel threatened to have the chamber's sergeant at arms "enforce the rules of decorum."

The audio clip crystallized the human dimensions of the family separation policy. In the weeks since Nielsen's decision, more than 2,500 children had been treated like the wailing voices captured on the recording. Under the new rules, children traveling with adults as they crossed without authorization into the United States were taken and reclassified as "unaccompanied minors." It was a mere bureaucratic designation, but it had a sinister effect that would prove disastrous as the number of separated families climbed; it essentially broke the linkage in the United States government's records between the migrant child and the parent with whom he or she arrived, making it extremely difficult to match them together later on. It also triggered a long process that, for many children like Alison, led them hundreds of miles away from their parents, to shelters for "tender-aged" children run by the Department of Health and Human Services. The shelters were mostly well maintained and staffed by caring employees. But they were already at capacity even before Nielsen's decision, forcing CBP to hold some children in detention for days or weeks before they could be transferred. Images of children sleeping under metallic blankets behind chain-link fences quickly captured the public imagination.

Like Miller, Trump was defiant, and refused to back down.

In an event in the East Room of the White House on space research, the president lashed out at Democrats and vowed that the United States would not become a migrant camp or a refugee holding facility like Europe. "Not on my watch," he declared, with Vice President Mike Pence standing silently to his right. "Remember," the president added, "a country without borders is not a country at all." And he dismissed the people crossing the southwestern border as lacking any qualities that might benefit the United States. Americans should want to let in people based on merit, he said, "not people that snuck across the border. And they could be murderers and thieves and so much else."

Nielsen was equally defensive during a little noticed speech in New Orleans to the National Sheriffs' Association on the morning of Monday, June 18. She complained about the "outcry and consternation" about the family separations and the refusal by Congress to give border agents more flexibility to detain families. "As a result of charging people for crimes they have actually committed, we must often separate adults from minors in their custody," she told the audience. She was unapologetic, insisting in the face of the swirling controversy that "there are some who would like us to look the other way when dealing with families at the border and not enforce the law passed by Congress, including some members of Congress. Past administrations may have done so, but we will not."

On the flight back to Washington, Sarah Huckabee Sanders called with an urgent request. Nielsen was needed in the White House briefing room, she said. You've got to go out there and defend the president and this policy. By the time she arrived in the West Wing, Nielsen was wary, as were her closest advisers. It was one thing to give a speech to a friendly audience full of supportive law enforcement officers. It was another thing entirely to face the White House press corps at the height of a full-blown scandal. Jonathan Hoffman, her spokesman, believed it was probably her job to do the briefing—a shitty job, but one she signed up for. Even so, he counseled her not to, knowing she would face a fierce grilling. Kelly, who was Nielsen's top protector in the administration, strenuously fought against the idea. You don't own this; don't do it, Kelly told her. Whoever goes out there is going to be the public face of this, and that shouldn't be you. "This is Sessions's shit storm," he told her. "Don't clean up his mess." Forget it, Nielsen said. I'm not doing it. But then she changed her mind again. She felt she owed it to the men and women in her department, who were being demonized for the family separations, to make the public case for them. And under immense pressure from Sanders and others in the White House, she relented. Nielsen got no preparation and little direction for her first solo appearance in the White House press room for a news conference that was carried on live TV. Try to call on someone in the middle, Sanders counseled. She didn't say why, but Nielsen later found out that the front rows of the briefing room are reserved for the highest-profile reporters, network correspondents and journalists from the top newspapers in the country.

Once at the lectern, Nielsen assailed Democrats and activists who were criticizing the administration, and declared firmly that "this administration did not create a policy of separating families at the border." But moments later, she acknowledged that "what has changed is that we no longer exempt entire classes of people who break the law. Everyone is subject to prosecution." Reporters in the room, clearly unsatisfied with Nielsen's evasive comments, peppered her with questions.

"Have you seen the photos of children in cages? Have you heard the audio clip of these children wailing, that just came out today?" one asked. Another pressed Nielsen on whether "this policy is not, by your definition, in any way cruel?" One simply wanted to know: "How is this not child abuse?" Nielsen got more and more defensive, her lips pressed tightly together. She deflected questions about the photos of children in cages and said she had not heard the audio recording. She repeatedly blamed Congress, suggesting that the government had no choice but to separate families as long as lawmakers refused to change asylum and immigration laws. When a reporter asserted that "we've never seen this under previous administrations," Nielsen seized on the inaccuracy and insisted that they "all separated families," too. She did not mention that prior administrations had taken migrant children from parents only on a case-by-case basis, when they had a specific reason to do so based on a concern for the child's welfare. It was a misleading answer that most viewers watching on television would not catch.

But it was Nielsen's answer to one of the last questions during her appearance that stood out as blatantly false, given the memo approving family separation that she had signed six weeks earlier. As reporters shouted to be heard, Steven Portnoy, a young and aggressive correspondent for CBS News Radio, broke through the din. "Are you intending for this to play out as it is playing out?" he asked, jabbing his hand in the air. "Are you intending for parents to be separated from their children? Are you intending to send a message?"

"I find that offensive," she said before declaring firmly: "No. Because why would I ever create a policy that purposely does that?"

"Perhaps as a deterrent," Portnoy said.

"No," she responded.

"AG Sessions says it was a deterrent," he said.

"The answer is, it's a law passed by the United States Congress. Rather than fixing the law, Congress is asking those of us who enforce the law to turn our backs on the law and not enforce the law. It's not an answer. The answer is to fix the laws."

It took only another forty-eight hours for Trump to cave.

In the weeks since Nielsen signed the memo, more than 2,500 children had been separated from their parents. (Officials later admitted that thousands more were separated prior to Nielsen making it a formal government policy.) The top human rights official at the United Nations condemned the practice as "unconscionable." The pope called it "immoral." Closer to home, Thomas J. Donohue, the CEO of the U.S. Chamber of Commerce, declared that "this is not who we are, and it must end now." The president's wife publicly chided her husband, saying the United States needed to be "a country that governs with heart."

Few people had more impact on the president than his daughter—and she was furious. As the mother of three young kids, Ivanka was flabbergasted at the idea that the government would purposely separate a mother or father from their children. And as the daughter of an embattled president, she was determined to stop the political damage that the policy was wreaking on her father. Ivanka blamed Trump's advisers, particularly Kelly and Nielsen, for getting him into the family separation mess by failing to appreciate the power of the devastating images that had for weeks been broadcast on television screens. She told her father that they had set the policy in motion without explaining the consequences to anyone, and now the president was paying the price.

On the morning of June 20, the West Wing was in complete chaos. The previous evening, Trump had admitted to Republican lawmakers that the optics of the family separations were "nasty" for him. His daughter Ivanka had told him the images were not good, Trump told the lawmakers. "The crying babies," he explained, "doesn't look good politically." By the time he woke up the next day, he had decided to throw in the towel on family separation. He told Kelly that he wanted to issue an executive order ending the policy that day. He instructed Don McGahn, the White House counsel, to draft the directive. He called Nielsen. "Come in to the White

House. We're doing this." When she arrived, nobody seemed to know what was happening. Miller was pacing around and popping in and out of McGahn's office to weigh in on the emerging draft, looking like he was having a meltdown. At one point, the vice president wandered through and buttonholed Nielsen. "What is this thing going to say?" he asked her. She didn't know. The whole process took less than an hour, and the result was a complete muddle. The 773-word order did not explicitly end family separation nor order the already separated children to be reunited with their parents. (A federal judge would later do both.) Instead, the document, titled "Affording Congress an Opportunity to Address Family Separation," pledged to continue aggressive enforcement of the nation's immigration laws while at the same time attempting to "maintain family unity." Parts of the order read more like a Miller-authored policy paper or speech than a legal document. "It is unfortunate that Congress's failure to act and court orders have put the Administration in the position of separating alien families to effectively enforce the law," the order said.

Still, Trump was clear with his staff about what this meant. He was sick and tired of the attacks and the controversy. He just wanted it to end. With Nielsen standing behind him at the Resolute Desk in the Oval Office, Trump signed the executive order overturning Nielsen's memorandum and directed the government to keep families together.

The retreat was the first real moment since taking office that Trump had backed down on a major immigration initiative, and some inside the West Wing saw it as evidence that Miller had finally gone too far. A few Republicans even called on Trump to dump him. "The President should fire Stephen Miller now," tweeted Mike Coffman, a Republican House member from Colorado who was facing a tough reelection race. For a time, Miller retreated into the background, content to be out of the headlines for a while.

Inside DHS, an odd combination of relief coupled with disappointment set in among top officials. On one hand, the white-hot controversy that had earned them condemnation from around the country and around the globe had ended instantly with a stroke of Trump's pen. But no one could shake the feeling that if the president had only been willing to hold out for a bit longer, as little as a week or two, the policy would have had its desired effect. The numbers of families showing up at the border would have started to fall as word reached Central America that the price of admission to the United States was having your child taken away. Instead, the opposite message would quickly reach the region: the Trump administration will never enforce the law against you. Homan, in particular, was disappointed. He thought the separations had been implemented disastrously, without the proper planning that he assumed would have taken place when he signed on to the memo for Nielsen. But he also thought that Trump had abandoned it too soon. He told colleagues that if the separations had continued for another thirty to forty-five days, it would have been the end of the Central American caravans.

Instead, Trump had buckled, causing what one senior official later called a "reverse boomerang effect." More families began flooding toward the United States.

— 24 —

ALWAYS A BOMB THROWER

OF ALL THE PUZZLING contradictions of Donald Trump's immigration agenda, there was none so profound as Stephen Miller, the young hard-liner with the over-the-top rhetorical style who held outsized influence inside the West Wing. Miller had spent most of his life rebelling against the establishment, styling himself as a provocateur willing to say what others would not, and relishing the shock and disgust of polite society with a self-satisfied smirk. But now, as a top adviser to the president of the United States, he *was* the establishment. Miller had real power in the Trump White House, and he spent much of his time struggling to figure out how to wield it effectively. In public, Miller's persona was that of an evil genius methodically plotting the most draconian immigration policies conceivable and bending the president to his will. Behind the scenes, the reality was more complicated.

Though he became the Trump-whisperer on immigration and spent years writing his speeches, Miller's views on immigration diverged in some significant ways from those of the president he served. Miller was driven by an ideology centered around the belief that legal and illegal immigration were detrimental to the United States and the fortunes of native-born Americans. He had long harbored a desire to radically reorder the system so that fewer immigrants could enter. By contrast, Trump's beliefs on the subject had no ideological core; they were a jumble of political instincts and personal observations that resulted in an aggressive posture—build a wall, crack down at the border, ban Muslims, fear a foreign "invasion." The resulting policy vision often dovetailed with Miller's own. But it hardly amounted to a cohesive agenda. In fact, Trump's natural impulses were in many ways the opposite of those that animated Miller and other immigration restrictionists like him, who were fixated on the plight of working Americans whose wages and jobs they argued were threatened by an onslaught of cheap foreign labor.

Trump was a business executive who prized cheap labor and readily available workers, no matter their legal status. While Miller and his low-immigration brethren routinely pressed for the mandatory use of E-Verify, the federal database for employers to check the immigration status of their workers, Trump privately railed against the tool. He was forced to use E-Verify when he was building the Trump International Hotel in downtown Washington, the president would often tell people, and it's "tough." It really raises costs, he would say. It nearly killed me, he said. It was the worst, most expensive thing ever—a total mess! It eventually became obvious that Trump did not use the system voluntarily; *The New York Times* reported in early December of 2018 that he employed many undocumented immigrants at his Bedminster, New Jersey, golf resort, and in the spring of 2019, that many more worked at his empire of resorts throughout the state of Florida.

Miller differed from Trump in another key way: he did not mind being seen by the public as a bad guy. The president, for all his tough talk, could not stand to be seen as mean or coldhearted, particularly when it came to children. It was why he shrank from a decision on the Dreamers and backed down from the family separation policy when the political heat got intense. Miller had no such qualms; he was happy to absorb the arrows even if it meant sharpening the caricature of him as the heartless, scheming architect of the administration's crackdown on immigrants. In fact, Miller fed the cartoonish impression himself, almost seeming to enjoy the notoriety. And the president loved him for it. Trump would later marvel at how different Miller was from his image in the media. "Stephen Miller has a press that's so different than he is. He's conservative, but he's a compassionate conservative, and if you read about him, they make him out to be something that he's really not," Trump said in an interview in June of 2019. "He's very intense, as you've seen, and I think probably the intensity gets him into a little problem, but he's intense in his love for the country." Miller wasn't completely immune to the criticism. When Ilhan Omar, a Somali American congresswoman from Minnesota who in 2019 became one of the first Muslim women to serve in Congress, attacked Miller on Twitter as a white nationalist, Miller—who is Jewish—told those close to him that he longed to respond with an explanation of why her attack made no sense. Instead, he let others defend him.

Thirty-three years old, with a slight build and a receding hairline, Miller was in some ways an unlikely champion of an anti-immigrant agenda: the middle child in an upper-middle-class Jewish family from a liberal, racially diverse Southern California enclave. Miller's great-grandfather fled anti-Jewish pogroms in Belarus at the turn of the century and arrived at Ellis Island in 1903, an immigrant who eventually brought his family to the United States and built a chain of supermarkets and grocery stores.

But despite his own personal history, Miller had been skeptical of immigrants and diversity of all kinds from a young age. And he had been waiting all his life for the kind of validation that being close to Trump provided. As a skinny kid in Santa Monica, he had grown up picking fights with liberals and with the establishment, and Miller became his high school's resident conservative and opponent of multiculturalism. Hispanics made up 30 percent of the student body at Santa Monica High School, and Miller would complain bitterly about announcements being made in both English and Spanish, suggesting that if students could not understand English, they should go elsewhere. He wrote a letter to the local newspaper branding bilingual announcements at his school "a crutch," complaining that there were "few, if any Hispanic students in my honors classes." Providing material in Spanish, young Miller wrote, "makes a mockery of the American ideal of personal accomplishment."

Even as a teenager, Miller understood the power of the media and the pull of an activist who was willing to buck convention and shock his audience. "I will say and I will do things that no one else in their right mind would say or do," Miller told his fellow students during a failed run for student government, with an insouciant grin on his face. He lost the race, but his speech was a memorable one. Miller criticized the school custodians, saying he was "sick and tired of being told to pick up my trash, when we have plenty of janitors who are paid to do it for us." So common were his rantings that his high school newspaper published an *Onion*-like parody of a letter to the editor in which they imagined Miller writing about the end of a multicultural club day. The school, the fake Miller wrote, "is much better off without that gross display of multiculturalism encroaching on our pure American values." Before long, Miller had caught the attention of Larry Elder, the conservative radio host based in California, who invited him onto his show. Elder would later say he had Miller on his program more than seventy times.

Miller went from California to Duke University, where he met David Horowitz, a right-wing provocateur and the founder of Students for Academic Freedom, which opposed progressive thought on college campuses. At Duke in 2007, Miller became the student president of the Terrorism Awareness Project, an effort backed by Horowitz, and warned of the looming dangers of Islamic jihad. "We will provide informational literature, films, posters, advertisements, speakers, and panel discussions whose purpose is to make our fellow students aware of the Islamic jihad and the terrorist threat, and to mobilize support for the defense of America and the civilization of the West," Miller wrote on the project's website. But it was his defense of several white Duke lacrosse players accused of raping a black woman that made him a fixture on Fox News. He called the case a "witch hunt" that was the result of "radicals" having taken over the campus. The players were exonerated, and after Miller graduated, Horowitz helped him find a job on Capitol Hill with Michele Bachmann, the conservative Minnesota congresswoman. By the time Miller landed in Sessions's office in the Senate, he was something of a mini-celebrity in conservative circles, a wunderkind of the anti-immigration right. He plotted strategy on how best to blow up bipartisan immigration deals and provided outlets like Breitbart with a steady stream of outrage-stoking stories singling out members of Congress—especially prominent Republicans like Paul Ryan—for being insufficiently hard-line. Fellow Republicans would roll their eyes privately at the earnest young aide who would arrive at strategy meetings and deliver passionate lectures about immigration policy, railing against "amnesty" for illegal immigrants.

Even like-minded immigration hawks on Capitol Hill found Miller to be over-the-top. Sessions's staff was regarded by many of them to be a bunch of nut jobs, nobody more so than Miller. He was on the right side of the issues, Miller's ideological allies knew, but he was so preoccupied with throwing bombs all the time, they thought, that he often rendered himself irrelevant—not to mention irritating. Miller, barely out of college and supremely confident in his grasp of immigration issues, was known for showing up in the offices of more experienced aides, putting his feet up on a desk and delivering lengthy lectures about whatever subject was on his mind. Then he would just get up and walk out. Miller could be a collegial team player when he wanted to be, with an intensive work ethic and a friendly demeanor that was the polar opposite of his reputation. But dealing with him was like being in the court of Nero, one former colleague said; one day the emperor is friendly and makes you his consul, and the next you're summoned at four in the morning and executed. You never know what mood Nero's going to be in. In that way, Miller was very much like Trump indeed.

Once he joined the Trump campaign, Miller was unleashed. Almost overnight, his know-it-all discourses on immigration policy were infusing a presidential candidate's speeches, and Miller himself was speaking to rallies that drew tens of thousands of adoring supporters—often with a row of attractive young women up front who seemed to be Stephen Miller groupies. And after Trump won, Miller was thrust into an entirely unfamiliar role. He was the senior policy adviser at the White House and his views were driving the entire debate around immigration. On a Sunday morning shortly after the travel ban took effect, Miller made back-to-back appearances on the morning television news talk shows to defend Trump and the policy. He delivered a series of hyperbolic rants about immigration and savaged the federal judges who had blocked Trump's order. Miller unleashed the kind of ideological broadsides that he used to attack past attempts at bipartisan immigration legislation. On Fox News, he called the travel ban rulings a "judicial usurpation of power." He said on *Meet the Press* that judges "cannot give foreign nationals and foreign countries rights they do not have." On CBS, he puffed out his chest and—with no hint of restraint—issued a blunt warning that was reminiscent of the over-the-top emails that he used to send to reporters and Senate staffers: "Our opponents, the media, and the whole world will soon see, as we begin to take further actions, that the powers of the president to protect our country are very substantial, and will not be questioned." It was the general public's first real glimpse of the Stephen Miller that lawmakers and aides on Capitol Hill had come to know well, a cocky, imperious, seemingly humorless ideologue who delivered an incendiary set of talking points in almost robotic, rapid-fire fashion.

Months later, on the day that Trump endorsed the RAISE Act, it was Miller who appeared at the lectern in the White House briefing room to explain the measure. He got into a spirited back-and-forth with Jim Acosta, the outspoken chief White House correspondent for CNN, about the Statue of Liberty and what it means to be an American. When Acosta quoted "The New Colossus," the Emma Lazarus poem that references "your huddled masses yearning to breathe free," Miller scoffed, saying the verse was added later, to the Statue of Liberty. He accused Acosta of revealing a "cosmopolitan bias." The exchange quickly went viral, adding to the Miller legend.

Inside the West Wing, though, Miller did not always live up to his villainous image. His closest colleagues saw him as brilliant, if not a little misunderstood. There was more to Miller than the one-dimensional anti-immigrant crusader people saw on TV and in the media, where he was often credited, accurately, for Trump's most radical and politically vicious ideas on immigration. For better or for worse, Miller wanted to get something done, and he was often torn between that instinct and the more destructive, outrage-stoking one that powered his rise. The struggle was evident after Trump ended DACA, when Miller began a months-long series of secret talks with lawmakers and congressional officials including Casey Higgins, a top aide to Paul Ryan, to try to cut a deal to preserve the program. During his years on Capitol Hill, Miller had rarely, if ever, engaged with mainstream Republicans on immigration issues, except to debate them publicly in the most aggressive of ways. But after a meeting of Ryan's immigration working group in October, he made a beeline for Mario Diaz-Balart, the Miami-area congressman who had been at the center of bipartisan immigration deals for years, and said, "We have to get together." Miller then spent the weekend texting with Diaz-Balart's top aide, who was mystified that he was actually having a substantive exchange with the same guy who had been his sworn enemy in past immigration debates. Miller began a series of meetings with the Florida congressman to try to forge an agreement.

It was puzzling to everyone who thought they knew Miller. At times during the DACA talks, he would flash an extraordinarily pragmatic side, seeming to understand that in order to accomplish his goal of tougher immigration restrictions, Trump would need to accept major concessions, such as providing a pathway to citizenship for the Dreamers. But the moment a compromise would begin to take shape, Miller would pull in a different direction, reintroducing controversial measures, like ending family visas for some immigrants, that shifted the debate to the right. After all his years of being the person to throw the grenade into the middle of an immigration negotiation, Miller did not seem to know how to break out of that role and cut a deal. He seemed genuinely conflicted, according to people who worked with him on DACA, between securing an agreement and his fixation with all of the concessions he could wring from Democrats in exchange for legalizing the Dreamers. They came away from the negotiations wondering whether Miller ever had any intention of reaching a compromise. Had he played them in the hopes of extracting the best possible deal, or had he genuinely wanted to find common ground? It was one of the enduring mysteries about Miller.

Still, there was nothing ambiguous about Miller's impatience; he wore it on his sleeve. From the earliest days of the Trump presidency, Miller exuded a sense of urgency about the need to move quickly to overhaul a system he saw as broken—a drive to action largely fueled by the resistance that he knew was coming. In the beginning, Miller's instinct toward rapid action was matched by the people he assembled to implement his immigration agenda. They were the true believers, his ideological allies in a bureaucracy he viewed as hell-bent on preserving the status quo. But most of them were lawyers, which Miller was not, and they were in jobs that required them to studiously follow a strict set of laws and regulations, to abide by court orders, and to work within practical and operational guardrails. That often put them at odds with Miller, leaving them to break it to Trump's top immigration adviser that they couldn't do what he wanted done.

Cissna, in particular, became a source of deep frustration. As the head of the agency that determines who gets a visa, who gets asylum or refugee status, and who can become a citizen, the director of USCIS was in a position to dramatically scale back legal immigration. Cissna agreed with Miller's broad goals of making the nation's immigration laws mean something again. But he repeatedly told Miller that he was limited in what he could do to make immigration tougher. He had no more right to bypass the law than his predecessors did when they moved unilaterally to weaken the rules during previous administrations. For Miller, it was a kind of betrayal. Regulations took forever. Memos suggesting aggressive action went nowhere. Presidential directives were tied up in endless legal debates. Miller, channeling Trump himself, had a maximalist view of executive power, arguing that whatever the president said must be obeyed, regardless of whether it was lawful, practical, or moral. So he would draft executive orders and arrange Oval Office meetings to set Trump's expectations sky-high, and then hammer away at top officials for failing to do what the president had said he wanted. Many of them began to tune Miller out, offering a perfunctory "Okay, we'll get right on that" and a silent eye-roll.

In some ways, it left Miller as the odd man out, an ideological purist who was nominally in charge of everything related to immigration but did not actually have hold of the levers of action on anything. He had the president's ear, which gave him political power. But in order to make something happen, he had to work through others, a reality that placed

limits on what he could accomplish. It was a challenge that he had antici-
pated during the transition, when he asked Cecilia Muñoz how she ma-
neuvered to cut the National Security Council out of the decision-making
process. In the months since, Miller had figured some things out on his
own, through trial and error. In prior administrations, the president and
his top advisers would usually identify their policy priorities and then put
the bureaucracy to work developing them, refining and debating them to
work out differences before the president gave his final sign-off. Miller
turned the process on its head, reverse-engineering it to reach his own
precooked conclusions. He would conceive of an idea, take it to Trump for
his buy-in, and only then start a policy review, often leaning on officials at
DHS or Justice to make it happen.

Miller even invented his own brand of policy committee to short-
circuit internal debates and ensure that he would be able to deliver the
results on which he had already sold Trump. They were called "pop-up
PCCs," but in reality they were nothing like the methodically managed
policy coordination committees of administrations past. Miller's pop-ups
were just that—groups hastily thrown together at the last moment with
relatively little planning and even less buy-in from inside the administration. Miller would handpick lower-level bureaucrats within the agencies
to invite for the pop-up PCC, issuing a vague agenda and running the
meetings himself. Invitees often could not speak on behalf of their agencies because they were too low on the organizational chart to know what
the front office thought of a given policy issue. Nielsen often would learn
only after the fact of Miller pop-ups in which her agency had allegedly
taken part.

But with people Miller liked and respected, he could be an extraordinarily, deceptively warm person, a wholly different character than his public persona or his internal reputation would suggest. Behind the scenes, he
didn't come across as mean-spirited. He could be funny and generous, not
the maniacal racist that his critics envisioned. He forged an unlikely—if
politically expedient—friendship with Ivanka Trump and Jared Kushner,
despite the vast gulf that separated them on immigration policy. He even
helped Ivanka with some of her policy initiatives, such as a proposal on

paid family leave. One day as Hope Hicks and Dina Powell joined Ivanka in her West Wing office to discuss the leave proposal, they gently ribbed Miller. "Okay, it's all the girls," they said. "Stephen, come on in."

And while Miller could be publicly brutal with his critics, he was privately gentle with his friends. Hicks was devastated in early 2018 when news surfaced that Rob Porter, the White House staff secretary she had begun quietly dating, had been accused by two ex-wives of physical abuse. Internally, Hicks pushed for the White House to defend Porter, which Kelly initially did. The episode quickly devolved into a public relations mess for the White House and a personal debacle for Hicks. At one point amid the furor, Miller pulled Hicks aside and gave her some blunt advice. Hicks said nothing, but the look on her face made it clear that she was devastated. A half hour later, Miller's assistant appeared in Hicks's office and handed her an envelope containing a note from Miller. I know what I said was harsh, Miller wrote, but I thought you needed to hear it. I really love you, and you are my friend, and I want you to succeed in all the ways that I know you can, he wrote. Hicks was moved. She kept the note, pinning it up in her office as a reminder that even when things got hard, there were people who cared about and loved her.

But even in his own personal life, Miller was unapologetic about who he was and what he believed. On New Year's Eve in 2018, Miller took Katie Waldman, then his girlfriend and a spokeswoman for the Department of Homeland Security, to an upscale restaurant in Washington's NoMa neighborhood for a romantic dinner. The government was shut down and the pair had been hoping to steal a few moments of privacy and downtime amid a swirl of chaos. Instead, Miller was spotted and recognized, and when he excused himself to use the restroom, two women at the next table began harassing Waldman. How can you be with such a horrible person? they said to her. He's a monster. He puts children in cages. You should be ashamed of yourself. You should leave right now. Waldman was dumbfounded, sitting helplessly as the two women railed against her boyfriend, calling him "evil." When Miller returned to the table, he saw that she looked ashen and upset. What's wrong? he asked. She told Miller what had happened. Let's get you another drink, Miller said, taking his seat and sliding his chair back into the table. We're not going anywhere. We're not going to let these people ruin our night.

So Miller and Waldman, who would marry in early 2020, stayed. Later that evening, one of the heckling women posted a picture on Instagram, boasting of how they had spent their New Year's Eve. "Just two queer femmes, enjoying a fancy dinner and ruining Stephen Miller's chances of getting laid tonight," she wrote. "We are patriots. Here's to 2019!"

"YOU'VE KIDNAPPED OUR KIDS"

THE PRESIDENT'S DECISION TO issue an executive order that would end routine family separation might have staunched the immediate political damage. But the effort to reunite the separated children was a looming disaster, and Alex Azar knew it.

Azar had been confirmed five months earlier as the secretary of health and human services. He was responsible for the facilities where the children were living while their parents sat in DHS holding facilities. Now the president said he wanted the families reunited, and it would be up to Azar to do it. On June 21, the day after Trump signed the executive order, Azar accompanied First Lady Melania Trump to visit separated children at the Upbring New Hope Children's Shelter near the Mexican border in McAllen, Texas. Melania's decision to make the trip set off a typical round of speculation and debate about whether Trump's wife, a sphinxlike figure who said little in public and almost never challenged her husband openly, was trying to send a subtle message that, like many Americans, she, too, was outraged by the president's policy. As she strode across the tarmac to her government-issued plane at Andrews Air Force Base, she sported an army-green anorak with a cryptic message scrawled in large white letters on the back: "I Really Don't Care. Do U?" Did she? Melania's East Wing staff later claimed that she wore the jacket to mock reporters, who were constantly trying to impart meaning onto her every move and garment. But behind the scenes, it was clear Trump's administration was scrambling to control the damage that the family separation policy had wrought.

Azar knew he needed help managing what had become a full-blown debacle for the administration, which had landed, almost without warning, in his lap. It was like a natural disaster in its scope and urgency, only it had been man-made. So he turned to a group of officials who were trained to manage disasters, in the Health and Human Services office charged with responding to epidemics, natural emergencies, and biohazards. Just before noon, Azar summoned Bob Kadlec, the assistant secretary for preparedness and response, known inside the department as ASPR. Azar gave Kadlec three tasks: Figure out which kids are separated; make sure they can talk to their parents for the next month; and then put them back together as quickly and safely as possible. Later, in a series of back-to-back meetings, Azar was blunt with the team, including Chris Meekins, Kadlec's chief of staff, and Jonathan White. It shouldn't be that hard, Azar told Meekins. We have databases to keep on top of such things.

The officials soon found out otherwise. The HHS computer system used to track the children in the department's care, called the ORR Portal, contained almost no information about a child's parents. Each child was given a unique identifier. But the Family Unit Number, which DHS assigns to families that cross the border illegally, was not consistently provided when children were separated from their parents and reclassified as Unaccompanied Alien Children. Occasionally, a case worker or a Border Patrol agent might have made a notation that the child came with a parent. But beyond that, there was no way of knowing for sure how many they were looking for. It was infuriating. Customs and Border Protection gave the HHS team one number; Immigration and Customs Enforcement gave them another; DHS headquarters offered a third. 1,000. No, 1,500. No. 2,100. Over several weeks, Azar and his team were given sixty different sets of data, each contradicting the others. The stakes got even higher near midnight on June 26, when Judge Dana M. Sabraw of the Federal District Court in San Diego angrily ordered that all children under five be reunited with their parents within fourteen days, and gave the federal government thirty days to reunite all other children in the care of the Office of Refugee Resettlement. If that didn't happen, Sabraw warned that he would hold Azar in contempt.

By Fourth of July weekend, Azar was furious. Kadlec, Meekins, and White—along with officials from throughout HHS, ICE, and the Border Patrol—had taken over the secretary's operations center, a large conference room filled with computers and giant television monitors, on the sixth floor of the Hubert H. Humphrey Building. But they still couldn't give him a solid number of how many kids had been separated. More than four hundred case files were inconclusive. "Give me a computer and I'll do it myself," Azar fumed. "I am not going to be held in contempt." That night, more than thirty officials—including the HHS chief of staff, the deputy chief of staff, and the department's counsel—worked past midnight in teams of two. Each team took thirty case files. At 11:15 p.m., Azar, who had attended a dinner, returned to the operations center and sat down in front of a computer with thirty case files of his own, still in his suit and tie. Despite all this, by the time Azar briefed reporters on a conference call July 5, the best he could do was say that "less than 3,000 children" had been separated. HHS is continuing to "work overtime" to determine which children belonged to which parents, Azar told the reporters on the call.

Azar eventually gave full control of the effort to Kadlec and the department's disaster team. Peter Urbanowicz, Azar's chief of staff, wrote an email to Scott Lloyd, the director of ORR: To be abundantly clear, ASPR has full operational control. You are now reporting to ASPR. But the disaster team struggled to reunite families once they identified them. In some cases, it was difficult to prove parentage. In other cases, parents had committed serious crimes, making it impossible to reunite them with their children. By July 10, the judge's deadline for reuniting children under five, officials had managed to bring together only about half of the families. That week, they began placing the older children on buses to be reunited with their parents at DHS holding facilities.

The first effort was bumpy at best. About thirty children in southwest Texas were placed onto a bus and driven to the Port Isabel Detention

Center, an ICE facility in Los Fresnos, Texas, only to be told by DHS officials that the parents weren't ready to be released. For weeks, there had been twice-a-day conference calls between HHS and DHS officials to coordinate the handoff. But somehow, the officials at Port Isabel had not completed the paperwork that needed to be done to release the parents. Worse still, the station didn't have anywhere the children could wait, so the Port Isabel officials turned away the bus. Thousands of miles away in Washington, Kadlec, Meekins, and White were awoken at 1 a.m. by telephone calls and urgent emails. "We have a problem," they were told. DHS won't release the parents, and we can't leave these kids. Unsure what else to do, the adults who were accompanying the children on the bus drove to a nearby Walmart and bought blankets, pillows, snacks, and other supplies for the children. As the final phase of their harrowing ordeal, these kids would have an impromptu sleepover inside a DHS bus in a barren parking lot on the border, waiting to be reunited with their detained parents. White, Meekins, and Kadlec spent the next several hours raising hell with DHS officials in a flurry of predawn phone calls. By morning, the official in charge of the facility had been removed. The moms, dads, and children had their joyful reunions. But the incident left everyone clear-eyed about what they were facing. Even in the best of circumstances, when they could match children with their parents and arrange for a reunion, the process was going to be anything but smooth.

Privately, Azar was as frustrated as his staff, many of whom were distressed as they sought to reunite traumatized children with their parents. Eventually, mental health counselors who normally tended to the needs of disaster victims were deployed inside the department to help the shaken staff. Publicly, though, Azar tried to put on the best face he could, arguing that his department was doing everything in its power to reunite children, while at the same time protecting the kids from adults with criminal records. Out of 102 children under five years old, they had discovered sixteen parents who had been convicted of serious crimes and five adults who had lied about being the child's real parent. "It is one of the great acts of American generosity and charity, what we are doing for these unaccompanied kids who are smuggled into our country or come across illegally," Azar told Wolf Blitzer in an appearance on CNN. "I'm proud of the work we do. I believe we are saving kids' lives."

The happy talk from the Americans was infuriating to the foreign ministers in El Salvador, Honduras, and Guatemala when Nielsen arrived in Guatemala City on July 10 for what she had hoped would be serious discussions about how the three Central American countries could do more to secure their borders and keep their citizens from heading toward the United States. Trump was continuing to hammer her on what more could be done to stop them from coming. Nielsen and a team of diplomats from the State Department had pushed for an agenda that included joint efforts to combat human trafficking, drug smuggling, and illegal immigration.

But that was wishful thinking. From the minute the American delegation arrived in the Guatemalan capital, Sandra Jovel, the country's foreign minister, insisted on making the issue of the separated families the primary topic of conversation at the ministerial conference, which also included Kevin McAleenan, the head of Customs and Border Protection, and Ronald Vitiello, the acting director of Immigration and Customs Enforcement. For weeks, officials in the three Central American countries had watched in horror as news reports from the United States showed children being taken from parents. And now the Americans apparently didn't know where all the children were, and which parents they belonged to. Why wasn't the United States sharing more information about the fate of the missing children? the diplomats demanded.

A cable sent several days later from the U.S. embassy to Secretary of State Rex Tillerson described the heated exchanges. "Jovel pressed for respecting migrants' human rights while ending family separation," the cable said. Facing off against Nielsen and the others, Jovel demanded that Guatemalan consular officers be notified about the whereabouts of the children so visits to the shelters could be arranged. Carlos Castaneda, the Salvadoran foreign minister, jumped in. He told the Americans that separating children from their parents causes permanent emotional and psychological damage. He demanded that the practice end, and raised objections to reports that the United States was using DNA tests to help reunite the children with their parents. That will only delay the process, he said. María Dolores Agüero, the Honduran foreign minister, said the Central American governments needed clarity about the fate of their children, and urged Nielsen to make sure the families were reunited quickly.

Nielsen tried to talk about other topics, to little avail. She assured the foreign ministers that officials were working to respond to a court order requiring the families to be reunited. She tried to reassure them that the United States government was working diligently to make it happen. But she denied that her department had made a conscious choice to separate families. "She also clarified that Congress had made crossing the border illegal decades ago, and that DHS does not have a policy of family separation," the cable said. "Rather, children are separated from their parents when they choose to cross the border illegally because children are not allowed to enter jails with their parents." It was hair-splitting at best, and it did little to mollify the Central American politicians.

The official DHS press release about Nielsen's trip read as if the topic of the children never came up. "The ministers and Secretary Nielsen reiterated their commitment to carry out concrete actions to enhance information-sharing best practices as well as collectively address security challenges and illegal migration flows," it said. In fact, the meeting—and the lack of solid information about the whereabouts of the children—only deepened the anger inside the foreign governments. When a team of DHS and State Department officials flew down to Tegucigalpa, Honduras, for a follow-up meeting two weeks later, they, too, were ambushed by their counterparts in the three countries. The United States was a party to the Convention on Consular Relations, which required that officials inform each other when they take another country's citizens into custody. But that didn't happen when the children were separated and taken away, the Central American officials complained. What do we tell our people? they demanded. What would you think if 2,600 American children were taken from their parents in our countries?

To the Americans who attended, the message from the Central American governments couldn't have been clearer: "You've kidnapped our kids."

"You're lying!" the congressman fumed at the homeland security secretary.

It was July 25, the same day that the American diplomats and DHS officials 3,400 miles away were being berated in Honduras. But this tirade was coming from Luis Gutiérrez, the Democratic congressman from Chicago, inside a small room on the second floor of the Cannon House Office Building, with pale yellow walls lined with wooden bookshelves, royal blue carpeting and drapes, and brass chandeliers. The Congressional Hispanic Caucus had invited Nielsen for a closed-door session to get concrete answers about how the family separation crisis had been allowed to happen, and expected an apologetic secretary ready with precise answers and a hefty dose of contrition. Instead, Gutiérrez stewed as Nielsen became defensive, unwilling to accept blame for the debacle and seeming to offer excuses instead of information. She primly told the lawmakers that they had nothing to worry about; the federal government had the situation under control, she said, and all of the children would be reunited with their parents by the court's deadline.

"You're never going to get these kids to go back together," Gutiérrez yelled. "You people have a thing against brown children."

After twenty-five years in the House, Gutiérrez had little patience for people like Nielsen, whom he viewed as an enabler of Trump's worst impulses. Known as a hothead, even among his friends and fellow Democrats, Gutiérrez had never cared much for the niceties of political decorum. He was an activist at heart. Early in 2017, Gutiérrez joined immigration advocates at an ICE office in Chicago and dared the agents to arrest them when they refused to leave. (Contacted in Washington, Kelly told the agents in no uncertain terms not to oblige the congressman.) In August, Gutiérrez was arrested along with about thirty other protesters as they sat on the sidewalk in front of the White House in the hopes of convincing Trump not to end the DACA program. A month later, after Sessions announced that the program would be terminated, Gutiérrez got himself arrested again, this time at a protest outside Trump Tower in New York City.

His blunt attack on Nielsen drew a rebuke from some of his colleagues in the room on that July day. "Luis, that's enough. You've gone too far," chided Michelle Lujan Grisham, a Democratic representative from New Mexico and the chair of the Hispanic Caucus. Nielsen took offense and defended herself, too. Nobody is working harder than I am to reunite these kids, she told the lawmakers. She recounted her repeated trips to Central America to try to resolve the migration crisis, and cited her personal friendship with Ana Rosalinda García Carías, the first lady of Honduras, as evidence of her effectiveness. When she was finished, Gutiérrez stormed out of the room. Recalling the incident later, Gutiérrez shrugged off Lujan Grisham's criticism and insisted that he has no regrets for what he said to Nielsen. "She's in charge. She can quit tomorrow and resign, right? And be a person of honor. No, she's not. She's allowing this to happen," Gutiérrez said.

But Nielsen had no intention of quitting. Nearly three months after the terrible cabinet meeting, she had survived what seemed to be the worst of the brutal family separation mess. Within days, government lawyers would tell the judge that most of the children had been reunited with their parents. An angry Democratic congressman like Gutiérrez was the least of her worries. As far as job security went, an infuriated president who was demanding more aggressive ways to crack down at the border was a far more immediate problem.

EVELYN AND AMBER

ON THE DAY THAT Jeff Sessions warned the world that the Trump administration's zero tolerance policy meant that immigrants apprehended at the border would be separated from their children, about 2,500 miles to the south, Evelyn took her seven-year-old daughter, Amber, and fled Guatemala. They were running for their lives.

Until recently, life had been relatively good for Evelyn in the small town on Guatemala's border near Chiapas, Mexico, where she and Amber lived with her parents, a six-year-old son by a different father, and four siblings. Evelyn had a reliable job at a cleaning company and a boyfriend. Scarcely five feet tall, with a round face and large, sparkling brown eyes framed by loose brown curls, Evelyn looked younger than her twenty-four years, especially when she smiled. Amber was a typical, chatty little girl. But in 2017, things had turned dark for them. Evelyn's boyfriend, a member of the Guatemalan military, had become abusive, and when she said she would leave, he threatened to kill both her and her daughter. Evelyn believed him.

She left her job and hid out at her parents' house for two months, terrified of being found by her boyfriend. She called family members in the United States to ask for their help escaping from her situation, but they all said the same thing: Sorry, we can't help. Then one Friday, she reached a cousin in a suburb on the East Coast who said Evelyn could come stay with her and her family. If you can make it here, we'll help you, the cousin said. Evelyn spent the weekend looking for transportation, scrounged together the fee of 27,000 quetzales, the equivalent of a little over $3,500, that her contact demanded, and made plans to leave on Monday.

"The situation got very dangerous, to the point where, when I was leaving the house, I didn't know if I would come back in the evening," Evelyn told us through a translator one afternoon in the spring of 2019, seated at a round dining table in her cousin's tidy suburban home, waiting to find out if she would be granted asylum in the United States. "With my faith in God, we left home, my daughter and I. I was risking everything." By the time of our interview, Evelyn and her daughter had made it to the United States and had been released by authorities with conditions, while they waited to see whether they would be allowed to stay. It was Friday, the day of the week when Evelyn must remain confined to her house under terms imposed by ICE, and Amber was at school, where she attended first grade and was learning English faster than her mother could believe. The only indication of Evelyn's ordeal was the bulky black electronic monitor strapped around her ankle, tucked under her black leggings. That, and the fear and anguish in her voice when she described what happened when they took Amber away from her.

Even before she left, Evelyn had to let go of a child. She left her six-year-old son with his father, where she felt that he would be safe and well taken care of. Amber had no father around to protect her; if she was going to survive, she would have to go with Evelyn. The journey north took ten days. With only the clothes on their backs, Evelyn and Amber woke up at dawn, and crammed into a red minivan driven by a Mexican man they had never seen before, and they drove for what seemed like forever. At one point, they switched to a bus, then back to another car, again driven by a stranger. They slept where they could—on floors, in people's houses along the way, and, one particularly terrifying night, in the woods. Amber would fall asleep in her mother's arms, worried but comforted by Evelyn's embrace. Evelyn slept only fitfully, watching over her daughter, anxious about what would come next. She told Amber little, just that they were leaving to get away from the people who had threatened them. As long as she was with her Mami, it was enough.

On Wednesday, May 16, 2018, around 8 p.m., Evelyn and Amber reached the U.S. border. Just days earlier in Washington, Nielsen had signed the memorandum ordering that all adults crossing the border without legal documents be prosecuted, even if they were traveling with children. At the San Luis Port of Entry in Arizona, in a yard with fencing on both sides, Evelyn and Amber presented themselves to CBP agents, who escorted them through a gate and asked for their identification documents, which Evelyn produced. They were put into the back of a patrol car and driven for about an hour until they reached a detention center in Yuma. The first thing Evelyn noticed when she entered the hulking facility was that it was freezing. A *hielera*, as they called it, or "icebox." After being asked to hand over her phone, belt, and shoes, Evelyn was led with Amber to a large room, with white concrete walls and a pale cement floor, long and narrow, like a squash court filled with women and children, some with silver Mylar blankets slung around their shoulders against the cold. As Evelyn gazed out a small window in the door, she overheard an ICE officer telling a distraught man that his son was going to be taken elsewhere because children were not allowed at this facility. When the man protested, the officer told him, "It's your fault that you're here. You use children to get into the United States." Would that happen to them? Evelyn wondered as she and Amber sat, munching on the only food they were given—juice and some biscuits.

At five the next morning, they were called in for processing. The officers asked Evelyn her name and where she was from. Then they confirmed her worst fear. They were taking her daughter, the officers said. Evelyn would be tried for illegal entry into the United States and Amber would be given to her relative on the East Coast. This place wasn't for kids, they kept saying, so she has to go somewhere else. Evelyn began to weep. She wasn't the only one. Sobs echoed through the holding room where the women waited with their children, sipping on instant soup, their breakfast, as they bided the time until their sons and daughters would be ripped away. Through her tears, Evelyn tried to put on a brave face for her daughter about what was about to happen. You're going somewhere with more food, and lots of kids, she told Amber. It will be better than here.

When the time came, Evelyn and Amber did not make a fuss. About an hour after eating another round of watery soup for lunch, an officer called Amber's name. "Look miss, you know what's going to happen now?" the officer said to Evelyn. "We're going to take your child away. So say goodbye to her." Don't be afraid, Evelyn told Amber, clutching her daughter and trying unsuccessfully to hold back her tears. "You won't be gone for very long, and I'll be here the whole time. You won't be alone," she told her daughter, who could not stand to be by herself. Amber cried and silently hugged her mom one last time before she was led out of the room and over to a group of seven other children, supervised by a man and woman wearing ID badges who gave them fruit juice. Evelyn watched, tears streaming down her face, as Amber receded down a long hallway with her minders and the other kids. Amber turned briefly to look in Evelyn's direction, a look of pure anguish and fear written in the big eyes on her small face.

And then she was gone. The next nine days were a blur of tears, cold, and nothingness. Evelyn and about fifty other mothers in the room at the *hielera* wept constantly. They never went outside, so nobody knew what time it was or what day it was. They stayed shut in, never showering or changing clothes, eating their instant soup. "It was like being lost in time," Evelyn recalled months later. "All we did was cry. We prayed to God that something would happen." The mothers were desperate to know where their children were, but most of the ICE officers had little patience for their questions. How would we know? the officers would snap, responding with disgust to what seemed like constant wailing. It's all your fault this happened anyway. You shouldn't have come, and you shouldn't have brought a child. One female ICE officer was more tender. She was a mother herself, she told Evelyn, and she was sorry for what was happening to them. But she had a job to do. And her job was to follow the law.

On the tenth day, guards shackled Evelyn's hands and feet and loaded her into a paddy wagon with ten other people. It was her first glimpse of the sun for more than a week, and after a three-hour drive, she arrived at

Florence Detention Center, midway between Phoenix and Tucson. She was given food and allowed to shower and finally change out of the clothes she had traveled in, which were badly soiled and smelled like it. But when she was given something fresh to put on, Evelyn was even more humiliated than she had been in her own filthy clothing; it was a bright orange prison uniform. She was taken to a jail in nearby Santa Cruz County, Arizona, and held for four days in a cell with a metal door, five bunk beds, and a metal table in the center. There were nine other prisoners in her cell, four of them mothers whose children had also been taken.

One morning out of the blue, Evelyn and her cell mates were awakened and told to put their old clothes back on. They were going somewhere, but nobody would say where. The guards slapped the shackles on again—wrists, ankles, and a belt around the waist—and herded the prisoners onto a bus. Evelyn started to panic. She had told her daughter she would be there when Amber came back, but now Evelyn had no idea where she was or where she was going. Was this it? Were they taking her back to Guatemala? Where was Amber? Had she made it to their relatives' house? When the bus arrived at its destination, the anxiety turned to terror. The bus had rolled to a stop on an airport tarmac, depositing the prisoners at the bottom of a staircase to a jumbo jet. Those are the planes they use to take people back where they came from, one woman said. Dozens of armed officers swarmed the plane—on the stairway and up and down the aisles—as the women, shackled and afraid, shuffled on board. It was like they were transporting El Chapo, Evelyn recalled, but this wasn't a hardened drug kingpin with a kill count, it was a bunch of distraught moms worrying about their babies. They kept asking where they were going, and Evelyn thought she heard an officer say they were headed to Los Angeles. As the plane hurtled down the runway and began lifting into the air, Evelyn's mind raced. She had never been on a plane before. "What if I die?" she thought. "What will happen to my children?"

They landed in San Diego, and after being searched, head-to-toe, she and the other detainees were taken by bus to the James A. Musick Facility near Irvine, a minimum-security detention center known as "The Farm." They gave Evelyn and the other ICE detainees green uniforms to distinguish them from the prisoners with red or blue uniforms on the other side of the corridor, who were there for things like DUIs or minor drug possession, failure to pay child support or prostitution. Here, there were no immigration officers; if she and her cell mates had questions, they could write them on slips of paper and tuck them into a small box in their cell provided for the purpose. Answers would often take several weeks, if they came at all. There were telephones in the cells, but you had to buy a phone card to use them, and Evelyn had no money. She had no idea that the separation policy had by then sparked an intense political controversy and generated global condemnation. All she knew was that it had been more than two weeks since the guards in Arizona had taken Amber away.

In early June, Evelyn finally spoke with an asylum officer by telephone, recounting her story of fleeing Guatemala. She would hear back in eight days, Evelyn was told. In the meantime, a cell mate took pity on her and lent her a phone card so she could contact her family. She called her cousin on the East Coast, praying to hear that Amber had arrived safely with her. But Amber wasn't there. Evelyn's cousin hadn't heard a thing about the little girl, and she and her husband were shocked by what had happened to them. They would investigate and see what they could find out, she promised in the brief call. Weeks later, on June 16—four days before Trump abandoned the family separation policy with an abrupt executive order—Evelyn was shackled again and taken to a courthouse in Los Angeles, where a judge asked her why she had come to the United States and whether she was afraid of returning home. Then he handed her a sheet of paper in English that Evelyn could not read. When she got back to her cell at Musick that night, another detainee translated the paper for her. It was a deportation order, she told Evelyn, handing it back. That night, Evelyn lay awake in her cell and agonized. "What happens if they send me back, and Amber is still here? Is she being treated well? Will I ever see her again?" When an ICE officer came to her cell a couple of days later with deportation paperwork for her to sign, Evelyn refused. She demanded to know what was going on with Amber. The officer left without her signature. Evelyn sent more slips of paper through the box, asking for the whereabouts and condition of her daughter, a number she could call to get in contact with her, any shred of information about Amber.

In early July, a lawyer came to visit Evelyn at Musick. He had been retained by her cousin on the East Coast and was handling Evelyn's case pro bono. The lawyer said he would make an official request to ICE for information about Amber and a phone number where she could be reached. They learned that the child was being held at Hacienda del Sol, a facility in Arizona run by a nonprofit organization called Southwest Key and funded by the Office of Refugee Resettlement, the HHS division that holds unaccompanied alien minors. Days later, Evelyn was allowed to speak with her daughter for the first time in nearly two months. Evelyn was overjoyed to hear Amber's voice. She sounded safe and well taken care of, and a feeling of relief washed over Evelyn for the first time in weeks. A social worker who was with Amber told Evelyn that she had a proper bed and was sleeping and eating well. But something was off. Evelyn's normally talkative, bubbly daughter was subdued, answering her mother with one-word answers.

"How are you?" Evelyn asked her.

"Well," Amber responded.

"Is everything okay?"

"Yes."

"How are they treating you?"

"Well."

After a couple of minutes, Amber began to cry, and the social worker ended the call. It lasted about five minutes. Evelyn did not know what to feel. The sound of her daughter's voice had buoyed her spirits, reassuring her that they were not so very far apart. But she still felt the intense ache of her children's absence and wondered whether she would ever see either of them again. Evelyn could not forget that piece of paper the judge had given her—a deportation order. What would happen to Amber if she were sent back to Guatemala?

Not long after, as she was watching the news on TV in the detention center, Evelyn learned that a federal judge in California had ordered the government weeks earlier to reunify parents who had been separated from their children at the border, and was now temporarily halting deportations of the reunited families. Evelyn's lawyer said he would file a motion to stop her removal order, and four days later he came back to Musick to give Evelyn the first good news she had since arriving in the United States: she was getting out, and would soon be reunited with Amber.

In late July, Evelyn was shackled again and transported to the Port Isabel Detention Center, an ICE facility sometimes known as El Corralón or "The Big Corral" on a former naval base in South Texas. At around midnight, they led Evelyn to a large room. There was Amber, standing quietly against a wall in a line of about thirty children, with a teddy bear and a small carry-on bag that Evelyn did not recognize. She grabbed her daughter and held on for dear life. She laughed and cried. "I love you," they said to each other over and over again. When she could catch her breath, Evelyn pulled away and asked Amber how she was, how she had been treated. She was fine, Amber said. There were teachers where she had been staying, she said, and she had made friends. People looked after her, she said. It was the middle of the night, and the little girl was exhausted, mentally and physically. That was about all the information that Evelyn was going to get.

Soon they were on the move again. ICE agents put Evelyn and Amber into a van with three other parents and their children and they drove through the night, although nobody would tell them where they were going. They wouldn't be separated, ICE officers said, but they weren't going to be released either. After about six hours on the road, they came to the South Texas Family Residential Center in Dilley, Texas, the largest such facility in the United States. Situated on fifty desertlike acres on brownish red dirt dotted with dry patches of brush, the detention camp consisted of dozens of tan-colored trailers housing the women and children being held there, as well as temporary classrooms, a cafeteria, and medical and legal visitation centers.

Evelyn and Amber were detained for four months. Life was monotonous and uncertain at Dilley, where the temperature often reached 100 degrees or higher. They lived in a trailer with six other mothers and their children, all of them happy to be reunited but depressed and frustrated with their limbolike status. Evelyn felt angry and betrayed; they had told her she would get Amber back and they would be let go, but now here they were in the middle of the desert, under the constant watch of guards, eating the same food every week and being in the same place all day, every day. Amber attended school in one of the trailers marked *escuela*, but Evelyn's days were broken up only by meals, TV, and playing with her daughter in a playground inside the heavily fortified fences of the detention center. In the afternoons, she would often visit the facility's lawyers, seeking legal advice and information about the outside world, and at times just to vent. It was from the lawyers that Evelyn finally learned that there had been a public outcry in Washington and throughout the country over the Trump administration policy.

And it was at Dilley that Evelyn first realized how profoundly Amber had changed during the time they had been apart. At night, her daughter was afraid and clingy, unable to fall asleep unless Evelyn sat with her and physically held on to her. By day, Amber was impatient and cranky, crying for her grandmother back in Guatemala and asking why they had to stay here. "Please forgive me—it's my fault this happened," Evelyn would tell her. After months, Amber had an interview with an asylum officer and her claim of "credible fear" of returning home was accepted. Both mother and daughter had met the threshold to be considered for asylum, and would be given the chance to have their cases heard. They were released in late November, driven to the airport in San Antonio, and boarded a flight to Houston, and then on to the city where Evelyn's cousin awaited.

Almost a year to the day after fleeing from her little hamlet in Guatemala, sitting in her cousin's house on a peaceful, wooded cul-de-sac in the United States, Evelyn was at peace, but she wasn't really free. The ankle monitor, which she was required to wear until her asylum case was decided, was designed to insure that she stayed within a restricted radius around her home, and she was required to check in with an immigration officer once every four weeks. She was barred from working or driving, preventing her from doing anything to provide for Amber. She was lucky to live with supportive members of her extended family who were helping her out, but it was not the same as having her own life. "It feels bad," Evelyn said. "It feels like someone . . ." She trailed off, making a jerking gesture with her hand and neck as if someone had her on a leash and was pulling on it.

The scars of the separation were still fresh. At first, Amber would not walk outside, for fear of being kidnapped, and was afraid to board the yellow bus to go to school, worried that she'd be taken away and not brought back to her mother. Those fears had faded somewhat, but the nighttime terror had not; Amber still could not fall asleep without her mother holding her.

Would Evelyn do it all again? Would she run for her life to the United States, knowing that her daughter could be forcibly taken from her and that they would be separated for months, maybe forever? Evelyn said she wouldn't. But then she hesitated.

"I would like to say to the other mothers first of all, one must not regret anything," Evelyn said. "There is God, and there is a reason for everything, and he's in our hearts, and he knows what we do and the reasons why we do things."

"I feel no resentment against the government—I don't blame the government for what they did," Evelyn added. "I just think that this experience has made me stronger, has made me the person that I am today. And one has to have patience."

"PENCILS DOWN"

ON THE EVENING OF July 11, a group of old friends gathered for happy hour at Blackfinn, a sports bar on I Street, a couple of blocks from the White House. Seasoned immigration experts who had worked together for years and now served in various senior positions in the Trump administration or on Capitol Hill, they were there to bid farewell to a colleague. Nick Perry, the lead immigration lawyer at the State Department, was leaving his plum post to escape to a quieter life in the Midwest. Perry had worked at the Department of Homeland Security before going over to State, and he had risen to the top echelons of the legal team there. But lately, he had become disillusioned and fed up with his job. He just wanted out of the pressure cooker of Washington, Perry told friends. He was leaving State to work as a low-level adjudicator at a USCIS service center in Nebraska. His former DHS colleagues who had come to send him off could sympathize. They had been toiling away for months on a pet project of Stephen Miller's, and it was a slog. As they sipped their cocktails and reminisced, the officials—including Francis Cissna, the USCIS chief, and Dimple Shah, a top lawyer at DHS—lamented how obsessed Miller had become with an arcane regulation called the "public charge" rule. Miller wanted them to stop everything else they were doing—"pencils down" on any other work, he had ordered—until it was finished.

Miller liked to tell people that he had been advocating for the public charge rule since he was fifteen. The idea behind it was simple, and Miller, along with Jeff Sessions, had sold Trump on it during the presidential campaign: immigrants should not be allowed to come to the United States and immediately go on welfare or use other aid programs paid for by American taxpayers. It wasn't fair, they argued, and it was bankrupting the country. The government should turn away immigrants who were likely to need public assistance when they arrived. And they should deport immigrants who became dependent on them. There was already a concept enshrined in immigration law that the government could consider whether someone might become a "public charge"—someone who is dependent on government programs to survive—when deciding whether they were eligible for admission. Now Miller wanted to vastly broaden the use of that criterion so that any immigrant who made use of any part of the social safety net could be blocked from entering, or turned out if they had already come in.

The concept of considering whether immigrants might become public charges—and barring them from the United States if they would—was nothing new. In fact, it dated back to shortly after the Civil War, when the first federal immigration statutes were enacted by Congress. In August of 1882, Congress passed a law that levied a 50-cent "head tax" on each immigrant entering the United States, and empowered the Treasury Department to collect the fee and oversee many aspects of immigration. But the task of regulating who could enter the nation's ports fell to the states. The law said that state officials were authorized to board ships landing at their shores to screen would-be immigrants, "and if on such examination there shall be found among such passengers any convict, lunatic, idiot, or any person unable to take care of himself or herself without becoming a public charge, they shall report the same in writing to the collector of such port, and such persons shall not be permitted to land." Later, Congress added provisions allowing for the removal of immigrants who became public charges within a few years of their arrival in the United States. The restrictive McCarran-Walter immigration overhaul enacted in

1952 stated simply that, "aliens . . . likely at any time to become a public charge" were inadmissible to the United States, and that immigrants who became public charges within five years of their arrival could be deported unless they could show that the cause of their reliance on government aid developed after they entered the United States. Immigration and welfare overhauls enacted in 1996 under Bill Clinton limited immigrants' access to welfare and stiffened requirements for them to be sponsored by someone who met a certain income threshold and would assume financial responsibility for them.

But even as the concept persisted over the decades, the term "public charge" had never been defined in American law. Left to its own devices, the government had interpreted it narrowly, confining it to immigrants who had a long-term mental deficiency or were primarily dependent on the government cash-assistance programs for survival. In 1999, the Immigration and Naturalization Service, the agency within the Justice Department that handled immigration prior to 2003, when DHS was created, tightened the definition still further, expressly excluding several of the most commonly used government aid programs from being considered evidence that an immigrant was a public charge. People could not be considered public charges, INS said, based on having used Medicaid, the federal health program for the poor; CHIP, the Children's Health Insurance Program; food stamps or other nutritional aid; or energy, housing, educational, or transportation assistance.

The idea of keeping immigrants out if they were not financially self-sufficient fit neatly into Trump's worldview and the political message that animated his campaign and invigorated his political base. It played on hostility among white working-class voters to immigrants who they believed were stealing their jobs, driving down their wages, and changing the culture and complexion of their communities and schools. Now they had to compete with immigrants for public benefits? That was too much to bear. The day that Sessions had turned his car around on a whim to join Trump at his rally in Mobile, Alabama, the topic had been on the candidate's mind. "Seven point five percent of all of the births in this country are illegal immigrants, okay?" Trump had said that day. "We can't afford it.

And they are supposed to stay." He railed against the Fourteenth Amendment to the Constitution, which confers citizenship on anyone born in the United States, and suggested that children born to undocumented immigrants should not get the same benefits as the native-born.

"So we have 300,000 babies a year—300,000!—that you have to take care of, we all have to take care of," Trump had said. "Other places don't do it. Very few places do it. We're the only place just about stupid enough to do it." It was, he added, one of the reasons he had decided to mount his improbable campaign for the presidency. "Is this crazy?"

Compared to his promises to build a wall, enact a Muslim ban, and unleash a deportation force, Trump's stated desire to jettison legal immigrants on welfare got little attention. But he never let go of the idea. In a little noticed section of Trump's big immigration speech in Phoenix in 2016, Miller had inserted a dramatic proposal: immigrants who were "public charges—that is, those relying on public welfare or straining the safety net"—would be priorities for removal, Trump said. In his first budget, the notion that immigrants were too reliant on the government's largesse was prominently featured. "Census data show that current U.S. immigration policy results in a large numbers [sic] of residents and citizens who struggle to become financially independent and instead rely on government benefits financed by taxpayers," the document said. "Focusing immigration policy on merit-based admissions has the potential to reduce federal outlays for welfare payments to lower-skilled immigrant-headed households."

In theory, Congress could impose new limits on public benefits for immigrants. But more than a year after the budget came out, and on the heels of several collapsed efforts to pass broad immigration policy changes, Miller was well aware that legislation to accomplish that goal had no chance of passing. Trump, however, had broad power to set immigration priorities on his own by redefining "public charge." And Miller wanted him to use it. It was a back-door way of accomplishing administratively what the president could not achieve legislatively. Miller had quietly begun to stoke Trump's enthusiasm for the idea early in 2018, when he had summoned Nielsen and Cissna to the Oval Office to brief him on the drafting of the rule. It was early January, and the West Wing was in a frenzy as Trump's senior staff tried to figure out how to respond to *Fire and Fury*, an explosive new book by Michael Wolff that portrayed the president as erratic and bumbling, and described the White House as a snake pit consumed by chaos. As a uniformed waiter served Trump Diet Coke from a two-liter plastic bottle, the president nodded along approvingly as the officials explained how they proposed to block immigrants who were likely to use government assistance, saying, "This is fantastic." And then, clearly having been prodded by Miller to inquire, Trump asked when the rule would be ready. Early spring? Nielsen said optimistically, although the professionals who were drafting it believed it would take much longer. Trump seemed thrilled.

Over the next few months, Miller had stepped up his pressure on US-CIS to finish the regulation. And he wasn't just insisting on a faster timetable. He was pushing for substantive changes to the rule to make it tougher on immigrants, and easier to bar them from staying in the country. The requests always came by telephone or in person—never in writing by email, text, or any other means that could later be traced back to him. Miller called Cissna at one point and told him he wanted the threshold for determining who was a public charge much lower—setting the bar for public benefits at 3 percent of federal poverty guidelines instead of the 15 percent or more that the agency was considering. That would mean that an immigrant who received more than about $30 worth of public assistance per month would be considered a public charge, and could be denied a green card. Miller's young aides from the Domestic Policy Council or Paul Ray, an official at the White House Office of Management and Budget, called USCIS officials frequently to weigh in on what Miller thought the rule should look like, pressing to push the threshold lower or include a wider array of social programs whose use could potentially disqualify an immigrant from gaining residency.

Still, much to Miller's dismay, the regulation seemed to be languishing in a never-never land of bureaucratic delay. At one point, a 250-page draft was delivered to top officials at USCIS with the urgent message that comments should be provided by the next morning at 8 a.m. "Showstoppers only," they were told, meaning they should only flag issues that were so problematic that they could stop the rule in its tracks. But since then, the momentum had faltered. It was being pecked to death, Miller complained, by civil servants who opposed its goals and by good, old-fashioned red tape. With midterm congressional elections only months away, Miller did not want to wait any longer. This is the most important thing that the department could be working on, he told officials at DHS. Miller was going to make sure that rule was finally finished.

"We need points on the board," Miller kept saying. "We've got to have some wins."

Like many of Miller's ideas, this one was based on a clever political calculation. For years, polling and focus groups had shown that, despite being divided about immigration in general, Americans shared a strong concern that immigrants were straining the social safety net by taking welfare benefits that should go to the native-born without paying into the system through taxes. In a survey released by the Bipartisan Policy Center in July of 2018, a majority—including a third of Democrats—cited the welfare issue as their top concern about immigration, ahead of national security, human rights, economic or cultural concerns. Picking a fight over whether immigrants should be able to use public benefits could introduce a powerful wedge issue into the bloodstream of congressional campaigns at a time when Republicans were battling to win the midterms. It would essentially dare the Democrats to defend what research showed was a divisive proposition. There were substantive reasons to press the public charge issue as well. Even if the rule were never finalized, it would strike fear into the hearts of immigrants throughout the country, making them think twice about using public benefits out of a concern that doing so might get them deported, or hurt their chances of gaining permanent legal status or citizenship.

Now the Trump administration was proposing to radically change the definition of a public charge. It would allow immigration officials to consider whether an immigrant used public benefits when officials were deciding whether to issue visas or green cards, and penalize those who had taken advantage of government assistance. Without any action by Congress, it would essentially give the Trump administration a way to blackball immigrants who depended on everything from food and infant nutrition services to transportation and housing subsidies. They could be deemed inadmissible because they were considered likely to become dependent on government help.

"Non-citizens who receive public benefits are not self-sufficient and are relying on the U.S. government and state and local entities for resources instead of their families, sponsors or private organizations," an early draft of the proposed rule said. "An alien's receipt of public benefits comes at taxpayer expense and availability of public benefits may provide an incentive for aliens to immigrate to the United States." The Trump administration was adopting the broadest possible definition of "public charge," holding that it applied to any immigrant who depended on "any government assistance in the form of cash, checks or other forms of money transfers, or instrument and non-cash government assistance in the form of aid, services, or other relief," the proposal said. The lengthy list of excluded programs that the Immigration and Naturalization Service issued in 1999 would be scrapped. If an immigrant depended on health insurance or nutritional subsidies; transportation, housing, or heating aid; or even government-funded preschool programs, he or she could be excluded or deported.

Inside the Department of Homeland Security, even Miller's ideological allies were deeply uncomfortable with the proposal. Dimple Shah, a top lawyer in the general counsel's office, advised her bosses that the rule's definition of "public charge" was so broad as to be crazy, and that it was certain to lead to an onslaught of litigation that the administration would almost certainly lose. If you wanted to limit legal immigration, she told colleagues, this is not the most efficient or effective way to do it. Cissna and his colleagues worried that, given the interference of White House officials and the rush to issue the rule, they had not developed a sufficient rationale for it, leaving it open to being struck down by the courts as "arbitrary and capricious." They all worried that they were being asked to sink hundreds of hours into putting together the regulation—time they could be spending on more impactful work—and would have little to show for it in the end other than a rule that would be tied up in the courts.

But Miller considered the rule critical. "This regulation will transform our society," Miller told his colleagues at one point. "It will be a transformative regulation." It was also a key component of Trump's midterm election approach, one that focused on juicing Republican enthusiasm by doubling down on the anti-immigration message that most animated his base. Defying the advice of Republican strategists who believed the election would be won and lost in the suburbs, at the hands of women and other independent voters, Trump and Miller were betting on a base strategy. So "pencils down" it was. And Trump began referencing the issue more frequently in campaign speeches, where he often lied by suggesting that undocumented immigrants could access taxpayer-funded benefits. "Democrats are also fighting to give welfare and free healthcare to illegal aliens, paid for by you, the American taxpayers, thank you very much," he told a crowd in Topeka, Kansas, drawing loud boos. "Republicans believe that the public benefits must be protected for the truly needy Americans— Americans that need help, not illegal aliens."

If Miller was running into internal resistance on the public charge rule, he was enjoying far greater success when it came to another of his pet projects: the drive to slash the refugee resettlement program. It was Round Two of the annual fight, which had ended in 2017 with a much smaller cut to refugee admissions than Miller had wanted, and this year he was determined to do more. In mid-August, aides to Nikki Haley, Trump's U.N. ambassador, discovered that deliberations had commenced about the refugee ceiling for the coming year, and she had not been included. When Haley asked for a seat at the table in the discussions, she was rebuffed. Haley had been a strong advocate for the refugee resettlement program in the past, and her exclusion from the process alarmed other supporters inside and outside the administration. Even more concerning, they were beginning to hear from well-connected colleagues that the cap was headed even lower than the previous year. On paper, Miller had lost his battle in 2017 to cut the number of refugees the United States would resettle to 15,000. Thanks to resistance from most of Trump's national security team, including Haley, the president had endorsed a ceiling of 45,000. But in practice, Miller had gotten his way. With new restrictions on the program in place and a clear directive from the president to keep refugee numbers as low as possible, resettlement had slowed to a crawl. The United States was on track to accept only 21,000 refugees in 2018, less than half of the limit Trump had set. As the deadline approached to come up with the ceiling for 2019, Miller was being ultrasecretive about the process, making sure that discussions on the issue were restricted to only a few of the most senior White House officials. Suddenly, meetings about how many women and children from war zones could be allowed into the United States were being treated with the same level of secrecy and exclusivity as planning sessions for high-stakes, clandestine military operations, like the Navy SEAL raid the Obama administration carried out to kill Osama bin Laden. It was one way in which Miller seized control of the process, essentially freezing out career officials who had opposed him the previous year.

By now, Miller had other advantages as well. Elaine Duke, who had been opposed to deep cuts in American refugee efforts, was no longer at the Department of Homeland Security; she had been replaced by Nielsen, a protégé of Kelly's, who privately questioned the need for more refugees. Even if Nielsen had wanted to preserve the refugee program at its current levels, she was already under siege by the president for her role in the family separation debacle and Trump held her responsible for the continued stream of migrants crossing into the United States at the southwestern border. Trump had fired Rex Tillerson via tweet from the State Department months earlier, and replaced him with Mike Pompeo, who was more politically aligned with the president. And Miller had powerful allies advising Pompeo. Andrew Veprek, who had been at the Domestic Policy Council during the prior year's refugee deliberations, was now the top political appointee in the Bureau of Population, Refugees, and Migration, at State. John Zadrozny, another of Miller's close allies from the DPC, had gone over to serve in the department's powerful Office of Policy Planning. Both shared Miller's priority of substantial cuts to refugee resettlement, and now they were in positions to influence a key player in the decision.

Miller even had a strategy for winning over Mattis, one of the refugee program's most stubborn proponents, who argued forcefully that refugee resettlement wasn't just a reflection of the country's humanitarian values, but also served a vital national security purpose. Mattis was particularly concerned about the impact of deep cuts to the refugee program on Iraqis who had risked their lives and those of their families by taking jobs working with the U.S. military or other parts of the American government in their country, in part based on a promise that the United States would protect them from the danger to which they had exposed themselves. In 2008, George W. Bush signed a law, the Refugee Crisis in Iraq Act, that created a special program for these Iraqis, known as "P2s" for "Priority 2," that essentially allowed them to bypass the line and apply directly for refugee status without a referral from the office of the United Nations High Commissioner for Refugees. They were vetted and interviewed extensively, just the way other would-be refugees were, but their service to the American government gave them a quicker and smoother path to resettling in the United States. Mattis would bring up the P2s without fail anytime the conversation turned to cutting back refugee admissions numbers. So Miller proposed a carve-out for the Iraqi P2s, which would essentially exempt them from the program cap and continue their special status. Mattis saw the idea for what it was—an attempt to buy him off and win his approval for slashing the refugee program—and refused. Mattis thought the program should remain at 45,000, and made sure that the president's team knew it. When Miller called the final meeting to discuss the refugee cap for a day when Mattis would not be able to attend, the secretary of defense took the unusual step of sending the Pentagon official who went to the White House in his place with a written memo declaring Mattis's support for maintaining the refugee ceiling at 45,000 and his rationale for doing so. It was the only way Mattis could be sure his opposition to Miller's efforts would be part of the presidential record.

But Mattis alone could not stand in the way. Miller had a new argument he was using to justify steep cuts to refugee admissions. He would say that a "migration crisis" was gripping the country—a flood of Central American migrants seeking asylum at the southwestern border by falsely claiming to be in fear for their lives. Most asylum seekers were illegal immigrants, Miller argued, and there was a huge backlog of asylum cases—700,000 people were in the queue, representing a wait time of several years—clogging the system. Immigration was a zero-sum game, he insisted. More refugees had to be weighed against all the other types of migrants who wanted to enter or stay in the United States. It was the culmination of Miller's effort to transform the refugee program—which had long been a bipartisan initiative, and was seen prior to Trump's presidency as a component of American foreign and national security policy—into a domestic political matter, and one more element of the partisan conflict the president was waging with Democrats.

Pompeo had initially argued for keeping the cap at 45,000 refugees. But by the time Miller, Veprek, and Zadrozny were finished with him, he had changed course and proposed a far lower number. On a Monday afternoon in mid-September, he went to the Treaty Room at the State Department to announce that the Trump administration would cap refugees at 30,000 for 2019—a 33 percent cut. In remarks that sounded as if they might have been drawn directly from Miller's own talking points, Pompeo defended the reduction by arguing that the United States had to give priority to hundreds of thousands of asylum seekers who were arriving at the border.

"Some will characterize the refugee ceiling as the sole barometer of America's commitment to vulnerable people around the world," Pompeo said. "This would be wrong. This year's refugee ceiling reflects the substantial increase in the number of individuals seeking asylum in our country," he added, "leading to a massive backlog of outstanding asylum cases and greater public expense."

The argument sounded right on paper: If the United States was being bombarded with people claiming to be refugees at its southern border, why shouldn't it pull back on admitting those applying from overseas? But the two populations were different and had always been treated as such. Refugees, by definition, had already been certified by the United Nations as having a well-founded fear of persecution in their home countries and submitted to a long and complex application process to win protection in the United States. Asylum seekers, by contrast, arrived at the border and asserted a credible fear of persecution, claims that would then be adjudicated by immigration authorities or judges. Many of them would never receive asylum. It was apples and oranges. But Miller believed they all belonged in the same basket, and Pompeo ultimately agreed.

A few weeks later, with little fanfare, Larry Bartlett quietly reclaimed his job at the State Department overseeing the refugee resettlement program at the Bureau of Population, Refugees, and Migration. The inspector general was still looking into allegations that he and others had been targeted for political retaliation, but Christine Ciccone, who had taken a job at the Department of Homeland Security, was refusing to be interviewed.

Refugees were hardly the only ones affected by Miller's push to lower immigration numbers. By late 2018, through arcane regulations, little-noticed policy guidance, and subtle changes in emphasis inside the agencies of the United States government, Trump had succeeded in making legal immigration slower and more difficult than it had been for decades. It started with the tone from the top, including the changed mission statement at USCIS, which manifested itself in dozens of small changes that carried large impacts.

In October of 2017, USCIS began requiring in-person interviews for any immigrant seeking a job-related green card, as well as spouses and children of refugees and people granted asylum. Many of those affected had been living legally in the United States for years, and undergone extensive security vetting, background checking, and interviews. In prior years, USCIS would typically waive in-person interviews for these kinds of applicants, except in cases where there was suspicion of fraud. In the Trump administration, the presumption was that extra screening was needed, whatever the circumstances. The agency made it more time-consuming and complicated for legal immigrants to submit applications, adding more pages to the forms they had to complete to adjust their status, bring a spouse from overseas, or become naturalized. Trump's DHS tripled the length of the I-485 adjustment of status form and added three times as many questions about criminal history, including tricky and exceedingly broad ones such as, "Have you EVER committed a crime of any kind (even if you were not arrested, cited, charged with or tried for that crime)?" The query went beyond the legal standard for blocking or removing an immigrant. Under the law, an immigrant can be considered inadmissible if he or she has committed certain "crimes of moral turpitude" and those involving drugs; in the Trump administration, anything that could ever have been considered a crime had to be included on the form.

DHS also made it more dangerous to make an error or omission on an application. Under a new policy, USCIS staff could immediately deny any application or request that lacked sufficient evidence or omitted official records. In the past, the agency had to give immigrants an opportunity to fix whatever was wrong with their application, by issuing either an official request for more evidence or a notification that the claim was going to be denied. Under the new policy, if immigrants wanted a chance to correct their mistakes, they had to submit an entirely new application, go to the back of the line, and pay a second steep application fee. In the press release announcing the new policy, Cissna called it a long-overdue change that would discourage "frivolous or meritless claims that slow down processing for everyone, including legitimate petitioners."

The impacts were substantial. The rate at which USCIS rejected applications for work permits, travel documents, and other grants of status jumped by more than one third during Trump's first year in office. Within a year of Trump's inauguration, wait times for immigrants seeking to become naturalized citizens had doubled, from about five months to an average of ten months, thanks to new requirements for green card holders, heightened scrutiny of applications, and the shifting of staff to other functions. The rate of naturalizations hit the lowest in a decade in 2019, according to an analysis by Boundless Immigration, a company that helps immigrants obtain green cards and become citizens. And Trump's administration went even further. With the cooperation of the Department of Justice, top officials established a new office, which came to be known as the "denaturalization task force," to accelerate a program begun during the Obama administration designed to strip naturalized Americans of their citizenship based on charges that they obtained it fraudulently.

The Trump administration was also fighting in court to be allowed to add a new question to the decennial census asking whether respondents were American citizens, a move that experts said would almost certainly lead to an undercounting of many Hispanics and other immigrants, potentially leaving their communities with less representation in Congress and fewer federal dollars. The idea had been pitched to Trump's transition team by Thomas B. Hofeller, a Republican political mapmaker who specialized in gerrymandering plans to solidify his party's dominance in districts around the country. In a 2015 study of Texas state legislative districts, Hofeller had argued that political maps that omitted noncitizens "would be advantageous to Republicans and non-Hispanic whites," undercutting the political power of Hispanics, who tended to vote Democratic. A citizenship question had also been a long-standing priority for Kris Kobach, the former Kansas secretary of state, who discussed it with both Trump and Bannon during the campaign and shortly after the inauguration in 2017. Bannon got in touch with Wilbur Ross, the secretary of commerce, and asked him to discuss the idea with Kobach, who made a forceful argument that a citizenship question—which had not been a part of the census since 1950—was vital. Omitting it, Kobach wrote to Ross in a July 14, 2017, email that was later turned over to a congressional committee investigating the issue, "leads to the problem that aliens who do not actually 'reside' in the United States are still counted for congressional apportionment purposes." But adding it, experts said, would almost certainly lead to an undercount of Hispanic households. That would be a boost for Republicans.

Ross was soon engaged in a quiet but intense lobbying effort to get the Department of Justice to recommend that the question be added. Census Bureau officials warned against the move; in a January 2018 memo to Ross, John Abowd, the chief scientist of the Census Bureau, said that adding the question is "very costly, harms the quality of the census count, and would use substantially less accurate citizenship status data than are available from administrative sources." But it was of intense interest to Trump and his inner circle, and by March of 2018, Ross had announced he was adding the question in order to improve enforcement of the Voting Rights Act. (Eventually, after several state attorneys general and advocacy groups sued to block the change, the Supreme Court temporarily prevented the addition of the question, with Chief Justice John Roberts writing in a June 2019 ruling that the administration's explanation for it "seems to have been contrived." The Court sent the case back to a lower court judge to be reviewed, but Ross relented, saying he would print the census without the citizenship question.)

Highly skilled foreign workers, the kind Trump was always saying he wanted more of, found themselves targeted as well. Trump had signed a "Buy American, Hire American" executive order in April of 2017 that ordered a top-to-bottom review of the H-1B visa program for high-skilled workers to ensure that it was admitting the most skilled and best-paid applicants. Before long, USCIS was making small but significant changes to the program that tightened eligibility requirements, freezing out computer programmers and raising new hurdles for engineers, accountants, lawyers, doctors, and others. New evidence requirements were piled on companies that employed H-1B holders who performed their work at another site. USCIS announced it was ending work authorizations for the spouses of H-1B visa holders, which would make it more difficult for foreign workers to support their families in the United States. DHS proposed killing a rule proposed during the Obama administration allowing foreign-born entrepreneurs starting businesses in the United States to gain temporary legal status.

And those were just the measures that received attention. Through regulations, memoranda, and guidance letters, the president's agenda, as translated by Miller and carried out by his allies throughout the bureaucracy, was filtering down to every aspect of immigration enforcement and policy. "Everything is grinding more slowly," said Doug Rand, the president and co-founder of Boundless. "It's a full-on assault in ways we haven't even fully been able to measure."

Civil rights and legal groups who were tracking the president's quiet assault on legal immigration sometimes referred to it as Trump's "invisible wall." Trump, however, was still preoccupied first and foremost with the real, bricks-and-mortar thing. And as the midterm elections crept closer, Trump became increasingly convinced that he needed to show his supporters, in the most tangible way possible, how aggressive he was willing to be in cracking down on immigration. The president was once again spoiling for a shutdown fight over the wall, and it was up to Paul Ryan and Mitch McConnell to talk him out of it. One afternoon in late July, they went to the White House to do just that. The polls were already flashing bright red warning signs for their party, the leaders said, and a shutdown in the weeks before voters cast their ballots would only make matters worse for Republicans. But you promised me I would get money for the wall, Trump said accusingly, recalling his anger in March over signing the massive spending bill. And you will, Ryan said, but this is not the time to force the issue. The two leaders laid out their strategy for pushing through the spending bills needed to fund the government for the coming fiscal year, which would begin in October. The Republican majority was making surprisingly good progress cutting deals with Democrats on bills to fund most of the government, they explained. For the ones they couldn't agree on, including the spending bill for the Department of Homeland Security, they would wait until after the elections, postponing the divisive fight for another day. Ryan tried to put the best face on the situation, telling Trump that money that he had requested was already being spent on border security. And the president had seemed to relent, agreeing that he would be patient and wait until after Election Day to force the wall issue. But days later, during an angry Sunday morning tweetstorm in which he also targeted Special Counsel Robert Mueller and the news media, Trump returned to the prospect of a shutdown fight over the wall.

"I would be willing to 'shut down' government if the Democrats do not give us the votes for Border Security, which includes the Wall!" he wrote, reprising his demand for substantial immigration policy changes. "Must get rid of Lottery, Catch & Release etc. and finally go to system of Immigration based on MERIT! We need great people coming into our Country!"

The leaders were petrified that the president was going to further imperil the party's electoral fortunes by forcing what they considered a ruinous shutdown fight over the wall. Even some members of Trump's own staff confided privately that they were unsure whether his desire for a public battle over the issue in advance of the midterms could be kept in check. So at McConnell's suggestion, Republican leaders decided to take out an insurance policy of sorts tailored to the president they had come to know and tendencies they had learned to manage. Trump loved campaigning, and from their perspective, he was great at it. Every time Trump held a campaign rally for a Republican candidate, McConnell, Ryan, or McCarthy would call the candidate in advance and ask him or her to deliver a message to the president. They were to thank Trump for being such an effusive and effective messenger for their campaigns, and for bringing out so many supporters. But they were also to make sure to warn the president against shutting down the government before the balloting. That would be awful for my campaign, the candidates were to tell Trump. As he traveled the country, the president received the message from virtually every candidate he campaigned for: Please do not shut down the government over the wall. "It was a very intense campaign to keep him from picking this fight," said one official involved in the effort. It seemed to work.

But if Trump was keeping himself in check in Washington, he was becoming increasingly vocal about his immigration views on the campaign trail. Like Miller, he believed the issue would resonate with his base, boost Republicans' chances of holding the House, and help save the party's majority in the Senate. Some of the most progressive Democratic candidates were campaigning on the idea of abolishing ICE, a notion that had gained new energy in the wake of the family separation crisis. Newspapers and social media were clogged with images of muscle-bound, heavily armed, uniformed agents confronting women and young children, and all of a sudden for many Democrats, "Abolish ICE" seemed like a politically salient issue. Miller and Trump saw it as a gift. Polls showed that most voters, whether they backed the president's immigration policies or not, were opposed to the idea of getting rid of the federal immigration enforcement agency. Miller began peppering Trump's rally speeches with broad generalizations about the Democratic Party—that it stood for abolishing ICE, opening the borders to criminals and terrorists, and giving violent immigrants refuge in American cities.

At his rallies, Trump began to speak of an illegal immigration onslaught that could only be stopped by Republicans. "A blue wave in November means open borders, which means massive crime; a red wave means safety and strength—that's what it is," Trump told thousands of supporters crammed into a civic center in Charleston, West Virginia. "The new platform of the Democratic Party is abolish ICE. A vote for any Democrat in November is a vote to eliminate immigration enforcement, throw open our borders, and set loose vicious predators and violent criminals. They'll be all over our communities. They will be preying on our communities."

And privately, the president was pressuring his top officials to find novel ways to keep immigrants out. The message to Nielsen and others was clear: I don't care what you have to do—just close it down. A new caravan of Central American migrants was forming and beginning to head northward through Mexico, adding urgency to the effort. The numbers were already making the president furious. DHS was at 97 percent capacity in its shelters for single adults, and running out of space in family facilities. Statistics gathered by the department showed that the number of family units apprehended at the southwestern border had hit a record in September—16,658—bringing the total number over the year to more than 100,000.

It was evidence of the reverse boomerang effect that DHS officials had worried about when the president abandoned family separation with his executive order in June. Word that Trump had caved to the pressure had clearly made its way down to Central America, where an increasing number of families were convinced that the United States would let them in if they could just make it to the border. It was not the invasion of armed and dangerous attackers that Trump claimed; the families were unlikely to bring with them the "massive crime" that he predicted. But it fed a migration crisis that would accelerate dramatically over the next six months, fueling Trump's fury.

Nielsen was desperate to figure out a way to quell Trump's anger at the eye-popping numbers, but she was also deeply frustrated with his approach. Trump had caved on family separation, the one thing that might have made a substantial dent in the numbers, and now Nielsen believed she was doing literally everything that she was legally able to do to get control of the border, and none of it was enough for Trump. He was an executive, accustomed to giving his underlings problems and ordering them to solve them—or else. But the situation at the border was complex and multifaceted. There were no simple solutions. Trump didn't care to hear about or understand any of the complicated specifics. His attention span was short and his tolerance for detailed explanations bordered on nonexistent. This was a president who would always rather trust his gut and take a drastic action than sit around listening to a long list of reasons why it was imprudent, unnecessary, or even illegal.

Nielsen was reminded of that one day in August, when she tried to persuade Trump to help pressure members of Congress to support new counter-drone legislation. DHS had been working for months on a bill to broaden the government's authority to take down a drone that was deemed an imminent security threat. For years, national security officials had worried and warned about the possibility of terrorists or other bad actors getting their hands on a drone, loading it with a bomb, and flying it over a stadium or other highly populated area, putting thousands of lives in danger. Just that month, assailants in Venezuela had loaded drones with four pounds of plastic explosives and tried to kill President Nicolás Maduro at an outdoor event in Caracas. Analysts called it the first case outside a war zone in which a drone had been used as a weapon. But under existing U.S. law, the government had no authority to take down a drone, because doing so would require intercepting the signals used to control it, and that would be a violation of wiretap laws written long before flying robots were invented. On the phone with the president that day, Nielsen asked Trump to tweet about the importance of passing the legislation. She explained that the bill had reached a critical stage on Capitol Hill and would need his backing to become law.

Growing impatient with her explanation, Trump cut her off. "Listen Kirstjen, you've got my approval to shoot them out of the sky, okay?" he said.

Nielsen paused, perplexed. "Let me explain it a different way," she began, trying again. "We legally can't, so that's why we need this law. We need your support, because—"

"Kirstjen, you didn't hear me the first time, honey," Trump interrupted. "Shoot 'em down. Sweetheart, just shoot 'em out of the sky, okay? You've got my permission."

The president was done with that discussion. He wanted to move on to the next thing. And that's just what Nielsen did.

— 28 —

USE OF FORCE

JUST AFTER 7:30 IN the morning on October 18, 2018, President Trump surprised his staff with a tweet that sent the White House and his entire administration into a tailspin. The president was angry about the caravan of migrants from Central America making its way north, and grasping for ways to show the public he was finally getting tough. "I must in the strongest of terms, ask Mexico to stop this onslaught," he wrote. "And if unable to do so, I will call up the U.S. Military and CLOSE OUR SOUTHERN BORDER!" Trump had barked privately about shutting down the border many times with senior officials in the White House and the Department of Homeland Security, and they had always managed to talk him down. They would explain that sealing the border was untenable—the logistics were nearly impossible and the economic pain that would result was extreme. Besides, his advisers told Trump, it would do little or nothing to solve the problem he was trying to tackle. Immigrants could still present themselves at the United States border and claim asylum, which is what the vast majority of people in the last caravan had done once they arrived. It was a matter of American and international law that Trump couldn't just order away. But lately, with the November elections approaching and news coverage about the caravan seemingly all over cable news, Trump seemed to be gravitating toward more and more radical ideas.

He began to issue direct orders to Nielsen and others in his administration: Do not let anyone from the caravan in. We have to keep them out, the president said. For Trump, it was a point of personal pride. This was my signature campaign issue, he told his advisers. I have said many, many times on TV that they're not coming in, I'm going to stop them from coming in. And now you people are telling me there's nothing you can do to stop it? The numbers from CBP showed that the migration flow was not only *not* dissipating, it was continuing to build. "You all are embarrassing me," Trump said during one particularly tense meeting in the Oval Office. Nielsen, who had flirted privately earlier in the year with resigning, began drafting a letter of resignation that she expected she would have to use sooner rather than later.

So when Trump announced abruptly that he was about to close the border that morning, it was not entirely surprising. He had raised it behind closed doors so frequently that senior officials at the Department of Homeland Security had discussed among themselves whether a presidential directive to seal the border would be a red line prompting them to resign in protest. They agreed it would be—if that time ever came. That Thursday morning, it seemed imminent.

Within minutes of Trump's tweet, John Kelly called an emergency meeting in his West Wing office down the hall from the Oval Office, with John R. Bolton, who had been named the national security adviser in April of 2018, and other aides. Nielsen rushed with her senior staff to the White House, where they had already been scheduled to attend a meeting in the Situation Room to talk about the border and their strategy for pressuring Congress to step in and do something to control the situation. But the president's alarming message was more urgent. Nielsen sent her aides downstairs to the Situation Room to huddle with Stephen Miller on the legislative strategy, while she stayed in Kelly's office trying to figure out how to walk Trump back from the brink of what she knew would be a disastrous declaration. They had to explain to Trump that Nielsen was, at that very moment, in the middle of exceedingly delicate negotiations with

Mexico on a deal that could actually help slow the flow of migrants into the United States, precisely as Trump had been demanding, and that shutting the border now would torpedo the plan. Her staff had been haggling quietly for weeks with Mexican officials on the agreement. It involved having UNHCR, the United Nations' refugee agency, build refugee camps in northern and central Mexico and requiring people to apply for refugee status there, rather than massing at the United States border to claim asylum.

Bolton scoffed. This is stupid, he said. Just send the military and seal the border. He was channeling Trump, and now it was clear that he had privately been egging the president on to take drastic action. John, you don't understand, Nielsen answered back to Bolton, the tension in the room rising. That's not how this works. You can seal the whole border and people can still show up and claim asylum—that's not going to fix it. As they argued, Kelly came to the defense of his protégé. She's the secretary of homeland security, he told Bolton, adding that Mike Pompeo, the secretary of state, supported what Nielsen was trying to do. At least give this a chance to work before you counsel the president to just shut it all down. By the time the meeting ended, Kelly and Bolton were both fuming.

They brought their bad blood into the Oval Office, where they were scheduled to meet with Trump and Pompeo about whether to lift sanctions on Turkey after the country had released an American pastor from jail. As Nielsen hung back in Kelly's office, the chief of staff made the case to Trump on her behalf. Let the secretary try to figure out whether this deal with Mexico works before you take the extreme step of sealing the border, Kelly said. Bolton pushed back, and the two men began shouting at each other. "Do what you want to do," Kelly said, exasperated. Trump asked an aide to get Jared Kushner, who had forged a close relationship with Mexican officials, on the phone. Kushner said he had his own idea about how to solve the border crisis. But before he could describe it, Kelly and Bolton were at it again, and this time the shouting escalated. "Fuck you," the chief of staff shouted at the national security adviser. And then, turning on his heel: "I'm out of here!" Kelly left the Oval Office and Bolton ran out behind him, believing that the chief of staff had just quit. The verbal altercation with Bolton had been so loud that aides throughout the West Wing had heard it. Kelly strode down the hall to his own office and told Nielsen and her staff, "I'm fucking out of here." And then, shortly after 10 a.m., the White House chief of staff left for the day.

The blowup in the West Wing underscored the sense of urgency inside the White House and throughout the Trump administration to deliver something—anything—that could fix a problem that was infuriating the president. Trump was getting increasingly agitated, and Miller was determined to deliver him results. His team began huddling regularly with officials from DHS, the Justice Department, and the State Department to explore their options for cracking down at the border. If they weren't allowed to forcibly separate parents from their children, Trump's team thought, could they do the same thing another way? One particularly harsh possibility would be to give parents what they called a "binary choice"—force them to choose between being detained with their children or voluntarily giving up the children to foster care and being held themselves. It was tantamount to reviving the family separation policy by coercing parents into consenting to it. Throughout the summer and fall, a discussion paper about possible reforms to the asylum system—including the binary choice option—had been circulating in the top ranks of officials at DHS, ICE, CBP, and the State Department. Few people had any doubt that Miller was the author, though he had been careful not to put his name on the document. It suggested tougher standards for granting asylum and raised the idea of requiring asylum officers to rely on State Department assessments of the current conditions in a country when making an asylum decision.

In a series of Tuesday afternoon conference calls with fifty or sixty officials from across the bureaucracy, Miller grew more and more impatient. The calls were officially hosted by May Davis, the deputy domestic policy adviser at the White House. But in practice, they were run by Miller. Now was the time, he insisted repeatedly, to put in place asylum changes that would make it more difficult for migrants to seek protection in the United States based on the legal standard of having a "credible fear." They should speed up the legal processing of newly arrived migrants, in order to get the word out that people arriving at the border were being quickly deported. And Miller insisted that the Central American countries whose nationals were showing up at the border had to be pressured into doing more. Trump had complained privately and publicly for months that the United States continued to provide foreign aid to El Salvador, Guatemala, and Honduras while they sent waves of migrants north to the United States. If the Central American governments refused to do more, the president said, the U.S. should simply yank their aid.

By the end of October, the number of families arrested at the border had spiked, rising to about 23,000 for the month, and Trump was on a nonstop tirade about sealing the border. Painting the migrant caravan as a national security threat, he warned on Twitter that "criminals and unknown Middle Easterners" were sprinkled among the migrants in the caravan making its way north from Honduras, suggesting that there could be terrorists in their midst. Inside DHS, the posting caused mass confusion. Where had Trump gotten his information? Within minutes of the president's tweet, officials throughout the department started getting phone calls from colleagues and reporters asking what Trump was talking about. It sounded like an assumption born of racism and xenophobia, the notion that a large group of Central Americans was filled with criminals, or that people of Middle Eastern descent would be more likely to be security threats. Were there any facts to back this up? Officials could not provide any. Customs and Border Protection steered reporters to the White House to ask what Trump meant. By the end of the next day, the president had walked back his statement, noting that there was "no proof" of Middle Easterners in the caravan. But by then, DHS had already developed an official statement supporting his initial tweet. Tyler Q. Houlton, a spokesman, said that "Citizens of countries outside Central America, including countries in the Middle East, Africa, South Asia, and elsewhere are currently traveling through Mexico toward the U.S." The disconnect between the president and his bureaucracy was as wide as it had ever been.

Trump ordered the Department of Defense to come up with a plan to deploy hundreds of active-duty Army troops to fortify the border. He wanted them armed and ready to push back migrants seeking to get into the United States. The prospect so distressed Jim Mattis, the secretary of defense, that he told colleagues he was potentially ready to resign over it. Mattis was not happy about having troops involved in any way in what most senior officials understood was a political stunt. But if American forces were going to play a role, Mattis made clear what the rules were: they could only go to the border in a support role to CBP, not as a phalanx of armed sentries brandishing weapons to target asylum seekers.

In a meeting at the White House, Trump gave Nielsen a direct order: Do not let any more people in. Nielsen told the president that she did not have that option. I can't just turn them back, the secretary told Trump, unless we invoke certain legal authorities. And that would take the co-operation of Mexico, Nielsen explained, otherwise they would become embroiled in a "literal Mexican standoff" over returning migrants that Mexico was refusing to accept. That, Nielsen said, was why he needed to give her negotiations time to work. As usual, the president seemed not to understand her pleadings or to simply ignore them altogether. Reasoning with Trump was often a futile endeavor. Sometimes he would yell and scream. Other times he would abruptly change topics. And on the rare occasion that he would agree to abandon an ill-considered idea, he often returned to it later as if he had never been talked out of it in the first place.

In this case, Trump was furious and wanted to do something more aggressive. Miller told officials at DHS they needed to speed up asylum rule changes that were due out in December, so that Trump could issue a high-profile public proclamation within days—just before the midterm elections—to bar Central Americans, including asylum seekers, from entering the United States. This was exactly what Nielsen had feared. She believed, and had been told by DHS lawyers, that such a move would violate U.S. laws that gave people the right to apply for asylum on American soil, regardless of their legal status or where they came from. Meanwhile, the National Security Council and the Office of Management and Budget were told to draw up plans for cutting off aid to the Central American countries. The president wanted a big, splashy event where he could highlight his toughness at the border and take Democrats to task for their opposition to his immigration agenda. Miller began planning for a major speech the following Tuesday, exactly one week before the congressional elections, where Trump would lay out his plans. In addition to sending the military to secure the border, he would essentially be declaring a national emergency to justify radical changes in American asylum policies that would bar many migrants from even seeking protection.

On Monday, October 29, the day before he was to deliver the address, Trump gathered cabinet officials and others in the Oval Office to discuss the caravan and his administration's response. Nielsen implored Trump to put off his announcement until she had had a chance to follow through on the negotiations with Mexico and reiterated her legal concerns about turning away asylum seekers. Trump wanted to invoke Section 212(f) of the Immigration and Nationality Act—the same authority he relied on to impose the travel ban days after taking office—to block the Central Americans from entering. It just wasn't operationally feasible, Nielsen insisted. To use that authority, you would have to know the specific identities of the people in the caravan, like ticketed passengers on a plane. There was no way to identify them. And there was another, completely unrelated reason to delay the speech. Over the weekend, a forty-six-year-old man had walked into the Tree of Life Synagogue in Pittsburgh and opened fired on worshippers there, saying that Jews needed to die. He killed eleven people and wounded several others before being taken into custody. The shooter had posted messages on social media blaming HIAS, a Jewish-affiliated refugee resettlement agency, for bringing "hostile invaders to dwell among us" and "kill our people." With the nation mourning the tragedy, it was hardly optimal timing to announce an immigration crackdown.

By the end of the meeting, Trump had agreed: the speech was off—for now. That afternoon, the Pentagon went ahead with its announcement that it was sending 5,200 active-duty troops to the border, as part of a new mission dubbed Operation Faithful Patriot. But the bigger announcement would wait. His advisers had bought themselves some time to talk the president out of sealing the border.

Still, Kelly was concerned about what the president might do or say. In a meeting with Trump later that day, Kelly tried to explain the limits of what the troops were allowed to do at the border. They could help fortify it with barbed wire and build tent cities to help ease the crunch on ICE and CBP, which were rapidly running out of space to hold migrants. But military personnel couldn't actually touch a migrant, either to detain one or to provide any kind of care or service. And they certainly could not use force to push them back, Kelly explained. Trump was not hearing him. He wanted the troops to keep the "illegals" out at all costs, he told Kelly, and he refused to acknowledge that there were any legal limits on what the military could do. Trump wanted to extend the travel ban he had put in place the previous year to all Central Americans, he told his chief of staff. That will do nothing to stop people from coming across the border, Kelly responded. But by then, the chief of staff had given up trying to reason with Trump. He later told colleagues in the White House and at DHS that he thought there was a very good chance the president might go out and announce the extreme measures he was suggesting, and there was little that Kelly or anyone else could do to stop it.

Kelly was right to worry. On Thursday, November 1, before leaving Washington for a six-day campaign sprint that would take him to huge rallies in eight states ahead of Election Day, Trump gave a speech in the Roosevelt Room about what he was doing to crack down at the border. He stopped short of announcing the executive actions on asylum he was weighing—and he did not announce a complete closure of the border—but he talked extensively about the role of the military, and, under questioning by reporters covering his comments, suggested that the troops might use lethal force to confront immigrants at the border. Asked what the American forces would do if migrants threw rocks, Trump answered: "If they want to throw rocks at our military, our military fights back," the president said. "I told them, 'Consider it a rifle.'"

Nielsen and her top aides, who were traveling to New York for meetings and had watched Trump's remarks on Fox News, were horrified. The president had just suggested, in comments carried live on TV, that American soldiers had license to shoot to kill migrants at the border. Once again, they dropped everything to head off a presidentially created crisis. Nielsen frantically asked her staff to find the CBP use of force policy and send it over to the White House immediately. Someone had to show it to Trump and get him to walk back his comments right away, she said. Kevin McAleenan, the CBP chief, called DHS lawyers to discuss the policy. The rules were very clear. They stated that DHS personnel "may use deadly force only when necessary, that is, when the officer/agent has a reasonable belief that the subject of such force poses an imminent danger of serious physical injury or death to the officer/agent or to another person." If migrants were throwing rocks, it would have to be met with commensurate *nonlethal* force—not live ammunition from rifles, as the president had suggested.

Trump appeared to get the message, and he backed off publicly from the idea of the military firing on migrants. When reporters asked him about it the next day, he said rock throwers would be arrested, and responded to a question about whether he could promise that the U.S. military wouldn't shoot at civilians at the border by saying, "Well, I hope they won't." But privately, Trump badly wanted to find a way that they could. A few days later, in a meeting with DHS officials, the president brought up the idea again. Listen, I get it, okay? he told them. If someone throws a rock, you can't shoot to kill. But would it be okay just to injure them? What if we shoot these migrants in the *legs*? To slow them down? That's not lethal force, right? Nielsen and her aides were flabbergasted.

No, they responded quickly. That's not allowed either.

HIJACKING THE MIDTERMS

IT WAS SIX DAYS before Election Day, and Trump was in a nasty shouting match with Paul Ryan. Over the last several weeks, the president had been steadily ratcheting up his anti-immigrant rhetoric, warning darkly about a second wave of caravans from Central America full of immigrants who were ready to invade the United States and bring drugs and crime to communities all over the country. At raucous rallies throughout the heartland, Trump was recapturing some of the energy of his 2016 campaign, whipping his crowds into a frenzy as they chanted "Build! The! Wall!" and he promised ever-more-aggressive measures to stop caravans of immigrants from entering the country. "Look, that is an assault on our country," Trump declared at a rally for Senator Ted Cruz in Houston, prompting loud boos from the crowd at the mention of the caravan. "That's an assault. And in that caravan you have some very bad people. You have some very bad people. And we can't let that happen to our country."

Republican strategists were looking at internal surveys that showed their candidates in key races badly behind or teetering dangerously on the precipice of losing. This was exactly the opposite of the message Trump needed to be delivering, Ryan had told the president in a series of conversations over the last several weeks. It's killing our guys, the speaker said.

We are going to win or lose this election in the suburbs, with educated women, Ryan told Trump. I understand the desire to play to your base, Ryan said, but those are not the voters we need to be worried about right now. Talk about the economy! Tout the massive tax cut you delivered with the help of Republican lawmakers who are running for reelection. But stop with the anti-immigration screeds. Through it all, Ryan never took Trump to task publicly for his rhetoric, believing it was better to make his case to the president privately.

This time, though, Trump had crossed a line. In an interview with the newsletter *Axios*, the president had said he was considering an executive order to eviscerate birthright citizenship, suggesting he would act unilaterally to undo the Fourteenth Amendment. "We're the only country in the world where a person comes in and has a baby, and the baby is essentially a citizen of the United States for 85 years, with all of those benefits," Trump said. "It's ridiculous. It's ridiculous. And it has to end." The president had his facts wrong; at least thirty other countries, including Canada, Mexico, and many others in the Western Hemisphere, grant automatic birthright citizenship. But he was unbothered by the details. Trump would bring up the idea every so often and Don McGahn would silently grimace and try to steer him away from it, saying while there might be a law review article somewhere that made the case that it was on shaky legal ground, it just didn't seem like the right thing to pursue. I'll keep looking into it, McGahn would tell the president, hoping that Trump would forget about it and move on. He had—until now.

Ryan was apoplectic. This went beyond the offensive or politically problematic statements Trump had been making about immigration at his campaign rallies and went straight to the heart of the Constitution and the separation of powers. A president could not simply wave a magic wand and erase a constitutional amendment. That would take action by Congress, and a painstaking process of ratification by the states—the kind of strict adherence to the letter of the Constitution that Republicans like Ryan were always preaching.

So Ryan broke his own rule against disagreeing publicly with Trump. During a campaign stop in Kentucky, Ryan told a radio reporter that the president "obviously" did not have the power to do what he was threatening. Republican candidates toiling to appeal to moderate voters in their districts, and those who represented substantial numbers of immigrant families, rushed to distance themselves from Trump's proposal as well. "Birthright citizenship is protected by the Constitution, so no @realDonaldTrump you can't end it by executive order," Carlos Curbelo, the Republican congressman from Miami, said on Twitter.

Ryan's rare bit of public criticism enraged Trump, and he was not about to let it go unchallenged. The next day, he picked a public fight with the speaker, posting a message on Twitter in which he said Ryan "should be focusing on holding the Majority rather than giving his opinions on Birthright Citizenship, something he knows nothing about!" The posting was an extraordinary airing of intramural bitterness, and fresh evidence less than a week before the midterm balloting of deep rifts between the president and leaders of his own party.

The tensions boiled over in the telephonic shouting match just before Election Day when Ryan called Trump. This is not the time for you to be getting into a public pissing match with me, he said. The president was unrepentant, arguing that the episode was Ryan's fault. You shouldn't be out there undermining me like that, he raged. Ryan was exasperated. Trump still didn't get it. He repeated what he had been telling Trump for weeks. You are not helping anything by talking about this kind of stuff. You are hurting your own people, and it will not end well.

The following week, Republicans lost the House, doing particularly poorly in the marginal districts where leaders had feared that Trump's anti-immigrant message would do the most damage. The president's jarring, out-of-nowhere musings about ending birthright citizenship had been a final, devastating blow to some of the most vulnerable Republicans. It cost Curbelo his seat, Ryan would later tell his colleagues. But his talk of sealing the border and having U.S. troops shoot at migrants had not helped either. Trump had made the congressional elections about him and his visceral message of fear and loathing toward immigrants, and voters in vital pockets of the country had recoiled, one of Ryan's associates later told a colleague.

"He had just hijacked the whole thing."

By the standards that Bannon had laid out five years before in his town-house behind the Supreme Court, Trump had been spectacularly success-ful. He had elevated immigration from an issue that hardly ranked among American voters' top concerns to one that preoccupied a substantial share of the public. Back in 2012, researchers at the Pew Research Center found that immigration was near the bottom of voters' list of priority issues—not even in the top ten, with only about 40 percent saying it was "very important" to their vote. The year Trump was elected, the Center found that that number had surged to 70 percent, and it eroded only slightly to 65 percent in the 2018 contests, on par with taxes, Social Security and Medicare, and racial equality issues. For some Republican candidates, that had been a good thing. In solidly Republican states like North Dakota, In-diana, and Missouri, conservative candidates who had embraced Trump's anti-immigrant message excelled, defeating Democrats and helping their party retain the Senate. In North Dakota, Kevin Cramer, a Republican congressman, went after Democratic senator Heidi Heitkamp in a televi-sion ad accusing her of having voted to allow federal money to go to cities "that hide illegal immigrants," including violent criminals. Heitkamp had voted against legislation that would have barred law enforcement money from going to any municipality that limited its cooperation with federal immigration authorities, but Cramer's description was misleading at best. And North Dakota, a state more than 1,000 miles from the border with Mexico that has a surpassingly low number of undocumented immigrants, does not have so-called "sanctuary cities." Still, Cramer's tactic resonated, and he beat Heitkamp in a state that Trump had won by 35 points in 2016.

Yet outside of deep-red America, the president's fear-filled immigration message fared poorly, taking with it the political fortunes of many Republi-can members of Congress. Stanley B. Greenberg, the Democratic pollster, found in a post-election survey that people who had voted Republican in the 2018 midterms gave "open borders" as their top reason. It was to them that Trump was speaking at his red-meat rallies, when he said the election was about the caravan, and warned that a vote for Democrats would be a vote for open borders. But a majority of voters rejected that formulation and voted for Democrats instead. Greenberg found that 54 percent of voters said immigrants "strengthen our country," and that three quarters of Democrats and a large majority of independents said that America gains from immigration. Miller's gambit to use the public charge rule to stoke anger at immigrants had failed as well, Greenberg found; only 34 percent of those polled viewed immigrants as a burden on the country.

"For their part, the Democrats embraced their diversity. They supported comprehensive immigration reform and the Dreamers, opposed Mr. Trump's border wall and opposed the separation of children from their families," Greenberg wrote in *The New York Times*. "In short, the Republicans lost badly in the House by running as an anti-immigrant party, while the Democrats made major gains as a self-confident multicultural party."

Republican analysts arrived at the same conclusion, albeit for somewhat different reasons. In the days after the midterms, David Winston, a Republican pollster, noticed something striking as he was poring over the results for clues of what went wrong for his party. Immigration and the caravan had overwhelmed the economic message that Ryan and other Republicans had been trying to highlight by a two-to-one margin. And that, Winston concluded, had been a massive missed opportunity for Republicans, pushing voters who had yet to make up their minds to break for Democrats by a 12-point margin. His data showed that Republicans loved the immigration focus, just as Democrats did their party's focus on health care and criticizing Trump. "What was surprising, however, was the similarity in the views of both parties' messages by key demographic/ geographic voters who helped determine the election: Independents, women, and suburban voters," Winston wrote in his post-election analysis. "They all saw the immigration issue as the Republicans' top message and the Democrats' as a health care message. They liked one; the other was not favorably received. . . . The data show the economy could have been a winning issue for the GOP. Instead, the Republican immigration message was not only poorly received by voters, it overshadowed what could have been a much more positive economic message for Congressional Republicans."

Ryan had been right.

Many candidates who styled themselves in Trump's anti-immigrant image fell short, including Kris Kobach, who lost his bid to become the governor of Kansas, and Lou Barletta, who tried and failed to unseat Bob Casey, the sitting Democratic senator in Pennsylvania. Some Republicans who embraced Trump's message in hopes of keeping their jobs found themselves swept out of competitive seats. And even those who, like Curbelo, desperately tried to distance themselves from the president, openly rejecting his attacks on immigrants and immigration, could not escape the dynamic. They became unwilling participants in Trump's base strategy, too, and paid the price for it with voters.

— 30 —

MEXICAN STANDOFF

THE WEEK AFTER THE disastrous midterm elections, Pompeo and Nielsen flew down to Houston, Texas, for a secret meeting with Marcelo Ebrard, the incoming foreign secretary of Mexico. They drove from the airport to the nearest hotel, where a large suite of rooms had been cordoned off for them. Security agents swept the area and pronounced it clear of threats, and the group got down to business. The deal they had been working on to create a refugee process in Mexico overseen by the United Nations had died during the transition between the administrations of Enrique Peña Nieto and Andrés Manuel López Obrador, who had won election in July and was set to take office within weeks. But Pompeo and Nielsen had not given up hope that a different agreement still might be possible to enlist Mexico in stemming the flow of migrants into the United States. Their idea was to keep migrants who were seeking asylum in Mexico—or to return them there once they arrived in the United States—while their claims were considered.

The plan had been months in the making, but discussions had intensified over the past several weeks. And they had taken on new urgency for the Americans after Trump had threatened to close the border and then abruptly imposed new restrictions on asylum two days after the elections.

The asylum changes were immediately challenged in court by the ACLU (and would be halted by a federal judge two weeks later), but the day of their secret gathering in Houston, they helped Nielsen and Pompeo underscore the stakes for Ebrard. Our president is willing to do absolutely crazy things if we can't get this deal inked, they said. We are going to start turning back migrants, and if you guys don't accept them, Trump will go apoplectic, and things will go very badly for you. He will shut down the border, they promised. It's not bullshit. It's not hyperbole. He really means it. We have to close this deal. Ebrard said he understood. His administration was willing to work out an agreement along these lines, but there were some important wrinkles to iron out. We have international obligations, he said. We have to offer people humanitarian protections. If you start turning people around at your border, we're not going to get into a physical altercation with the forces on your side. But we've got to do it in an orderly way.

Both sides saw the meeting as a breakthrough of sorts. The fact that the Americans had been able to extract a commitment from the Mexicans to begin taking back migrants meant there was space for an agreement. Above all, it was the threat that Trump was as crazy as he sometimes seemed that got them there. Nielsen and Ebrard deputized their top aides to iron out the details.

What followed was weeks of clandestine shuttle diplomacy between Miles Taylor, a top aide to Nielsen, and Javier López Casarín, Ebrard's right-hand man, on the terms of the deal. They met in person in Mexico City and Washington, D.C., huddling in hotel rooms, restaurants, and bars to hammer out how the program would work. What did the laws of each country dictate? How can we actually return people? What are our humanitarian obligations, and how do we make sure we are both living up to them? For the United States, that meant that people had to be given the opportunity to claim asylum. For Mexico, it meant that anyone on their soil had to receive a humanitarian visa and certain protections. Taylor had to convince López Casarín that the American government would actually process the migrants' asylum claims eventually, rather than leaving them to languish in Mexico indefinitely. And López Casarín had to swear to

Taylor that the Mexicans wouldn't simply turn the migrants loose to be targeted by the brutal drug cartels that were a major reason they were fleeing to the United States in the first place. The deal would not be legal if American officials believed people were going to die as a result.

On Thanksgiving Day, they hit a major setback. *The Washington Post*, citing multiple officials inside DHS, reported that the Trump administration was in the final stages of talks with Mexico to put in place a program known as "Remain in Mexico." The story, which ran on the front page of the *Post* and dominated news coverage over the holiday, quoted an internal DHS memo that explained the parameters of the emerging deal. "If you are determined to have a reasonable fear of remaining in Mexico, you will be permitted to remain in the United States while you await your hearing before an immigration judge," officers were to tell migrants who arrived seeking asylum. "If you are not determined to have a reasonable fear of remaining in Mexico, you will remain in Mexico." The story angered and spooked the Mexican negotiating team. They were already getting political blowback at home for even pursuing negotiations with the Trump team, the Mexicans said, and now that the details had leaked, the resistance they faced was intensifying. Olga Sánchez Cordero, the incoming minister of the interior in López Obrador's government, issued a terse statement saying there was "no agreement of any kind between the future federal government of Mexico and the United States of America." The negotiations stalled.

When talks picked up again days later, both teams agreed they had to rebrand their plan. It couldn't be called "Remain in Mexico," a name that conjured up politically problematic images of the United States blocking asylum seekers and of Mexico being forced to hold them. Instead, they would call the agreement the "Migrant Protection Protocols," a mind-numbingly bureaucratic title that instead put the focus where both governments wanted it: on providing humanitarian relief for asylum seekers. Taylor begged López Casarín and his team to keep the negotiations on track. *Trump is going crazy about this. This is our last best hope of preventing him from doing something truly terrible.*

The Mexicans said they were still open to the plan, which both teams were now referring to by the shorthand MPP—with two major conditions. The United States would have to commit to a $10 billion development plan for Mexico and the Central American countries that would be announced first. That would allow Mexico to point to an upside for its cooperation with the new arrangement. Secondly, there would be no treaty or official agreement signed between the two sides. The Trump administration would unilaterally declare that it was going to return migrants to Mexico in a diplomatic note sent to the government in Mexico City. The Mexicans would reply with a diplomatic note of their own making it clear they would not object. It was politically advantageous to both sides; Trump got to look like the tough-talking American president, demanding that the Mexicans do their part to stop migrants before they reached the border, while the Mexicans could avoid looking complicit, and instead say they were simply doing their humanitarian duty.

The talks came down to the wire, with Trump's team unsure until the very last moment whether they would come together. The negotiations were so delicate and shrouded in so much secrecy that at one point, to avoid detection or leaks, Pompeo printed out a hard copy of a final draft of one of the diplomatic notes that was to be exchanged and quietly hand-delivered it to Taylor during an unrelated meeting in the Oval Office.

On the day the deal was to be made public, the week before Christmas, there was a careful rollout plan in place. Nielsen was scheduled to testify in front of the House Judiciary Committee, and she planned to announce it in her opening remarks. Press releases were ready to go out, a briefing was scheduled, and Pompeo was going to be interviewed by Laura Ingraham of Fox News and Steve Inskeep of NPR. But even as Nielsen made her way to the hearing room in the Rayburn House Office Building on Capitol Hill for the hearing, it was not clear that the Mexicans had signed off. With the clock literally ticking the seconds until Nielsen faced the lawmakers on live television, John Creamer, the top American diplomat in Mexico City, sent the Obrador administration's diplomatic note to Nielsen's aides, who were standing by her side in the holding room outside the congressional hearing. Unfortunately, it was in Spanish, and none of them was proficient enough to tell what it said. Did it say they would comply? Did it say they would refuse? Nielsen was about to take her seat at the witness table and her staff had no idea. Finally, a State Department colleague who was fluent in Spanish sent the final word. They said yes! A Nielsen aide shoved a sheaf of papers into her hands—a new version of her testimony that described the just barely confirmed deal—and she made her way to the witness table.

"Today, I am announcing historic measures to bring the situation under control," Nielsen told the House Judiciary Committee that morning. "Effective immediately, the United States will begin the process of invoking Section 235B2C of the Immigration and Nationality Act. Once implemented, individuals arriving in or entering the United States from Mexico illegally or without proper documentation may be returned to Mexico for the duration of their immigration proceedings. They will not be able to disappear into the United States. They will have to wait for approval to come into the United States. If they are granted asylum by a U.S. judge, they will be welcomed into America. If they are not, they will be removed to their home countries."

Just as the two sides had planned, Nielsen presented the deal as a unilateral decision by the Trump administration that the Mexicans had essentially been forced to accept. "We have notified the Mexican government of our intended actions," she said. "In response, Mexico has informed us that they will commit to implement essential measures on their side of the border to facilitate this process by providing humanitarian assistance."

The aid package that the U.S. had agreed to went unmentioned.

— 31 —

SHUTDOWN

TWO WEEKS EARLIER, ON the morning of Tuesday, December 11, Chuck Schumer and Nancy Pelosi had headed to the White House for what was billed as a private meeting with President Trump. It was to be the first face-to-face encounter between the president and the Democratic leaders since the now infamous "Chuck and Nancy" Chinese-food dinner more than a year before, where the president had nearly cut a deal to preserve DACA, only to be pulled back by his advisers. But now, the Democratic takeover of the House had rotated the political world on its axis, and the three were preparing for an era of divided government, which would require the kind of bipartisan compromises that Trump had mostly been able to avoid during his first two years in office. The president was conflicted about the prospect. On the one hand, he fancied himself a consummate dealmaker, and felt that if given the chance he could strike big bargains with Democrats that would be immensely popular with the public and boost his image. But Trump was also deeply angry about the outcome of the elections and how it was being interpreted—as a rebuke of his leadership and his agenda, particularly his closing argument about the evils of immigration. He was as determined as ever to extract the ultimate concession from the Democrats. He wanted his wall, and he wanted it now.

Ryan and McConnell understood the dangerous dynamics at play. For most of his presidency and particularly the past several months, the Republican leaders had managed, just barely, to steer Trump away from what they considered a disastrous government shutdown fight over money for his border wall. But lately, it had become abundantly clear that time was running out. The president's patience for signing bills without a huge sum for his signature campaign promise had worn thin. They had averted the shutdown in the immediate run-up to the election, but the chances of preventing it again in the waning days of all-Republican rule on Capitol Hill were 50-50 at best. "Everybody knew that you're walking a tightrope to pull it off," a senior aide said.

The last near miss had come in mid-September, just as the president was blazing his way through campaign rallies warning of an invasion of migrants. Ryan had gone to the White House to discuss a stopgap spending resolution with Trump. Yet another deadline was coming at the end of the month for funding the government, and Ryan had to appeal to the president, once again, to support a spending measure to keep money flowing for a few more weeks—until after the November elections—to provide time for a longer-term agreement. Wall money wasn't in this bill; that would have to wait for another day, Ryan explained. But that was all Trump seemed to care about.

Do you know how I first started talking about the wall? Trump asked the House speaker. Ryan confessed that he did not. The president began reminiscing about how a mnemonic device invented by one of his advisers had, almost by accident, become the animating idea behind his presidential campaign. One of his campaign aides had put the line in a speech—"I will build a wall!" Trump told Ryan, doing a campy impression of himself speaking to a campaign crowd. So he went out there and said it, the president recalled. And do you know what happened? People went crazy—absolutely crazy, Trump said. They ate it up. It was the biggest applause line you can imagine. My people love it, the president told Ryan, and I can't let them down. I made a commitment that I was going to build the wall, and I've got to deliver on it. Ryan said he understood all of that—he wasn't asking the president to abandon his promise—but a shutdown was not the way to go about achieving it. All a shutdown would do would be to guarantee political defeat going into the midterms, Ryan explained. It would be better to keep talking about the wall and use it as a cudgel against Democrats in hopes of defeating them in the coming elections, the speaker said, so Republicans could be in a better position to push through funding for it when the midterms were behind them. Trump said he would sign that bill, but he was clearly not happy about it.

Now, in the wake of an election that had cost Republicans their House majority, Trump wanted to extract substantial money from Democrats to pay for his border wall. But what exactly did that mean? As ever in Trump-world, the details were murky. Shahira Knight, who had taken over from Marc Short earlier in the year as Trump's chief liaison to Capitol Hill, told top Republican aides that the White House was coalescing around a stopgap spending measure that would include around $2 billion in funding for the wall. It was more than the $1.6 billion they had requested in Trump's budget, but Knight said the president would be satisfied with the increase—at least until the new year, when they would have another opportunity to push for more money. But in early December, when Ryan and McCarthy went to the White House to see Trump, he was fixated on a far higher number. He wanted $5 billion for the wall. There wasn't a clear White House position.

On the morning of Tuesday's Oval Office meeting with Pelosi and Schumer, the president was spoiling for a battle. On Twitter, he issued a series of lies and threats about the wall, saying that large portions of his "Great Wall" had already been built (they had not), and that even without acquiescence by Democrats in Congress, his administration could continue construction. "People do not yet realize how much of the Wall, including really effective renovation, has already been built," Trump wrote. "If the Democrats do not give us the votes to secure our Country, the Military will build the remaining sections of the Wall. They know how important it is!" Trump had been musing privately for months about diverting money from the Department of Defense to build the wall, something that he had repeatedly been told was not possible without express authorization from Congress, which had sole power to allocate money and say how it could be used. Trump had become preoccupied with the idea of transferring revenue collected by government agencies—pots of money that Congress does not control—into a fund to pay for the wall, and administration lawyers were scrutinizing ways for him to do so. They had yet to find a way. No matter what the president said publicly, he was going to need Congress if he wanted that wall.

Schumer and Pelosi, who had met the previous evening to plot out their strategy for the meeting, were prepared to tell Trump that his demand for $5 billion for the wall did not have the votes to pass either chamber. He could have the $1.3 billion Congress had approved the previous year for border security, which included some money that could be used for fixing or extending fencing—no more. Everyone knew that the stakes for the meeting were high. Republicans would continue to hold the House, Senate, and White House for a couple more weeks, but this was to be the initial touching-of-gloves for Trump and the two Democratic leaders, a trio thrown together by political chance and constitutional necessity. Trump, as was always the case, was going from his gut; Schumer and Pelosi had a plan of action for the closed-door confrontation with the president.

There was just one hitch: Trump wasn't in the mood for a private negotiating session. He wanted a televised confrontation with the newly empowered Democrats. Moments after Schumer and Pelosi took their seats on cream-colored sofas in the Oval Office, Trump invited reporters in for an unscheduled glimpse of the meeting, allowing them to snap pictures and capture video of the three exchanging pleasantries and talking in generalities about legislative business: a criminal justice overhaul that was about to be finalized; an emerging agreement on a farm bill. "And then we have the easy one, the wall," Trump said, turning to taunt Schumer. "That will be the one that will be the easiest of all—what do you think, Chuck? Maybe not?"

"It's called 'funding the government,' Mr. President," Schumer answered sharply. He was sticking to the plan that he and Pelosi had cemented the previous evening. They would make it clear that their priority was the orderly functioning of government, and that Trump's new demands for more wall money would only stand in the way of achieving that goal. The make-nice-for-the-cameras portion of the encounter had obviously ended, but Trump was not dismissing the reporters. With the cameras still broadcasting live, he launched into an elaborate defense of the wall, repeating his lie that much of it had already been built and saying that illegal border crossings were down "virtually 100 percent" in areas where it had been erected. He claimed, without offering any evidence, that his move to shut down the caravan in the weeks before the election had been extraordinarily successful. Then Trump turned to Pelosi to ask if she wanted to say anything. She, too, stuck to the talking points, saying that the public wanted to avoid a lapse in federal funding, but Pelosi also added a dig at the president.

"I think the American people recognize that we must keep government open—that a shutdown is not worth anything," Pelosi said, "and that you should not have a Trump shutdown."

"Did you say 'Trump'?" the president protested. "I was going to call it a 'Pelosi shutdown.'"

Pelosi was having none of it. "You have the Senate," she told Trump. "You have the House of Representatives. You have the votes. You should pass it right now." Pelosi tried repeatedly to get Trump to dismiss the reporters in the White House press pool so they could haggle privately over the issue. "I don't think we should have a debate in front of the press on this," she said, and then a few minutes later, with the cameras still rolling, "let us have our conversation, and then we can meet with the press again."

But Trump wanted to have a public fight. "There are no votes in the House—a majority of votes—for a wall, no matter where you start," Pelosi told Trump, practically daring the president to try to muscle a bill through the House to pay for the wall. She knew that privately, Republican leaders had begun to worry that they would not be able to muster enough votes to pass the bill, with many of their rank-and-file members—particularly those who had been defeated in the midterm elections the previous month—in no mood to return to Washington weeks before Christmas to wage war over Trump's wall. Trump needled Schumer that he had gotten "killed" so badly during January's "Schumer shutdown" over DACA that he had been forced to back down in just a day ("I don't want to do what you did," Trump said). And the president sought to undercut Pelosi, who had just headed off an internal Democratic rebellion and been nominated by her colleagues to reclaim the distinction as the first and only woman to serve as speaker of the house—a job she had relinquished in 2011 after Republicans took control of the chamber. There were still rumblings that Pelosi would face a challenge in January during the official floor vote, and Trump, ever the bully, went straight for what he considered Pelosi's weak spot.

"I don't think we really disagree so much," Trump said. "I also know that, you know, Nancy is in a situation where it's not easy for her to talk right now, and I understand that."

Schumer gazed silently at Pelosi across the coffee table, which was adorned with an arrangement of red roses, and raised his eyebrows dramatically in her direction. "Mr. President," Pelosi said with barely disguised disgust, wagging a finger as she spoke. "Please don't characterize the strength that I bring to this meeting as the leader of the House Democrats who just won a big victory."

It was clear that Trump wanted to show that he was driving this conversation, and Schumer, sensing an opening, was happy to oblige. Schumer had come to the White House that day armed with a tally compiled by his staff of twenty separate instances in which the president had publicly threatened to shut down the government if he did not get his way on funding the wall. How hard could it be to get Trump, who had invited the press in to watch as he browbeat Democrats over the issue, to say so again?

"You want to shut it down—you keep talking about it," Schumer said, as Trump objected repeatedly. "You've said it . . . You said it." Finally, Trump had had enough.

"Okay, you want to put that on my—I'll take it," the president said. "You know what I'll say: Yes, if we don't get what we want, one way or the other—whether it's through you, through a military, through anything you want to call—I will shut down the government. Absolutely."

"Okay," Schumer said, the look on his face barely disguising his joy at having extracted Trump's admission. "Fair enough. We disagree."

Then Trump went even further. "And I'll tell you what, I am *proud* to shut down the government for border security, Chuck, because the people of this country don't want criminals and people that have lots of problems and drugs pouring into our country. So I will take the mantle. I will be the one to shut it down. I'm not going to blame you for it."

When the cameras departed, Trump's demeanor appeared to change as if with the flip of a switch. Leaning in conspiratorially toward the Democratic leaders he had just sparred with relentlessly on live TV, the president brightened considerably and said he was eager to work with them in the second half of his term to strike great deals. The new Congress could be the "greatest Congress in the history of Congress," Trump told Schumer and Pelosi. And don't worry about Mitch, Trump told them, speaking of McConnell; if they could compromise on measures that could get through the House, he would force Republican senators to back them so he could sign them into law. Was this the same president who had said just minutes before that he wouldn't even agree to fund the government unless Democrats agreed to his demands for a border wall?

Even as he tried to make nice with the Democrats privately, Trump was still spouting misinformation and threats about the wall. If they wouldn't agree to fund it, the president told Pelosi and Schumer, Mexico would pay for it through money that would flow into the United States as part of a new North American trade agreement, the United States-Mexico-Canada Agreement, or USMCA. That's never going to happen, Schumer said. The agreement still had to pass the House, Pelosi pointed out, and besides, any economic gains from it should go to American workers and businesses, not a border wall. "Well," Trump insisted, "they're going to pay for it one way or the other."

The Democrats had another idea. Trump's attempts to win wall funding would fail, they assured him, and the government would suffer a partial shutdown, as he had just publicly threatened it would. Then when Pelosi took over as speaker of the house in January, her first order of business would be to pass legislation to reopen the government, essentially daring the Republican-led Senate to reject it. "What do you think Mitch will do?" Schumer asked Trump. "Keep it shut down another month? Another week?" Trump sat silently, pondering the thought.

At the White House and in Republican offices on Capitol Hill, Trump's performance was met with rueful shakes of the head and shrugs. The president had just made a shutdown more likely, and preemptively taken credit for what was certain to be a politically damaging outcome for his party— and all over a border wall that most Republicans did not consider to be worth the trouble. What was worse, Trump did not seem to comprehend what he had just done, or have any sense of urgency about extricating himself from the predicament. Following the meeting, as she commiserated with senior Republican officials on Capitol Hill about the televised debacle, Shahira Knight, Trump's liaison to Congress since July, reported perhaps the most unbelievable piece of all. "He thinks it went really well," she said. The president, she said, "thinks it went spectacularly."

Democrats shared that assessment, but for very different reasons. On his way out of the West Wing, Schumer stopped to tell reporters that Trump had thrown a "temper tantrum" over this wall. Video of Pelosi striding out of the White House in a red cashmere coat and donning a pair of sunglasses with a grin went viral and spawned dozens of GIFs, solidifying a public sense that the session had been a moment of triumph for her. When she returned to Capitol Hill, Pelosi met privately with senior Democrats and regaled them with a mocking description of a president she described as unhinged and toddler-like.

"This wall thing," Pelosi told her colleagues, is "like a manhood thing for him—as if manhood could ever be associated with him."

"I was trying to be the mom. I can't explain it to you—it was so wild," Pelosi recounted, painting the remarkable scene even as she chose her words demurely. "It goes to show you, you get into a tinkle contest with a skunk, you get tinkle all over you."

The following day, Ryan received a call from Trump. They had much to discuss. How were they going to play this government funding debate with Democrats now that Trump had admitted publicly that he was the one courting a shutdown? It seemed like a no-win situation. But Trump, true to Knight's description, was ebullient. Did you see how great the ratings were for that Oval Office meeting? Trump asked Ryan. The speaker was dumbfounded. They have ratings for that already? he asked. Oh sure, the president told him, they have ratings for everything. This is why people loved me on *The Apprentice*, Trump told Ryan. Because people love the drama that I create.

That may have been true of viewing audiences across America. It was not true of Republicans on Capitol Hill, who had ten days to find a way to push through spending legislation before a partial shutdown three days before Christmas. The White House had no plan for how to resolve the impasse, and Ryan was having a hard enough time keeping his rank-and-file members in Washington following a crushing electoral defeat that had swept a large portion of them out of their seats, rendering them lame ducks. They were sick of Washington, sick of looking at each other, sick of showing up to cast votes on legislation that might not have any chance of passing the Senate. Ryan decided to shutter the House of Representatives for nearly a week, until there was something to vote on—or at least a plan of action.

On December 17, just days before Nielsen's hearing before House lawmakers, she and Pompeo went to the White House to brief Trump on their emerging deal with the Mexicans. Trump was irritated. He didn't like the deal, and he was particularly livid about the $10 billion aid package, of which Mexico would get about half, the rest going to the three Central American countries. He had been telling people for years that the Mexicans were going to pay for his border wall; the last thing in the world Trump wanted to do was have to pay them $5 billion instead. Pompeo tried to explain that a lot of the money was private investment—American companies going down to Mexico would turn a profit and create jobs. And he and Nielsen told Trump that the aid package was essential if he wanted the rest of the deal to go through. It is the only way we are going to get Mexico to take back large numbers of migrants, they said. Showing little enthusiasm, Trump reluctantly agreed.

By the next day, however, he was furious again. In another meeting with Nielsen and her staff, Trump trashed the agreement with Mexico. I don't want to do it, he told his aides. I want to close the border. "Let's stick it to the Mexicans." By then, it was too late. The agreement had been finalized, and word had begun leaking out about the aid package, which the Americans had agreed would be made public first. The timing could not have been worse. Just that morning, in an interview on Fox News, Sarah Huckabee Sanders, the White House press secretary, had signaled that the president might be willing to back down on his demand for $5 billion for the border wall, the first indication that Trump might actually blink in his standoff with Congress and steer clear of a government shutdown. Conservatives were up in arms. Now that it had gotten out that the United States had agreed to send nearly that much aid to Mexico, the outrage factor shot up exponentially. The right-wing website *Drudge Report* ran a headline that blared, "WALL FUNDING OFF TABLE. U.S.A. GIVING $4.8 BILLION TO MEXICO." Someone printed it out and handed it to Trump.

The president blazed into a rage. "My fucking friends are calling me," he yelled. "This is the stupidest shit you've ever done. Why the fuck would we do this? I'm not getting $5 billion for the wall, and instead I'm paying Mexico $5 billion? What the fuck am I getting out of this?" Trump's team spent the next several hours frantically trying to tamp down another presidential blowup. The last thing they needed was for Trump to see *Drudge*'s story line reinforced and echoed on every news program he watched that night. Taylor, Jared Kushner, and Bill Shine, the former Fox News executive who had been installed over the summer as White House communications director, began working the phones, calling every producer at every conservative TV outlet they could think of and begging them not to run with the *Drudge* headline. There was more to the story, they promised. Please trust us.

It hardly mattered. Later that night, Trump told his staff that he was going to tweet against the Migrant Protection Protocols deal and blast the State Department for giving money to Mexico, announcing that he was taking the money back. Pompeo called Trump to implore him to reconsider. We are on the precipice of this thing, he said. Let's give it a chance to work.

On Capitol Hill, Mitch McConnell was single-mindedly focused on trying to avert a government shutdown, and had decided to take matters into his own hands. There was no clarity from the White House on what Trump would accept, but it seemed as if the president was at least open to the idea of dropping his demand for $5 billion in wall funding. Sanders's interview had been a hopeful sign, signaling for the first time that Trump was looking for ways to avoid a shutdown. McConnell began making arrangements for a bill that would simply postpone the debate to the new year—a short-term spending measure to keep the government open until early February, while lawmakers and the president continued to haggle over border security.

In the age of President Trump, Sharon Soderstrom, McConnell's chief of staff, kept a calendar in her office with roller coasters on each page, one for each month, and she would pull it out from time to time and say to colleagues, "Here's today." December 19 was one of those days. There were about forty-eight hours before the deadline to fund the government, and McConnell was about to make a last-ditch effort to get Trump to accept a bill without his $5 billion for the wall. That day, Pence had come to Capitol Hill to huddle with Senate Republicans at a lunchtime gathering just off the Senate floor. You've done a great job this year, the vice president told the Republican senators, and the president really appreciates it. McConnell, who had met privately with the vice president, briefed the senators seated around the rectangular wooden table about his plans for a temporary funding bill. His understanding from the vice president, McConnell told his colleagues, gesturing at Pence, was that the president is going to support this. Pence said nothing, but nodded his head slightly as if to acknowledge what McConnell had just said. Republican senators left the meeting with the distinct impression that Trump was on board and would sign the measure.

But McConnell knew better than to be certain of anything when it came to Trump. The Senate leader had two overriding instincts about dealing with this president. First, McConnell was only ever as confident as his last conversation allowed him to be. In this case, his last conversation with Pence had left him confident that Trump would sign the spending bill. McConnell's other rule of thumb was that when he thought he had a deal that was workable, he needed to act quickly to lock it in before the president could change his mind. The idea, as described by someone close to McConnell, was, "Move fast, because we might wake up the beast."

McConnell's staff spent the rest of the day quietly laying the groundwork for speeding the spending bill through the Senate without any fanfare and without a roll call vote. If the president was going to turn around and veto this bill, McConnell did not want Republican senators to have to go through the politically risky exercise of casting a vote in favor of it, putting them in danger of drawing the wrath of Trump's wall-obsessed base. His strategy worked; as the hours ticked by, nobody registered an objection. And just after 10 p.m., McConnell asked for—and received—unanimous consent to pass the measure. In the blink of an eye, with no debate or dispute and before most senators could figure out what was happening, the famously sluggish Senate had given lightning-fast approval to a stopgap spending bill to avert Trump's promised shutdown. Republican officials were stunned and relieved when Democrats did not request a roll call vote that would have forced their members to go on the record on whether they supported the move.

Now the ball was in Ryan's court, and it was still unclear whether the president would accept the measure. The Senate bill was causing a mini-revolt in the House, where conservative members of the Freedom Caucus were up in arms about it. If Trump signed the Senate bill, they argued, he would be selling out his signature promise and relinquishing the last of the Republicans' leverage in the fight over the wall and other restrictive immigration policies. Mick Mulvaney, the former South Carolina congressman who ran Trump's budget office and had recently been named acting White House chief of staff following Kelly's resignation, rushed to Capitol Hill to meet with the Freedom Caucus. Mulvaney had been one of the founding members of the caucus, which prided itself on being willing to defy Republican leaders and take down legislation its members considered insufficiently conservative. They told him that the president should not, under any circumstances, capitulate. That night, Mulvaney showed up at the Capitol Hill Club to hobnob with his former colleagues. He came bearing an ominous message from the White House. You guys better put up a big Republican number on this bill when you vote on it tomorrow, Mulvaney warned, or else the president might veto it. The message was clear: they could not count on cover from Trump on this vote. If they were going to defy his wishes for a wall, they were taking their political fate into their own hands.

Early the next morning, just before heading into a closed-door meeting with House Republicans in the Capitol basement, Ryan placed a call to Trump. If he was okay with the temporary spending bill they were about to vote on, the president was going to have to say so publicly, thereby ending the debate within the party about whether or not to support it. But the president was unreachable, so Ryan went into the meeting without any idea what to tell his members. As it turned out, the issue was moot. As the gathering unfolded, lawmaker after lawmaker rose to register dismay over McConnell's stopgap measure in the Senate, saying they should back the president's demands for a wall. Some lawmakers even called for votes on a far-reaching immigration overhaul that would impose new restrictions and sharpen Trump's crackdown. Freedom Caucus chairman Mark Meadows and other members of his group said they should stand and fight for the president's immigration agenda now—not *after* Democrats take control of the House in the new year. We're starting out the day in a hole, Republican officials said privately. People don't want to vote for this thing.

As the discussion grew more tense, Ryan's cell phone rang. It was Trump returning his call, and the speaker stepped out of the Republican Conference meeting to take it in a small room down the hall. Ryan cut to the chase. You need to sign the Senate bill, and we need you to make clear that you are going to, he told the president. But Trump was in no mood to do that. This is our moment of maximum leverage, the president said, echoing his conservative allies in the meeting. Now is when we should have this fight, before the Republican majority is gone. Building the wall is an 80-20 issue, Trump said. (That wasn't even close to true. The public was divided over building a wall on the southwestern border to keep out illegal crossers, and only a fraction of voters—about the same third or so who adored Trump the most—liked the idea of shutting down the government to accomplish it.) Not long after Trump and Ryan hung up, the president used Twitter to take a thinly veiled swipe at Ryan, who had one day earlier given his farewell address as speaker. "When I begrudgingly signed the Omnibus Bill, I was promised the Wall and Border Security by leadership," Trump wrote in his post. "Would be done by end of year (NOW). It didn't happen!" It was an ironic ending to Ryan's career in Congress, where he had always been a quiet advocate for a broad immigration compromise, including a pathway to legal status for millions of undocumented people. Instead of finding a way to negotiate a deal like that, he was spending his last hours in power on Capitol Hill making a futile stand for a border wall. In the midst of the legislative chaos, Nielsen was in an office building just across from the Capitol, announcing the new arrangement for migrants to be returned to Mexico while their cases were heard. Amid the intraparty revolt, it got little attention.

Around noon, Ryan, McCarthy, and Steve Scalise, the House Republican whip, went to the White House for a hastily called meeting with Trump. They were accompanied by more than a dozen other House Republicans, including Meadows, who were agitating for Trump to stand his ground and refuse to sign any spending bill until he got more wall money. The gathering in the Cabinet Room was ostensibly about weighing the pros and cons of a shutdown, and Trump made a cursory show of listening to arguments on both sides. But he was soon diverted when one of the lawmakers said Republicans should be debating a whole host of other measures to crack down on illegal immigration, including making it mandatory for employers to use E-Verify, the federal database that checked workers' legal status. With only hours left until parts of the government were to run out of money, the president launched into his familiar diatribe about the program, rehashing what a pain in the ass it had been to use it while building the hotel bearing his name in Washington. "It's a disaster!"

If it hadn't been clear before then, it was pretty clear to everyone around the table that a shutdown was happening.

On December 21, the day of the shutdown deadline, things were eerily quiet in the Capitol. These moments were usually times of intense negotiation and shuttle diplomacy between the two parties and the two houses of Congress, in which legislative language was carefully crafted and controversial details were painstakingly ironed out. There was none of that. It was four days before Christmas, less than twelve hours before appropriations expired, and there was very little happening. The House had passed a bill adding $5.7 billion for the border wall, and McConnell had reluctantly called his members back from states around the country to vote on the measure, knowing that it was doomed to fail. From the White House residence, Trump was on a Twitter tear, praising House Republicans for backing him and trying to cast blame preemptively on Democrats for a shutdown. But he also singled out McConnell, instructing him to take extreme measures to push through the wall money, even if that meant changing long-standing Senate rules that require sixty votes to advance most major legislation. "Mitch," Trump tweeted, "use the Nuclear Option to get it done! Our Country is counting on you." Several Republican senators quickly issued statements rejecting the idea, and McConnell's staff shot it down, telling reporters the party did not support it.

In a meeting with Trump that morning at the White House, McConnell reiterated what he had repeated for the president so many times before: The votes simply are not there in the Senate to deliver what you want. McConnell would bring up the bill the House had passed, complete with Trump's cherished wall money, he explained, but it would not draw anywhere close to the sixty votes needed to advance in the Senate. Trump would soon learn that the news was even worse. The spending bill could not even draw a majority of the Republican-held Senate. For hours on Friday afternoon, as the clock ticked ever-closer to a shutdown, McConnell was forced to prolong what was to have been a standard fifteen-minute-long roll call while senators arrived back in Washington to cast their votes and a pair of Republicans pondered siding with Democrats to block the bill from even advancing to a final vote. Jeff Flake of Arizona and Bob Corker of Tennessee, two of the only Republicans who had dared criticize the president publicly—both of whom were retiring—spent hours agonizing over how they should vote, reluctant to join Republicans in endorsing a measure that was going nowhere. Should they vote no, and force Trump and their own leaders to draft a new version without the wall money? Or would it be better to allow the measure to fail along party lines, potentially paving the way for negotiations that could produce a compromise to break the impasse?

For several hours, with the vote still under way, uncertainty reigned on the Senate floor as lawmakers milled about and held hushed conversations. At one point about two hours in, the Senate clerk, wearing a necklace adorned with miniature Christmas lights in a nod to the season, hunched over the dark green marble dais in the front of the Senate chamber, gazing with puzzlement at a laptop used to count the time elapsed during votes. The overtime clock had reached 100 and did not seem to have the capacity to go any higher. After a few moments, it started counting backward again. Would the bill be allowed to advance or be blocked? It hardly mattered; in either case, there was no way it was going to pass the Senate. And there was no Plan B for what to do to fund the government past midnight.

That evening at the White House, Trump was in the Oval Office signing bills and fuming about the prospect of a shutdown. He had a brief moment of happiness when Nielsen showed him the mock-up she had produced of the border wall Trump had so meticulously detailed to her weeks earlier. And that is how it came to pass that the president of the United States, who had brought the nation to the brink of a government shutdown over funding for his border wall, tweeted out a fantasy version of the edifice that would never be built, hours before government funding lapsed. Around the same time, Flake and Corker decided to side with their party and vote to keep the wall funding bill alive. They voted yes, bringing the tally to a tie, which Pence was on hand to break. After a little over five hours, Pence banged the gavel. The vote was 48–47 to begin debating the bill, but it was now abundantly clear that the votes did not exist to pass it.

Trump's wall had not been able to garner the support of a majority of the Senate. There would be a shutdown, the only question now was for how long.

Jared Kushner was exhausted. The senior White House adviser and presidential son-in-law had spent the past few months quarterbacking quiet discussions with the Mexicans over trade and border issues, and several intense weeks cementing a bipartisan deal in Congress on criminal justice reform legislation. He was eagerly anticipating jetting off to Florida with Ivanka and their three children for some badly needed rest and relaxation over the winter holiday. This squabble with Congress over the wall could wait until 2019, he told colleagues. But his father-in-law had other plans. Trump asked Kushner to cancel his vacation and remain in Washington to negotiate a deal on the wall. Along with Vice President Pence and Mick Mulvaney, the budget director now doing double duty as acting chief of staff, he was dispatched to Capitol Hill that night to try to strike a compromise.

Senior Republican officials called them the "three wise men," with more than a hint of irony. Pence, Kushner, and Mulvaney began making the rounds on Capitol Hill that evening without warning. They exuded an air of urgency, eager to lay out for congressional leaders what they believed was a fresh way out of the mess in which they found themselves. Their first stop was Paul Ryan's ceremonial office, steps from the House floor, where they arrived with Meadows and fellow Freedom Caucus leader Jim Jordan to pitch a potential solution. Pence, Mulvaney, and Kushner outlined a deal in which they would get a total of $2.5 billion for border security measures, including about $1 billion that Trump could access in the future to pay for his immigration priorities. It was similar to a proposal that Republicans had offered Democrats privately the previous week and they had rejected out of hand. But Trump's team, particularly Kushner, either did not know that or didn't care. Kushner seemed particularly confident in his ability to break the logjam. The president's son-in-law brought up the bipartisan criminal justice reform legislation that Trump had just signed into law earlier that day, which had united an unusual coalition of liberal Democrats and conservative Republicans. Having navigated the tricky politics of that debate, Kushner assured the Republicans that he could cut a deal with Democrats on immigration. Besides, I am completely unburdened by all the history and knowledge you guys have on this subject, he said. Ryan was blunt. We can live with anything the president is willing to sign here, he said. If you can get buy-in from the Democrats, we won't be your problem. But it was clear nothing was going to be settled that night. As the meeting broke up and darkness fell in Washington around six thirty, the House adjourned, a sure sign that nobody expected a deal before the midnight deadline.

The wise men strode purposefully across the Capitol, where they had requested a meeting with Schumer. Pence told the Democratic leader that they were prepared to accept $2.5 billion for the wall—half what the president was publicly demanding. But Schumer was not in the mood to haggle over numbers. Any measure that includes money for the wall can't pass the Senate, he said. Take our offer of $1.6 billion for other forms of border security and call it a day. As the haggling continued, Trump was at the White House recording a video.

"We're going to have a shutdown," Trump said, standing in front of a pair of flags and a mantelpiece decorated with pine and holly branches. "There's nothing we can do about that." Ten days earlier, in the Oval Office meeting whose ratings he celebrated, Trump had told Democrats he'd be "proud" to shut down the government for his wall. Now, though, he shifted blame. It was Democrats' fault, Trump said in the video, circulated to his tens of millions of followers. As images of brown-skinned men rushing fences and banging on barriers were interspersed with video of crowds of migrants swarming, Trump returned to the same themes he had hit upon two and a half years earlier when he had announced his candidacy in the lobby of Trump Tower, denouncing Mexican immigrants as drug dealers and rapists. The border was a war zone. Immigrants were to be feared. Trump would finally fix it. Now, instead of coming from a long-shot novice presidential candidate in a glitzy office tower, the message was coming directly from the White House and the president himself.

"It's very dangerous out there. Drugs are pouring in, human trafficking, so many different problems, including gangs like MS-13.

"We don't want 'em in the United States," Trump continued. "We don't want 'em in our country."

Over the next few days, as the reality set in that the president had plunged the country into what was likely to be a lengthy shutdown with no clear path to resolution, Trump's best hope at blocking immigrants from entering the country stalled. The deal with Mexico, so meticulously negotiated by Nielsen and her top aides, was in a kind of legal limbo. A partial shutdown meant that many functions of government had to cease, although there were exceptions for certain diplomatic matters and areas that affected life or property. After four days of panicked phone calls about whether the Migrant Protection Protocols fell into either of those gray areas, the verdict came back from the lawyers: it didn't. While much of the program could proceed, the Trump administration could not issue directives to finalize the deal and put it into practice while the government was partially shuttered.

Trump's obsession with the wall had, for the time being, effectively stymied his best hope of controlling immigration.

"WE'VE WASTED THE LAST TWO YEARS"

THE PARTIAL GOVERNMENT SHUTDOWN was thirteen days old, and there was no obvious way out. It was January 3, 2019, the first day of the 116th Congress, and Nancy Pelosi, wearing a hot-pink dress and a beaming expression, was starting her new term as speaker of the house, waving the gavel triumphantly as Democratic lawmakers used the roll call vote to stand and take swipes at Trump and his wall. Kushner sat in his West Wing office with several senior officials getting a tutorial on immigration policy and politics, something of an Immigration 101 crash course for a senior White House adviser who was discovering, in real time, how little he understood about the extraordinarily complex and politically charged issue.

"Holy shit—this is pretty complicated!" Kushner said at one point, as the officials walked him through the basics, and the dysfunctional history of attempts by the Trump administration to cut deals with Congress to overhaul immigration laws. "Man," he said later. "This thing has more landmines than Afghanistan." Kushner was starting to panic. The more the officials told him, the more convinced he became that Kelly and Nielsen had left the president in an untenable position, having failed to lay the groundwork for a deal with Democrats, or even identify what the ultimate goal should be.

Kushner had good reason for alarm. The day before, Trump had invited congressional leaders to the White House Situation Room for the first in what would be a series of meetings called to resolve the shutdown impasse. It had been a disaster. Inside the bunkerlike room in the basement of the West Wing, Trump had made the case to Pelosi and Schumer for his border wall and insisted the Democrats must provide more money for it. Nancy, you must understand the need for a wall, Trump said, turning to Pelosi, who is Catholic. The Vatican has walls! But when the president called on Nielsen to give a presentation on the challenges at the border, Schumer interrupted her and deferred to Pelosi. The newly installed speaker said Nielsen had her numbers wrong, and Pelosi took control of the meeting, laying out her plan for ending the shutdown. The next day, she said, she would be offering legislation in the House to reopen the government, and the administration should support it. Republicans had backed similar measures just the month before, Pelosi said. Why wouldn't Trump do the same now? Schumer asked Trump.

"I would look foolish if I did that," Trump responded. "The wall was why I was elected."

The problem was, Democrats were dug in, too. Most of them regarded the wall as the embodiment of Trump's hard-line immigration policy, a monument to the president's hateful messages about immigrants and the physical manifestation of the approach that brought about family separations at the border and all of his other draconian policies. "The wall," Pelosi said on her first day as speaker, "is an immorality." The more Trump insisted he must have his wall, the more determined Democratic leaders became that they would never agree to it. And as the days wore on and federal employees began missing paychecks, it began to dawn on Trump's inner circle that he had gotten himself into a predicament it would be difficult to get out of.

Days later, Kushner gathered the negotiating team in his West Wing office and posed a question. If I could get you every bit of money you needed to build a wall across the entire southern border, how much would that reduce illegal immigration? And separately, if we could close all of the loopholes that govern how we deal with families, children, and asylum claims, how much would that affect the numbers? McAleenan, the CBP commissioner, was matter-of-fact. A wall across the entirety of the southern border would cut illegal immigration about 20 percent, maybe 25 percent at the most. If we could close those loopholes, we're talking about a decrease of 75 to 80 percent.

Kushner nodded, his jaw tight and his eyes wide. "Okay," he said quietly. "So we've wasted the last two years." Miller looked stunned. Trump had taken the wrong hostage, and now they were all stuck demanding a ransom that everybody knew would never be paid. How were they going to get out of this?

In their swing space in the Ronald Reagan Building near the White House, DHS staff kept a whiteboard that bore a graph that top officials would regularly update in different colors of dry-erase marker. It plotted the strength of the administration's negotiating position on immigration starting in the spring of 2018, and its sharp drop-off resembled a terrifyingly high cliff or a giant stock market crash. Early in the year, the chart had a dot high on the "negotiating power" axis for the deal that would have provided $25 billion for the wall and several policy changes in exchange for legal status for DACA and TPS recipients. That was the compromise Trump had abruptly rejected in the spring. By January 2019, the dot was much lower, at $1.3 billion for border security and no policy changes. At some point, someone had taken an orange marker and scrawled "MORALE," with a roller-coaster-like wavy line that hit a high at the end of 2018 but then fell precipitously. In blue marker was another line that started out high and stayed there for a while, until plunging into the abyss in early 2019. That one was labeled "DHS Ability to Secure Nation." The chart served as a visual reminder to Nielsen's staff of how little leverage the administration had left on immigration, and how depressed and exhausted senior officials had grown trying to squeeze a deal, or any practical security measures, from a position of weakness.

At the White House, it was clear that Trump was losing politically on the shutdown. Polls showed that the public blamed him and Republicans for it, and wanted the president to back down. Desperate to show that Trump and his team were working toward a solution, White House officials threw together a weekend negotiating session with senior congressional staff. On the first Friday of 2019, two days after Trump's disastrous Situation Room meeting with Pelosi and Schumer, aides received an email inviting them to a rare Saturday meeting in Pence's office in the Eisenhower Executive Office Building. It wasn't clear who was going to be there or what the exact agenda would be, and those invited assumed that the vice president's role would be limited to a quick drop-by to welcome them and then leave the haggling to White House and congressional staff. But when they arrived that Saturday morning, aides were shocked to find that Pence himself was presiding over the meeting—and he was staying. An evangelical Christian, Pence wanted to start off with a prayer, so Sharon Soderstrom, McConnell's chief of staff, offered a brief, anodyne invocation that tried to set the tone for an amicable discussion, asking that God "bring us together." But the Democrats made it clear from the start they were not there to give any ground. Dick Meltzer, Pelosi's policy director, said the Democrats hadn't come to negotiate or make a deal that day—that would have to wait until their bosses returned the following week—but that some sort of compromise to reopen the government had to be struck by Tuesday, the payroll deadline for allowing federal workers to receive their checks that Friday. The three-hour meeting yielded no progress, but Pence asked everyone to return the following day for another round.

That Sunday, Joe Zogby, Dick Durbin's chief counsel, asked if he could be the one to offer the opening prayer. It was Epiphany, a major feast day for Catholics, and Zogby's remarks doubled as an implicit rebuke to Trump and his administration. He prayed that the group reflect on the fact that Jesus and Mary were refugees, and that as Christians, they were called to recognize that in the eyes of their brothers and sisters was where they would find God. The negotiators spent another three hours talking around each other, but nothing got done.

Trump wasn't budging either; in fact, he was in the mood to double down. He believed that he was winning on the issue of border security, and some of his top advisers agreed. After all, the whole country was now focused on the flood of migrants crossing the border, and for better or for worse, the border wall was the subject of daily conversation around the nation. Trump and his communications team began planning for him to give a prime-time Oval Office address that would crystallize the issue for the public. It would be the first time that Trump used the traditional venue that for decades presidents had chosen to deliver speeches on matters of grave national importance, such as somber declarations of war or expressions of grief during times of national tragedy.

Trump had his doubts about the speech. Early in the day on January 8, in an off-the-record lunch with TV journalists, the president conceded that it was probably pointless, blaming Bill Shine, the communications director, as well as Kellyanne Conway and Sarah Huckabee Sanders, for talking him into it. On the night of the address, the mood was anxious in the Oval Office. Shine was pacing nervously. Sanders, Ivanka, Miller, and Conway were all gathered for the big moment. The president was still worried about what he would say. Is Miller done with the speech? he kept asking. Trump asked whether he should riff off script. Nobody on his senior staff answered, the closest West Wing aides would usually come to telling him no. He fussed about the lighting, directing aides to make sure it was flattering enough. Where are the lights I had in Iraq? the president wanted to know. I liked how I was lit for that video in Iraq, he said, referring to an official White House video of a visit he had made there over the holidays. I want to look like that. An aide rushed in with a small framed picture of Trump's parents and one of his wife and son to place on the chest behind him, where they would be visible in the shot of the president. With the speech finished, the final version was loaded into the teleprompter. Trump took a sip of his omnipresent Diet Coke, placed just off camera, and began.

"My fellow Americans," he said, "tonight I'm speaking to you because there is a growing humanitarian and security crisis at our southern border."

As Trump predicted, the speech did nothing to change minds about the shutdown. The Democrats were dug in against the wall, and some Republicans in Congress were becoming increasingly uneasy about the situation, worrying that the shutdown was becoming untenable and deeply unappealing to their constituents. Senator Lisa Murkowski of Alaska complained to Trump that the shutdown was hurting her state, which has a heavy concentration of federal workers who were now not being paid. Other Republican moderates were raising questions privately as well. Trump felt trapped. The day after his televised speech, on January 9, he opened a meeting in the Situation Room with Pelosi and Schumer by handing out miniature Butterfinger and Baby Ruth candy bars, ready to cut a deal. But his mood darkened when it became clear that the Democrats had not moved in his direction. You've supported barriers before, Trump told the Democratic congressional leaders—why won't you give me my $5.7 billion? Pelosi and Schumer said they were happy to talk about border security funding, but the wall was a nonstarter—and in any case, the first order of business should be ending the shutdown. "You are using people as leverage," Schumer told Trump. "Why won't you open the government and stop hurting people?" "Then you won't give me what I want," Trump shot back, insisting he was trying to do the right thing for the country. Bottom line, Nancy, the president asked the speaker, if I were to agree to reopen the government, would you give me money for the wall? Pelosi would not budge. No, she told the president. With that, Trump thumped his hands abruptly on the table as if to declare the meeting adjourned, rose, and said, "Bye-bye," walking out of the room.

Inside the White House, the mood among Trump's negotiators was grim. It was clear by now that Democrats were not going to agree to any more border security money, even if the administration was willing to throw in sweeteners like legal status for Dreamers and TPS recipients. Kushner had hatched a plan to do just that, and Trump scheduled a rare Saturday evening speech to pitch the plan. But even before the president opened his mouth, Democrats were denouncing the plan, which would have made substantial changes to the DACA program and included scores of changes to asylum law that would have made it more difficult for migrants to seek protection in the United States. As the talks stalled in private, it got personal. Pelosi disinvited Trump from his own State of the Union address and the president responded in a fit of pique by revoking the speaker's government jet for a trip to Afghanistan. It was clear that the president was going to have to accept what his team considered a crappy deal to get him out of the shutdown. But to get him to do so, his top aides knew they would need to deliver Trump some credible way of spinning the defeat as a victory.

Russ Vought, the acting director of the Office of Management and Budget, was given a herculean task: Find us every possible bucket of money we could use to pay for the wall without an appropriation from Congress. There were Treasury asset forfeiture funds, a pot of money that had grown to about $700 million. There was Defense Department counterdrug funding that added up to another $2.4 billion. And if the president declared a national emergency, as he had been publicly threatening to do, that would unlock even more money—enough to total somewhere around $5 billion.

By the end of the fifth week of the shutdown, federal workers were facing a second pay period without checks, Transportation Security Administration personnel were calling in sick, and the Federal Aviation Administration was laboring under staffing shortages, warning that it would soon have to begin delaying or rerouting flights. Republicans were in open revolt over the dysfunction. Frustrations boiled over during a tense meeting of Senate Republicans with Pence on a Thursday afternoon, as the senators vented about the shutdown and made clear how damaging the situation had become. "You put us in this position," Senator Ron Johnson of Wisconsin said to McConnell, who snapped back, "Are you suggesting that I'm enjoying this?" The Senate leader reminded his colleagues that he had never favored a shutdown and never believed it would have a good outcome. McConnell phoned Trump that day. I don't think I can sustain this any longer, the majority leader told the president. Senators are balking at the shutdown. By that evening, Trump had agreed.

The following day, Trump stood in the frigid cold in the White House

Rose Garden and announced he was ending the shutdown. He would sign a three-week funding extension and continue fighting for the wall. "We really have no choice but to build a powerful wall or steel barrier," the president told reporters that day. But it was clear that nobody on Capitol Hill had the stomach for another shutdown, and three weeks later, Trump ended where he had begun, having to agree to a deal that provided about $1.4 billion for border fencing. At the same time, he declared a national emergency, availing himself of the ultimate face-saving option his aides had prepared for him.

"We're going to confront the national security crisis on our southern border, and we're going to do it one way or the other," Trump said in the Rose Garden. "It's an invasion."

The legal response was swift and overwhelming, setting up yet another constitutional confrontation for Trump. By the beginning of the following week, sixteen states, including California and New York, had returned to federal court in San Francisco to argue that the president was perpetrating a fraud by claiming an emergency that didn't exist. Xavier Becerra, the California attorney general, used Trump's own words from the Rose Garden address the previous week: "I didn't need to do this, but I'd rather do it much faster," Trump had said, essentially admitting to the ruse. Once again, the fate of Trump's immigration agenda was in the hands of judges. Just days earlier, the ACLU filed a separate suit challenging the Migrant Protection Protocols that had been so painstakingly negotiated with Mexico. Trump and his aides viewed all of the legal challenges as desperate and unfair attempts to subvert the will of the people. But for his adversaries, they were a bulwark against an out-of-control president. If Trump was going to keep asserting his power to go around Congress in his quest to limit immigration, his opponents were going to keep heading to court to stop him.

At the border, the migrant surge was becoming overwhelming. Thousands of people, most of them families from Central America, were arriving each day, and there was no place to put them. Despite Trump's well-known anger about "catch and release," Border Patrol agents had no choice but to arrest and then quickly release many of the families with orders to appear in court. Bus stations in communities like El Paso became crowded drop-off points for hundreds of families, as churches and other nonprofit relief agencies struggled to feed, clothe, and shelter them. In December, two young children from Guatemala—seven-year-old Jakelin Caal Maquin and eight-year-old Felipe Gómez Alonzo—had died in CBP custody, raising questions about the agency's treatment of migrants. By the end of February, Border Patrol agents had apprehended 36,000 families crossing the border in a single month, a record that would be broken the next month and the month after that.

Throughout February and March, Miller tried to make sure that everyone in the administration was treating the border crisis like a national emergency. He and his staff told top officials at USCIS that they would be expected to surge all nonessential staff to the border to help with credible-fear interviews to vet asylum seekers and police the border. It could not be "business as usual" during the border crisis, Miller told the officials at one point. Beyond helping to process the glut of asylum claims at the border, the move would achieve another of Miller's goals. He told his colleagues he wanted the Democrats to "feel the pain." If USCIS sent scores of staffers to the border, that would mean fewer officers available to process green card requests and naturalization applications. That would disproportionately affect Democratic members of Congress who had large communities of immigrants in their districts, many of whom would see their own claims and those of their families stalled. McAleenan and Cissna both balked at the idea, but a version of it survived and ended up in a presidential memorandum Trump issued a few months later.

It was not Miller's only idea for how to make Democrats pay for their intransigence about funding the border wall, and their rejection of policy changes that could end "catch and release" once and for all. He also resurrected a plan his staff had first floated in November in which ICE would transport migrants slated to be released from its custody to sanctuary cities, including Pelosi's San Francisco district. ICE had pushed back hard on the proposal when it first surfaced months earlier. In an email, Matthew

Albence, then the agency's acting director, had told the White House that the plan would impose an "operational burden" on ICE, and said he wasn't sure how the substantial costs of transporting the migrants to cities far from the border would be considered a "justified expenditure." Besides, Albence had warned, ICE could be opening itself to massive liability exposure if a migrant were injured during such a journey. The White House had backed off, but now the idea resurfaced. DHS officials were exasperated. If this is a political stunt, one senior official said during a conference call about it, then just do the stunt. Write a letter to lawmakers declaring you're going to do this. But don't make us operationalize an absurd plan and divert our limited resources to make it happen.

The plan never materialized, but months later, when it became public and the White House denied that it was on the table, Trump tweeted that he was giving "strong consideration" to it, and soon after, during a giant arena rally in Green Bay, Wisconsin, the president told his supporters that the practice was already under way for immigrants who entered the country illegally. "We're sending many of them to sanctuary cities, thank you very much," Trump said. "They're not too happy about it. I'm proud to tell you that was actually my sick idea."

"What did they say? 'We want them,'" Trump said, mocking Democrats. "I said, 'We'll give 'em to you.'"

— 33 —

THE PURGE

ON THE EVENING OF Wednesday, March 27, Lou Dobbs, the seventy-three-year-old Trump intimate and anchor at the Fox Business Network, kicked off his 7 p.m. broadcast with a scathing takedown of the administration's efforts to secure the border. For several minutes, Dobbs painted the picture for his viewers of a strong president who was demanding to get tough against illegal immigrants but had been stymied at every turn by a weak and ineffectual bureaucracy either unable or unwilling to execute on his orders.

"What has happened to our Department of Homeland Security, the department that slow-walks the president's demands to secure our southern border, while simultaneously releasing tens of thousands of illegal immigrants into United States?" Dobbs asked, his voice dripping with disdain. "President Trump has declared a national emergency, sent the military to the border, yet DHS is paralyzed. The world's only super-power now appears suddenly defenseless and on its knees before Central American and Mexican illegal immigrants. Has the Department of Homeland Security SOLD OUT AMERICA?" His top story, Dobbs told his audience that night, was "the Department of Homeland Security surrendering our border."

"DHS secretary Kirstjen Nielsen is whining about the inability of her department to protect the homeland despite the president's best efforts to provide the department with every means necessary," Dobbs said. He mentioned that the secretary had served in several staff positions in the administration of George W. Bush, a distinction that had sown suspicion with Trump from the outset. "The worsening border crisis makes it all too clear," Dobbs added, "that Secretary Nielsen is in way over her head."

CBP Commissioner McAleenan had been at the border in El Paso that day, and it was his comments that inspired Dobbs's damning assessment. A Fox correspondent who reported on McAleenan's appearance said that the commissioner had "basically raised the white flag, saying his agency is overrun and overwhelmed." McAleenan had, indeed, painted a portrait of dysfunction and crisis at the border. "On Monday, we saw the highest total of apprehensions and encounters in over a decade with 4,000 migrants either apprehended or encountered in ports of entry in a single day. That was Monday. Yesterday, we broke the record again with 4,117," McAleenan had said. The agency was on pace to apprehend or encounter 100,000 migrants in the month of March, he said, the highest since 2008. "The breaking point has arrived," McAleenan reported. He said his agency would begin releasing more migrant families with notices to appear in federal court, and that he would divert 750 uniformed officers from ports of entry to help with the care and custody of migrants. That was described on Dobbs's show that night by the Fox correspondent as "processing, babysitting, and providing a taxi service for migrants needing hospital care or rides to the bus station."

Later in the broadcast, Dobbs invited Kris Kobach, the former Kansas secretary of state who had long been whispering in Trump's ear on immigration, to comment on what Dobbs called "failed leadership at DHS." Kobach was equally scorching. "It's shocking," Kobach said. "We are on track to have the highest level of border apprehensions in twelve years—higher than anything we saw under the two terms of the Obama administration—and the great irony here is President Trump is the strongest president we have ever had on the issue of illegal immigration. He campaigned on it. He has made clear where his stands. Yet we have his

DHS apparently sitting on its hands." Dobbs and Kobach were now practically finishing each other's sentences. "Why are we permitting these people to continue this charade?" Dobbs asked. "The Department of Homeland Security looks like a joke. They're acting as a joke. Kirstjen Nielsen—in my opinion, she is utterly unqualified for the job." What should Trump do? he asked Kobach. "He's got to have an agency that is aggressively restoring the rule of law in immigration," Kobach responded. "I don't know what's going on inside."

Trump was mortified, and not for the first time. He had told Nielsen dozens of times before that, "Lou Dobbs hates you. Ann Coulter hates you. You're making me look bad." He had run on a hard-line immigration policy, put in place dozens of harsh orders and policies, declared a national emergency to execute a crackdown, and promised to keep immigrants out of the country at all costs, with nothing to show for his efforts but a giant spike in migrants crossing the border? The next day, before he left the White House for a rally in Grand Rapids, Michigan, Trump summoned several officials for a meeting in the Oval Office. Nielsen, McAleenan, and Pompeo were there, along with Kushner, Mulvaney, Miller, Russ Vought, the acting budget chief, the strategic communications director Mercedes Schlapp, and May Davis, the deputy White House policy coordinator. The president was as furious and unhinged as his inner circle had ever seen him. What had been planned as a thirty-minute meeting dragged on for two hours as Trump ranted and raved about the skyrocketing border-crossing numbers. "You are making me look like a fucking idiot," Trump told the senior officials. I ran on this—it's MY issue. How could the numbers be so high?

Nielsen pushed back forcefully, arguing that the only way to deal with the crisis at the border was for Congress to close legal loopholes that created the incentives for migrants to reach the United States and allowed them to stay. We need you to push Congress, she said. We're sending a bill to them, along with a supplemental spending request to deal with the border emergency. But Trump had no patience for it. How the hell did we get to this point? he kept asking. Turning to Pompeo, he began lambasting the deal with Mexico that had been painstakingly negotiated a few months before. "The worst fucking deal we've ever made. How stupid. You guys made me look like an idiot. All my friends think I'm an idiot!"

Miller attempted several times to get the meeting back on track. They were supposed to be discussing the legislation the White House was planning to send to Capitol Hill, along with a variety of other measures they were considering to get control of the border. But Trump was hearing none of it. That's it, he finally said. We're shutting down the border. Nielsen tried reasoning with him. We can literally close the whole thing, she said, and it's not going to fix anything, because people can still claim asylum. She proposed closing just one port of entry so that the president could witness in real time what the effects would be. But in Trump's mind, closing the border meant no one could come in—period. Kushner tried interrupting, echoing Nielsen's point. This wasn't going to solve anything. But Trump swatted him down. "All you care about is your friends in Mexico," he told his son-in-law. I've had it—they're full of shit. We're going to start shutting down the border. I want it done at noon tomorrow. And then the meeting was over.

As Trump flew west on Air Force One to his rally in Michigan that evening, panicked officials at DHS and the White House swung into action, desperate to delay what they saw as a reckless and potentially catastrophic border shut down. There's no way we can do this, DHS officials told their White House counterparts. We need to buy time to find him another alternative that will work. On the flight back, Miller and others convinced Trump to delay the border closing for one week. But Miller also picked up where Dobbs and Kobach had left off the night before, telling the president that he needed to completely overhaul DHS and purge senior officials there who were slow-walking measures aimed at blocking immigrants. They had dragged their feet on a whole host of regulatory changes, Miller said, from the public charge rule—his attempt to limit welfare benefits for immigrants—to one that would revoke work permits from certain immigrants. They were always citing legal hurdles to explain why they couldn't deliver on what the president had promised. It was time for fresh leadership.

By now, Miller knew Trump was fed up with Nielsen, but he argued the problem went deeper than her. Cissna, the head of USCIS, had become intransigent. Miller kept telling Cissna that he needed to effect a "culture change" at USCIS, where Miller believed the asylum officers were a bunch of saps who would approve anyone. But Cissna would push back, saying that his people were just following the standards laid out in the law; he couldn't just snap his fingers and make them start rejecting people. Miller had also turned against Ron Vitiello, a top CBP official whom Trump had nominated to lead ICE. In a meeting weeks before in the White House Situation Room, Miller had lashed out at Vitiello for failing to push through new rules that would gut court-ordered protections for migrant children, known as the Flores settlement for the young teenage girl whose case inspired them. "You ought to be working on this regulation all day, every day," Miller shouted at Vitiello in front of other senior administration officials. "It should be the first thought you have when you wake up. And it should be the last thought you have before you go to bed. And sometimes, you shouldn't go to bed!" John Mitnick, the DHS general counsel, was also on Miller's list. In his view, they were all problems.

As Miller plotted a purge of their department, DHS officials scrambled to come up with a plan of action to divert Trump from his fixation with closing the border. They touted their effort to reassign border agents from ports of entry, which in turn would increase wait times and slow the flow of migrants without having all the negative economic effects of a full border closure. They leaned on Mexico to increase apprehensions of Central American migrants inside their own country so they could show Trump that the deal that had been struck was working as planned.

In frank telephone calls with their Mexican counterparts, DHS officials begged for cooperation. Look, we know we've cried wolf on this a thousand times, but this time it's real, they said. The president is about to shut down the border, and you need to step up. The Mexicans understood the stakes. They had discussed the idea of creating what they called a "third border," effectively detaining migrants in southern Mexico to keep them as far as possible from the U.S. border. The Mexicans figured it would take forty-five to sixty days to implement the plan, but now Trump administration officials told them there just wasn't time. We need you to do this NOW.

With the week-long reprieve from the border shutdown quickly running down, senior DHS officials spent the next several days sending daily emails to Mulvaney, Kushner, and Miller showing that the Mexicans were apprehending more migrants and that wait times at U.S. ports of entry were getting longer. Print these out and show POTUS, the officials implored Trump's team. Business executives and members of the U.S. Chamber of Commerce were enlisted to call Trump and impress upon him how horrific the effects would be for them and their businesses if Trump were to close the border.

They crossed their fingers that it would all work. In the meantime, Trump was getting anxious. On Friday, March 29, the day after the Oval Office blowup, Trump made public what he had threatened behind closed doors the day before. "If Mexico doesn't immediately stop ALL illegal immigration coming into the United States through our Southern Border, I will be CLOSING the Border, or large sections of the Border, next week," he said in a pair of tweets from his Mar-a-Lago estate in Palm Beach. Later in the day, while touring Lake Okeechobee, he announced he had halted $500 million in aid to Guatemala, Honduras, and El Salvador, the three Central American countries who were sending the most migrants. The timing was, as usual, inopportune. Nielsen had just concluded a painstakingly negotiated regional agreement with the three countries in which they had agreed to try to help stem the flow of migrants to the United States. And as was so often the case, Trump's abrupt decision contradicted his own government. As he spoke, several State Department officials were on Capitol Hill briefing senators on the department's fiscal 2020 budget request, which included $484 million in aid to Central America. Now the president was saying those countries were cut off. We need to get off the Hill as soon as possible, one of the officials told his colleagues when he saw news reports about what Trump had said. Before somebody asks us about this.

———————

Days later, in the wee hours of a Monday morning in London, Nielsen was asleep in her hotel room when a call came through from the White House. It was Trump looking for his homeland security secretary, who had arrived there late that night for several days of meetings on counterterrorism and cybersecurity. A military aide traveling with Nielsen in London asked the White House operator whether it was an emergency. No, the operator said. Later Monday, Nielsen was at the U.S. embassy when she returned the president's call. Trump was furious. "I called you, and you didn't answer!" he snapped. She apologized, explaining that she had not been aware he had tried to reach her until she had woken up that morning. "I don't know why you're there—we're in a crisis," Trump said. "You have to get back here." Instead of finishing her meetings and continuing on to Stockholm and Paris, where she was due to have additional talks, Nielsen headed back to the United States. She stopped to survey the situation on the border in Texas and Arizona, then planned to join Trump in Calexico, California, where he was scheduled to pose in front of a section of completed wall and meet with Border Patrol agents.

Nielsen and her staff kept up a steady drumbeat of emails to the White House to lobby Trump against closing the border. Members of Congress and more executives were weighing in privately as well. This is a terrible idea, they all said. We will take an enormous hit, and it won't get you the results that you want. By midweek, the president was getting cold feet, clearly looking for ways to avoid following through with his threat. Nielsen was in El Paso when she heard from Trump: Maybe there's another way to do this, he told her. How about if I impose tariffs on the Mexicans, or threaten to impose tariffs? Tariffs are great! Trump said. We're doing it with China, and *we* don't lose money, but *they* lose money. That wasn't quite the way tariffs worked, but Nielsen and her staff were relieved. Maybe they had succeeded in talking the president out of closing the border.

The same day, a baffling thing happened. A contact on Capitol Hill called Nielsen to ask her why she had pulled the nomination of Ron Vitiello to be the director of ICE. The odd part was, she hadn't. Vitiello had gotten wind of a rumor earlier in the day that he was being ousted, but when he had called over to the White House, Miller and Sean Doocey, the head of presidential personnel, had played dumb. It's just a paperwork screwup, they said. Vitiello thought he was fine. Nielsen placed a call to Doocey, and never got a callback. Late that night, though, he informed her staff that there had, in fact, been a paperwork mix-up—Doocey never said what it was—but it was too late to fix it. Vitiello was out.

The next day, as they boarded Nielsen's plane to fly to Yuma, an issue of *USA Today* was on a seat bearing a headline that so thrilled one of her top aides that he pulled out his iPhone and took a picture of it. "President Trump Says US May Never Close the Mexico Border, Would Try Tariffs First." Until that moment, the secretary of homeland security had not been completely sure whether the president of the United States actually intended to follow through with the order he had given the previous week to seal the border with Mexico. She and her team heaved a sigh of relief. They had lived to fight another day.

Their celebrations were premature. As Trump made his way to Calexico aboard the presidential aircraft on Friday, he turned to McAleenan, his CBP chief. I want you to stop letting migrants cross the border—no exceptions, the president told him. If you get into any legal trouble for it, I'll pardon you. If Nielsen was not going to shut the border, Trump was determined to find somebody at DHS who would. Once on the ground, Trump and his entourage met up with Nielsen, who had flown in from Arizona, and as they all gathered in a hallway at the Border Patrol headquarters to begin a roundtable with agents and other personnel, Kushner and Miller both did something out of the ordinary: they each gave Nielsen a big hug. It would be the first indication that her days as secretary of homeland security were numbered.

Once inside, Trump worked the room, greeting Border Patrol agents with attaboys for the great job they were doing, and repeating to them what he had told McAleenan on the plane. They should start turning away migrants at the border. My message to you is, keep them all out, the president said. Okay? Every single one of them. Turn them around. Can't come. When reporters were led in for the public portion of the visit, Trump took his place at a long, narrow table covered with a forest green cloth, flanked by CBP and Army Corps of Engineers officials, and delivered a similar refrain. "This is our new statement: The system is full," the president said. "Can't take you anymore. Whether it's asylum, whether it's anything you want, it's illegal immigration. We can't take you anymore. We can't take you. Our country is full. Our area is full. The sector is full. Can't take you anymore, I'm sorry. Can't happen. So turn around. That's the way it is." Later, Trump singled out Dave Shaw, the ICE special agent in charge of the Homeland Security Investigations office in San Diego, who had described for the president how the influx of migrants was overstraining his agency. "You know, Dave, you were mentioning before about, you know, people coming in, and they come in and they come in. You don't have to take them in," Trump said. "You can't take them? You can't take them. There's nothing you can do, okay?"

Trump continued schmoozing with the border agents after the media had been led out, and he repeated his advice. That's it—just start turning these people away. Once the president had left the room, McAleenan and other top DHS officials did a frantic round of cleanup. All that stuff he said about turn everyone away? That was not a direct order, they told the agents. Don't do it. You absolutely *do not* have the authority to simply stop processing migrants altogether.

As Nielsen flew back to Washington on her Coast Guard plane Friday evening, she called Trump. "Sir, I know you're really frustrated," she told him. "Let me come in and talk to you about what we can do." Trump was surprisingly magnanimous. "It's not your fault," he told Nielsen. "You're great." Come see me on Sunday in the Yellow Oval Room, he told Nielsen. "They call it the Yellow Oval," he said again, as if it were the name of a secret clubhouse. "It's in the residence." She spent much of the flight back huddling with aides to put together a point-by-point plan to show the president—a Hail Mary pass—scrawling it on a sheet of notebook paper that she would tear out and bring to the White House forty-eight hours later. She called it the "Six C's"—Congress, Courts, Communications, Countries, Criminals, Cartels—and it was a multifaceted strategy for getting control of the border. Her staff quietly started work on another document: Nielsen's letter of resignation.

The afternoon of her meeting with Trump, Nielsen was led into the Yellow Oval for what she thought would be a one-on-one meeting. But Mick Mulvaney, Trump's acting chief of staff, was there to greet her as well, a sign that this would not be the conversation she had envisioned. Nielsen launched into her presentation, touching on her extensive negotiations and the deal she had reached with the Mexicans to decrease the flow of migrants by 50 percent. "You see what I mean, Mick?" Trump said, turning to his chief. "That's ridiculous. I told them 100 percent." It was clear the two had talked about Nielsen before the meeting—and not in a good way. That's just not possible, Nielsen replied. The Mexicans could not physically stop 100 percent of the migration flow even if they were willing to, which they weren't. Trump grew exasperated. "Why do you always fight me on this stuff?" he asked. She tried to get through the other items on her list. They needed a legislative push that would actually make a dent in the problem, Nielsen said. Well, Trump said, Jared's been working on a whole plan for comprehensive immigration reform. Maybe *you* should have done that. And another thing, Trump said. We need a cement wall.

Nielsen looked at the president, whose dreams of a wall had morphed from cement to steel slats to bollards to trenches and now back to cement. Two years into his presidency, he was back where he had started, bent on keeping immigrants out of the country, determined to take the toughest, most extreme measures regardless of whether they were legal, moral, or even possible, torn between feuding advisers giving him conflicting advice on what policies to embrace, and obsessing over a beautiful, hulking, concrete wall. They couldn't build that now even if it would work, which it wouldn't, Nielsen told Trump. The designs for steel barriers had long since been finalized, the contracts bid and signed. Work was under way in some places. "Sir," she said, "I literally don't think that's even possible."

It was too late anyway. It was clear the president had already made up his mind to get rid of her. "Kirstjen, I want to make a change," he told her. This is not going to work. We're just not going to be able to do it. Then I'll resign, Nielsen said. In an interview months later, Trump recalled that moment as a "sad meeting, because she worked so hard." Nielsen had a "very hard job," he acknowledged, especially doing it for him. "I'm demanding a lot on that job, because I understand what I want." She did not know it yet, but a purge of her agency's senior staff was already underway. In the coming days, Trump would also fire Claire M. Grady, the undersecretary for management, who by statute was designated to take the top post in the event the secretary's position became vacant. Trump wanted McAleenan instead, so Grady, an acquisitions specialist who had spent her entire career in government, was unceremoniously pushed out. Within two months, Cissna would also be out, replaced by Kenneth T. Cuccinelli II, who had pushed for an end to birthright citizenship and allowing police officers to investigate the immigration status of anyone they stopped who they suspected might be undocumented. The purge was just beginning.

By the time Nielsen emerged from the thirty-minute meeting in the Yellow Oval, before she had left the White House grounds or had time to sign a resignation letter, Trump's aides had already begun leaking that she was out.

"Secretary of Homeland Security Kirstjen Nielsen will be leaving her position," Trump wrote on Twitter, "and I would like to thank her for her service."

EPILOGUE

SUNSHINE POURED IN THROUGH the curved windows of the Oval Office on the steamy day in late June 2019 when President Trump sat down with us to talk about immigration. He was in a sunny mood as well, preparing for a big summit in Asia followed by a giant Independence Day party in Washington, complete with tanks, fighter jets, and fireworks over the Lincoln Memorial. American flags were already draped all around the White House grounds to mark the occasion. Trump was here to put a positive spin on his immigration record; to tell us how wrong his critics were when they condemned his policies as racist; to cast himself as a humanitarian who only wanted a more orderly system; to insist that he was helping the country, not hurting people.

But as we took our seats, the ugly and tragic consequences of his immigration policies were playing out in dramatic fashion. Photographs of migrant children, their clothes and hair caked with dirt and snot in squalid and overcrowded detention centers, played incessantly on cable television. Reports from lawyers who had visited the migrants told a macabre story of Third World conditions in the shelters, where the children, some as young as toddlers, had no soap, diapers, toothbrushes, or toothpaste. Soon, the internal DHS watchdog would issue a report confirming the grim accounts of holding centers where children went without showers or hot meals and migrants were crammed into standing-room-only cells. It quoted a senior manager in one of the facilities who called the conditions "a ticking time bomb." And it included visual evidence of the disaster, including one photograph showing dozens of men packed into a locked room, some shirtless and many pressed up against a glass wall, with one holding a scrap of paper on which he had scrawled, "HELP." It was clear that the large-scale migration of families seeking protection in the United States was continuing to overwhelm the country's capacity to receive them, deepening a humanitarian crisis that Congress was racing to address through an emergency funding bill. Tent cities were being built in the scorching desert to house the scores of migrants who were pouring into facilities that were never designed to hold this much humanity.

But Trump, seated behind the Resolute Desk, was in a parallel universe of his own making. He had a page-long list for us of his immigration success stories: *Travel Ban . . . Significantly reduced refugee ceiling . . . National Emergency on the Southern Border . . . Terminated TPS designations . . . DACA rescission (tied up in court) . . . Border Wall . . . Giving ICE officers full license to do their jobs . . .*

In the president's telling that day, the horrible conditions playing out at the border in the third year of his presidency were the fault of Barack Obama, and of Democrats in Congress who refused to change the law to make it more difficult to claim asylum and easier for the United States to quickly turn people away at the border. It was Obama, Trump claimed falsely that afternoon, who first separated families, and Trump who decided—against his better judgment, he was quick to add—to end a practice he acknowledged was inhumane. In Trump's warped account, he was absolved of responsibility for the most brutal of his immigration policies. In fact, he wanted credit for ending family separation even though he knew doing so would encourage more Central American migrants to surge north in even greater numbers.

"I don't regret it, because it was terrible," Trump said of his decision to abandon the policy in the face of global outrage. "But from the standpoint of numbers of children and people, it brings the people. A family that says, 'Well, I'm going to be separated from my children,' they don't come up.

When you say, 'We're going to be together,' then they're willing to take their chances. I said that at the time. I said, 'Look, I'm doing this. And I'm doing it also on a humanitarian basis.' But I did say more people are going to come up. And that's what happened."

It was the only time during our thirty-five-minute interview when Trump acknowledged even a shred of responsibility for a decision that had made the nation's immigration challenges worse. Nearly two and a half years after Trump took office vowing to fix the broken system, it was as dysfunctional as ever—and, in some ways, more so. And as he sat across his desk from us, the president was grappling in real time with the contradiction that had been at the heart of his assault on immigration all along. "I have absolute power to shut down the border," Trump declared. But in the next breath, he conceded that his authority was not as sweeping as he would like it to be. American troops couldn't use force against immigrants, he said regretfully, nor could he keep people out of the country the way he would like to do. "The problem you have with the laws the way they are, we can have 100,000 of our soldiers standing up there—they can't do a thing," Trump said, his voice rising slightly with a note of incredulity. "They can't engage in any way, shape, or form. We're the only country where you can't. I mean, most countries say, 'I'm sorry, you can't come in.' With us, the people can walk in; touch the land; in theory, they go to court. The problem is, they never come back."

Trump was once again dangling a fearsome threat to break that cycle. The week before, on the eve of his official reelection kickoff rally in Orlando, Florida, he had warned on Twitter that he was about to order mass deportation raids throughout the country, to remove "millions of illegal aliens." He had since said he was delaying the operation, but only by a couple of weeks, to leave time for Democrats to agree to changes in asylum law. They wouldn't, of course, and Trump thought he knew why. "It should be easy," the president told us. "They just don't want to do it. I honestly believe they think it's a good political point. I don't! I think it's a bad political point for them." In the end, for Trump, it all came down to politics.

The border was at the center of some of Trump's biggest failures and disappointments: the children ripped from their parents' arms; the fights over a wall that plunged the country into its longest-ever government shutdown; the futile attempts to stop growing waves of migrant families from pouring into the country. But the border, Trump knew, also provided the raw fuel for his political brand. It was ground zero for the rage about immigrants that he tapped to whip up his supporters, using the marketing prowess that he had developed over decades to sell himself as a business executive and a celebrity TV star. For Trump, the obstacles were the point. The more the courts, the Democrats, the political establishment, and even his own government resisted his efforts to crack down at the border, the starker his message became. The harder he fought, the more extreme his tactics, the more his supporters loved him. It is a quintessentially Trumpian formula that is at the heart of a reelection campaign in which the president's border wars are a defining theme.

Under Trump, America presented a different face to the world, one that was far less welcoming and more fearful of the risks of a diverse society. He rewrote the political playbook on immigration in ways that are likely to have lasting impacts on both parties, deepening the partisan divide and increasing the costs of compromise. All the while, he rejected pleadings from fellow Republicans and gambled that his take-no-prisoners approach would be a political winner—a bet that he has so far lost, but one he still believes will pay off for him as he seeks a second term.

And yet here he was, insisting that he had nothing against immigrants. "No, I don't at all—just the opposite!" he said with a faint note of disappointment in his voice that suggested he had expected the question. "But I do have something against people, when they come up and use our system and come in and they're unchecked." He was in the midst of trying to whitewash the harsh legacy of his immigration policies—and he was letting us in on the strategy. "I do believe in immigration. That's maybe why I'm doing the interview, right?" Trump said with a half smile and a squint of his eyes.

What about all of the harsh policies and dark rhetoric about immigration? we asked. Would his legacy be that of a xenophobic president who closed America off to immigrants? "I hope not, because I'm not that way," Trump replied. "I think you're right. I think the perception might be more that way than the other. I hope not. I would like to have a great immigration policy, I'd like it to be fair, I do not want criminals coming into our country. I don't think you do, either."

After all this time, Trump was admitting, in his own way, that he did not yet have the immigration policy that he wanted. As we spoke, the Department of Homeland Security was reeling from a second shake-up that had abruptly elevated officials aligned with the president's hard-line approach, and Kevin McAleenan, the acting secretary who succeeded Kirstjen Nielsen, was clinging to his job after having pleaded privately with the president not to carry out his deportation raids. The crackdown on asylum seekers had continued as the administration moved to impose new fees and deny them work permits. A new rule had been proposed to force undocumented immigrants out of public housing, and officials said they were still considering the plan to drop off thousands of migrants in sanctuary cities. The Social Security Administration had sent letters to tens of thousands of employers informing them that the names of some of their employees did not match their Social Security numbers—a not-so-subtle threat designed to drive undocumented workers out of their jobs.

Just days before our interview, Trump had walked back from the brink of yet another crisis point with Mexico, having threatened to impose tariffs if they did not stop migrants from crossing into the United States, and then backed down when officials there promised to do more to police their own borders. The president was celebrating a federal court's decision to throw out a lawsuit by the House of Representatives challenging his power to declare a national emergency so he could spend money to build his wall. "I just won that case!" Trump exulted. But within days, another court would halt some of the funds permanently, and the Supreme Court would temporarily block the addition of the citizenship question to the census. When Wilbur Ross announced that the survey would be printed without the controversial query, Trump insisted that such reports were "FAKE!" and within days was plotting to draft an executive order to add it anyway. But by mid-July, as his administration struggled unsuccessfully to find a legal strategy to preserve the question, Trump accepted defeat and abandoned the effort. The executive order he did issue simply directed agencies to compile citizenship data they already had.

The president was simultaneously in the midst of a recalibration of his message on legal immigration. Weeks earlier, he had endorsed an overhaul plan drafted by Jared Kushner. It had some of the trademark elements of Stephen Miller's hard-line agenda—cracking down on asylum seekers and ending chain migration—but its focal point was a moderate-sounding immigration proposal: a "merit-based" system that would draw skilled workers and was designed to appeal to corporate titans who see immigrants as critical to their economic success. "It's just very simple: I want people to come into our country legally, and I frankly happen to believe in the system of merit," Trump told us. "We need workers in our country." Never mind that he had endorsed a huge cut to legal immigration two years earlier during a ceremony in the East Room of the White House. "I disagreed with that aspect of it," Trump told us, almost as an aside. This was the nightmare scenario of the low-immigration hawks who had always worried that this president secretly shunned their agenda.

As for the Dreamers, Trump swore that it was the Democrats, not he, who had walked away from a deal to preserve their protections, after a federal judge found in favor of DACA. "We came very close to having a deal on DACA," Trump said, crediting himself with the idea of offering the protections to 1.8 million Dreamers, something that Democrats had insisted upon from the start. "We were going to take in more people than they even thought. I was the one that brought up the number. I said, 'Here's what we're going to do: 1.8.' It's a nice number, good number, everybody was on board. And the judge ruled against. And after he ruled against, I said, 'They'll never make a deal now,' and they didn't." But when we pressed, Trump admitted that he had been the one to jettison the deal. "Well, you could say I walked away because all of a sudden, they gave me a deal that was much tougher than the deal that they would have had."

Trump seemed genuinely regretful about the fate of DACA, even though he had been the one to end it, leaving nearly 800,000 young immigrants who have lived most of their lives in the United States vulnerable to deportation. He returned again to the bigger number—"1.8!"—as if clinging to the idea that he had been magnanimous. How could someone that generous be accused of being anti-immigrant? he seemed to be saying. And if we needed convincing, he had proof. "One thing's happened that's interesting," the president said, leaning in as if he were letting us in on a big secret. "Hispanics love me. Everyone thought it was going to be the opposite." It was more evidence, in Trump's mind, that he was on the right track on immigration, and that there was no political price to be paid for his harsh rhetoric and policies.

It had only been about a half hour since we had entered the Oval Office, and in the time it took Trump to defend his immigration policies, yet another disturbing image that would come to symbolize their consequences had gone viral. In the photograph, the drowned bodies of Óscar Alberto Martínez Ramírez and his twenty-three-month-old daughter, Valeria, lay facedown on the muddy banks of the Rio Grande, the little girl's lifeless arm draped around her father's neck. Valeria and her parents had fled El Salvador but had grown frustrated by the long wait in Mexico to apply for asylum. Desperate, Óscar had taken matters into his own hands and tried to cross the river to Texas with his daughter, only to be swept under by the strong current.

Trump had just finished telling us that he didn't feel responsible for the horrific conditions in which migrants were being held by the U.S. government, and he wasn't likely to take any ownership of this latest tragedy. He had nothing to apologize for, not even about the birther claims that he stoked before entering office, which he said had no connection whatsoever with his hard-line immigration agenda.

"Hey, I have a wonderful life," Trump said when we asked if he regretted his claims that the nation's first African American president was not, in fact, American. "And I've done a great job as president. I'm very happy with the job I've done as president. We have the strongest economy we've ever had."

He was hoping this book would help people see it his way.

"If I like it," he said as we turned to leave, "I'll tweet it out."

AFTERWORD TO THE PAPERBACK EDITION

In early 2020, the week after President Trump was acquitted by the Senate in his impeachment trial, he made the short walk across the driveway from the West Wing of the White House to speak to the National Border Patrol Council. He entered the drab-looking auditorium full of uniformed border agents to chants of "Four! More! Years!" and a standing ovation. "Say 'Thank you, Mr. President,'" Trump told the group, a union that had endorsed him in 2016. He held up pictures of portions of the wall that were under construction, boasting about the black paint that kept it too hot to touch—the very kind he had demanded incessantly from Kirstjen Nielsen—and spoke in detail about the materials being used to erect it. He talked about the dangers of criminal immigrants and so-called sanctuary cities, citing the horrific case of a ninety-two-year-old woman, Maria Fuertes, who had been raped and murdered in New York. Her assailant was an undocumented man with an arrest record for misdemeanor assault. Immigration officials said they had requested two months earlier that the suspect be turned over for possible deportation, but New York's policy is to honor such requests only for people who have been convicted of violent or serious offenses.

Trump did not mention it that day, but, quietly, his Department of Homeland Security was preparing to unleash a tactical force of border agents trained in SWAT team–like fashion—with sniper certifications and armed with equipment like stun grenades—on sanctuary cities around the country. With little fanfare, the White House had just informed Congress that it was renewing the national emergency at the border that Trump had declared a year earlier so he could spend money Congress refused to allocate on the border wall. At DHS, officials were moving to speed up wall construction by waiving federal contracting rules that required open competition and gave losing companies the right to appeal. And the Pentagon had announced that another $3.8 billion intended for military equipment would instead be used to pay for building the barrier, drawing bipartisan howls of outrage that would amount to nothing.

After five months spent under the cloud of impeachment, Trump had declared himself "liberated" by the Senate's not guilty verdict and he was acting like it. He was aggressively pushing the limits of his power as he began a campaign of retribution against those who had testified against him and used his Twitter feed to pressure the Justice Department to do his bidding in federal investigations. He was stepping up the pace of his arena-style rallies around the country as well, trolling Democrats who were locked in an intense intraparty battle for the privilege of challenging him for the White House. And he was pressing forward with the immigration agenda that had powered his political rise and was emerging once again as the centerpiece of his campaign.

Because just as his acquittal had convinced the president that there was no real check on his power, Trump saw ample evidence that his no-holds-barred immigration crackdown—as rocky as its execution had been—was having the effect he wanted. During his first two years in office, he had presided over a 350 percent increase in apprehensions at the border, an infuriating reminder for Trump of the pace of unauthorized crossings that vividly illustrated his failure to deliver on a central campaign promise. But thanks to the draconian set of policies Trump had managed to put in place during his third year in office, the numbers had been on a steady decline for months, and apprehensions were now about 1 percent lower than they had been when he became president. Legal immigration—something that Trump had always insisted he loved and welcomed—had fallen more precipitously, declining about 11 percent since 2016. The courts had blocked some of his actions and Congress had tried to intervene, but neither proved a match for the president's sheer determination to scale back the number of immigrants who came into the country.

To those who had lived through three years of immigration policy-making under Trump, the events that had given rise to the impeachment saga looked and sounded familiar. Just as Trump had demanded in a 2017 phone call that the president of Mexico help him politically by saying his country would pay for the border wall, he used a call with Ukraine's president to ask for a political favor, too: investigations of his campaign rivals, including former Vice President Joseph R. Biden Jr., who at the time of the call was regarded as his most likely challenger. Trump's relentless campaign to pressure Ukraine to do what he wanted shocked and horrified career professionals and even some of his own advisers who were charged with carrying out United States policy toward Ukraine, much as his obsession with the wall and ever-more-aggressive tactics for cracking down on immigration had stunned the civil servants and political appointees who had to implement them. In both cases, Trump dismissed the naysayers as disloyal, and ultimately purged them.

Maybe most importantly, there was another common thread: Trump got away with it, ultimately suffering no lasting consequence for either set of actions. The Democratic-led House had impeached him for abuse of power and obstruction of Congress based on the Ukraine affair, leaving Trump's legacy stained with the distinction of being only the third president in American history to be charged with high crimes and misdemeanors. But the Republican-led Senate had acquitted him, even as some members of his own party conceded that he had acted inappropriately, and even shamefully. (In a twist that reflected how dramatically Trump had changed his party in just a few years, Senator Mitt Romney of Utah—whose 2012 loss had persuaded Steve Bannon, Jeff Sessions, and Stephen Miller that an anti-immigration presidential candidate was needed to revive their party—was the only Republican to cross party lines and vote to remove Trump.) On immigration, too, Trump had suffered some setbacks. His harsh rhetoric and extreme policies had contributed to Republicans losing the House of Representatives in the 2018 midterm elections. Federal courts continued to block some of his policies. And Congress voted every six months to terminate the national emergency he had declared on the southwestern border. But by the beginning of 2020, many of his most sweeping changes were firmly in place and his job approval rating heading into his reelection campaign was at 49 percent, the highest level of his presidency.

Even as the Ukraine scandal stole the media spotlight away from most other subjects, Miller and the immigration hardliners he had installed during the spring purge of 2019 had been moving forward aggressively.

In late summer 2019, after nearly two years of waiting, Miller finally got the public charge rule he so badly wanted. Standing in the same White House briefing room where Nielsen was savaged while trying to defend the family separation policy, Kenneth T. Cuccinelli, the new director of United States Citizen and Immigration Services, announced that immigrants would now have a higher burden to prove they would not be a drain on the American economy. To make his point, Cuccinelli brashly recast the famous Emma Lazarus poem inscribed on a plaque on the Statue of Liberty's pedestal: "Give me your tired and your poor who can stand on their own two feet and who will not become a public charge," he told reporters. The comment became instant fodder for late-night comedians, and by October three federal judges had blocked the rule. Judge George B. Daniels of the federal district court in Manhattan called it "repugnant to the American Dream of the opportunity for prosperity and success through hard work and upward mobility." But three months later, in January of 2020, the Supreme Court, without comment, allowed the rule to go into effect while the cases moved forward.

The administration continued its push to turn off every spigot that controlled the flow of immigration into the United States. On a rainy day in late August, Kevin K. McAleenan, then the acting secretary of homeland security, unveiled a new rule designed to get around the twenty-day limit for detaining immigrant families. A month later, a federal judge blocked it, calling the government's reasoning "Kafkaesque." But in September, the Supreme Court temporarily cleared the way for another Trump administration program to ban asylum seekers who had not first sought refuge in another country. By the end of that month, the Trump administration had announced it was once again slashing the number of refugees that could be admitted to the United States in the coming year, this time reducing the number to eighteen thousand, almost half the previous year's cap. The president signed a new executive order that for the first time barred refugee resettlement in any state that did not explicitly approve, effectively handing states veto power over welcoming people fleeing violence and persecution around the world. The Republican governor of Texas, Greg Abbott, quickly announced his state was closed to refugees.

In October, the Department of Homeland Security announced it would begin collecting the DNA of migrants who were already detained, and entering the data into a nationwide criminal database that would aid efforts to deport those in the country illegally. Within months, the State Department would task consular officers with preventing "birth tourism" by denying visas to women who were pregnant or appeared to be. In their ongoing effort to crack down on those already in the country illegally, officials looked for every opportunity to keep undocumented immigrants from finding a legal way to stay in the United States. Applicants for the U visa, which was created to encourage immigrants who are victims of violent crimes to report them, were rejected if they failed to fill out every field on the application form, even if it didn't apply to them. Lawyers began urging the applicants to write "n/a"—not applicable—in every blank field, just in case.

Not everything went according to plan. When the Trump administration's lawyers arrived at the Supreme Court in November 2019 to defend the president's decision to end DACA, they discovered something that Jeff Sessions had been worried about from the start. Elaine Duke's reluctance to fully embrace the termination of the program had weakened the administration's legal justification, just as Sessions had predicted it would. Under pressure from Sessions and Miller to end DACA, she had agreed to do so, but instead of offering a considered set of policy reasons, she wrote a bare-bones memo stating simply that the attorney general had declared the program unconstitutional and illegal. She refused to endorse the claims by Sessions and Miller that the program encouraged illegality and disrupted legal immigration flows. At the Supreme Court, proponents of the program used Duke's position to argue that the government had no legitimate reason to end the program, making its elimination "arbitrary and capricious," and therefore invalid. Still, by the end of the hour-long argument, the court's conservative majority—which now bore Trump's stamp— appeared ready to side with the president. Justice Brett M. Kavanaugh said that he assumed the move to end the program was "a very considered decision." Justice Neil M. Gorsuch appeared to have little appetite for extending the legal battles over the program: "What good would another five years of litigation over the adequacy of that explanation serve?" he asked.

For Miller, Cuccinelli, and their allies, the legal and regulatory progress was finally yielding some positive results. Despite a series of mixed court rulings on funding, the administration slowly moved forward on construction of Trump's wall. Along parts of the border between Texas and Mexico, government officials accelerated negotiations with private landowners so construction could proceed. The travel ban, which had been so controversial when it was initially imposed during Trump's first week in office, was expanded in early 2020, adding Nigeria, among other countries, Africa's most populous nation and the subject of the president's rant in the summer of 2017, when he complained that citizens of that country would not want to "go back to their huts" if they were allowed to visit the United States.

But perhaps most significantly, the president's threat to impose tariffs on Mexico finally triggered the response he wanted from that country's leaders. Desperate to avoid economic calamity, they agreed to increase their own military's efforts to stop migrants from heading north toward the United States. And under duress, they consented to more rapidly implement the Migration Protection Protocols, which Nielsen and Mike Pompeo had begun negotiating during secret meetings in Houston. By the beginning of 2020, close to sixty thousand migrants who hoped to win asylum in the United States were waiting in squalid camps on the Mexican side of the border, many with no access to legal counsel. Advocacy groups reported hundreds of violent attacks, and sexual assaults against the migrants, as well as abductions, prompting House Democrats to announce an investigation into what the Judiciary Committee called "a dangerously flawed policy that threatens the health and safety of legitimate asylum seekers." At the end of February 2019, an appeals court blocked the policy, calling it "invalid in its entirety." But it seemed likely that the government would appeal, leaving the program's fate in the hands of the Supreme Court.

By denying migrants the rights they have had for decades to access the American asylum system, the administration ensured that border apprehensions—the number that Trump fixated on endlessly, driven to rage when Fox News reported it was increasing—declined for eight months straight. In January of 2020, about 36,000 migrants were apprehended at the border, down nearly 75 percent from the high of 144,000 in May of 2019. Heading into his reelection campaign, Trump could finally boast—accurately—that he had succeeded in fulfilling the promise he made in 2016. During his State of the Union address the night before his acquittal in February 2020, he did just that, bragging that his administration "has undertaken an unprecedented effort to secure the southern border of the United States" and claiming vindication in the border wars he had been waging for three years.

"Our borders are secure," Trump declared.

Unleashed after his impeachment acquittal and convinced that his policies were a political winner, Trump was laying the groundwork for yet another election season in which his harsh immigration agenda would be a rallying cry for his candidacy. And Democrats, consumed with internal conflicts over health care and economic issues, were saying little about their own immigration plans, leaving Trump an opening to portray them falsely as "open borders" extremists who were bent on defanging border enforcement and encouraging more waves of undocumented immigrants by offering free benefits to all comers.

"Every day, Democrats' open borders policies are harming and killing innocent lives," Trump bellowed at a campaign rally in Phoenix in February of 2020. "Right here in Phoenix, an illegal alien chased a man through a parking lot and shot him in cold blood, then walked over to the victim and shot him four more times right in the face as he laid dying in the street. This savage animal had previously been deported after serving six years in prison." When the novel coronavirus reached the United States later that month, Trump—who in 2015 had compared illegal immigrants pouring into the country to "vomit"—capitalized on fears about the illness to portray Democrats' immigration stance as dangerous. "The Democrat policy of open borders is a direct threat to the health and well-being of all Americans," he said. "Now you see it with the coronavirus." The next day, he told reporters at the White House that he was considering closing the United States border with Mexico in light of the virus. (He did not mention the idea of sealing the northern border.) Before long, Trump was capitalizing on the spread of the virus to clamp down still further, sealing American land borders to nonessential travel, refusing almost all migrants who tried to enter, and halting green-card processing at American consular offices. Miller had long sought to use the president's broad public health powers to impose strict new immigration restrictions; the pandemic finally gave him the legal rationale he needed.

Even after three years of Trump's anti-immigrant rhetoric and policies, surveys showed that the American public was still overwhelmingly in favor of immigration, with majorities calling it a net positive for the country, saying they were in favor of admitting refugees and expressing support for allowing undocumented immigrants to stay in the United States and gain legal status. Majorities still opposed building a wall and Trump's declaration of a national emergency to pay for it. But most Americans believed illegal immigration was a crisis or a serious problem, and under Trump, the partisan divide over immigration had deepened. Republicans held more negative views of immigrants and immigration than Democrats or Independents did.

What was unmistakable, though, was the degree to which Trump had changed the country's posture toward immigrants during his years in office, putting it on a trajectory to dramatically reduce the number of people from around the world who could come to the United States, legally or illegally. In the Oval Office in 2019, Trump had expressed admiration for the harsh immigration policies in other countries. "I mean, literally, if you have even the slightest infraction, they won't let you in," he said. "And then you have other countries, if you've had a cold in your life, if you've ever been sick, if you've ever—they won't let you in." He paused. "You know, it's a much different world out there." Eight months later, he was moving the United States in that direction. As president, he had only begun to build small sections of the wall he had promised on the southwestern border, but Trump had begun to erect a far more consequential barrier of restrictive policies that would be an indelible part of his legacy.

ACKNOWLEDGMENTS

When we first began contemplating writing this book, over a couple of glasses of wine at a noisy bar not far from the *New York Times* Washington bureau, we were intimidated by the challenge and excited about the possibilities. Could we pull this off? As first-time authors, we couldn't imagine how. A year and a half later, we have learned that it was, indeed, achievable, but only because of the generosity, support, and thoughtful participation of sources, colleagues, friends, and family.

Peter Baker, our friend and colleague and an accomplished author in his own right, was the first to nudge us toward turning our years of immigration reporting into a book, and one of the earliest readers of the book you hold in your hands. His relentless cheerleading, sharp advice, and thoughtful comments along the way made this book possible. We are also indebted to Peter for connecting us with our agent, Rafe Sagalyn at ICM. Endlessly optimistic and incredibly patient, Rafe was generous with his time and wise guidance at every step.

It was Rafe who introduced us to Bob Bender, our editor at Simon & Schuster. Bob is the type of editor that writers dream of: kind and supportive, inquisitive and attentive, careful and enthusiastic. His astute advice and counsel, and his endless encouragement, improved our book immeasurably. Johanna Li and the team at Simon & Schuster were a pleasure to work with, and we owe a special debt of gratitude to Jonathan Karp, who took a particular interest in our book from the very beginning and stayed involved throughout the process.

Outside of our families, no one bore the brunt of the demands of writing this book more heavily than Elisabeth Bumiller, our bureau chief, whose herculean job of managing more than one hundred reporters in one of the busiest newspaper bureaus on the planet is made even more difficult when two of them ask for months off to tackle a big project. She handled the disruption, as she does everything else, with her typical grace and aplomb (and maybe a touch of gallows humor). We could not ask for a more inspiring editor—fearless in the face of immense pressure, gifted with a reporter's raw copy, protective of our journalistic ethics, and understanding that we have lives outside of the paper. (And a fabulous chef to boot.) The book would never have happened without the other editors in the bureau, too, especially Bill Hamilton, who for years has been our primary editor on White House coverage and never failed to make our stories smarter and more sophisticated (and shorter). There isn't anyone in Washington with a sharper eye when it comes to politics, and the book benefited from the advice and counsel we received daily from him. Jonathan Weisman, the *Times's* talented congressional editor and an author himself, made Julie's transition from the White House beat to Capitol Hill, to book leave and back again as painless as it could be—no easy feat. His deft hand as an editor and his ruthless efficiency with time were both deeply appreciated. We are exceptionally grateful to Dean Baquet, whose exacting standards as an editor, boundless appetite for great coverage of Washington, and unfailing support even in the most stressful of circumstances have helped us produce our proudest work, including the story that was the inspiration for this book. He and the other editors in New York—Matt Purdy, Joe Kahn, Alison Mitchell, and many more—have given us the remarkable opportunity to write about national politics on a daily basis. We are forever thankful.

Covering Washington is a team sport, and we have been lucky to be part of one of the best teams ever. Peter Baker, Mark Landler, Katie Rogers,

Annie Karni, Maggie Haberman, and Mike Tackett are the most talented White House reporters anywhere, and working alongside them has been the honor of our careers. They are gracious, funny, smart, perceptive, sassy, and—particularly during the past year—accommodating, especially when we disappeared for two-hour interviews or begged for a weekend-duty trade. It's hard to imagine covering the chaos of the Trump administration without them by our side. Likewise, Sheryl Stolberg, Nick Fandos, Emily Cochrane, and Catie Edmondson have welcomed Julie to the congressional team with grace and generosity, and their hard work, sharp eyes, and distinctive writing have helped make her return to Capitol Hill a truly rewarding one. Without our colleagues' support, *Border Wars* would not have been possible. Nor could we have done it without the endless patience of the bureau's other editors like Mikayla Bouchard, Amy Fiscus, Margaret Ho, Lara Jakes, Justine Makieli, Teshia Morris, Andy Parsons, Thom Shanker, Deborah Solomon, Jaime Swanson, and Nathan Willis. Tahirah Burley helped us navigate the book leave process, and Ari Isaacman Bevacqua has been a creative and energetic booster of our work.

We are fortunate to work alongside many brilliant journalists in the Washington bureau, and even luckier to have benefited from their help and advice at key moments. Carl Hulse has been a mentor and inspiration ever since Julie was a twenty-something baby reporter on the Hill, and his own maiden voyage into book writing preceded ours by only a few months; we benefited tremendously from his advice and lessons learned. Helene Cooper and Mark Leibovich, who have each written successful books of their own, provided sage counsel and, when needed, stern lectures, reminding us to stay true to ourselves and our vision for this work. Maureen Dowd inspired us from her office around the corner from our desks, offering real-time demonstrations of how to be a keen observer and elegant chronicler of our times. David Sanger and Binya Appelbaum offered words of wisdom about hiring researchers and fact-checkers. David Leonhardt's first contribution to this book came when Julie was in high school, when he was gracious enough to tour her through the hallowed halls of the *Yale Daily News*, which became her first and only journalism school. Some twenty-five years later, he reprised the role of wise guide, offering to read an early draft and providing thoughtful advice that made it better. Our many colleagues at the *Times* who cover immigration and the border on a regular basis shared their sources and smart analysis in ways that helped us shape the stories we told. They include: Ron Nixon, Caitlin Dickerson, Miriam Jordan, Zolan Kanno-Youngs, Kirk Semple, Nick Kulish, Azam Ahmed, Kim Murphy, Mark Lacey, Manny Fernandez, Liz Robbins, and Eileen Sullivan. Michael Barbaro and his fabulous team at *The Daily* repeatedly gave us a forum to discuss the themes we explore in this book.

We are indebted to Karen Donfried and Derek Chollet of the German Marshall Fund for housing us in a quiet office in Washington, D.C., our home away from home (and much more peaceful than our actual, kid-filled homes!) while we did our work. Nicola Lightner made us feel like part of the GMF family, and we were honored to be included in the stable of researchers and fellows there who are doing important work on issues of democracy, global institutions, and transatlantic cooperation.

Any mistakes in the book are ours alone. But there are many fewer than there might have been because of the painstaking work of Hilary McClellan, who fact-checked every page. Cynthia Colonna transcribed several of our longer interviews, making it far easier for us to recall the best details. Matt Mendelsohn made us look good in our author photos. Trina Realmuto at the American Immigration Council helped us connect with Evelyn, the young mother from Guatemala who shared her story of being separated from her daughter under the zero tolerance policy. Hiram Soto, of Alliance San Diego, helped guide us during a visit to the border and added to our understanding of the situation there, as did Enrique Morones of Border Angels. Both connected us with contacts in the migrant shelters of Tijuana during our visit.

For Michael, no one has been a closer friend and newspaper partner for the last twenty-seven years than Peter Baker. He is a remarkable journalist, a compassionate author and historian, an inspirational father, a warm and generous colleague, and a dedicated fan of superhero movies—in short, the best friend anyone could have. Michael was introduced to journalism in 1985 by Nick Ferentinos, the faculty adviser to *The Epitaph* at Homestead High School. Nick instilled a lifelong respect for writing, reporting, and politics and became a dear friend before cancer took him in 2016. He would have been proud. Michael's parents, Steve and Suzy, raised their son to be curious, determined, ambitious, caring, fun-loving, and fair—attributes that have served him well throughout life and during the process of writing this book. To say that they were the ones who inspired Michael is an understatement; it is their examples that he strives to emulate every day. His sister, Jody, never doubted that her big brother could succeed in this venture, and for that Michael is endlessly grateful. His father-in-law, Dale, cheered him on from Nebraska. For the last quarter century, Michael's wife, Caitlin, has been the love of his life and his best friend. No one could ask for a more supportive spouse, whose good cheer and patience throughout the entire book-writing process was remarkable. And it was her wise advice at key points that helped shape the proposal that we wrote and improved the final book. Finally, Michael can think of no better reason to have worked so hard on *Border Wars* than his two children, Sam and Sophie, who every day deliver the kind of smarts, humor, kindness, and decency that is in short supply in the world.

Above all, Julie is grateful for her family. In this book as in everything, she has been inspired and nurtured by the memory of her mother, Janet, who had the sharp eye, probing curiosity, and deep compassion of a great writer, plus the work ethic and deadline addiction of the most ambitious journalist—even though neither of those were her chosen profession. Her father, Jimmy, a talented storyteller in his own right, taught her to trust her creative instincts and surround herself with good people, and his unconditional love and relentless support have made this project possible. Her sister, Jennie, has been a sounding board, confidant, and cheerleader, never doubting for a moment that this was possible (or never saying so!) even when Julie did. This book could not have happened without the support, generosity, and good cheer of Cécile Roussilhe, who has become a member of the family and an indispensable support. Julie's children,

Claire, Harry, and Rose, are extraordinary, and they amaze her more every day, teaching her new heights of love and wonder. Finally, there are no words to adequately express Julie's love and gratitude for Jonathan, the best and most supportive partner a person could have. His love, encouragement, perspective, excellent cocktails, and gourmet cooking have made this book possible, not to mention a whole lot more fun.

SOURCES

This account of the battles over immigration inside President Trump's government is based on more than 120 extensive interviews we conducted with current and former White House and administration officials, lawmakers, and legislative staff from both sides of the aisle, immigration activists, diplomats, and law enforcement and national security officials. In some cases, senior aides shared contemporaneous notes or audio recordings of meetings that provided us key insights into the often heated debates over the president's immigration policies. We were also able to review many never-before-seen documents including emails, diaries, letters, calendars, speech and hearing transcripts, and memo drafts that helped us to understand how the events we describe played out.

Many of the stories in this book are the result of our own reporting specifically for this project and have never been told before. We also relied on extensive reporting on Trump's immigration agenda that we produced for *The New York Times* starting just days after the 2016 election and continuing throughout his first two and a half years in office. But *Border Wars* also benefited greatly from the many accounts of the president's immigration policies by other reporters that have appeared in the *Times*, *The Washington Post*, and elsewhere. In particular, we have learned much from the reporting of *New York Times* reporters Caitlin Dickerson, Zolan Kanno-Youngs,

Miriam Jordan, and Ron Nixon and *Washington Post* correspondent Nick Miroff. Whenever we have relied directly on the valuable reporting of others, we have attempted to say so in these notes.

Most of the people we interviewed agreed to talk to us on the condition that they not be identified. Their anonymity provided them the freedom to speak in great detail about the meetings they attended and the discussions they participated in. We have attempted to corroborate recollections by seeking multiple, independent descriptions of the same events. In many cases, we were able to confirm key details, including direct quotes, with contemporaneous documents or notes. But we take responsibility for any misinterpretation or factual errors.

PROLOGUE

We talked to many people during the course of our reporting over the past year who related, often in vivid detail, Trump's obsession with the appearance of his border wall and the materials out of which he thought it should be built. Those conversations helped us describe for readers how Trump thought the wall should look. In some cases, lawmakers or members of the administration described meetings in which the president interrupted conversations about other topics to discuss the status of the wall and his desire to make sure that immigrants were not able to climb over it.

CHAPTER 1: THE VESSEL

Many people associated with Donald Trump's early thinking about running for president were gracious with their time, as were those who later joined the president's campaign. All of them helped us understand how immigration became central to Trump's political identity. We relied on two Trump biographies to understand his personal history: Michael D'Antonio's *The Truth About Trump* and Gwenda Blair's *The Trumps: Three Generations of Builders and a President*. The young Dreamers who met with Trump at his Manhattan tower described that meeting for us. Robert Draper provided key insights into the dinner at the Breitbart Embassy in his March 26, 2017, article "Trump vs. Congress: Now What?" in *The New York Times Magazine*. Also instrumental to our understanding of the alliance among Bannon, Sessions, and Miller was Ryan Lizza's 2017 piece in *The New Yorker*, "The Rise and Fall of Steve Bannon." Joshua Green's *Devil's Bargain* (Penguin, 2017) was similarly helpful in understanding Bannon and his role in Trump's rise. We benefited greatly from seeing early drafts of campaign speeches, internal memoranda, and emails that helped us understand Trump's deliberations about immigration before and after he decided to run for president.

CHAPTER 2: BREAKING THE APOLOGY-RETREAT CYCLE

Several people helped us reconstruct key moments during the president's campaign, including Trump's response to terror attacks in December of 2015 and the internal debates about what Trump should say in a major immigration address that he delivered in Phoenix in September of 2016. Others shared with us stories about the immediate aftermath of Trump's election victory. Matt Flegenheimer unearthed fascinating background about Stephen Miller's upbringing in his October 9, 2017, piece in *The New York Times* called "Stephen Miller, the Powerful Survivor on the President's Right Flank." We interviewed Miller at length in October and November of 2017 to discuss Trump's immigration agenda, the power of his immigration rhetoric, and the ways in which the administration had begun to implement his vision.

CHAPTER 3: THE HAMILTON GROUP

Current and former administration and congressional officials helped us reconstruct the efforts of a small group of advisers who worked to draft immigration executive orders during the transition. Veterans of legislative battles in Washington recalled for us the long history of divisive immigration debates and the people who fought them behind the scenes. Several former Obama administration officials, including Jeh Johnson, the outgoing homeland security secretary, and Cecilia Muñoz, Obama's domestic policy adviser, talked with us about the transition and the interactions they had with the "landing teams" from the incoming Trump administration. *Vox* published the earliest drafts of the incoming administration's executive orders on January 25, 2017, in a piece titled: "Read Leaked Drafts of 4

White House Executive Orders on Muslim Ban, End to DREAMer Program, and More." Representative Luis Gutiérrez of Chicago shared with us his reasons for choosing not to attend Trump's inauguration and his impressions upon returning to Washington that evening.

CHAPTER 4: FORTY-THREE MINUTES
Many sources close to the process provided us detailed accounts of the president's decision to impose a ban on travel from several mostly Muslim countries during his first week in office. Some shared notes, emails, and documents from that chaotic period that were invaluable in helping track who knew about the president's travel ban order and when they knew it. We reviewed documents from the Office of Legal Counsel at the Justice Department as well as intra-office memos that were distributed by officials at the NSC, the State Department, and other agencies. The transcript of Trump's call with Mexican president Enrique Peña Nieto was available to us because of the great reporting by *Washington Post* reporter Greg Miller in his August 3, 2017, piece entitled "Trump Urged Mexican President to End His Public Defiance on Border Wall, Transcript Reveals." Several people who were present described in detail the travel ban briefing in the DHS conference room on January 26, 2017, at the moment that Trump signed the ban.

CHAPTER 5: "BRING OUT THE CRAZIES"
Several people with direct knowledge about the reaction to Trump's travel ban inside the Justice Department shared information with us. We were helped immensely by Kara Swisher's excellent interview with Sally Yates, the former acting attorney general, conducted for *Recode* on November 14, 2018. That piece was entitled "Former Deputy Attorney General Sally Yates Explains How Donald Trump Is Trying to Corrupt the Justice Department." Lee Gelernt and others at the ACLU were helpful to us in describing the actions they took to respond to the president's travel ban. Charlie Dent, the former Republican congressman from Pennsylvania, shared the story of how the Assali family got caught up in the ban. Several

administration officials described for us White House meetings that took place in the immediate aftermath of the ban.

CHAPTER 6: "A FUCKING WATERED-DOWN VERSION"

The argument about whether Iraq should be on the banned travel list was described to us in detail by several people with direct knowledge of it. The report by the DHS intelligence office, entitled "Citizenship Likely an Unreliable Indicator of Terrorist Threat to the United States," was first published by the Associated Press on February 24, 2017. Numerous officials familiar with the travel ban discussed the fallout from it inside their departments. Multiple sources with knowledge recounted the president's angry Oval Office tirade about the travel ban in early March, as well as the efforts by Sessions, Bannon, and others to convince Trump to replace it with a second executive order and his resistance to doing so.

CHAPTER 7: SHACKLES OFF

We talked to a number of people familiar with Stephen Miller's Friday immigration meetings at the White House. In describing Trump's early crackdown on immigrants, we benefited greatly from the reporting of our colleagues at *The New York Times*, like this piece from Nicholas Kulish, Caitlin Dickerson, and Ron Nixon: "Immigration Agents Discover New Freedom to Deport Under Trump." The development of a presidential address to Congress involves many people in an administration, and several sources described for us the internal debates over the language that Miller wanted to use, as well as the concerns about the lack of support for certain assertions that Trump made. We had access to some emails about the president's address written by Justice Department officials thanks to a Freedom of Information request filed by Benjamin Wittes, the cofounder of the "Lawfare" blog. We were able to reconstruct contentious meetings between John Kelly and Democratic members of Congress with the help of several members and aides who attended the meetings, some of whom took detailed, contemporaneous notes with portions recorded verbatim. We also reviewed notes of Miller's Friday meeting with administration officials. The confrontations between sheriffs and Kelly and Sessions about the declined detainer reports were described to us in detail by several people familiar with them, including one who kept detailed notes that we reviewed.

CHAPTER 8: ANGELS AND DEMONS

Our reporting on the Angel Families was supplemented by the excellent story in *The New York Times* by Kenneth P. Vogel and Katie Rogers published on July 4, 2018, under the headline, "For Trump and 'Angel Families,' a Mutually Beneficial Bond." The data about the rate at which immigrants commit crimes is drawn from a July 2015 report released by the American Immigration Council, written by Walter A. Ewing, Daniel E. Martinez, and Rubén G. Rumbaut. The discussion of the economic impacts of immigration and where they are felt was informed by the research of George Borjas, including his 2004 paper, "Increasing the Supply of Labor Through Immigration: Measuring the Impact on Native-born Workers." We also cite the findings of *The Economic and Fiscal Consequences of Immigration* (The National Academies Press, 2017), edited by Francine D. Blau and Christopher Mackie.

CHAPTER 9: NO LEGAL BASIS

Our recounting of the history of anti-immigrant sentiment in the United States was informed by Tom Gjelten's exceptional book, *A Nation of Nations: A Great American Immigration Story*, and Daniel Okrent's fascinating look at the dark consequences of eugenics in *The Guarded Gate*. We also relied on statistics from the Center for Migration Policy and a paper by the Urban Institute titled *Immigration and Immigrants: Setting the Record Straight*, by Michael Fix and Jeffrey S. Passel. We also found helpful passages about the history of immigration in the *Congressional Record* and in *Immigration Wars: Forging an American Solution* by Jeb Bush and Clint Bolick. Lee Gelernt talked with us at length about the legal fights that he and other ACLU lawyers engaged in over the fate of several small minority communities targeted by ICE for deportation soon after the start of the

Trump administration. We also reviewed legal briefs filed by both sides in the cases and obtained transcripts of several of the hearings that provided insights into the arguments made by Trump administration lawyers and the reactions by the judges.

CHAPTER 10: THE TRUMP EFFECT FADES

Several people told us about the brainstorming session that Hamilton led and the list of action items he wanted done in forty-eight hours, including the idea of routinely separating families. We covered the border crisis involving unaccompanied minors during the Obama administration, and several former Obama officials recalled for us the debates inside the White House about how to respond, some of which we detailed in our June 16, 2018, piece headlined "How Trump Came to Enforce a Practice of Separating Migrant Families." Since the beginning of the Trump presidency, we have covered scores of Trump's rallies. During the course of reporting for the book, we reviewed video and transcripts of many more, including his June 21 rally in Cedar Rapids, Iowa. In December of 2017, we were the first to report for *The New York Times* the Oval Office scene in which the president asserted that all Haitians "have AIDS" and musing that Nigerians living in the United States would not want to "go back to their huts." The White House disputed that the president used the words "AIDS" and "huts" at that time. For this book, we talked to additional people with knowledge of it, adding detail that we had not reported before.

CHAPTER 11: THE ADMIRAL'S ALMANAC

To understand Garry Hall's role in refugee issues, we talked to numerous people inside and outside the administration who interacted with him. We also spoke with former NSC officials who helped us understand how the work that Hall did differed from that of his predecessors. We reviewed internal memoranda and emails that Hall exchanged with associates. Details about Hall's podcast were first obtained by Nahal Toosi of *Politico*, who listened to it and wrote about it in an article entitled " 'Leadership, Fitness and Sex': Trump Aide Moonlights as Podcast Host." The podcast episode has since been taken offline, but a one-and-a-half-minute trailer for it remained at the time of publication on a website at http://admiral .libsyn.com/introducing-the-admirals-almanac.

CHAPTER 12: REFUGEES NOT WELCOME

Several sources intimately familiar with the discussions helped us re-create the debate over the refugee ceiling, including the meeting in which Miller demanded evidence that refugees cost too much. The report by the Center for Immigration Studies on the cost of Middle Eastern refugees can be found here: https://cis.org/sites/cis.org/files/camarota-refugees-15_0.pdf. The study that Bartlett cited from Cleveland, entitled "Economic Impact of Refugees in the Cleveland Area," can be found here: http://www.hias .org/sites/default/files/clevelandrefugeeeconomic-impact.pdf. The draft HHS report on the cost of refugees, which was rejected by Miller, was never released. But Julie and our colleague Somini Sengupta acquired a copy and wrote about it in a September 18, 2017, story headlined "Trump Administration Rejects Study Showing Positive Impact of Refugees." A copy of the draft report can be found here: https://www.nytimes.com/in teractive/2017/09/19/us/politics/document-Refugee-Report.html?_r=0. We reviewed many of the discussion documents that were exchanged among officials during the debate over the refugee cap, and interviewed several key players. They informed our understanding about the internal tensions inside the National Security Council and the pressure from Miller and his allies to keep the cap low. Jonathan Blitzer of *The New Yorker*, whose coverage of immigration issues has been groundbreaking and informative, was the first to report parts of the 2015 exchange about refugees between Sessions and Anne Richard of the State Department in his May 1, 2018, piece, "The Trump Administration's Hard Line on Refugees Comes Under Fire." Tom Bossert, the president's first homeland security adviser, denied he used the words attributed to him on the phone call with Duke.

CHAPTER 13: A NOT-SO-GLOBAL COMPACT

The debate inside the White House about whether to remain part of the Global Compact for Migration was related to us by several people close to the months-long discussions. The article cited by Miller and Veprek about international law and the global compact can be found here: https://blog.harvardlawreview.org/how-to-help-the-migration-crisis-and-make-international-law/.

CHAPTER 14: BLIND SPOT

Much of Trump's agonizing over what to do about DACA played out in the open, through Twitter and his own statements. But many of those involved in private conversations with the president about DACA and the Dreamers shared their recollections with us. That provided us important insight into Trump's thinking as he was pulled by advocates on each side within his administration. Former Obama administration officials helped us to reconstruct the conversation about DACA between Obama and Trump in the Oval Office after the election. They also recounted the actions they and others took to try to protect the Dreamers from what they expected would happen to the DACA program once Trump took over. In describing the meeting between Kelly and Hispanic lawmakers, we were aided by contemporaneous notes that were taken by two people familiar with those discussions. Kushner's once secret discussions with Dick Durbin about DACA became well known inside the White House and on Capitol Hill, and several knowledgeable sources described them to us in detail. Trump told us in an interview in the Oval Office on June 25, 2019, that he had always opposed cutting legal immigration.

CHAPTER 15: NO WAY OUT

We talked to many administration officials about the pressure on Elaine Duke to end the DACA program. We reviewed Duke's daily calendar, which was released by DHS in response to FOIA requests by American Oversight, the nonprofit ethics watchdog that has devoted itself to such litigation, and can be found here: https://www.dhs.gov/publication/s1-calendars. Many people described to us the efforts by members of Congress, lobbyists, and business executives to dissuade Trump from ending DACA and the negotiations among lawmakers and with the White House to salvage the protections through legislation once he had terminated it.

CHAPTER 16: LIFE IN TWO-YEAR INCREMENTS

Itzel Guillen Maganda sat down with Julie in early April 2019 for an interview in her office in San Diego about what it was like to grow up undocumented, obtain DACA protections, and have that status threatened when Trump moved to end the program.

CHAPTER 17: FORCED REMOVAL

In piecing together the story of Elaine Duke's struggle over Temporary Protected Status, we were aided immensely by documents filed with courts as part of discovery in several lawsuits challenging the termination of TPS programs, including by the ACLU, the American Immigration Council, the Northwest Immigrant Rights Project, and individual TPS holders. Nick Miroff of *The Washington Post* was the first to obtain from the ACLU internal emails and cables exposing the dispute over ending TPS, including Francis Cissna's correspondence with Brandon Prelogar pointing out the inconsistency of the government's rationale for ending TPS for the Sudanese. They appeared in his August 23, 2018, piece headlined "Government Emails Reveal Internal Debates over Ending Immigrant Protections." We were able to obtain additional material, including emails, internal memoranda, and diplomatic cables. We interviewed several key players in the decision to end grants of TPS, and many others with direct knowledge of the deliberations, who filled out our understanding of how the debate unfolded and the decisions were ultimately made.

CHAPTER 18: "JUST BITE THE BULLET"

Our portrayal of Elaine Duke's dilemma over ending TPS status for several nationalities and the pressure she endured from Trump's White House and other administration officials to do so is based largely on interviews with people who were close to the matter. Congressman Jim McGovern of Massachusetts, one of the authors of the statute that established Temporary Protected Status, was generous with his time and insights during an interview in his office on Capitol Hill, in which he recounted his unsuccessful efforts to get Kirstjen Nielsen to reconsider her decision. Documents submitted as part of discovery in the litigation, including handwritten notes that Duke took during meetings and conference calls and emails from her and John Kelly, helped us to fill in the blanks of how it took shape.

CHAPTER 19: "SHITHOLE COUNTRIES"

Julie reported for *The New York Times* on Trump's Oval Office blowup over an emerging DACA deal the day it happened and for several days afterward. We were later able to fill out our understanding of how the meeting came about, how it unfolded, and what happened as a result through extensive interviews. Some of our sources shared written notes and emails to help us understand the context.

CHAPTER 20: ASH AND TRASH

For our re-creation of the behind-the-scenes negotiations on legislation to save DACA, we relied on many hours of interviews with people who were involved, including officials who kept detailed notes and referred to them as they walked us through the blow-by-blow of how the discussions proceeded.

CHAPTER 21: "NO MORE DACA DEAL!"

This account of the ultimate demise of a bipartisan DACA deal was also pulled from interviews and contemporaneous notes, as well as text messages we reviewed from people involved at key moments. People close to Sessions said the attorney general's suggestion that they simply ignore the Flores settlement and let the judge come after them was never seriously considered.

CHAPTER 22: ZERO TOLERANCE

We reported in real time on the family separation policy for *The New York Times*, and our colleague Caitlin Dickerson was the first to document the practice in her April 20, 2018, piece headlined "Hundreds of Immigrant Children Have Been Taken from Parents at U.S. Border." The government watchdog groups Open the Government and the Project on Government Oversight were the first to obtain a redacted copy of the memo Nielsen ultimately signed adopting the tactic, through an FOIA request that led to its release in September of 2018. We subsequently obtained an unredacted version, which contributed greatly to our understanding of the options under discussion and the internal debate over how to proceed. We also obtained the six-page memo sent by staff of the DHS Office for Civil Rights and Civil Liberties detailing the human rights concerns of officials there about family separation. NBC was first to report on the 2017 internal discussion document titled "Policy Options to Respond to Border Surge of Illegal Immigration," which revealed the roots of the decisions made by Nielsen and White House officials. We conducted several interviews with people close to the process, who added important insights and specifics about how the policy came to fruition.

CHAPTER 23: REVERSE BOOMERANG

We based much of this chapter on our exclusive interview with Stephen Miller in June 2018, and where we drew from other news reports, they are credited in the text. We also benefited greatly from interviews with several central figures who detailed the extraordinary events that led to Trump's decision to rescind the family separation policy, and the consequences of that move.

CHAPTER 24: ALWAYS A BOMB THROWER

Our portrait of Stephen Miller was drawn from years of covering him during his tenure on Capitol Hill and at the White House, including many interviews with him and extensive discussions with people who dealt with him in various capacities during these periods. We benefited from the insights contained in several pieces about Miller's upbringing and professional development, including: Fernando Peinado's February 2017 piece about him for Univision News, which first unearthed his high-school-era letters to the editor of his local newspaper and referenced his later writings, during his time at Duke University, about his sense of alienation; Matt Flegenheimer's *New York Times* profile of Miller from October 9, 2017; McKay Coppins's May 2018 profile in *The Atlantic* entitled "Stephen Miller: Trump's Right-Hand Troll"; and a piece in *Politico* by Miller's uncle, David S. Glosser, published on August 13, 2018. Where possible, we went back to read Miller's early writings for ourselves to verify their authenticity and get additional context. In one case, we reviewed video of a speech he delivered at Santa Monica High School during his run for student government. Trump shared his personal impressions about Miller during our June 25, 2019, interview.

CHAPTER 25: "YOU'VE KIDNAPPED OUR KIDS"

Once again, the reporting of our colleague Caitlin Dickerson about the bureaucratic reasons behind the government's inability to keep track of separated children and parents so they could be quickly reunited informed our own reporting and interviews about the depths of the dysfunction that plagued the effort. Her July 5, 2018, *New York Times* story headlined "Trump Administration in Chaotic Scramble to Reunify Migrant Families" provided important leads for our work. A January 2019 report by the Health and Human Services Office of the Inspector General has since detailed portions of the effort we wrote about here. Our interviews with several important people close to this chapter of the family separation drama were pivotal to our understanding of both the domestic and international dimensions of the crisis.

CHAPTER 26: EVELYN AND AMBER

This account of one mother and daughter impacted by the family separation policy was reconstructed from a lengthy in-person interview with Evelyn. It was also informed by legal briefs prepared by her attorneys for a lawsuit challenging the family separation practice. Both names have been changed to protect their identities, in light of their continued fear of retribution for having fled Guatemala, and to protect their privacy during the ongoing litigation. While theirs is only one deeply personal story, we were struck during our research and interviews by how similar these accounts were. Thousands of families went through nearly identical experiences and faced the same impossible choices Evelyn did at the hands of the United States government.

CHAPTER 27: "PENCILS DOWN"

This chapter was largely based on primary-source interviews with people close to the events. The discussion of the legislative history of the public charge concept comes from a review of the 1882 statute as posted on the website of the University of Washington Bothell. The proposed rule is available in the *Federal Register*. Yeganah Torbati of Reuters was the first to report in February of 2018 on the Trump administration's efforts to overhaul the public charge standard. Michael reported for *The New York Times* on the proposed rule and its political and policy implications later that year. The public opinion perspective revealing Americans' belief that immigrants cost taxpayers too much is gleaned from several surveys, including an April 2018 BPC Action Immigration Survey by the Bipartisan Policy Center. The account of Miller's efforts to bring about further cuts to the refugee resettlement program was based on several interviews with people knowledgeable about it. The discussion of subtle but consequential changes to legal immigration was informed by Doug Rand at Boundless Immigration, who was generous with his insights and shared research tracking those efforts. The American Immigration Lawyers Association's April 24, 2018, report, "Deconstructing the Invisible Wall," was similarly instructive. The discussion of the addition of a citizenship question to the 2020 Census is based in part on documents obtained by the House Oversight and Reform Committee in the course of their investigation into the matter. Michael Wines of *The New York Times* was the first to report on Hofeller's study detailing how drawing political maps based only on citizens would benefit Republicans, in his piece headlined, "Deceased G.O.P. Strategist's Hard Drives Reveal New Details on the Census Citizenship Question." The account of the rising tensions between Trump and Nielsen on a variety of fronts is based on interviews with several sources.

CHAPTER 28: USE OF FORCE

Our re-creation of Trump's late-2018 desperation about how to gain control of the border is based on extensive interviews, including with sources who kept contemporaneous notes and shared key portions to help us understand what was happening behind the scenes as the president tweeted and made increasingly aggressive public declarations on the topic. We have quoted directly from the *CBP Use of Force Policy, Guidelines and Procedures Handbook*, last updated in May 2014 and available on the agency's website.

CHAPTER 29: HIJACKING THE MIDTERMS
This account of how Trump's anti-immigration message played in the midterm congressional elections was drawn almost entirely from primary-source interviews. Where we have borrowed analytical themes from pollsters in both political parties, we have cited the sources in the text.

CHAPTER 30: MEXICAN STANDOFF
The secret negotiations between the Trump administration and Mexican officials were described to us by multiple people with knowledge of them, who were generous with their recollections and in one case consulted contemporaneous notes to help reconstruct key scenes.

CHAPTER 31: SHUTDOWN
The account of the hours leading up to the longest government shutdown in history was informed by extensive interviews, including of Democratic and White House officials who provided contemporaneous accounts of the events.

CHAPTER 32: "WE'VE WASTED THE LAST TWO YEARS"
We interviewed a wide array of officials and other sources knowledgeable about the negotiations between the White House and congressional leaders during the shutdown. We viewed a picture of the whiteboard graph described in the chapter, in which the administration's negotiating power, morale, and ability to secure the country were tracked by DHS officials in dry-erase markers. Senior White House and congressional officials provided detailed accounts of the discussions, as chronicled in our stories for *The New York Times* during this time period.

CHAPTER 33: THE PURGE

Our account of the events leading up to Trump's purge of his Department of Homeland Security, including the ouster of Kirstjen Nielsen, was drawn almost entirely from extensive interviews with many sources close to the situation. Trump talked to us about Nielsen during our interview on June 25, 2019.

AFTERWORD

Our colleagues Caitlin Dickerson and Zolan Kanno-Youngs were the first to report on the Trump administration's plan to deploy tactical border agents into sanctuary cities, in a February 14, 2020, article entitled "Border Patrol Will Deploy Elite Tactical Agents to Sanctuary Cities." Catherine Rampell wrote about the stricter rules for U visa applications in the *Washington Post*. We relied on statistics compiled by Customs and Border Protection and posted on its website to calculate the levels and percentage change of border apprehensions during Trump's tenure. Stuart Anderson of the National Foundation for American Policy was generous with his insights and data, including his calculation of the sharp decline in legal immigration under Trump, presented in the foundation's January 2020 policy brief entitled "Analysis of FY 2018 Legal Immigration Statistics." That analysis found that legal immigration to the United States declined by 7.3 percent between fiscal year 2016 and fiscal year 2018. When refugees who physically arrived during that period but had been admitted before Trump became president were excluded, the analysis said, the decline was 11.5 percent. In assessing the public's attitudes about immigration and partisan divisions about the issue, we consulted a number of publicly available polls, including Gallup research and a November 12, 2019, analysis by Andrew Daniller of the Pew Research Center entitled "Americans' Immigration Policy Priorities: Divisions Between—and Within—the Two Parties."

PHOTO CREDITS

INDEX

Justice Department, U.S. (DOJ) (*cont.*)
family separation policy and, 253, 254, 257, 261–62, 263–64
and frustrations with immigration policies, 103, 104
and Global Compact for Migration, 153, 154
Hamilton group and, 43
Miller working group and, 93
and options for cracking down on border, 332
and refugees, 143
sanctuary cities grants and, 105
and slowing of naturalization processing, 321
TPS and, 212–13
travel ban and, 61, 68–70, 78–80, 86, 87, 89
and Trump speech to Congress, 98
Trump sued by, 20
zero tolerance policy and, 255, 257
See also specific person or division

Kadlec, Bob, 292, 293, 294
Kaine, Tim, 234
Katz, Jeremy, 167
Keene, New Hampshire: Trump speech in, 137
Kellogg, Keith, 61, 132, 205
Kelly, John
and Bannon-Kushner relationship, 164
and blame for immigration crisis, 265, 267
Bolton disagreement with, 331–32
and border closings, 330, 331–32
and border security, 241

congressional appearances of, 100–102
and DACA/Dreamers, 162–63, 164, 166–67, 172, 173, 174, 177–78, 179, 221, 222, 226–27, 229, 230, 231–32, 250
Democrats' meeting with, 100–102
family separation policy and, 124, 253, 263, 264, 275, 277
and government shutdown, 230
and Gutiérrez arrest, 297
Hicks-Porter case and, 289
and Homan appointment, 96
ICE directives of, 96–97
and increase in immigrant crossings, 241
influence on Trump of, 226
Kushner views about, 368
and local law enforcement efforts, 105–6
Mexico-U.S. relations and, 97
and military for border security, 245, 336
Nealon relationship with, 122
and Nielsen resignation, 267
omnibus spending bill and, 238
professional background of, 101
and refugees, 139
reputation of, 101
resignation of, 360
responsibilities of, 121
and sanctuary cities, 105–6
TPS and, 195–97, 207–10
travel ban and, 65, 66, 71, 75, 76, 80, 81, 83–84, 87, 90, 91, 164
and Trump outbursts, 126, 128

ABOUT THE AUTHORS

Julie Hirschfeld Davis is the congressional editor at the *New York Times*. She has covered politics and policy from Washington for twenty-three years. She joined the *Times* in 2014 as a White House correspondent after stints at Bloomberg News, the Associated Press, the *Baltimore Sun*, and *Congressional Quarterly*. She won the 2009 Everett McKinley Dirksen Award for Distinguished Reporting of Congress.

Michael D. Shear is a White House correspondent in the *New York Times* Washington bureau. A veteran political correspondent, before coming to the *Times* in 2010 he spent eighteen years writing about local, state, and national politics at the *Washington Post*, where he was also part of the Pulitzer Prize–winning team that covered the Virginia Tech shootings in 2007.